MEDIEVAL ENGLISH POETRY

Longman Critical Readers

General Editors:

Raman Selden, late Emeritus Professor of English,
Lancaster University and late Professor of English,
University of Sunderland;

Stan Smith, Professor of English, University of Dundee

MEDIEVAL ENGLISH POETRY

Edited and Introduced by

STEPHANIE TRIGG

LONGMAN
LONDON AND NEW YORK

Longman Group UK Limited,
Longman House, Burnt Mill,
Harlow, Essex CM20 2JE, England
and Associated Companies throughout the world.

Published in the United States of America
by Longman Publishing, New York

First published 1993

ISBN 0 582 08260 9 csd
ISBN 0 582 08261 7 ppr

British Library Cataloguing-in-Publication Data

A catalogue record for this book is
available from the British Library

Library of Congress Cataloging-in-Publication Data

Medieval English Poetry/edited and introduced by Stephanie Trigg.
        p.   cm. – (Longman critical readers)
    Includes bibliographical references and index.
    ISBN 0-582-08260-9 (csd). – ISBN 0-582-08261-7 (ppr)
    1. English poetry–Middle English, 1100-1500–History and criticism.
    I. Trigg, Stephanie.   II. Series.
    PR313.M43   1993
    821'.109–dc20   93–10072

Set in 10/11½ Palatino by 15
Produced by Longman Singapore Publishers (Pte) Ltd.
Printed in Singapore

Contents

General Editors' Preface

The outlines of contemporary critical theory are now often taught as a standard feature of a degree in literary studies. The development of particular theories has seen a thorough transformation of literary criticism. For example, Marxist and Foucauldian theories have revolutionised Shakespeare studies, and 'deconstruction' has led to a complete reassessment of Romantic poetry. Feminist criticism has left scarcely any period of literature unaffected by its searching critiques. Teachers of literary studies can no longer fall back on a standardised, received, methodology.

Lecturers and teachers are now urgently looking for guidance in a rapidly changing critical environment. They need help in understanding the latest revisions in literary theory, and especially in grasping the practical effects of the new theories in the form of theoretically sensitised new readings. A number of volumes in the series anthologise important essays on particular theories. However, in order to grasp the full implications and possible uses of particular theories it is essential to see them put to work. This series provides substantial volumes of new readings, presented in an accessible form and with a significant amount of editorial guidance.

Each volume includes a substantial introduction which explores the theoretical issues and conflicts embodied in the essays selected and locates areas of disagreement between positions. The pluralism of theories has to be put on the agenda of literary studies. We can no longer pretend that we all tacitly accept the same practices in literary studies. Neither is a *laissez-faire* attitude any longer tenable. Literature departments need to go beyond the mere toleration of theoretical differences: it is not enough merely to agree to differ; they need actually to 'stage' the differences openly. The volumes in this series all attempt to dramatise the differences, not necessarily with a view to resolving them but in order to foreground the choices presented by different theories or to argue for a particular route through the impasses the differences present.

The theory 'revolution' has had real effects. It has loosened the grip of traditional empiricist and romantic assumptions about language and literature. It is not always clear what is being proposed as the new agenda for literature studies, and indeed the very notion of 'literature' is questioned by the post-structuralist strain in theory. However, the uncertainties and obscurities of contemporary theories appear much less worrying when we see what the best critics have been able to do with them in practice. This series aims to disseminate the best of recent criticism and to show that it is possible to re-read the canonical texts of literature in new and challenging ways.

RAMAN SELDEN AND STAN SMITH

The Publishers and fellow Series Editor regret to record that Raman Selden died after a short illness in May 1991 at the age of fifty-three. Ray Selden was a fine scholar and a lovely man. All those he has worked with will remember him with much affection and respect.

Acknowledgements

The editor would like to thank Stephen Knight, Greg Kratzmann and James Simpson for their generous advice, and Ros Harris for her invaluable assistance in preparing this volume.

The Editor and Publisher are grateful to the following for permission to reproduce copyright material:

AMS Press, Inc. for 'English, Latin, and the Text as "Other": The Page as Sign in the Work of John Gower' by Robert F. Yeager in *Text: Transactions of the Society for Textual Scholarships* **3** (1987): 251–67; Colleagues Press Inc. for 'The Rhetoric of Excess in *Winner and Waster*' by Stephanie Trigg in *Yearbook of Langland Studies* **3** (1989): 91–108; Cornell University Press for '"Truth's Treasure": Allegory and Meaning in *Piers Plowman*' by Laurie A. Finke in *Medieval Texts and Contemporary Readers* ed. Laurie A. Finke and Martin B. Schictman. Copyright © 1987 by Cornell University; the Editor of *Essays in Criticism* for 'Price and Value in *Sir Gawain and the Green Knight*' by Jill Mann in *Essays in Criticism* **36** (1986): 294–318; Garland Publishing Inc. for 'Leaving Morgan Aside: Women, History and Revisionism in *Sir Gawain and the Green Knight*' by Sheila Fisher in *The Passing of Arthur: New Essays in Arthurian Tradition* ed. Christopher Baswell and William Sharpe vol. 781 (1988): 129–51; Local Consumption Publications and the author, Stephen Knight, for a revised version of the essay 'Why was *Lady Isabel and the Elf-Knight* the Most Popular Ballad in Europe?' from *Not the Whole Story: Tellings and Tailings from the ASPACLS on Narrative* ed. Sneja Gunew and Ian Reid (1984), pp. 5–13; Manchester University Press for 'The Romance of Kingship: *Havelok the Dane*' from *Medieval Literary Politics: Shapes of Ideology* by Sheila Delany (1990), pp. 61–73; The Pennsylvania State University Press for 'The Narrator in *The Owl and the Nightingale*: A Reader in the Text' by R. Barton Palmer from *Chaucer Review* **22** (No. 4): 305–321. Copyright © 1988 by The Pennsylvania State University; Routledge for 'Imagination and Traditional Ideologies in *Piers Plowman*' from *Chaucer, Langland and the Creative Imagination* by David Aers (1980), pp. 1–37, 196–204 (notes); the Editor of *Speculum* for 'The Idea of Public Poetry in the Reign of Richard II' by Anne Middleton from *Speculum* **53** (No. 1) (1978): 94–114; University of California Press and the author, Steven Justice for 'The Genres of *Piers Plowman*' from *Viator: Medieval and Renaissance Studies* **19** (1988): 291–306. Copyright © 1988 by the Regents of the University of California; the Editor of *Philological Quarterly* and the author, Alexandra A. T. Barratt for '*The Flower and the Leaf* and *The Assembly of Ladies*: Is There a (Sexual) Difference?' from *Philological Quarterly* **66** (No. 1)

Acknowledgements

(1978): 1–24; The University of Wisconsin Press for 'The Romance of History and the Alliterative *Morte Arthure*' from *Negotiating the Past: The Historical Understanding of Medieval Literature* by Lee Patterson (1987), pp. 197–230.

1   Introduction
Medieval Poetry and Literary Criticism

To define the scope of this book is in one sense straightforward: the essays
printed here offer critical readings of a range of poetry written in English
between the twelfth and fifteenth centuries, with the exception of the works
of Geoffrey Chaucer. Many authors and critical approaches have had to be
excluded, but these essays represent some of the exciting new developments
in medieval studies over the last fifteen or twenty years. As the title of this
introductory essay suggests, the concerns of this volume are very firmly
clustered around literary criticism and critical methodology, and the ways in
which medieval literary studies borrows from and contributes to the theory
and practice of literary criticism in the 1990s. This is not to say that other
fields of inquiry such as prosody, editorial theory, economic and social
background, source and influence studies do not set their own agendas in
medieval studies: simply that the principal concern of this book, and this
series, is with the dramatic changes to the theory and practice of literary
criticism over the last twenty years. Yet some of these changes throw up
challenging questions about the very discipline of medieval literary studies in
English, and indeed, about some of the principles by which this book is
organised. The collection accordingly has two aims: to represent the growth,
if not of a new medievalism, of at least a rich and interrogative vein of
criticism in this field; and secondly, to consider this movement in the rather
broader contexts – and crises – of criticism and historicism in the 1990s.

The critical traditions of medieval poetry

Cross-disciplinary investigations and other movements in cultural studies
continue to put pressure on the 'discipline' of medieval studies, yet the
boundaries of the field remain relatively stable. The body of texts described

1

as 'medieval' hasn't changed, of course; and medievalists still name themselves with reference to this historical period, rather than a critical methodology, for example. At the same time, contemporary medieval studies is certainly not marked by a single, dominant critical mode, and nor is there a single narrative thread we could trace in the criticism of the various genres, and authorial or textual modes of medieval poetry. But if a complete diachronic history and an exhaustive survey of medieval studies are beyond the scope of this introduction, it may still be useful to sketch out some of the oppositions and debates, the issues and questions around which the criticism of medieval literature has been, and is still, generated. The field has been transformed so swiftly that an attempt to chart these movements in relation to Middle English poetry seems timely, even if such an account can be at best only provisional.

One way of approaching this task would be to survey the different, and rival, reading practices used by contemporary scholars to interpret medieval literary texts, and the changing trends in criticism. Using fairly broad strokes of the pen, we could outline a decisive shift from both an older historicism and formalism in favour of newer forms of historicism and materialist critique which seek to explore medieval literature against a range of historical discourses and contexts.[1] This opposition is easy to trace in the study of later literature: medieval criticism presents a rather more complex picture.

Medieval studies took its formative shape in the latter part of the nineteenth century, organised around the scholarly and sometimes nationalist imperatives of philology, literary history and, most significantly, the inauguration of English literature as a university discipline. At Oxford, for example, Anglo-Saxon had been taught since the seventeenth century,[2] but Middle English was introduced only with the new English School, established in 1894. Accordingly, the study of Middle English literature is deeply implicated in nineteenth-century debates about the propriety of literary studies as an academic discipline, and a sufficiently rigorous subject of examination.

In addition to research into the language and dialects of Middle English, the earliest forms of historicist criticism were committed to identifying the original circumstances of production of medieval poetry: the names and geographical or cultural provenance of its poets, their patrons, the events to which they referred, or occasions for which they wrote. The enthusiasm with which the early scholars discovered literal, topical references in, and consequently, firm dates for passages which we now read as allegories, or conventional *topoi*, may amuse us, but this insistence that medieval literature has a social and historical – not just an aesthetic – meaning has been, in one form or another, the hallmark of medieval studies.

It is hard to imagine, now, what it must have been like to read a poem when so little was known about its provenance or authorship, its relation to other texts and, in many cases, the very language and dialect in which it was written. So many texts have survived in just one manuscript, with few later references, and certainly no tradition of critical reception. Many of the manuscripts with which we are now so familiar – through direct access, or reading accounts of them, or working with microfilms and facsimiles often in countries far removed from England – were unknown. And if their existence was known, their contents were often uncatalogued, or catalogued inaccurately. The modern culture of the book, in the specific form of the catalogue, has inscribed itself, as it were, on the medieval manuscript. While there are still manuscripts that are less frequently read and consulted, and while the specific experience of any one reader encountering any one manuscript may be as baffling and confusing as an originary moment of scholarship and rediscovery, the fact remains that our expectations of the sense manuscripts ought to make is largely driven by our expectations of the modern book.

Thanks to the labours of those early scholars, we have been able to move beyond purely empirical studies and experiment with more theoretical methodologies. But it is worth reminding ourselves that the history, or even, the archaeology of what we now know as Middle English literature had first to be written. In this, the history of medieval studies bears a closer resemblance to the historical recovery and reception of classical texts than early modern literary studies, and its criticism has, until very recently, depended on scholarship of a more positivist cast. These relations have not always been straightforward. Lee Patterson has revealed, for example, an almost complete split in the work of John Livingstone Lowes, between his detailed historical research into the contexts of medieval literature and his discussions of Chaucer's poetry, published in the 1930s, which make virtually no reference to this material.[3]

Similarly, there is no simple 'New Critical' moment in the reception of medieval English literature. The fragmentary and uncertain life of medieval poems in their manuscripts has perhaps worked to their advantage, since, unlike renaissance literary studies, Middle English studies was never so firmly driven by the ahistorical imperatives of formalist criticism. The texts were far from being the 'well-wrought urns' of organicist aesthetics; they were often acephalous or atelous, their metre seemingly random or incompetent, their authorship uncertain, their ethic moralistic or didactic, their unfamiliar, troubling conventions worn heavily, and their uncompromising forms of address often far from transcendent. Translation, a favoured medieval mode, also found little favour in the era of New Criticism. Moreover, poetry and verse in the Middle Ages have many uses which could be described as downright unpoetic. Epic poems, the *Siege of Jerusalem*, Lydgate's *Siege of Thebes* and *Troy Book*, for example, retold the classical and biblical epics, primarily as translations and adaptations, shoring up a classical heritage rather than reinventing epic tradition. Many of these works were linguistically difficult, of course, which put up a barrier to the Arnoldian dynamics of Poetry as a secular religion,[4] though I would also want to argue that this linguistic barrier is in part an effect of discursive and pedagogical traditions that read them *as* inaccessible without the benefit of specialist training.

And yet, the influence of New Criticism is clearly evident in the popular, and popularising Chaucerian criticism of E.T. Donaldson and others whose main concern was to capture the ways in which Chaucer, and selected other medieval poets, could make meaning for modern readers; that is, to efface what was alien and other, and to embrace the familiar – those elements which might transcend historical difference. Accordingly, Donaldson opened up an ironic, knowing distance between Chaucer and his narrative voices, establishing an easy, flattering perspective for the modern reader, who was thus freed from many of the more scholarly demands of medieval studies and encouraged to respond to the broader 'human' concerns of the poems, and the genius of their author. Chaucer's texts were powerfully brought to life for modern readers, though often at the expense of their own historical specificity.[5]

In England, the more programmatic work of John Speirs took up F.R. Leavis's emphasis on criticism as a total engagement of intelligence, sensibility, judgement and experience, 'both of literature and of life', warning that medievalists were too ready to insulate themselves in their specialist study, 'still too anxious and preoccupied to keep their studies safe from the literary critic'.[6] 'To insist that the scholar should be a critic, and the critic a scholar, seems rather what is needed,' he wrote, defending his own interest in anthropological research and its importance for reading medieval literature. Like Donaldson, though, Speirs assumed a stable, human response to literature, arguing that medieval texts occupy the same cultural and aesthetic space as *King Lear* or *Anna Karenina*. 'The judgement of one who has never experienced these and other greatest things in literature could not be trusted among medieval works either.'[7]

If we accept this opposition between criticism and scholarship for the moment, the most outstanding example of the latter – for the sometimes acrimonious debates that troubled medieval studies in the 1950s and 1960s – is the work of D.W. Robertson and Bernard Huppé. They were not alone, of course, in paying increased attention to the intellectual contexts of medieval literature, and insisting on the cultural differences that separate the medieval from the modern, but their theory was articulated more forcefully and more programmatically than others. They argued that medieval poets composed their works to chime in harmony with the reading practices of scriptural exegesis and, more specifically, Augustine's identification of *caritas* as the desired allegorical meaning of every biblical text.[8] Armed with sufficient information about those reading practices, the modern reader could steer clear of modern concerns and preoccupations – at best distracting and at worst treacherous – and attain an authentic and correct reading. No longer an opportunity for the engaging, confessional criticism of writers like Donaldson – the 'hedonistic' identification with medieval characters, in Robertson's phrase – medieval poetry was forced into an almost monastic existence, as it were, enclosed in a single, orthodox medieval world view, organised around a series of 'quiet hierarchies'.[9] The 'method', still hotly contested even thirty years later, is probably the single critical theory, or science of interpretation, developed specifically around the site of medieval literature, not borrowed from other areas of English literary criticism.

I began by sketching an opposition between formalism and historicism, but it is apparent that in the field of medieval studies this opposition is cut across by a different, related tension, this time between criticism and scholarship, particularly the exegetical kind. Speirs articulated the polarity in 1957, as we saw above, and, five years later, Elizabeth Salter came to a similar conclusion in her survey of *Piers Plowman* studies, suggesting that those historical or scholastic readings which neglected the poem's status as 'a product of the creative imagination' were severely restricted.[10] Like many medievalists, Speirs and Salter were haunted, though for different reasons, by the fear that medieval studies might somehow be left behind, that New Critical methods were burgeoning elsewhere, and medieval scholarship was not keeping up. In part, it is another version of the debate about historicism, and the categories through which we read and even define 'poetry' and 'literature' in the medieval period. Salter contemplates the kind of 'surgery' that a purely aesthetic reading might effect on *Piers Plowman*, and concludes that scholarly findings should 'vivify, not simply . . . chart more accurately, the meaning of a medieval poem'.[11] In espousing this middle path, Salter writes from a similar rhetorical position as scholars as diverse as Speirs and, more influentially, Rosemary Woolf.[12] Naturally, it is rare to find anyone openly espousing either extreme of pure scholarship or pure criticism; what is fascinating is the way in which these writers redefine their field and their methodology as the proliferation of critical methods gradually makes an impact on medieval studies.

A.C. Spearing, for example, in *Criticism and Medieval Poetry* (1964), first set out to reconcile techniques of close reading with the distinctive features of medieval poetic style, work extended in his 1970 study, *The Gawain-Poet*. In 1985, his *Medieval to Renaissance in English Poetry* interrogated the assumptions and implications of periodicity in medieval studies, and explored Harold Bloom's work on poetic misprision in relation to Chaucer and his followers, while more recently, his essays in *Readings in Medieval Poetry* (1987) work eclectically with aspects of narratology and hermeneutics.[13]

Dissatisfied with such experiments, though, and the very oppositions around which most of these movements are organised, contemporary historicism attempts to refigure completely the relationship between text, context and reader, in both conceptual and political terms. Accordingly, 'criticism' can be seen as increasingly irrelevant or outdated, if it is defined simply as a 'response' to the literary text. Once it is reconceived, though, as a set of strategies for reading a range of literary, cultural, social and historical texts, it is the bread and butter of modern cultural studies. The medieval poem can thus be situated amidst a number of conflicting cultural and textual milieux, not just the dominant expressions of orthodoxy (the traditional object of 'scholarly' research), as it negotiates a range of ideological demands and generic or intertextual affiliations. And further, because medieval verse occupies a different, far broader social and cultural role than the more purely aesthetic realm to which poetry is customarily relegated, it can even help us redefine our theories of the workings of cultural production. In different ways, the work of David Aers, Sheila Delany, Louise Fradenburg, Stephen Knight and Lee Patterson can stand as exemplary in this regard, as we shall see later. Some of these studies are specifically Marxist, concerned to examine not only the beginnings of capitalism and the relation of literary production to changing economic circumstances; but they also consider more generally the relation between literature and ideology, the various roles of medieval texts in either supporting or challenging dominant ideologies.

A different, in some ways analogous, narrative would describe a shift from a textual philology whose imperatives were almost purely empirical, to a contemporary textual criticism organised around a range of generic, intertextual, social and even psychological concerns. Medieval manuscripts are no longer regarded simply as artefacts, or as imperfect witnesses to an ideal, never fully recoverable work and are increasingly seen – however 'corrupt' – as primary documents for the study of the reception and representation of medieval texts.[14] It is a movement particularly associated with the school of medieval studies at York University. B.A. Windeatt's four-column edition of Chaucer's *Troilus and Criseyde* is a fine example of how productive such an intertextual treatment can be.[15] This edition provides an instant measure of Chaucer's textual indebtedness and the manner in which he compiled extracts from Boccaccio, Petrarch and Boethius. At the same time, it destabilises the hypothetical ideal of a single, authorially validated text, since the inclusion of commentary and textual variants on the same page insists on the *edited* nature of the text, and the history of interpretation which we cannot escape. Robert Yeager's essay in this volume is just one example of a number of similar developments in this newer philology.

Another avenue of approach would be to chart the influence of structuralism, modern narratology, psychoanalysis, deconstruction and other forms of post-structuralism on medieval studies. Once more, this would certainly lead us into the broader fields of literary studies, and might lead us to the unhappy conclusion – rehearsing the early complaints of Speirs and Salter, perhaps – that medievalists have been relatively slow to react to changes and challenges in other areas. The influence of structuralist analysis has certainly been felt in metrical and stylistic studies,[16] though some of the more speculative methods of interpretation and analysis have found it harder – or less attractive – to gain a foothold in this area, and the list of influential monographs is short, though Eugene Vance and R.A. Shoaf have been trailblazers in Middle English studies.[17] As recently as 1981, for example, Morton Bloomfield was able to take a long-distance view of contemporary theory, surveying it from a distance to determine 'what aspects of modern disciplines are, in my opinion, useful in interpreting and evaluating literature . . . I shall conclude by suggesting some approaches to Chaucer that may be helpful in understanding and appreciating him.'[18] While Bloomfield's willingness to examine 'theory' seems commendably modern, the purposes to which it will be put – interpretation, evaluation, understanding and appreciation – reveal a deep unwillingness to consider the implications of contemporary methods, which might well challenge the assumption that understanding or appreciating an author is any longer possible, or the desired end of criticism. Any discussion which regards modern theory merely as a decorative supplement to the interpretation of medieval literature is necessarily blind to its more profound critical implications. In *Medieval Theory of Authorship*, for example, A.J. Minnis suggests that medievalists who borrow terms derived from modern literary theory are tacitly admitting defeat, in using 'concepts which have no historical validity as far as medieval literature is concerned'.[19] His scholarly work on medieval literary theory is more than welcome, of course, and Minnis is duly aware that his window onto medieval authorship theory can be at best only 'unclear and distorting', yet his work is founded on the assumption that the acts of reading, summarising and interpreting his source materials are unproblematic, that 'medieval theory of authorship' is indeed objectively accessible to the attentive scholar who is prepared to forego modern theory.

More recently, however, a number of critical anthologies and journals bear witness to a more provocative and challenging relation between medieval texts and modern theory, starting from just such an opposition and instituting a series of dialogues between the two: a dialectic which has borne substantial fruit.[20] This question is of increasing importance once we acknowledge the difficulties inherent in the hermeneutic project, of establishing a set of reading practices that might be, indeed, hermetic, that might exclude the present, and its own pressing concerns. If we no longer concede the possibility, or indeed the desirability, of suspending modern attitudes and knowledge and becoming 'medieval' in order to read medieval literature, what position does the modern historicist assume when reading a medieval text? Minnis's 'window' is much more likely to be conceived now as *both* window and mirror, as we ask: What kinds of dialogue with the past are possible? And what kinds of dialogue are inevitable?

An avenue of inquiry that is only rarely taken up would be to consider changes in attitudes to the process and limits of interpretation, to consider scholarly dealings with the past, less for their conclusions and readings of individual texts than for the rhetorical voices and political strategies in and by which they situate themselves both in regard to the past and within their own contemporary, usually institutional, context. And if we ask this question from an even broader perspective, we would need to consider both the relation of contemporary medieval studies to the social, national and institutional origins of 'English' as an academic discipline, and the changes that have consistently marked that field and challenged its boundaries.

Modern feminist and cultural studies press their claims most loudly here, since their impact is felt not only on readings of individual texts, but on the silences and gaps in medieval literary history, as well as the strategies of interpretation we bring to bear on those texts which do survive. It is also under the influence of these movements that we are starting to pay attention to traces of popular culture in the medieval period, and less obviously 'literary' works.[21] Recent inquiries into the forms and expressions of medieval women's spirituality, for example, owe a good deal to these movements (though as prose texts, they fall outside the scope of this volume). Feminist theory and practice represent probably the most profound critique of and methodological challenge to medieval literary studies, since their impact is felt on all forms of historicist, political and textual criticism. It is no longer possible to dismiss feminism as historically anachronistic, 'irrelevant' to medieval literature on the grounds that there was no recognised women's movement in the period. This argument can be mounted only when the starting point of interpretation is narrowly conceived as determining authorial intention in the context of dominant ideology, and usually indicates only a complacent resistance to the broader forms of feminist critique of literary and cultural institutions. Even leaving aside the area of women's history, considerable work remains to be done in recovering women's writing, women's voices in medieval texts, or examining the means by which those voices are repressed, in considering specifically gendered forms of spirituality, of orthodoxy and heterodoxy, and of the textual representation of women and misogynist obsession in fictional and poetic texts, especially those which claim to foreground women's issues.[22] Feminism is also a crucial reading strategy in approaching the critical traditions through which medieval literature is still mediated for us, as we shall see below.

So while it is possible to set up a number of grids by which to read the critical histories of medieval studies, it is also true that all our dialogues with the past continue to change. We must now consider precisely that structure of 'dialogue' between past and present, between medieval and modern. How, and why are such divisions formed? And how are they maintained?

Defining the medieval, and the medievalist

Mediæval, medieval *a.* and *sb.* Of, pertaining to or characteristic of the Middle Ages. Of Art, Religion, etc.: Resembling or imitative of that of the Middle Ages.

The invention of the middle ages, as everyone knows, dates not from the medieval period itself but from renaissance scholarship, a strategic motive and effect of its own cultural and literary agendas. Needing to strengthen the ties between the classical past and their own endeavours, renaissance scholars wrote freely and easily of the period of cultural illiteracy, alienation from the classical masters, and unquestioning faith from which they saw themselves as liberating knowledge, extending the borders of exploration and inquiry — both geographically and philosophically — and forming a stronger sense of the individual or private self, distinguished from the public office or public sphere, or indeed, from outward personal demeanour.

As far as medieval vernacular literature is concerned, some aspects of the renaissance reception of Chaucer bear eloquent witness to the esteem in which he was held, and indeed, rewritten as an 'ancient', a classical author worthy of praise, attention, and scholarly commentary. Naturally, this is a two-edged sword. From this kind of attention, we can trace the formation of a canon of medieval literary texts, and the singling out of Chaucer as the pre-eminent, more or less atypical medieval poet — he who gave birth to English poetry. On the other hand, the perceived need for scholarly and linguistic commentary, and the sense that it was later poets who truly refined and polished English poetic language, pushed him back further into an ever-receding, increasingly inaccessible medieval past.

Situating the medieval as irreparably lost without specialist expertise has been one of the most powerful acts of naming and categorising in Western cultural history, and contemporary renaissance studies, with its emphasis on self-fashioning on a series of linguistic, discursive and epistemic breaks with the medieval past, reveals itself as still being written, in large part, by the stated concerns and self-definitions of the period it studies.[23] Of course this is a large generalisation to draw, and yet the willingness of renaissance and modern scholarship to dispense with, or seal off, the medieval is a curious phenomenon to which no other cultural explanation will answer. At the same time, to the extent that this blindness forces medievalists to answer to the criticism, scholarship and methodology of other historical fields, it may turn out to be productive, rather than limiting, and a cause for increasing engagement, rather than high-minded retreat into the discourses of truth and the authenticity of our own historical vision.

From the very beginning, though, we must concede the extent to which our historical period is named, organised and even written by later interests. A useful reminder of historical difference is to consider the various acts of nomination which organise the past for us. So many of the words and phrases we use to describe our period — medieval, middle ages, Middle English — date not, in fact, from the renaissance, but from later periods, mostly the nineteenth century.

As an example, consider the word 'mediæval'. First recorded in English in 1827, its first gloss from the *Oxford English Dictionary*, quoted at the beginning of this section, reveals a curious doubleness in this word. To begin with, the digraph in the older spelling testifies, perhaps, to the archaising desires inherent in the very conception of writers like Ruskin, to whom the *OED* attributes the first use of *mediæval* as noun, of *mediævalism*, and of *mediævalist*. I want to underline, though, the dual definition of medieval as 'characteristic of the Middle Ages' and also as 'resembling or imitative of . . . the Middle Ages', where we note the idea of the modern imitation of the medieval. To define or to demarcate this historical period is simultaneously to suggest the possibility of a simulacrum, of imitation and replication, of effacing the past at the same time as marking it as Other. We could perhaps take this as an unwitting allegory of a great deal that is typical in modern medieval criticism; the desire to approach ever nearer, without ever fully realising, medieval presence.

In all that I have said so far, I have used the category 'modern' without challenge. Like 'medieval', though, it is a signifier whose signified shifts constantly, according to context. In the preceding paragraph, I have wanted to distinguish it from 'renaissance' in order to mark a difference between Ruskin and the earlier commentators, though there is also a crucial sense in which we have accepted the renaissance's self-definition *as* the modern, in so far as it effects that break between itself and its past.[24]

As a counter to this tradition, it became fashionable, during the 1970s and 1980s, to locate parallels between some aspects of medieval theories of language and signification, and modernist or post-modernist theory and practice. Instead of condemning, it was now possible to commend the medieval, because it seemed to have anticipated so many of modernism's concerns with intertextuality, representation, semiotic theory and textual instability. From this period date a number of radical comparisons between Augustine and Saussure, for example, or studies which extend the discipline of semiology back into medieval philosophical tradition. The work of Umberto Eco, both theoretical and fictional, is central to this fashion, and indeed, the current fashionability of the medieval.[25] Some of the most original and influential modern theorists – Jacques Derrida, Luce Irigaray, Julia Kristeva and Jacques Lacan among them – also read medieval texts or cultural practices in ways which blur the discursive boundaries between the medieval and the modern.[26]

And once we shift our attention in this way to European developments, we find a number of medievalists who, from different perspectives, work to interrogate the quasi-anthropological nature of research into medieval cultures, and the effects of our reading of the past as both Other to us, and also antecedent. Scholars such as Hans-Robert Jauss, Paul Zumthor, R. Howard Bloch, and Brian Stock consider the nature and status of writing and textuality in the medieval period, the tensions between Latin and vernacular cultures, and different ways in which the modern medievalist situates himself or herself with respect to these cultural forms.[27] Not only is the scope of inquiry thus

broadened considerably beyond the field of culturally privileged forms of
expression – the aesthetic, or the ethical, for example – but the implications
for the inquirer are thus foregrounded. No longer the neutral, objective
scientist of the past, the contemporary medievalist not only gives a shape to
knowledge, but is also in turn fashioned by the questions he or she finds it
possible to put to the medieval text, eliciting various responses and
eliminating others.

Once we turn to the specific concerns of this volume, we must nevertheless
acknowledge that many of these more adventurous studies derive from a
tradition of scholarship very different from the Anglo-American stream; only
rarely do they consider medieval English texts. Medievalists working in the
English tradition seem more reluctant to branch out into this more speculative
research, and to extend their own, perhaps more specialised training. While
the borders between 'literature' and 'history' as discursive fields are being
broken down, the medieval academy still guards its boundaries with some
care, as hostile reviews of the more progressive and experimental books in
English medieval literature reveal.[28]

Lee Patterson argues persuasively that medieval studies tends to adopt the
authority structures of the dominant medieval institutions of knowledge and
doctrine. Medieval studies is a 'clerisy', he says, a discipline to which one must
be 'trained, not educated'.[29] One is inducted into its specialist mysteries, its
skills, its languages, to the point – and perhaps this is the point – where
critique from inside is impossible, such is the investment in one's training and
the debt to one's superiors, one's fathers. Patterson does not expound the
socio-political implications of the word 'clerisy', but it is worth noting its
powerful interpellation of the medievalist as male, Christian and, by implication
in this context, white. While women scholars and students increasingly find an
important and independent voice in medieval studies, it is true that the field
has little to say directly or in a straightforward way to non-Europeans, to the
indigenous inhabitants of Australia and New Zealand, for example, where
medieval literature is widely taught in the university curriculum. We might
also consider the nature of medieval studies when taught in Asian countries,
and offer a critique of the appreciative subject of literary studies, that finely
honed, well-educated reader who is set up as an ideal which can be successfully
imitated only by other white, male, Anglo-Saxon reading subjects. Again,
Chaucer studies leads the field here: perhaps it is a function of poetry which is
so clearly 'authored' to address its readers in such a determined, and determining
fashion, and in turn, to generate the critique of such interpellation.[30]

Louise Fradenburg has published a series of articles in which she develops
Patterson's analysis by a detailed diagnosis of masculinist bias in medieval
studies, in the very structure of those historicist studies which argue that the
past is irreparably lost to us. Fradenburg is concerned with the exclusivist
implications of a medieval scholarship which stresses the inaccessibility and
authoritative self-presence of the past:

The textual object has acquired its value insofar as it is, in some profound way, *lost* to us by its very pastness; critical and scholarly acts accordingly gain their legitimacy by means of reparation, by making up for that loss, by recovering an impossible relation to the alterity of the West's own past. Moreover, the notion of the alterity of the medieval past has all too often become a means of asserting the unapproachability and inviolacy of that past – of constituting it as an ideally pure and unchanging object, besieged by a variety of philosophical, political and sexual perversions. When this happens, the historicisation – we might say, the *mortification* – of the past, has the effect of preserving the past for the few who know how properly to revere it.[31]

Fradenburg calls for a feminist deconstruction of the hierarchical opposition between past and present and a critique of the 'construction of authority in the practice and theory of historical knowledge', those traditional practices which rule out of court any consideration of the position from which the critic speaks. She thus insists that contemporary feminist and post-structuralist debates about knowledge and critical method should be a *starting*-point, not an optional extra, for medieval studies. The essays in this book represent a number of different ways of approaching medieval literature in this way.

Non-Chaucerian poetry?

It is perhaps not in keeping with the spirit of this volume that many of my examples of critical trends have been drawn from Chaucer criticism and Chaucer scholars. The main reason is practical: change is much more legible over the same site. Still, I would also want to argue that most trends in medieval studies find their first and most influential expression among Chaucerians. This is not the place to discuss the reception of Chaucer, except to remark on the enormous critical investment in him above all other medieval poets, as the benevolent, lovable and enabling father at the head of the English poetic tradition. But since all medievalists of the English-speaking tradition are readers of Chaucer and Chaucer criticism, all are influenced, to some degree, by the dominant and traditional patterns of Chaucer scholarship.

What does it mean to define a body of poetry – Medieval English Poetry, Excluding Chaucer – in negative opposition to such a strongly defined canonical figure? Like the old phrase, Poetry of the Age of Chaucer, such a definition sets up the single canonical figure not only as exceptional, but also as exemplary in some way, a way which reflects more on the sixteenth-century poets and scholars than on Chaucer's own contemporaries. During the fifteenth century, Chaucer's name rarely appeared without those of Gower and Lydgate following close behind, or even leading the lists of medieval poets singled out for praise and commendatory verses; while Lydgate and Hoccleve, for example, both describe Chaucer as their poetic master. As long as a learned, high style was in vogue, it was hard to separate the three, but once such writers as Sidney and Spenser started looking for a creative challenge in English tradition, a poetic space to inhabit, Chaucer's self-conscious modernism dated Lydgate's poetry very rapidly, and both he and Gower, who was never fully committed to the development of an English poetic, were relegated to a second rank of competent or less competent imitators of Chaucer, from whose shadow they are only just emerging. Of Chaucer's other contemporaries, the *Gawain*-poet's work was isolated by its regionalism, and the absence of a manuscript tradition. Langland presents a different picture altogether. *Piers Plowman* had considerable contemporary manuscript success, but Crowley's printed edition of 1550 was probably a highly motivated act directed to a Reformation context, where Caxton's decision to print *The Canterbury Tales* in 1476 was simply a question of translating into a different medium a work whose continued popularity was well established and assured. Earlier poetry is even more deeply marked by the vicissitudes of political repression, chance and historical fashion. And of course, given the restricted access to manuscript copying and book production in this period, in the most material sense, we must constantly remind ourselves that what we read is not only an incomplete and partial record of what was written, and that writing itself represented only one aspect, or means of textual production.

Given the comparative obscurity into which Chaucer scholarship has thrust the rest of medieval English poetry, we are in a good position to consider the status of the non-canonical text. The situation of our poetry seems difficult to define in political terms: it does not form part of the great named tradition, and yet nor does it speak in any obvious way for minorities and other groups excluded from the very conception of canonicity as traditionally maintained. We can hardly mount a sustained claim on behalf of these mostly white, male, heterosexual, medieval poets that might be based on blindness to questions of race, gender or sexual orientation. Are we reduced to aesthetic judgements, then, to account for the pre-eminence of Chaucer, or are there other questions at issue? This is too large a question to be fully examined here, but we can perhaps provide a partial answer, which has some interesting implications for the relation between criticism and literary history.

As we are increasingly recognising, the production and reception of medieval poetry are organised very differently from the author-based models with which we are familiar. Most poetry was written by scholars and clerks, not 'writers' in the modern sense, and was often disseminated in large, anonymous collections and anthologies. Even when an author or scribe felt his name was worth recording, it was usually on that part of the manuscript, the beginning or end, which was most vulnerable to loss and decay. In short, there is no cult of the author: the 'author-function,' to quote Michel Foucault, is undoubtedly something we have imposed on, and attributed to selected texts of medieval literature, while formulations such as 'the *Gawain*-poet' reveal very clearly our desire to attribute poetry to a personality, even if all the specific information we have about him is derived from the works we cluster under his name.

Two important works of the 1970s attempted to rethink the divide between the Chaucerian and the non-Chaucerian, though in radically different ways. J.A. Burrow's *Ricardian Poetry*, published in 1971, expresses a willingness to shift critical emphasis from ways of distinguishing between the poets writing in the last decades of the fourteenth century, and to emphasise what they might have had in common.[32] And if, as his title reveals, he defined a stylistic movement in regnal terms, his work nevertheless drew the attention of literary critics to a productive socio-cultural milieu about which we have a great deal of information. Another remarkable book to appear in the 1970s was Thorlac Turville-Petre's *The Alliterative Revival*.[33] Here was an alternative way of organising the poetry of the medieval period, according to verse form, and the implications of that verse form for the literary history of the period. Turville-Petre's thesis, that the fourteenth-century did see a 'revival' of alliterative verse forms, is based on the formal necessities, structures and limitations of writing in English without rhyme, as opposed to a cultural and nationalist nostalgia for Anglo-Saxon poetry, the view of many nineteenth-century historians. Both these works represent attempts to see English poetry differently, to look closely at style, in particular.

There have been a number of other attempts – some more self-conscious than others – to break this stranglehold of the 'author' over medieval poetics. Derek Pearsall's *Old and Middle English Poetry*, and John Burrow's more recent *Medieval Writers and Their Work* (less a history than an account of the contexts of production and reception of Middle English literature) are useful introductions to the field of medieval literature which pay scrupulous attention to manuscript contexts, for example, and are less willing to promote individual authors as personalities.[34]

In more speculative and theoretical studies, medieval aesthetics and poetics are foregrounded, sometimes in sympathy with the work of Robertson, sometimes wishing to offer less prescriptive, alternative medieval models of interpretation, and nearly always stressing the intertextual contexts of production. Leaving aside those many works which explore newer possibilities for Chaucerian poetics, we could name, for example, the volumes of A.J. Minnis; Judson Boyce Allen, *The Ethical Poetic of the Later Middle Ages: A Decorum of Convenient Distinction*; and Jesse Gellrich, *The Idea of the Book in the Middle Ages*.[35] These works are all characterised by their interdisciplinary approach, and their willingness to rethink the category 'literature' and its occasionally anachronistic implications for reading medieval textuality. The next step is for the insights of these new literary histories, and these studies of medieval poetic theory and its contexts to be brought together with a criticism informed by contemporary literary theory. This is one of the endeavours that link the essays in this book.[36]

Contemporary criticism

It has been necessary to consider the history of medieval criticism, in order to sketch the contexts of the essays reprinted here, and the movements they represent. These essays certainly do not form a single, coherent narrative, for they often speak from opposing points of view. They are linked, however, in their attempt to interrogate and rethink some of the traditional categories of criticism, to explore other possibilities, to open up, rather than foreclose interpretation. The texts they cover also vary widely, from the well known to the virtually unknown, from early to very late Middle English texts. Needless to say, this range is not designed to be inclusive or exhaustive. But bearing in mind that this is just one of a number of narrative threads we could chart, these essays strike unusual chords in relation to one another. Any selection, any choice, inevitably lays claim to some kind of canon, and I have often been influenced in my choice by wanting to include an essay by an author whose work seems to me to represent a particular style of being a medievalist, for as I have argued, that is an aspect of current critical formations that is too often overlooked. These essays sometimes foreground theory: more often, they work by establishing a more intimate relationship between the text and their chosen critical method.

The first essay reprinted here, by Anne Middleton, in some respects takes John Burrow's *Ricardian Poetry* as a starting point, in its attempt to move away from author-based studies in the most narrowly conceived sense. Best known for her work on *Piers Plowman* and Chaucer, Middleton has always stressed both linguistic and stylistic analysis while becoming increasingly attentive to the historical contexts of the works she studies. A recent, ground-breaking essay on *Piers Plowman* stresses both the linguistic dispersal of the poet's name throughout the text, and the interrelations of revolutionary social and revolutionary poetic acts.[37] In one sense Middleton's work is closely allied to that of the 'new historicists', though it is not driven by quite the same Foucauldian agendas of locating linguistic or structural acts of power. *Piers Plowman*, after all, is not written as part of an elaborate court machinery for propping up, or mounting a critique of a government. On the contrary, Langland's political criticism is far more overt than covert. And as this earlier essay reveals, Middleton has long been interested in the public rhetoric of medieval poetry, and the ways in which it defines its own place in the public sphere. Tracing similarities between Gower and Langland, Middleton applauds Burrow's shift of emphasis away from Chaucer as the governing or most typical or influential poet of the period, and defines the 'impassioned direct address' of his contemporaries which is only indirectly

voiced through some of Chaucer's characters. This essay is concerned with
the 'institution' of poetry and the kinds of rhetorical positions that institutional
space allows or licenses. It is not simply a question of style: Middleton's
work is an advance on Robertson or Muscatine's diagnosis of the appropriate
style for the appropriate level. In this essay, style is equally a question of
ethics, and in this, Middleton's work chimes closely with the ideological
analysis of Jacques Le Goff and David Aers, concerned to examine the ways
in which the middle classes found a voice and developed a mercantile
ideology.[38] Middleton suggests, in fact, that this voice is most
characteristically concerned with 'the turning of worldly time, that essential
middle-class commodity, to "common profit"'. It is a voice that seeks to
harness wisdom, to give guidance, concerned with ethics: 'experientially
based, vernacular, simple, pious but practical, active'.

Middleton's essay stands at the head of my collection because it ranges
over this most productive period for both literature and criticism – the latter
part of the fourteenth century – and because it considers a number of issues,
especially rhetoric and politics, and the relation between them. It sits in
fascinating, complementary conjunction with the work of David Aers, which
follows it.

Aers has been one of the most prominent medievalists to emerge from
Britain in the last twenty years, and his work traces an interesting trajectory.
His first book, *Piers Plowman and Christian Allegory* offered a critique of the
Robertsonian exegetical model, and set in its place a more subtle and flexible
understanding of medieval figurative expression in *Piers Plowman*.[39]
Throughout his prolific publishing career, Aers has always resisted the allure
of ahistorical, hierarchical models of interpretation and criticism, and his
studies of medieval texts are typically informed by detailed research on
medieval economic and social conditions. At the same time, Aers is fascinated
by the active engagement of the poetic imagination with social change, and
his work can be usefully read against studies by thinkers as diverse as
Raymond Williams and Pierre Macherey. In the essay reprinted here, Aers
argues that Langland's poetic energies give more persuasive life to
revolutionary forces, to the merchants and wasters who challenge the
hierarchic, tripartite ideology of medieval society. In later works, Aers has
also mounted rigorous challenges to some of the traditional formations of
medieval criticism.[40] In his most recent work, he has become more attentive
to feminist questions, and in offering a critique of Renaissance 'new
historicism'. In particular, his latest book, *Community, Gender and Individual
Identity*, interrogates precisely the relation between an emerging sense of self
and changing concepts of community in the medieval period.

In many respects, the work of David Aers finds its closest affinities in
medieval studies with that of Sheila Delany and Stephen Knight. Although
they have never worked together, and until recently, have been based,
respectively, in England, Canada and Australia, they form a radical triumvirate

of leftist politics and interpretation in medieval studies, offering a sustained challenge to some of the more pious orthodoxies of traditional scholarship. In 1986, for example, both Aers and Knight published brief introductions to Chaucer in separate series, both concerned with re-reading the canonical text in radical, socio-historical ways. A little earlier, in 1983, Delany had published *Writing Woman: Essays on Women, Medieval and Modern*, a collection of essays which considered texts by and about women, though not primarily or solely from a feminist reading position.[41] Delany has always described herself as a Marxist with a special interest in the oppression of women within pre-capitalist and capitalist socio-economic structures. Stephen Knight's strongest critical affiliations are probably with the Raymond Williams school, if we may call it that, of cultural studies and critique. Alert to the linguistic and semiotic structures of the texts they study, all three critics have written on Chaucer, to re-politicise his poetry, and the criticism it has generated. It was Delany, for example, who in *Writing Woman*, mounted the first great challenge to some of the pieties of Chaucerianism, reintroducing authorial, albeit unconscious, intention, to approach Chaucer's misogyny, and its displaced representation in *The Manciple's Tale*. This essay has paved the way for a good deal of contemporary feminist criticism of Chaucer.

Knight's essay on *Lady Isabel and the Elf-Knight* typically combines close attention to the text with an examination of the historical contexts of the early ballads, and their reception in later periods, insisting that the 'meaning' of the text is to be found in its attempts to articulate with social and cultural, and in this case, gender problems. Like Aers and Delany, Knight also researches and publishes in areas other than medieval studies.

I have chosen Delany's essay on *Havelok the Dane* because it exemplifies, in very concise form, the strength of her reading strategies. Instead of focusing on source studies or structural and comparative analogues, as so many studies of romance do, Delany hones in on the politics of kingship as represented in this romance, through its content and its style, as a form of cultural wish-fulfilment, while at the same time tracing challenges to traditional theories of kingship as divine right, as a contractual theory of kingship emerges in response to thirteenth-century royal politics.

In addition to considering less well-known works like *Havelok* and the ballads, I have also chosen to foreground two more familiar medieval poems, and a selection of recent essays to compare and contrast. *Piers Plowman* and *Sir Gawain and the Green Knight* are my sample texts here. In contrast to Aers's essay, Laurie Finke considers *Piers Plowman* in the light of post-structuralist criticism, a discipline with which Aers, Knight and Delany, for example, often have little sympathy. Setting medieval against modern and post-modern thought about allegory, Finke tackles the vexed question of anachronism, tracing a number of contradictions and tensions in Augustine's theories of representation, used as the basis for so much exegetical criticism. She argues, not that post-structuralism can produce productive readings of medieval texts; but that 'the contradictions and silences within Augustine's theory of allegory are archetypal and hence may illuminate the Yale Critics' interest in allegory'. The problem of anachronism disappears, in one sense, and *Piers Plowman* can be read as itself an allegory of language's ability to represent truth.

Like Aers and Finke, Steven Justice sees the poem as an experimental work, but approaches the problem from a slightly different angle, focusing on Langland's composition of a narrative that is in a way provisional, trying out different genres and the forms of narrative authority they invoke. The pilgrimage of the poem, then, is a poetic pilgrimage, a search for 'a genre that will accommodate an authority neither abusive nor idiosyncratic'. This is where Finke and Justice differ from Aers, in that they both read *Piers Plowman* as a more self-consciously poetic work, as in part about the problems of writing poetry. These concerns are not simply the concerns of modernism warped over the medieval text: in both cases, they stem from problems Langland raises in the poem itself.

A salient contrast is found here in the essay by Barton Palmer, on *The Owl and the Nightingale*. Surveying the many conflicting interpretations that have been offered of this poem, Palmer argues that critical expectations of a 'singular and valid interpretation' of medieval poems probably reflect expectations formed around the site of realist fiction, for example, where a hierarchical range of speaking voices, dominated by that of the omniscient author, organises meaning and validity of interpretation for the reader. Medieval texts, he argues, can more productively be read as interrogative texts, and an unresolved debate poem such as *The Owl and the Nightingale* surely discourages a single, straightforward 'answer' to the problems it sets.

My own essay on *Winner and Waster* also considers a debate poem. Because this poem is incomplete in the single manuscript, the problems of closure and final interpretation are compounded. Like Aers's work, my essay considers the poet's attempts to reconcile traditional ideologies with contemporary realities, and like Steven Justice, I've tried to be attentive to the different genres employed by the poet, and their associated narrative voices. In company with many modern scholars, my work seeks to bring together an emphasis on language and linguistic patterns informed by post-structuralist criticism, with detailed attention to the work's social and political contexts.

As we saw above, recent developments in manuscript and textual studies in this period work to demystify the notion of a transcendent text of the poet's work. Robert Yeager works from the base of these studies but goes further in exploring the spatial and visual semiotics of the medieval page, when the Latin glosses of Gower's *Confessio Amantis* seem to be incorporated into the design of the poem from the very beginning. Thus the hierarchy of text and commentary is put into question from the very beginning of the work's production and reception.

This process of demystification might be identified as a common thread linking many of the essays collected here. In general, these scholars work with a willingness to unpack and rethink traditional critical attitudes and practices, especially where literary criticism has the effect of locating, endorsing and even perpetuating a dominant, single world view.

The two essays on *Sir Gawain and the Green Knight* demonstrate this process in different ways. This poem has been the subject of a wide range of critical approaches: it is still regarded, though for different reasons, as an exemplary medieval romance. Like many readers, Jill Mann compares the competing worldviews presented in the poem, but is more sympathetic than many critics to the bourgeois world of Hautdesert, and argues that the poem can be read as an attempt to synthesise mercantile with knightly values. Sheila Fisher's more speculative essay reads not just the overt tensions in *Sir Gawain*, but also the covert ones, with specific reference to the different ways in which the female characters in the Arthurian narrative have been displaced in this poem from their crucial roles in that tradition. Reading medieval texts as part of broader cultural patterns is a most pressing concern for a number of the authors represented in this volume.

Feminist literary analysis in medieval literature has tended to concentrate on Chaucer's female characters, or on women writers, when they can be positively identified. Alexandra Barratt questions the traditional ascription of most anonymous medieval poems to men, and examines the implicit assumptions and conclusions of such ascriptions in two fifteenth-century poems, which used to be described as 'Chaucerian' works. Barratt's essay is modest in scope, but exemplary in the care with which it examines our working assumptions.

Lee Patterson's essay on the alliterative *Morte Arthure* brings together a number of concerns raised by other authors in my collection. Part of his ground-breaking study, *Negotiating the Past*, Patterson's essay combines medieval theories of history with modern theories of historicism; and finds a self-reflexivity in this poem, as a meditation on the problematic use of historical precedent. It is an approach he has expounded further, in his *Chaucer and the Subject of History*, especially in his reading of Chaucer's *Troilus and Criseyde*.

Naturally, there are many omissions and gaps in this collection, and I hold the usual reservations about seeming to establish or confirm a canon of either poetical works or critical authors. At the same time, by putting well-known against less well-known works and authors, this volume goes some way towards breaking down such an opposition. The questions raised by these essays are critical ones. I have chosen them as detailed readings of texts to exemplify current reading practices: more thorough examinations of methodology and theory belong in longer, more sustained works. The reader is obviously free to read the essays in the order most useful to his or her needs: if I have ordered them to move from familiar, fourteenth-century works to the less well known, both earlier and later, it seems to me, all the same, that these essays could be ordered and read in a number of different ways, all productive of different dialogues with one another, and with the texts they study.

Notes

1. This opposition is examined with respect to Chaucer studies by LEE PATTERSON, *Negotiating the Past: The Historical Understanding of Medieval Literature* (Madison: University of Wisconsin Press, 1987).

2. D.J. PALMER, *The Rise of English Studies: An Account of the Study of English Language and Literature from its Origins to the Making of the Oxford English School* (London: Oxford University Press, 1965), pp. 71–7.

3. PATTERSON, *Negotiating the Past*, pp. 17–18.

4. See CHRIS BALDICK, *The Social Mission of English Criticism 1848–1932* (Oxford: Clarendon Press, 1983); and TERRY EAGLETON, *Literary Theory: An Introduction* (Oxford: Basil Blackwell, 1983), pp. 22–7. For an alternative perspective, see IAN HUNTER, *Culture and Government: The Emergence of Literary Education* (Houndmills: Macmillan, 1988).

5. E. TALBOT DONALDSON, *Speaking of Chaucer* (London: Athlone Press, 1970); and his selected edition of Chaucer, *Chaucer's Poetry: An Anthology for the Modern Reader*, 2nd edn (New York: John Wiley & Sons, 1975).

6. JOHN SPEIRS, *Medieval English Poetry: The Non-Chaucerian Tradition* (London: Faber & Faber, 1957), pp. 25, 16.

7. SPEIRS, p. 15.

8. D.W. ROBERTSON, *A Preface to Chaucer: Studies in Medieval Perspectives* (Princeton: Princeton University Press, 1962); D.W. ROBERTSON and BERNARD F. HUPPÉ, *Piers Plowman and Scriptural Tradition* (Princeton: Princeton University Press, 1963).

9. ROBERTSON, pp. 41, 51.

10. ELIZABETH SALTER, *Piers Plowman: An Introduction* (Oxford: Basil Blackwell, 1962), pp. 1–7.

11. ELIZABETH SALTER, *Fourteenth-Century English Poetry: Contexts and Readings* (Oxford: Clarendon Press, 1983), pp. 3, 11.

12. ROSEMARY WOOLF, *The English Mystery Plays* (London: Routledge and Kegan Paul, 1972); *The English Religious Lyric in the Middle Ages* (London: Oxford University Press, 1986); and *Art and Doctrine: Essays on Medieval Literature*, ed. Heather O'Donoghue (London and Ronceverte: The Hambledon Press, 1986).

13. A.C. SPEARING, *Criticism and Medieval Poetry* (1964; 2nd edn, London: Edward Arnold, 1972); *The Gawain-Poet: A Critical Study* (Cambridge: Cambridge University Press, 1970); *Medieval to Renaissance in English Poetry* (Cambridge: Cambridge University Press, 1985); *Readings in Medieval Poetry* (Cambridge: Cambridge University Press, 1987).

14. See, for example, Derek Pearsall (ed.), *Manuscripts and Readers in Fifteenth-Century England: The Literary Implications of Manuscript Study*. Essays from the 1981 Conference at the University of York (Cambridge: D.S. Brewer, 1983); Pearsall (ed.), *Manuscripts and Texts: Editorial Problems in Later Middle English Literature*. Essays from the 1985 Conference at the University of York (Cambridge: D.S. Brewer, 1987); Pearsall (ed.), *Studies in the Vernon Manuscript* (Cambridge: D.S. Brewer, 1990).

15. B.A. Windeatt (ed.), *Geoffrey Chaucer, Troilus and Criseyde: A New Edition of 'The Book of Troilus'* (London, New York: Longman, 1984).

16. See, for example, Susan Wittig, *Stylistic and Metrical Structures in the Middle English Romances* (Austin: University of Texas, 1978); Evelyn Birge Vitz, *Medieval Narrative and Modern Narratology: Subjects and Objects of Desire* (New York: New York University Press, 1989); Robert William Sapora, Jr, *A Theory of Middle English Alliterative Meter with Critical Applications*. Speculum Anniversary Monographs 1 (Cambridge, Mass.: Mediaeval Academy of America, 1977).

17. Eugene Vance, *Mervelous Signals: Poetics and Sign Theory in the Middle Ages* (Lincoln and London: University of Nebraska Press, 1986); R.A. Shoaf, *Dante, Chaucer, and the Currency of the Word: Money, Images, and Reference in Late Medieval Poetry* (Norman, Oklahoma: Pilgrim, 1983).

18. Morton W. Bloomfield, 'Contemporary Literary Theory and Chaucer', in *New Perspectives in Chaucer Criticism*, ed. Donald M. Rose (Norman, Oklahoma: Pilgrim Books, 1981), p. 24–5.

19. A.J. Minnis, *Medieval Theory of Authorship: Scholastic Literary Attitudes in the Later Middle Ages*, 2nd edn (Aldershot: Scholar, 1988), p. 1.

20. Laurie A. Finke and Martin B. Shichtman (eds), *Medieval Texts and Contemporary Readers* (Ithaca and London: Cornell University Press, 1987); Allen J. Frantzen (ed.), *Speaking Two Languages: Traditional Disciplines and Contemporary Theory in Medieval Studies* (Albany: State University of New York Press, 1991); Julian Wasserman and Lois Roney (eds), *Sign, Sentence, Discourse: Language in Medieval Thought and Literature* (Syracuse: Syracuse University Press, 1989); Marina S. Brownlee, Kevin Brownlee and Stephen G. Nichols (eds), *The New Medievalism* (Baltimore and London: The Johns Hopkins University Press, 1991). See also the essays collected in 'The New Philology', *Speculum*, **65** (1990), and 'Reflections on the Frame: New Perspectives on the Study of Medieval Literature' *Exemplaria*, **3** (1991).

21. Thomas J. Heffernan (ed.), *The Popular Literature of Medieval England*. Tennessee Studies in Literature 28 (Knoxville: University of Tennessee Press, 1985).

22. See, for example, Alexandra Barratt's edition of *Women's Writing in Middle English* (London: Longman, 1992).

23. For example, see Stephen Greenblatt, *Renaissance Self-Fashioning: From More to Shakespeare* (Chicago: University of Chicago Press, 1980); Catherine Belsey, *The Subject of Tragedy: Identity and Difference in Renaissance Drama* (London: Methuen, 1985). For commentary, see David Aers in *Community, Gender and Individual Identity: English Writing 1360–1430* (London: Routledge, 1988), pp. 16–19 and Lee Patterson, *Chaucer and the Subject of History* (London: Routledge, 1991), pp. 7–8.

24. There is a fascinating discussion of the concept of modernity and tradition in recent medieval studies in Stephen Nichols' introduction to *The New Medievalism*, pp. 8–12.

25. ALEXANDRE LEUPIN'S review of the work of Roger Dragonetti, 'The Middle Ages, the Other', in *Diacritics* (Fall 1983), pp. 22–30; UMBERTO ECO, *The Name of the Rose*, trans. William Weaver (London: Secker & Warburg, 1983); ECO, *Travels in Hyperreality*, trans. William Weaver (San Diego: Harcourt Brace Jovanovich, 1986); ECO and COSTANTINO MARMO (eds), *On the Medieval Theory of Signs* (Amsterdam: John Benjamins, 1989); ECO, *Semiotics and the Philosophy of Language* (Houndmills: Macmillan, 1984); THERESA COLETTI, *Naming the Rose: Eco, Medieval Signs, and Modern Theory* (Ithaca and London: Cornell University Press, 1988); EUGENE VANCE, *Mervelous Signals*, and with LUCIE BRIND D'AMOUR (eds), *Archéologie du Signe* (Toronto: Pontifical Institute of Medieval Studies, 1983); and MARCIA COLISH, *The Mirror of Language: A Study in the Medieval Theory of Knowledge*, rev. edn (Lincoln: University of Nebraska Press, 1983).

26. For example, consider JACQUES DERRIDA's discussions of the mythology of the book, in *Of Grammatology*, trans. Gayatri Chakravorty Spivak (Baltimore: Johns Hopkins University Press, 1976); LUCE IRIGARAY's discussions of female mysticism in *Speculum of the Other Woman*, trans. Gilliam C. Gill (Ithaca: Cornell University Press, 1985); JULIA KRISTEVA's analysis of romance and early novels in *Desire in Language: A Semiotic Approach to Literature and Art*, trans. Leon S. Roudiez (Oxford: Basil Blackwell, 1981), and of courtly love in *Tales of Love*, trans. Leon S. Roudiez (New York: Columbia University Press, 1987); and JACQUES LACAN's discussions of courtly love in 'God and the *Jouissance* of The Woman: A Love Letter', in JULIET MITCHELL and JACQUELINE ROSE (eds), *Feminine Sexuality: Jacques Lacan and the école freudienne* (London: Norton, 1983), pp. 138–48. Another important collection is MICHEL FEHER (ed.), *Fragments for a History of the Human Body: Part One* (New York: Zone 3, 1989).

27. To consider only the most well known of these studies, see HANS-ROBERT JAUSS, 'The Alterity and Modernity of Medieval Literature', *NLH*, **10** (1979): 181–227; PAUL ZUMTHOR, *Essai de poétique médiévale* (Paris: Éditions du Seuil, 1972); R. HOWARD BLOCH, *Etymologies and Genealogies: A Literary Anthropology of the French Middle Ages* (Chicago and London: University of Chicago Press, 1983); BRIAN STOCK, *The Implications of Literacy: Written Language and Models of Interpretation in the Eleventh and Twelfth Centuries* (Princeton: Princeton University Press, 1983).

28. Cf. DAVID AERS (ed.), *Medieval Literature: Criticism, Ideology and History* (Brighton: Harvester, 1986), pp. 3–8.

29. LEE PATTERSON (ed.), introd. *Literary Practice and Social Change in Britain, 1380–1530*. The New Historicism 8 (Berkeley and Los Angeles: University of California Press, 1990), p. 3.

30. CAROLYN DINSHAW, *Chaucer's Sexual Poetics* (Madison: University of Wisconsin Press, 1989); ELAINE TUTTLE HANSEN, 'Fearing for Chaucer's Good Name', *Exemplaria*, **2** (1990): 23–36.

31. LOUISE FRADENBURG, '"Voice Memorial": Loss and Reparation in Chaucer's Poetry', *Exemplaria*, **2** (1990): 173. See also, her 'Criticism, Anti-Semitism, and the *Prioress's Tale*', *Exemplaria*, **1** (1989): 69–115.

32. J.A. BURROW, *Ricardian Poetry: Chaucer, Gower, Langland and the 'Gawain' Poet* (London: Routledge and Kegan Paul, 1971).

33. THORLAC TURVILLE-PETRE, *The Alliterative Revival* (Cambridge: D.S. Brewer 1977).

34. DEREK PEARSALL, *Old and Middle English Poetry*. The Routledge History of English Poetry 1 (London, Henley and Boston: Routledge and Kegan Paul, 1977);

J.A. Burrow, *Medieval Writers and Their Work: Middle English Literature and its Background 1100–1500* (Oxford: Oxford University Press, 1982).

35. Judson Boyce Allen, *The Ethical Poetic of the Later Middle Ages: A Decorum of Convenient Distinction* (Toronto: University of Toronto Press, 1981); Jesse M. Gellrich, *The Idea of the Book in the Middle Ages: Language Theory, Mythology and Fiction* (Ithaca and London: Cornell University Press, 1985).

36. A recent essay by Anne Middleton, 'Medieval Studies' in *Redrawing the Boundaries: The Transformation of English and American Literary Studies* (New York: MLA, 1992), pp. 12–40, considers a number of issues raised in this section, but appeared too late to be discussed fully in the text.

37. Anne Middleton, 'William Langland's "Kynde Name": Authorial Signature and Social Identity in Late Fourteenth Century England', in Lee Patterson (ed.), *Literary Practice and Social Change in Britain, 1380–1530*, (1990), pp. 15–82.

38. Charles Muscatine, *Chaucer and the French Tradition: A Study in Style and Meaning* (Berkeley: University of California Press, 1969); Jacques Le Goff, *Time, Work and Culture in the Middles Ages*, trans. Arthur Goldhammer (Chicago: University of Chicago Press, 1980).

39. David Aers, *Piers Plowman and Christian Allegory* (London: Edward Arnold, 1975).

40. David Aers, 'The Good Shepherds of Medieval Criticism', *Southern Review*, **20** (1987): 168–85. See also his *Chaucer* (Brighton, Sussex: Harvester, 1986).

41. Sheila Delany, *Writing Woman: Women Writers and Women in Literature, Medieval to Modern* (New York: Schocken, 1983).

2 The Idea of Public Poetry in the Reign of Richard II*

ANNE MIDDLETON

Resisting the emphasis of traditional criticism on author-based studies, Middleton's influential essay locates and defines a characteristic speaking voice shared by a large body of late fourteenth-century poetry. Such poetry situates itself as steering a middle course between the courtly and clerical traditions, and consistently addresses the question of the common good, based on a shared understanding of ethical and social concerns. The poet's speaking position is an 'implicated' one, which invokes not only the formal addressees of the poem (the king, for example), but also the readers, as members of the same worldly community. At the same time, these works also attempt to create a distinctive space for poetry — and the poet — in public affairs.

'Ricardian' poetry is a term that has entered our critical vocabulary only recently, since the admirable study by J.A. Burrow.[1] He uses it in order to further the kind of critical thought which has for some time comfortably referred to 'Elizabethan' or 'Edwardian' poetry. The term implies a willingness to seek broad connections between social and literary history, rather than the 'influence' of one writer upon another. Unlike the earlier phrase, 'the age of Chaucer', the notion of a 'Ricardian period' in literature enables Burrow to identify some common themes and features of style as characteristic of the era, without subordinating other writers' achievements to either the stylistic preferences or the idiosyncrasies of personal development of its crowning genius. The shift in perspective that follows this simple change of names has already been salutary for Chaucer criticism, as well as for the understanding of his major contemporaries, each of whom can be seen to have a coherent sense of his purpose, his audience and his world.

---

* Reprinted from *Speculum*, **53** (1978): 94–114.

In this same spirit I attempt here to identify and describe a kind of poetry, and an ideal of literary eloquence implicit in it, that makes its first appearance in the Ricardian period, but is only indirectly and intermittently represented in the work of Chaucer. The social and literary values that found expression in the mode I call 'public poetry' are presented in Chaucerian fiction only, as it were, in indirect discourse, assigned in various ways to several characters in the Canterbury fiction – and thereby greatly qualified.[2] The impassioned direct address that was the characteristic voice of public poetry among Chaucer's contemporaries was, however, a considerable expressive achievement in its own right, and it is in its simpler form that it will be described here. The general social dispositions of its most effective spokesmen have been noted by historians. These attitudes, which constitute the foundations of a secular and civic piety, are attended in the poetry by explicit and coherent notions about the nature of poetry, about poetry's worldly place and purpose. In brief terms, poetry was to be a 'common voice' to serve the 'common good'. The realised presence of the poetic speaker in this literature became a stylistic means of expressing that purpose, and it produced a new kind of experientially based didactic poetry, tonally vivid and often structurally unstable.

Public poetry is a mode quite distinct from the homiletic or satirical poetry often grouped with it as 'complaint' or 'verse on contemporary conditions'; indeed, the strength and consistency of its 'voice' frequently strain against the formal frameworks that it adopted from earlier didactic genres. It will be the task of this paper to note such distinctions and to describe the characteristics of this new form of vernacular eloquence. A brief survey of an important part of Ricardian literature cannot, of course, supply an interpretation or complete reading of any of the poems in the tradition, particularly of those two 'baggy monsters', the *Confessio Amantis* and *Piers Plowman*, that provide my chief illustrations. It can perhaps suggest what is new in the social and literary imagination informing both works and show what influence this had on their successors writing on public ethical themes.

The public poetry of the Ricardian period is best understood not as poetry 'about' contemporary events and abuses, whether viewed concretely or at a distance, from the vantage point of a universal scheme of ideal order[3] – it is rarely occasional or topical, and it is indifferent on the whole to comprehensive rational systems of thought or of poetic structure. Rather it is poetry defined by a constant relation of speaker to audience within an ideally conceived worldly community, a relation which has become the poetic subject. In describing their mode of address, the poets most often refer to the general or common voice, and the ideal of human nature that sustains this voice assigns new importance to secular life, the civic virtues, and communal service. The voice of public poetry is neither courtly, nor spiritual, nor popular. It is pious, but its central pieties are worldly felicity and peaceful, harmonious communal existence. It speaks for bourgeois moderation, a course between the rigorous absolutes of religious rule on the one hand,[4] and, on the other, the rhetorical hyperboles and emotional vanities of the courtly style, whether that style is conceived in its narrower sense of a distinctive manner of speech or as the mode of living and personal values associated with the noble estate.[5] This poetic voice is vernacular, practical, worldly, plain, public-spirited, and peace-loving[6] – in a word, 'common', rather than courtly or clerical, in its professed values and social allegiances.

Such values are certainly audible in Chaucer's Franklin, but they are equally clear in the lives and literary interests of the so-called Lollard Knights, that distinguished group of pious laymen who, like Chaucer and Gower, with whom some of them were closely associated, were highly literate and conscientious public servants in both military and diplomatic capacities. They exemplify an ideal of communal responsibility founded not primarily in an estates conception of one's duties, but in an altruistic and outward-turning form of love that might be called 'common love' to emphasise its symmetry and contrast with that singular passion which expresses itself in literature in the inward self-cultivation sometimes called 'courtly love'. 'Common love', for these men, was an emotion as fully natural and universal as *eros*, but it defined man as a social being, and, unlike its private counterpart, was turned outward to public expression. This kind of love is non-transcendent, practical, active; it issues in acts of social amelioration rather than in the refinement of inwardness. It manifests itself in mutual 'suffraunce' – toleration, compromise, forgiveness – and in public service.

It is this love that prompts Thomas Usk to direct his confession of misery to Lady Love, in imitation of Boethius's initial complaint to Lady Philosophy. He is prompted to model his *Testament of Love* on the *Consolation of Philosophy* not only by reverence for a literary prototype, but also by the close parallel between Boethius's situation and his own. He is a civil servant who considers himself wrongly accused and betrayed by his devotion to public office and to London, not unlike the imprisoned Boethius who found himself in need of Philosophy's support.[7] (Usk met, in fact, a similar fate: he was executed, along with the mayor Nicholas Brembre, in 1388.[8]) His destiny as public man, not the cruelties of an indifferent mistress, informs his somewhat clumsy effort to be a vernacular philosopher of love. Likewise Gower's long devotion as a moral poet to civic virtue and social accord occasions the confessional dialogue between the Lover and the Priest of Venus that he evidently considered his own 'testament of love'; within the *Confessio Amantis*, Venus bids Gower return to the world to 'gret wel Chaucer' and urge him to make a testament of his own. In both cases love as communal and historical bond, not as transcendental force or as erotic servitude, is the impetus to literary creation.

Usk explains to his instructress that she has always been his motive for undertaking public service – the 'office of commen doinge' as he calls it: 'For you, Lady, I have desired such cure' – that is, for love, not for fame.[9] 'That', the Lady replies, 'is a thing that may draw many hertes of noble and voice of commune into glory.' This interesting formulation – 'hearts of noble and voice of common' – is thematic in the poetic and social values I am describing. The 'hearts of noble' are incited by love to intense self-cultivation; the 'common', however, shows its heart in its voice, enlisted in the furtherance of virtue in 'commen doinge'.

The love that issues in worldly action is a central conception in Ricardian public poetry, where it is treated as an emotional and ethical force no less powerful and fundamental to human life than its more familiar counterpart in courtly literature. The literary eloquence best suited to expressing that conception will itself be an instance of such public work, inspired by communal love rather than by anger or indignation. Its rhetorical strategy attributes to the audience a ready reserve of good will toward secular harmony, despite diversity of 'craftes'.

These social values, and the notion of the place and purpose of secular literature that follows from them, are deeply characteristic of both the *Confessio Amantis* and *Piers Plowman*. Some common features of these two long poems offer the best possible conditions for examining this essentially public notion of literature. Both poets are essentially 'one-poem' writers (Gower clearly saw his entire output as one continuous effort).[10] Both are inveterate revisers, and in both cases their revisions seem largely dictated not by formal considerations, but by matters of social fact and currency. Gower, whose alterations in the *Confessio* have incurred the suspicion of political trimming, has been defended against this charge by Fisher, who points out that his changes have an internal and principled political coherence; they consistently display 'the sentiments of a London citizen', rather than a narrowly expedient shift from Richard to Henry of Lancaster.[11] Similarly, Donaldson has argued that fullness and clarity, not changes in political allegiance or personal beliefs, determine the C-revisions of *Piers*.[12] (I would add that the Rising of 1381 probably gave a good deal of urgency to his effort to mend ambiguities.) What is significant, though, is that what the poet alters, what in his view most needs improving, is the poem's adequacy to his world, not only as a representation of it, but, even more important, as an address to it.

Their poetry, and Ricardian public poetry generally, speaks 'as if' to the entire community – as a whole, and all at once rather than severally – rather than 'as if' to a coterie or patron. By its mode of address and diction it implies that the community is heterogeneous, diverse, made up of many having separate 'singular' interests. It envisions a society composed of members whose differing stations, functions, and ways of life yield different perspectives on the common world, which it is the aim of the speaker to respect, to bring to mutual awareness, and to resolve into common understanding. What common understanding – that is, 'we', each of us in the presence of the others – can see about our common condition, the world we share *as a people*, becomes the poetic subject. The style, which is distilled out of all the disparate special languages of society's parts, will be offered as the 'common voice' – the 'commun worldes speche', to use one of Gower's several variants of the notion. It will be a plain style, by choice and on principle, and will justify itself as both socially and psychologically well suited to the presentation of lay morality and large experiential truths.

What distinguishes public poetry among the genres that are mimetic of direct speech is,[13] first, the imagined character of the participants in this transaction, the 'I' and the 'you', and, second, the effort at comprehensiveness derived from that perception. 'Your' experience gives each of you a partial, but solidly based, view, to be completed by attention to the views – similarly based in worldly experience – of others. Here the Canterbury pilgrims' strong but comically disparate views of what the burning issue of their day *really* is exemplify this sense of the world, a model of public poetry's sense of its audience; Jill Mann has argued that it is precisely this that Chaucer learned from Langland.[14] Chaucer, however, gives a different fictional form to that sense of his audience, addressing them as an empathetic familiar, much as Chaucer the pilgrim reacts, in 'close-up', to each of his traveling companions. The 'I' of public poetry presents himself as, like his audience, a layman of good will, one worker among others, with a talent to be used for the common good. It is his task to find the common voice and to speak for all, but to claim no privileged position, no special revelation from God or the Muses, no transcendent status for the result, and little in the way of special gifts beyond a good ear. The 'I' is otherwise like 'you' and includes himself and his poetic endeavor in the world's work. As a 'character' he makes himself nearly invisible, but not in the chameleon-like manner of Chaucer the pilgrim, who takes his color, his moral partialities, from whatever hobbyhorse his fellow travelers happen to be riding. Rather he occupies the whole field of moral vision spanned by the several views of all those who make up the 'commune', by stretching himself, as it were, to the point of transparency.

In this mode there is little room for speculation or epistemological self-doubt; however partial the view of each may be, it is complemented by the view of others to form a firm fabric of worldly experience shared by all, and thereby reliable. Corresponding to this faith in worldly experience is a high degree of confidence in – even insistence upon – ordinary language, not learned or refined speech. It is often quite pointedly contrasted with the insulated jargon of the professions, of advanced learning, or of high rhetorical poetry, as on the whole the best medium for keeping moral knowledge active and heartfelt. It avoids mistakes precisely by being the language of the whole, 'common', not 'special'.

In partial corroboration of this distinction, the divergence of Chaucer's fortunes as a poetic influence from those of our two major examples is instructive. Despite the obvious fact that Chaucer's diction is to us as lucid, 'plain', and in places colloquial, as that of either of these contemporaries, he became to his aureate imitators a paradigm of refined style, justifying any amount of inkhorn inventiveness. Gower and Langland, though in other ways subjected to different critical fortunes, share a common later estimate of their style: both are seen as masters of 'plainness'. For Ben Jonson, Gower is the model of English plain style; and Churchyard's comment (1568) that

> Peers Plowman was full plaine
> and Chausers spreet was great.[15]

neatly summarises both Langland's critical reputation in the Renaissance and after, and the felt distance between his kind of achievement and that of Chaucer. It is apparent from these remarks that by 'style' these later readers must mean something more than diction or verbal and visual texture. As Churchyard's reference to 'spreet' (spirit) suggests, style implies something much broader: a set of social, moral, rhetorical, even political attitudes which together constitute a characteristic kind of perception, a mode of self-presentation, and a manner of speaking. In this broader sense, these readers are right to see a kinship between the two in their 'plain style'. What they are remarking on is the characteristic 'voice' and basic effect of what I have called public poetry: the sense it gives of offering 'common truth' in 'common speech'.

The notion of the 'common' or 'commune' is central to this poetic mode, and essential for understanding Gower's and Langland's use of the speaker in their English fictions. Like 'plain' in the instances I have cited, 'common' seems to denote a 'style' broadly considered. Its resonance in fourteenth-century usage is at once social and moral, political and rhetorical – and, on the whole, evidently positive. 'Common profit' is the usual translation of *res publica*, and its range of meanings in English is well described by Cicero's account of *res publica res populi*: 'the public good, or commonwealth, is the people's affair, in the sense that "people" are considered not as a herd, assembled in any sort of way, but as *a people*, bound by agreement as to law and rights, and associated for mutual benefit or expediency.'[16] 'Common', in other words, can denote the commonwealth as a whole, a community or fellowship, the populace or citizenry, as well as the 'common people', a class distinguished from either nobility or clergy or both as the 'third estate'. What is noteworthy in all uses of the term is its uniformly non-abstract, non-speculative cast. The 'commune', like the 'public' for Cicero, is not a theoretical or logical construct, derived from postulates about human nature; it is an association neither ideal nor fully voluntary, but evolved, historical, and customary, a creature of time, place, event, and language. It is society regarded experientially, an immanent rather than a transcendent notion.

The same aura of worldliness and experiential solidity clings to the wide range of adjectival uses of the term: 'public' (as opposed to private), 'lay' (as opposed to clerical), 'popular' (as opposed to learned), 'vernacular' (as opposed to Latin), 'general' (as opposed to special); also 'shared', 'usual', 'customary', 'familiar' or 'widely known' – and, it seems, therefore true: 'this proverbe is ful soth and ful commune' – it means all of these things as well as 'non-noble'.[17] And the same benign, even approving, attitude toward this array of qualities emerges from the *Middle English Dictionary*'s several illustrations of them, examples thickly clustered around the Ricardian period. True, phrases such as 'common criminal' and 'common whore' exist and have survived, but there is little to suggest that 'common' is usually a pejorative term in relation to its associated opposite; in fact, quite the reverse. There is on the whole less testimony to the negative senses of the term familiar to us in Modern English: 'low', 'mean', 'coarse', 'ignoble'. The range of meaning of the word, its field-of-play, delineates a coherent, and on the whole positive, cultural 'idea', suggesting that such phrases as 'common soth' and 'common voice' stand within a stylistic norm, for living and for speaking, that has gained some currency and distinctness, a special force and luminosity, in the last quarter of the fourteenth century.

Dictionary citations are not by themselves a sufficient base upon which to posit a cultural ideal. There is, however, ample literary testimony to the perceived ethical and stylistic coherence of these qualities, taken as justifying a homegrown eloquence, an elected plainness of expression, associated with active commitment to worldly service. In the literature of the Ricardian period each sense of the term seems to call up the others with a consistency that suggests an established locus of value.

This complex of social and rhetorical values is accompanied in all of the major Ricardian poets by a good deal of explicit speculation on the place of poetry-making as an activity in the world. Gower, Langland, and Chaucer incorporate into their long poems a considerable amount of 'thinking out loud' about this matter, and, despite their vast differences in artistic temperament, they are in striking agreement: for all of them, poetry is a mediating activity. This notion of the poetic enterprise reinforces the social ideals I have described and contributes along with them to the forming of a tonally felicitous middle style that was consciously chosen as appropriate to a particular expressive purpose.

All three of these London poets have a vivid sense of poetry's medial position in almost all the schemes they use for talking about it. Typically, the poet's enterprise – or some aspect of it – is described as 'between this and that'. The *Canterbury Tales* move, in the narrator's terms, back and forth between 'sentence and solas', though it is to be some ideal marriage of the two that will take the prize for the best story. Narrative tone oscillates between 'ernest and game'. The terms seem to correspond to polarities in the speaker's own attitude in the earlier poetry, particularly the *Troilus*, where the narrator strives for both the serene cosmic perspective of the historian and bibliophile, and the interested sympathy of the man of simple feeling; a version of this contrast becomes the Canterbury dialogue between experience and authority. These Chaucerian dualities have, of course, been in the critical spotlight for some time; Gower's and Langland's terms are, however, remarkably similar in structure.

For Gower, who has a great deal to say on what he is about, poetry is made 'between work and leisure' (*inter labores et ocia*)[18]; in the *Confessio*, where he acknowledges that for his last long poem he has taken a new approach to his lifelong concern with virtue and vice in the realm, he proposes to speak 'sumwhat of lust, sumwhat of loore', writing a book 'betwen the tweie', that may be 'wisdom to the wise, and pley to hem that lust to pleye'.[19] This medial course implies a moderate reach, a perspective less exclusively detached and cosmic, more implicated in, and circumscribed by, the mortal world:

> I may not strecche up to the hevene
> Min hond, ne setten al on evene
> This world, which evere is in balance.
>
> (*Conf. Am.* 1, 1–3)

As if to embody this axiom, he uses for the first time an invention characteristic of Ricardian poetry, an implicated speaking presence. In the *Confessio*, his voice is no longer that of the prophet, satirist, or moral historian, but that of a lover, and his style is conscientiously pitched to take a 'middel weie' between earnest and game. Gower's matter, too, is compounded of two sources: what old books have given us, 'whereof the world ensaumpled is', and 'the world which neweth everi dai'. More is implied by this mixure than the familiar trick of enlivening ancient lore with newsworthy 'modern instances', the dubious pedagogical practice of Chaucer's Eagle. For Gower, the meeting of old and new matter in poetry is entailed in its very nature as a social art. The whole poetic enterprise is a 'middle weie' between past and future, between truth and our need for it. As we are 'ensaumpled' by fine old books, it behooves us to write 'of newe som matiere' that will,

> When we ben dede and elleswhere
> Beleve to the worldes eere
> In tyme comende after this.
>
> (*Conf. Am.* Prol., 9–11)

'Lore' lives to posterity, not by the transcendence of the contemporary and immediate, but only as it is validated by and intermingled with our own experience, which acts both as a witness to events and as testimony to our investment of feeling in what we need to know. An implicated narrator, far from a rhetorical trick, becomes a nearly inevitable part of Gower's poetic program, as he finally comes to explain it, entailed by his moral sense of the poet's role and of the equivocal nature of poetry itself.

Care for the human future implies the speaker's willing acceptance of involvement in its present course, its daily work. Few have articulated this sense of personal moral responsibility as clearly as Gower: 'Because anything should be shared with others in proportion as one receives it from God', Gower writes in the Latin colophon to the *Confessio*,[20] he means, as he puts it – here echoing the scriptural text of Wimbledon's famous 1388 Paul's Cross sermon on the duties of the estates[21] – to 'give an account of his stewardship' (*villicacionis sue racionem*), and this stewardship turns out to be the production of his three large and, as some might say, 'tediously instructive' books in verse. The view that poetic composition 'for the notice/knowledge of others' (*ad aliorum noticiam*) is a fully legitimate way of doing his share of the world's work, the activity which binds him to the 'commune', lends surprising confidence and dignity to the otherwise fairly modest claim that poetry itself is of mixed birth, neither wholly 'lore' nor wholly 'lust'.

The same form – a way between paired extremes – for thinking about poetry and the poet's role haunts *Piers Plowman* as well, but more in the way of a bad dream than an achieved synthesis. There the terms are largely implicit in the general account of 'doing well'. What the speaker is doing in and for the world is addressed as a subclass of this larger category, and though his mode of life is on occasion both a model and a test case for the adequacy of the broader moral terms, the speaker does not within his work differentiate himself from his literary offspring – his 'book' or 'making' – in order to ask questions about the 'good' of it, as Chaucer and Gower do. He does not speak of his work as a product, a 'book' to leave for posterity, a now-autonomous creature with a life of its own among humankind, but as if 'making' itself were a never-ending process (a view perhaps exemplified in the author's nearly continuous tinkering with his poem), a continuous action rather than a finite production, which *as a mode of life* must be justified before God and man. The familiar paired terms, work and play, lore and lust, define the range and shape of his thought on the subject – as they shape his fictive treatment of the commune's alternating approach to, and falling away from, truth – but they manifest themselves in endless ambivalences: they are the upper and nether millstones between which the one work of a lifetime is ground out, and ground increasingly fine.

That Langland means his utterance to be taken completely seriously by his hearers is apparent, but what the task of 'making' is – whether work or a form of play – for its 'maker' is left ambiguous. Committed with an even greater vehemence than Gower to a view of the world which prescribes that 'everi man his oghne werkes shal bere', he is hard pressed to find for poetry a 'middle weie' in the world, a legitimate place between the idle entertainments of minstrelcy ('lust') and the serious, systematic and learned enterprise of instruction in the faith (significantly called 'clergye' a good deal of the time rather than a more general term like 'lore' or 'wisdom'), which he can only see as properly belonging to the ordained cleric. Disdaining the former and excluded from the latter, both by circumstance and by a temperamental disaffection with book-lore as it is husbanded by its traditional guardians, he remains an anomaly among the workers on the field.[22] Though the speaker, Will, is twice asked by his instructors to confront the problem of his 'making', to justify its meaning and worth, the results are very hard to interpret. In one, the Imaginatyf episode in the B-text,[23] 'making' appears at best a harmless solace until full knowledge somehow comes by other means. It is not, in other words, itself a way to truth, a distinct mode of knowing, either for the maker or for his hearers. In the other episode, Will is invited by Reason and Conscience, who seem about to charge him under the Statutes of Labor as an 'idle man', to account for his stewardship. Somewhat surprisingly, he is released upon his resolution to begin to 'turn his time to profit'.[24] But if the activity he intends is 'making', its nature, subject, and place among other human crafts and estates are left maddeningly unclear, though some analogy between poetry and prophecy is several times suggested.

Between minstrelcy and 'clergie', it seems, there remain to the ordinary layman only prayer and psalm-singing by which he can enlist the human voice and its eloquence as tools with which to share the burden of the world's work. Secular poetry is never completely justified within the poem, except minimally, as it is the mode of life of the poet. The nature and form of literature's perpetuation in the world once out of its creator's reach, its status as a work conducing somehow to human enlightenment or comfort, is not resolved. The kind of resolution desired, however, is quite clear: a poetry which would have the moral authority and scope of vision of 'clergial' systematic learning, and the immediate common appeal of popular tales. The stylistic synthesis expressive of this aim is achieved only sporadically in the poem, most notably in the Easter Passus, which survives the stylistic Scylla and Charybdis of the two extremes, pedantry and plain garrulousness, that constantly threaten it. The reprieve Will wins from his interrogators does not win for the speaker the consistent assurance of tone his ideal demands, but the poet and the reader remain confident that they know what that 'treasure' is, and how to recognise it.

What is striking, though, especially in the face of the widely differing success each poet has in dealing with this question of the nature and place of poetry as a worldly activity, is the structural uniformity in the way it is posed. Both – indeed all three – writers are conscious of the 'middle state' of the lay and vernacular poet of serious moral intentions, and believe that poetry justifies itself within society, or ought to, as a moral force, in essentially public terms. Further, they seem to see its role and effects as potentially mediating and meliorative. Their terms for exploring these matters are essentially social rather than epistemological or metaphysical, transactive and relational rather than absolute. While they are not equally at ease within the confines of these paired terms – Langland certainly the least of the three – they are in general agreement as to the shape in which the matter presents itself to thought. What is even more remarkable is the fact that they all think at length about it in their poems for the first time in English literature.

The positive value attached to secular communal life, and the 'middle way' assigned to the poet's enterprise within it, entail for these writers the choice of specific dictional and formal means explicitly justified in the poetry itself as proper to their intentions. In his Prologue to the *Testament*, Usk explains that

> for rude wordes and boystous percen the herte of the herer to the innerest point, and planten there the sentence of thinges, . . . this book, that nothing hath of the great flode of wit ne of semeliche colours, is dolven (engraved) with rude wordes and boystous.[25]

He goes on, altogether in the manner of the Wife of Bath defending barley bread, to uphold the utility of such drawing in 'coles and chalke', to excite men to 'thilke thinges that been necessarie'. Usk's defense of his simple style is not simply another instance of the old modesty *topos*, which is usually a profession of unworthiness – of person or skill or both – pure and simple. It argues, rather, the fitness of plain means for an end seen as wholly consonant with the life of a good citizen. In a similar way, the Franklin's self-deprecation about his lack of 'Scitheronian' eloquence becomes in his tale a consistent undertone of skepticism about the grievous power of illusion wielded by such eloquence and implicit in the extravagant rhetoric of romantic love.

In the Prologue to the *Confessio*, Gower explicitly associates the middle style of his poem with his moral and social vantage point as a recorder of the 'common world's' truth. 'I take to record [i.e., as witness] . . . the common vois, which mai not lie' (Prol. 124). Though the common sees that division is rife, its healing begins in attending to this voice. To assent to what it says is to reaffirm common grounds for understanding, to begin to will the restoration of mutual peace and concern for the common profit.

> To him that wolde resoun seche
> After the comun worldes speche
> It is to wondre of thilke werre . . .
>
> (*Conf. Am.* Prol., 173–5)

War is the very antithesis of community, the pursuit of singular profit. Gower takes this same line not only in his admirable short poem *In Praise of Peace*,[26] but also as Amans within the Lover's confession, in opposition to the Priest's counsel that war confers glory which wins love. That this 'fictive person' as Gower calls him in the Latin gloss in the poem, the authorial voice, and that of the colophon are to all purposes identical in the very foundations of their ethical and social style, ought to be registered; I will consider its significance in a moment.

The reliability of what the 'common' see, the solidity of the general view, is axiomatic in public poetry generally. What validates experience is not its particular intensity, but its 'commonness'. Gower repeatedly declines to catalogue specific abuses in the manner of a satirist, for

It nedeth noght to specifie
The thing so open ys at eye.

(Conf. Am. Prol., 33–4)

A similar refusal to descend to a bill of complaint, an insistence that the general view is truer, more rhetorically effective, and ultimately more humane than an anatomy of abuse, appears repeatedly in poetry of social criticism from about 1400 on, whereas there is no trace of such self-conscious and principled restraint in earlier political poems, which tend to be occasional or topical. In an otherwise fairly undistinguished poem from Digby MS 102 – which also contains a copy of *Piers Plowman* – on 'What Profits a Kingdom' (dated by Robbins 1401), the speaker, who reminds us of the duty to speak truth and assures us that he does not wish to be a mere tale-teller, says that he will not speak 'in speciale' but 'hool in general'.[27] In the alliterative poem *Crowned King*, dated 1415, and clearly influenced by *Piers*, a truth-telling cleric presents himself before the king, who has just asked his 'commons' for a subsidy for a war. The cleric offers the king a larger view of his duty, to 'shewe you my sentence in singular noumbre; To peynte it with pluralites my prose wolde faile.'[28] A similar sense of stylistic pressure to maintain the common view is evident in *Richard the Redeless*, though more in the breach than in the observance. The speaking voice, which has been rehearsing Richard's misdeeds at merciless length, is interrupted by Reason, who reminds him of the loftier view of his task of correction. The speaker seems to accept this, but the reminder of the sense of community he *ought* to feel with all, including the king, only maddens him the more: he soon loses himself again in Richard's past sins, admitting that he is unable even to attribute generous if misguided motives to them:

> ȝif that was ȝoure purpos   it passeth my wittis
> To deme discrecioun   of ȝoure well-doynge![29]

The other fragment of this poem has as its subject the practical problem of giving truthful counsel.[30] What is striking in all these poetic remains after 1400 is the clear sense they all show of a 'right way' to talk about public matters, an already established decorum of language, social posture, and voice. They are, I think, testimony to an ideal of the 'common voice' established largely by the complex experiments of Langland and Gower, and not derived from earlier Latin satire or pulpit oratory, to which they are sometimes compared.

    The examples I have mentioned so far are of poetic speech ostensibly addressed to the king, rather than to the 'comune' directly. This is true, too, of Gower's *Confessio*, at least in its earliest form. It is later changed in two separate stages of revision, first from a book 'for King Richardes sake' – said to have been written at Richard's express request – to a 'bok for Engelondes sake', and later commended in general terms to Henry of Lancaster.[31] That this change requires little other adjustment perhaps proves my point: the mode of address I am describing is not a matter of deferential politeness to a ruler, but of rising to sufficient largeness of mind and of reference for a public occasion, and a broad common appeal. The king is not the main imagined audience, but an occasion for gathering and formulating what is on the common mind. (Gower's cancellation in the final revision of the famous reference to Chaucer may have been dictated by the same consideration, namely, that coterie references were out of place in a work now explicitly meant for the 'comune' at large).[32] Gower's *In Praise of Peace*, evidently his last poem, addressed to Henry the Fourth, and Hoccleve's commemorative poem on the interment of Richard II in Westminster in 1413[33] use 'I' and 'we' respectively with a luminous generality and self-respect that speaks for an active and well-disposed citizenry, not for 'subjects'. Taken together they make the point: a dead king will do as well as a living one as an occasion for the common voice to reassert, and remind itself of, the highest view of its own responsibilities.

No such occasion, real or imaginary, offers itself for *Piers Plowman*, but it is apparent that the poetic voice is similarly grounded in worldly experience, a commitment to active well-doing, and to 'common wit' rather than more learned routes to truth. (As a corollary to this, poetry itself is seen as action, not as a treasury of wisdom.) The poet might have had less difficulty in maintaining tonal consistency had he been able to imagine concretely an occasion such as might have placed him in the royal presence or on a public platform – had he, in other words, been able to attribute a more secure social standing to his poetic aspirations. Here his ambivalence about poetry as a human activity undermines his belief in his own ability to instill 'well-williness' toward the common good in his audience, and the assured tone of the ideal public voice deserts him. On such occasions – almost always those involving the intrusion into communal harmony of some form of willful 'speciality', such as learnedness, greed, wasting and the like – Will becomes aggressively erudite, authoritarian. The speaker does not explicitly identify his presence as 'common', but his impassioned sense of advocacy on the common world's behalf never leaves him, and it is always portrayed by the process of the fiction as superior to the imposition of corrective authority from above. His emotional allegiances are all on the side of the experiential idea of common truth: Dowel is at one point defined as a 'comun lyf'; Christ redeeming mankind comes 'to drinke of common coppes all Christen soules'. Throughout the poem, the right to speak to one's fellow man comes from conscience and imagination, not 'clergye'.

I could – anyone could – multiply examples from *Piers* to illustrate the presence of such sympathies and the coherence of all senses of 'common' in a substantial vision of the world, though it has become embarrassingly old-fashioned, even 'sentimental,' to do so. But the central critical question is –

and in one way or another has always been, since first the rebels of 1381, then the Protestant reformers, took up the poem in their cause – whose sympathies are they, and what follows from them? For Langland, like Gower, it has been argued, does not speak in his own person, but *quasi in persona aliorum*. As Gower puts it in his Latin marginal gloss on the *Confessio, fingens se auctor esse amantem* – 'the author presents himself fictionally as a lover; feigns himself to be a lover'.[34] And Will, it is said, the would-be cleric, painfully conscious of the morally equivocal, event fraudulent, character of his own mode of life, expresses opinions, and reveals himself in acts, that ultimately betray his own worldliness and impatience, which it is the goal of the process depicted in the fiction to overcome.[35] In that overcoming lies the 'meaning' of the poem.

Much ink has been spilled over the issue of the *persona* in all the major poems of this period – Chaucer-the-pilgrim, Gower-the-lover, Will-the-truthseeker – and I do not wish to sully the same premises further. These premises are encompassed in the question: are the views expressed those of a fictive character and therefore dramatically circumscribed as are the opinions of a character in a play, or are they those of the author? Chambers argues that such a distinction is at best anachronistic,[36] and Kane contends that the distance or identity between the two is *by design* indeterminable: these voices are those, he says, of 'speculative lives, without historical necessity',[37] a formulation I could not hope to improve upon. But the *literary* issue is what we do with this *demande* besides puzzle over it. It's bearing on the meaning of the work is not whether we take this presence, these views, as those of the author, but whether we take them seriously: what are the consequences of our entertaining, not only with sympathy but *with assent*, this voice's sense of the world? Framed in this way the question turns around to face the questioner and becomes: what reason is there for *not* taking Will or the Lover seriously?

An answer to this question would take us deeper into the intellectual history of twentieth-century criticism than fourteenth-century literature. I can only suggest in passing that in bending over backward to avoid imposing modern values on medieval works in the cause of historical fidelity, criticism has committed a kind of emotional infidelity to them. Belief that the only medieval *loci* of serious literary values and styles are either courtly or 'clergial' has led to the perception (correct as far as it goes) that the poetic voice in these poems does not fit either system. From that it has been concluded that we are asked to see the values these speakers express as weighed in the balance in the course of their instruction, and found wanting. I do not think such a conclusion is necessary, nor is it any more historically rigorous or justifiable than the one I am proposing.

What I hope this exercise suggests is that the problem of the *persona* virtually disappears if we take these voices seriously, as expressions not only of feelings, principles, and sympathies we happen to be tempted to indulge because they are ours as flawed human beings, but of the social and ethical ideals of the work itself. The 'voice' presented by these poets is offered not as the realization of an individual identity, but as the realization of the human condition. Furthermore, this characteristic voice provides a tonally secure center of reference for allegorical structures that have gone weak in the philosophical foundations, and become spectral and over-subtle as pedagogic devices. What Will and Amans represent is not only 'speculative lives, without historical necessity', but a 'common life', a rhetorical embodiment of their audience's best and most actively responsible selves as members of the human community. It is a voice neither 'universal' nor 'personal', to use John Peter's terms for the speaker's stance characteristic of 'complaint' and 'satire' respectively. The universal voice is the one Gower explicitly renounces for his long English work. Rather the voice in both of these poems is 'between the tweye', a middle way, embodied in worldly experience, to be sure, but also inviting us to share this common vantage point, the only one we *can* bring to the instruction the speakers undergo in the course of the poem. They are implicated speakers, but the suggestion they offer is that we shall never be otherwise while the world lasts; yet in that time much remains to be understood. The question they ask on our behalf, with an earnestness we are, I think, meant to take very seriously, is: what *in the world* shall we do and say? While this world endures, how shall we live? Their effort as participants in allegorical fictions is to attain universal reach by a distinctly mortal grasp. It is a heroic effort, and not satirically treated. I think we are meant, as readers, to stand with both Will and Amans to the end, and not to regret having done so.

True, these speakers reveal their worldliness. As I have indicated, I do not think it follows that we are meant to see them as fundamentally in error. True, they also reveal some impatience with their instructors. As well they might: much of what they offer is distraction itself. In both poems, the instructors — who are, after all, the creations of a writer's free imagination working in a long tradition of wonderfully wise personified abstractions — are on the whole a remarkably inept lot and not especially well disposed to help the seeker. Gower's Genius is fundamentally muddled about the ethical terms of his priesthood — ultimately, with the reappearance of Venus, somewhat embarrassed by them — and the lover is not so far gone in erotic self-absorption that he fails to notice it. Study scolds her husband Wit for 'casting pearls before swine' in offering to teach Will, and Scripture scorns him, sending him into despair.[38] It is not that Will and Amans do not hear their instructors: they do, and are understandably puzzled. It is rather that their instructors don't hear them, and their questions are serious and worth asking. It is true that some of Will's instructors are kinder, and that Genius is benevolent. Much of what they say is true and orthodox. They even say it beautifully. But somehow what is *said* doesn't help much; it is what happens to these dreamers that makes all the difference. A vision of the Redemption takes Will in his own experience downward into darkness, and back into the common light of Easter morning in Cornhill. Amans is cast out of Venus's 'comune', his suit for favor refused; love, though unrequited, is not renounced, and certainly not repudiated, but transformed to a labor of love in another form: the making of books for the 'common profit'. In both poems, the events reflect back upon, if not the authority, certainly the practical adequacy, of the instructors' catechism.

What shines through the worldliness and impatience of these voices is their ardor, an 'embarrassing purity' of motive which endures in some form to the last in both poems and constitutes their exalted and truly memorable 'story'. A result of the interest and consistency of the voice, as the most reliable one in the poem, is a secondary effect of some importance: the voice and the human story to which it testifies, rivals the pedagogical progress which in both cases forms the 'plot', as a locus of meaning. The voice of worldly experience and need acts as a critique of the encyclopedic mode of instruction – its unresponsiveness (striking in both poems) to the seekers' earnestness of purpose, their genuine and on the whole fairly high-minded yearning to 'do well'. This is something new in didactic allegory: it is as if all the good songs had been given to Boethius.

A consequence, in turn, of these two incommensurable centers of interest and meaning in both poems is a fundamental problem of poetic closure. It is fairly easy to create an end to a pedagogic-progress plot: present your speaker with an ultimate vision or revelation which will make intellectual and emotional coherence of all that has led to it; the model for this is of course the *Divine Comedy*. But what end is there to a worldly voice, except death, either of the speaker or of the world itself? (It is significant that in both poems the speaker is an old man, of failing powers, at the end.) There can be no end to the human voice's testimony to its own experience before the end of time. And it is that testimony which in both poems comes to interest us as a 'story'. The structure is more closely analogous to that of *Der Ackermann aus Böhmen*, with its impassioned plowman, nature's nobleman, in his exalted and touching care for human bonds, locked in irresolvable rhetorical warfare with scurrilous Death. That debate can only be ended by the direct intervention of God as Judge, who, incidentally, allows merit to both sides of the case.[39]

In both the *Confessio* and *Piers* the ending is intensely problematic – indeed, equivocal endings seem to be deeply characteristic of major Ricardian poetry. But in these two cases, the question that presents itself is: why do both poems go on *past* two of the most ravishing, most emotionally satisfying, possible endings in all of medieval literature: namely, Gower's banishment from Venus's train, and the Easter Passus? In both cases, the poem continues past this visionary climax, and ends not in world-transcendence, but in some form of return to the world. Will dreams past Christ's triumph to the ravaging of the world by Antichrist; the last action of the poem before Will's last dream ends in Conscience's renewed search through the world for Piers Plowman, to restore Unity. Amans is not 'cured' of his love, but is told to turn his time to making a last testament to the power of love as the common bond. It is noteworthy that the famous lovers of the world's history who dance in Venus's company plead in vain, on Gower's behalf, for Venus's favor; their plea perhaps expresses a recognition that their stories rest in his hands. It is he who will make the power of their loves – of 'courtly love' – intelligible to the common world and, through the power of pathos, a force for good within it. Venus's refusal is a judgement of her cult, not of Gower – as Chaucer, in the *Legend* (which Fisher believes is the product of the same royal request)[40] similarly, if more indirectly, judges the God of Love by assigning him a literary sensibility as narrow as the Man of Law's.[41] It repudiates, not earthly love, passionate commitment, or the world's variety, but the formalising of passionate devotion into a game, the reducing of law to mere rules. From love as the obsession of the noble heart, Gower is cast back on love as the expression of the common voice, in the furtherance of peace.

For if the natural expression of the noble heart is pity – the grand result to which all courtly self-cultivation tends, and all its rhetoric is designed to bring about – these two poems imply that the 'common voice's' highest expression, the end of all its labors, is peace. As pity 'runs' in the gentle heart, peace flows from the common tongue. Peace is virtually the highest good in these public poems. The Digby poem I have mentioned interprets the Pearl of Great Price as Peace. The Langlandian millennium is when 'Love and Peace be maistres' (Langland, though a great advocate of compassion, empathy, fellow-feeling, is singularly uncomfortable with pity, which he often portrays as an interruption in the process of justice, and always seems to him halfway to lawlessness). Gower argues before Henry IV that the highest goal of rule is not conquest or display of power, but Peace. They are related – pity and peace, the goals of 'courtly' and 'common' virtues – as the Franklin knows well. The noble axiom 'pitee renneth soone in gentil herte' has its more pragmatic bourgeois counterpart – the same 'sentence' at bottom, but framed as if taught by experience of the world: Since 'on every wrong a man mai nat be wreken',

> Lerneth to suffre, or elles, so moot I goon,
> Ye shul it lerne, wher so ye wol or noon.[42]

'Suffrraunce' in the Franklin's world of love is not the grand passion of self-immolation, but mutual tolerance, compromise, forgiveness. As Hannah Arendt reminds us, these are the great beginners of action in the world, and they, too, confer glory.[43]

If there is a 'bourgeois style' in late fourteenth-century literature, it lies, I believe, somewhere within the territory I have been describing, not in the literature of fabliau, jest, or minstrelcy.[44] And if it can be called a style, it is not in the narrower sense of a characteristic verbal or visual *decor*, but in the broader social sense we have been using: a coherent set of ethical attitudes toward the world – experientially based, vernacular, simple, pious but practical, active – and the poetry that gives expression to this essentially high-minded secularism. Its most characteristic concern is the turning of worldly time, that essential middle-class commodity, to 'common profit'. Will promises to 'turn all times of my time to profit'; Amans regrets, not his passion, but 'only that I hadde lore my tyme . . .'. Its values are meant to be taken seriously among those whose lives make it necessary to ask 'How shall the world be served?'

I leave it to others to speculate, beyond these brief suggestions, as to the causes, both in social fact and social myth, that made the last quarter of the fourteenth century especially congenial to the development of a poetic 'common voice', the flowering of an English vulgar eloquence. The high hopes entertained for the boy king Richard, which soon turned to the pious fiction of a king in need of counsel, may have provided reason for this outpouring of large-minded, paternal, and heartfelt guidance. Perhaps, as Jusserand suggested, the petitioning voice of the commons had something to do with the development of the common voice of *Piers*.[45] The social station of the major poets – commoners to a man – in relation to the traditional audience for literary recreation may have dictated the wisdom of a broader view that embraced both as a 'public' for the first time and appealed to common experience rather than to abstract, and now largely non-functioning, chivalric literary ideals as grounds for accord. But when all this is said, it is still true that public poetry is, as a literary mode, simply an extention of the incipient realism in these Ricardian writers' views of what poetry is: like man himself 'a creature of a middle state', and serving its highest function as a peacemaker, and as an interpreter of the common world.

Appendix

The voices of both Langland and Gower as presences in their poems have been called 'universal,' similar to those of the Old Testament prophets. For this quality, both have been invidiously compared to Chaucer, who is said to have mastered the more 'individualised' approach of satire, which works in the 'concrete particularities of real life' rather than in the 'conceptual', 'impersonal' mode of 'complaint'. The comparison, the notion that medieval literature of social correction speaks with a 'universal' voice, and this definition of the terms 'complaint' and 'satire' are those of John Peter (*Complaint and Satire in Early English Literature* [Oxford, 1956], passim). John Hurt Fisher adopts them essentially without question in his study of Gower. It will be apparent that 'public poetry' as I define it coincides in some ways with what

Peter calls 'complaint', chiefly in that Peter emphasises, as I do, the universal and systematic scope of the social criticism in 'complaint' and its corrective aims, contrasting them with satire's punitive tone and focus on concrete abuses. However, he evidently values those qualities by which he defines 'complaint' less than the concreteness and scornful indignation which characterise satire, and he implies a kind of evolutionary development in the literature of social criticism in which satire – a kind which, like the term for it, did not emerge in literary usage until the Renaissance – is as it were a more highly developed form of literary life, higher on the phylogenetic ladder, and more 'sophisticated'. He is certainly right to distinguish universal scope as a defining feature in medieval literature of social criticism, and to try to respect the medieval term 'complaint', but it would have been still more accurate to have noted the connection between the two – between the term and the ideal of universal reach, which is in fact implicit in it. Complaint, or *planctus*, is not merely a protest or acknowledgment of a wrong but a lament, and by its very nature delivered only by someone implicated in, affected by, the grievance regretted. It implies, as satiric scorn need not, a sense of something lost, yet at least in principle retrievable, if only by an act of the imagination. A complaint – often, interestingly enough, associated in medieval philosophical fictions with a scene of confession – suggests, as does confession itself, an acknowledgment of deviation from the right or true, accompanied by a wish or hope that this act itself be restorative, instrumental in making things right again. It aspires to have this effect, not through the application of the lash, but by an appeal to a reawakened vision of former and still possible integrity.

Satire may indeed be the favored and therefore more highly developed mode of social criticism in later literary periods – in part, one suspects, because by then writers have given up hope for universal coherence, striving instead to correct by means of individual embarrassed recognitions – but in middle English it is the effort to attain morally compelling universal vision that receives the most serious attention from major writers, and with more interesting and sophisticated results; the verse addressed to particular abuses is on the whole far cruder in structure and tone. In other words, in the Middle Ages it is what Peter labels 'complaint' that is the more developed form, as it will be again in any literary era with the values and aims that 'complaint' or lament implies. It could be argued that Romantic social criticism aspires to the condition and effects of complaint rather than satire, for example. There is no single ladder of development according to which a step away from the conceptual and universal to the telling concrete detail, an interest in the offender rather than the nature of the offense, is necessarily a step upward. It depends on the effect desired, and its commensurability with the rhetorical means of achieving it. The rhetorical effect of complaint is, broadly speaking, to keep our attention on the total harmony which gives reason to all particular recommendations. Public poetry's chief effect is to make the quality of that attention, which amounts to a kind of social self-awareness, the cutting edge of reform. The means of achieving it is implicit in the voice.

Does attention to the whole necessarily require what Fisher calls, in Gower, the 'universal voice'? If the only imaginable antonym for that is the voice of a particular and fully characterised fictional 'personality', as Peter suggests — something like Chaucer-the-pilgrim — perhaps yes, but the poverty of his contrasted terms for describing what either Gower or Langland is doing is nowhere more evident than here, for neither Fisher's 'universal' nor Peter's 'impersonal' adequately describes the characteristic embodied voice of Ricardian public poetry. As Peter uses them, the opposed terms 'universal' and 'personal' refer not to the speaker's relation to his audience and the grounds for his interaction with his hearers, but to the amount of particularity or concrete detail used to present the personality of the speaker. These two things are not the same: a writer may mention any number of idiosyncrasies and historical details, either in his subject or himself, without thereby establishing the basis of his rhetorical appeal to his audience, the terms within which he proposes to have an effect on them. Peter's terms denote a style of self-reference, but they do not consider the mode of self-presentation intrinsic to the author's voice and effect. His terms, in other words, are not interactive, but those used by the middle English poets themselves are — intensely so.

What both Gower and Langland develop in their long English works is a voice neither universal nor personal, but — and here I adopt their way of looking at it — a 'middel wei' between the two, a common voice, implicated in the ills it describes, yet capable of entertaining cosmopolitan complexities and a vision of communal harmony. Its social tone with respect to us is that of an observant and enlightened citizen among peers.

Notes

1. J.A. BURROW, *Ricardian Poetry* (New Haven, 1971).

2. The materials of the literary synthesis described here were all fully available to Chaucer; he simply made a quite different use of them in his fiction than any of his contemporaries. The Man of Law and the Franklin, public men of a social station closely comparable to that of Chaucer and several of his literary associates, embody in dramatic form several of the social and literary values I describe below. In their acute awareness of the social standing of their own literary tastes and their concern to enhance their public virtue through the tales they tell, they present in a highly condensed, and possibly satirical, form the social origins, affinities, and emotional appeal of the ethos of Ricardian 'public poetry'. Chaucer the pilgrim, offering the irreproachable Tale of Melibee as a more edifying replacement for the aborted 'drasty rime' of Sir Thopas, may perhaps be similarly understood. But precisely because of the fictional indirection and complexity with which Chaucer reflects upon a literary situation he shares with his contemporaries, I must exclude consideration of those reflections from this paper, and treat the matter separately

at greater length. For a brief general description of this technique in the *Canterbury Tales*, see my article, 'The Physician's Tale and Love's Martyrs: "Ensamples Mo than Ten" as a Method in the *Canterbury Tales*', *Chaucer Review*, **8** (1973): 9–32; and DEREK BREWER, 'Towards a Chaucerian Poetic', *Proceedings of the British Academy*, **60** (1974): 219–52.

3. See Appendix.

4. Sir John Clanvowe, one of the 'Lollard knights' associated with Chaucer's circle, wrote a moral treatise in English called *The Two Ways* (ed. V.J. Scattergood, *English Philological Studies*, **10** [1967]: 33–56), which contrasts the 'broode wey of helle' with the 'streit wey to hevene' in the traditional manner, but recommends as a rule of life a 'meene' between instances of these two ways – between, for example, abstinence and gluttony, between 'mistruste yn the mercy of god' and overconfidence in that mercy. Clanvowe is hardly an original thinker, but perhaps precisely for that reason he affords an interesting testimony to the mental habit of defining the middle way as the course of virtue, even where, as here, it somewhat interferes with the two-fold conceptual scheme by which the exposition is organised. See also K.B. MCFARLANE, *Lancastrian Kings and Lollard Knights* (Oxford, 1972).

5. The relation between style as a linguistic category – as the characteristic mode of verbal expression of an individual work or writer, capable of being described by noting features of diction, syntactic patterns, and the like – and style in its broader sense, an array of forms of social behavior referred to within a work, expressing the shared attitudes of a group, has been a controverted question in medieval literary studies generally for some time. That there is an essential continuity between verbal and social style has been – properly, I think – a fundamental assumption of the most illuminating modern studies of Chaucer. See, for example, CHARLES MUSCATINE, *Chaucer and the French Tradition* (Berkeley, 1957), and DONALD HOWARD, *The Idea of the Canterbury Tales* (Berkeley, 1976). The theoretical complexities of this position are not germane to the present purpose.

6. The assigning of paramount value to peace, rather than to the glory conferred by chivalric conquest, is utterly consistent with what I take to be the ultimate social origins of this complex of social and literary values – the civic order required by the commercial state, and the social ethos, expressed in civic humanism, most appropriate to it. Marsilio of Padua insists that the 'sufficient life' rather than a crusading or transcendent mission is the goal of secular societies (*Defensor Pacis*, tr. and ed. Alan Gewirth [New York, 1956], ch. 4). Nearly 200 years later, Machiavelli still finds it necessary to argue that the virtues of a chivalric leader have become disruptive and dysfunctional in an urban commercial state (*The Prince*, trans. and ed. T.G. Bergin [Northbrook, Ill., 1947], ch. 16). The literature on the infusion of the earlier vocabulary with changed meaning, appropriate to a shift in social fact and social values, is vast; JOHAN HUIZINGA, *The Waning of the Middle Ages* (New York, 1954) is only one among many large general treatments of a phenomenon that took very different forms in different countries.

The value these poems assign to peace and peace-making has more concrete resonances, closer to home. It is consonant as well with two tendencies in English political life and society frequently remarked by historians: the consistent opposition of the Commons to continued foreign military exploits, expressed concretely in their repeated refusal to grant the taxes necessary to support them requested by the Crown; and a growing strain of pacifism as a religious ideal within Wycliffite thought generally, expressed with particular complexity in the life patterns of the 'Lollard knights', whose largely military and diplomatic careers seem nevertheless to have been remarkably detached from any glorification of valor in their literary interests or productions. See McFARLANE, *Lancastrian Kings*, pp. 177–85; and ANTHONY TUCK, *Richard II and the English Nobility* (London, 1973).

7. THOMAS USK, *The Testament of Love* 1.6, in *The Complete Works of Chaucer*, **7**, ed. W.W. Skeat (Oxford, 1897), pp. 27–9.

8. *DNB*, 'Thomas Usk'; also JOHN H. FISHER, *John Gower, Moral Philosopher and Friend of Chaucer* (New York, 1964), p. 62 and n.

9. USK, *Testament* 1.8, p. 36.

10. See FISHER, *John Gower*, pp. 115, 135.

11. FISHER, *John Gower*, pp. 116–24.

12. E. TALBOT DONALDSON, *Piers Plowman: The C-Text and Its Poet*, Yale Studies in English 113 (New Haven, 1949; repr. Hamden, Ct, 1966), esp. chs 3 and 4.

13. See NORTHROP FRYE, *Anatomy of Criticism* (Princeton, 1957; repr. New York, 1967), pp. 248–50.

14. JILL MANN, *Chaucer and Medieval Estates Satire* (Cambridge, 1973), pp. 207–12.

15. T. CHURCHYARDE, *The Works of John Skelton*, ed. A. Dyce (London, 1843), l:lxxvii; cited by Marie Jacobus Hertzig, 'The Early Recension and Continuity of Certain Middle English Texts in the Sixteenth Century', unpub. diss., University of Pennsylvania, 1973, p. 252.

16. CICERO, *De Re Publica*, 1.25.39. Loeb Classical Library (New York, 1928). The translation is mine, expanded to emphasise the relevant distinction. The definition follows upon Africanus's remark that his inquiry into the commonwealth will not pursue the subject to its first elements, 'as the schoolmaster does', but that he will proceed as if speaking to intelligent men of practical affairs, experienced in public service 'both in the wars and at home'.

17. *OED*, s.v. 'common'; *Middle English Dictionary*, ed. Hans Kurath and Sherman M. Kuhn (Ann Arbor, 1954), s.v. 'commune'.

18. *The English Works of John Gower*, ed. G.C. Macaulay, EETS, ES 81–2 (Oxford, 1900–01; repr.1957), 2:479. For an account of the three extant versions of this colophon, see FISHER, *John Gower*, pp. 88–91.

19. *Confessio Amantis* Prol. 84–5, *Works*, ed. Macaulay.

20. *Works*, ed. Macaulay, vol. 2, p. 479; FISHER, *John Gower*, p. 89.

21. *Wimbledon's Sermon: Redde rationem villicationis tue*, ed. Ione Kemp Knight (Pittsburgh, 1967). Langland also uses this text, and possibly alludes to the sermon. See *Piers the Plowman, in Three Parallel Texts*, C.X, line 274, ed. W.W. Skeat (Oxford, 1886); and MORTON BLOOMFIELD, *Piers Plowman as a Fourteenth Century Apocalypse* (New Brunswick, NJ, 1962), p. 87.

22. DONALDSON's chapter, 'The C-Reviser and the Occupations of the Folk on the Field,' in *Piers Plowman: The C-Text and Its Poet*, pp. 121–55, remains the best account of Langland's view of the 'maker' in society.

23. *Piers* B.XII: see esp. lines 16–52, which are omitted in C.

24. *Piers* C.VI, lines 1–108. A detailed account of this scene – its relation to labor and vagrancy laws (particularly the Statute of 1388), and to Langland's theories of poetry – will appear in my forthcoming paper, '*Piers Plowman* and the Statutes of

Labor', presented in abbreviated form to the Middle English Section of the Modern Language Association in December, 1973.

25. USK, *Testament*, Prol. (Skeat, *Oxford Chaucer*, 7:1).

26. *Works*, ed. Macaulay, Vol. 2, pp. 481–92.

27. *Historical Poems of the Fourteenth and Fifteenth Centuries*, ed. Rossell Hope Robbins (New York, 1959), No. 13, lines 49–52.

28. ROBBINS, *Historical Poems*, No. 95, lines 46–47.

29. *Richard the Redeless* in SKEAT, *Piers Plowman*, 1:612, lines 109–110.

30. *Mum and the Sothsegger*, ed. Mabel Day and R. Steele, EETS 119 (London, 1946).

31. FISHER, *John Gower*, pp. 116–24.

32. For a similar view, see PAUL M. CLOGAN, 'From Complaint to Satire: The Art of the *Confessio Amantis*', *Medievalia et Humanistica*, 4 (1973): 219.

33. ROBBINS, *Historical Poems*, No. 40.

34. *Works*, ed. Macaulay, vol. 1, p. 37; the comment refers to *Conf. Am.* 1.60.

35. Though perhaps somewhat overstated, this is essentially the premise of such otherwise diverse critical studies as JOHN LAWLOR, *Piers Plowman: An Essay in Criticism* (London, 1962), p. 88 and passim, and D.W. ROBERTSON, Jr and BERNARD F. HUPPÉ, *Piers Plowman and Scriptural Tradition* (Princeton, 1951; repr. New York, 1969), p. 106. Whether Will is seen as a dramatic entity or an abstract of human moral faults, this view implies that he is a created or hypothetical character, and skirts the question of authorial voice as a presence in the poem.

36. R.W. CHAMBERS, 'Robert or William Langland?' *London Medieval Studies*, 1 (1948, for 1939): 430–62.

37. GEORGE KANE, *The Autobiographical Fallacy in Chaucer and Langland Studies*. Chambers Memorial Lecture, 1965 (London, 1965).

38. *Piers* B.X, lines 1–10 (cf. C.XII, 1–8); B.XI, lines 1–10 (cf. C.XII, 163–72).

39. *Der Ackermann aus Böhmen*, ed. Alois Bernt and Konrad Burdach, in *Vom Mittelalter zur Reformation*, ed. Konrad Burdach (Berlin, 1917), 3; p. 1.

40. FISHER, *John Gower*, p. 235.

41. See ALFRED DAVID, 'The Man of Law vs. Chaucer: A Case in Poetics', *PMLA*, 82 (1967): 217–25; and my article, 'The *Physician's Tale* and Love's Martyrs', n. 2 above.

42. Franklin's Tale, V (F), lines 777–8; in *The Work of Geoffrey Chaucer*, ed. F.N. Robinson, 2nd edn (Boston, 1957).

43. HANNAH ARENDT, *The Human Condition* (Chicago, 1958), esp. pp. 236–47.

44. For discussion of 'bourgeois realism' see MUSCATINE, *Chaucer and the French Tradition*, ch. 3; and D.W. ROBERTSON, JR, *A Preface to Chaucer* (Princeton, 1962), ch. 3.

45. J.J. JUSSERAND, *Piers Plowman: A Contribution to the History of English Mysticism*, trans. M.E.R., rev. edn (London, 1894; repr. New York, 1965), p. 71.

3 Imagination and Traditional Ideologies in *Piers Plowman**

David Aers

Aers examines the ways in which aspects of Langland's poetic imagination cut across and press against the dominant hierarchic ideologies of the second half of the fourteenth century. Accordingly, his dramatisations of newly emerging social groups, or aspects of economic change, for example, are marked by a poetic energy in comparison with which the traditional representatives of the feudal order seem flat and powerless to resist change. The poet's refusal to subordinate his creative imagination to inherited ideologies eventually results in the poem's apocalyptic movements, and opens the way for the poem to be read as a revolutionary document in the rising of 1381.

And þoruȝ hir wordes I wook and waited aboute,
And seiȝ the sonne euene South sitte þat tyme,
Metelees and moneilees on Maluerne hulles.
Musynge on þis metels a myle wey ich yede.
Many times þis metels haþ maked me to studie
Of þat I seiȝ slepynge, if it so be myȝte . . .

Piers Plowman (B version), VII. 145–50

Traditional ideologies expressed the patterns through which self and world were perceived and understood. They depicted the features of legitimate authority and practice in different areas of the culture; they presented conventionally accepted beliefs, standards and values; they naturalised certain symbols and images which helped shape individual and collective experience.

---

* Reprinted from David Aers, *Chaucer, Langland and the Creative Imagination* (London: Routledge and Kegan Paul, 1980), pp. 1–37, 196–204.

In short, they encouraged certain ways of seeing and thinking while discouraging others. No one has ever doubted the fundamental importance of traditional ideologies to Langland's perception and judgement. What has been less well recognised is the way writing poetry constantly released his imagination to embrace realities which pressed against received ideologies, his art putting these into solution despite the essential place they held in his conscious values and hopes. This is the relationship I wish to explore, between affirmation of established ideologies and their negation in the same poem, for this interplay turns out to be a central factor in the organisation and magnificent achievement of *Piers Plowman*. I hope the study may also contribute to a more general discussion of the interactions between literature, social change and strains in received ideological structures. For Langland's great poem does invite attention to the ways in which traditional ideologies were themselves historical phenomena subject to diverse processes of change. With the gradual emergence of new social and economic situations, ideologies generated in earlier periods inevitably came under strain. Their authority was challenged and slowly undermined in the face of fresh problems, anomalies and confusions, leaving the community the long task of constructing ideologies and institutions appropriate to living in the changed circumstances.[1]

In the present chapter we shall be especially concerned with the major social ideology of Langland's world. This envisaged society as a static hierarchy of estates, fixed in occupations which were organically related, mutually beneficial, harmonious and divinely ordained. Society was often presented as a human body, with head and hands as king and nobility, feet as peasantry, and so on. As common was the tripartite division into those who pray, those who fight and those who labour to maintain fighters and praysters. Thomas Wimbledon states the view typically in 1388:

> in þe chirche beeþ nedeful þes þre offices: presthood, knyȝthod, and laboreris. To prestes it falliþ to kutte awey þe voide braunchis of synnis wiþ þe swerd of here tonges. To knyȝtis it falliþ to lette wrongis and þeftis to be do and to mayntene Goddis Lawe and hem þat ben techeris þerof, and also to kepe pe lond fro enemyes of oþer londes. And to laboreris it falleþ to trauayle bodily and wiþ here sore swet geten out of þe erþe bodily liflode for her and for oþer parties. And þese statis beþ also nedeful to þe chirche þat non may wel ben wiþouten oþer. For ȝif presthod lackede þe puple for defaute of knowyng of Goddis Lawe shulde wexe wilde on vices and deie gostly. And ȝif þe knythod lackid and men to reule þe puple by lawe and hardnesse, þeues and enemies shoden so encresse þat no man sholde lyuen in pes. And ȝif laboreris weren not, boþe prestis and knyȝtis mosten bicome acremen and heerdis, and ellis þey sholde for defaute of bodily sustenaunce deie.

He develops this picture of mutual dependence adding that 'euery staat shul loue oþer'.[2] Traditional divisions of labour, distribution of products and forms of life are presented as eternal, while the hierarchy of power and privilege is to remain absolutely static. Thomas Wimbledon, for example, adds, 'ʒif þou art a seruant oþer bondman, be soget and low in drede of displesynge to þy Lord', just as Gower, using the corporate image, asserts

> Quant pié se lieve contre teste,
> Trop est la guise deshonneste;
> [When the foot rebels against the head
> the behaviour is wholly illegitimate]

Similarly, another conventional preacher reminds 'knyʒthes and oþur gentils' to concentrate on 'good gouernaunce' and military efficiency, priests on Christ's law, 'lower men' on labour, and concludes: 'iff euery parte of Cristes churche wold hold hem content with here own occupacions and not to entermet farþur þan reson and lawe rewels hem to, þan þe grace of almyghty God shuld floresh and þe more freshly contynue among.' So fixed are the boundaries that it seemed natural to perceive human identity almost completely in these classifications: 'There be in þis world þre maner of men, clerkes, knyʒthes, and commynalte.'[3] When writers criticised deviations from this order in sermons or 'estates satire' their vision was firmly structured by the normative paradigm which never came into any kind of question: deviations were sinful and frequent, but corrigible. This attitude is evident in Lollard texts and Wyclif's work as well as in the orthodox writers referred to above.[4] The leading ideology thus made the inherited social world, with its distribution of power, work and wealth, so natural that any opposition to it seemed literally monstrous, as well as iniquitous.[5]

Of course, there was opposition and some signs of alternative social ideologies significantly at odds with the dominant one, as the Peasants' Uprising of 1381 indicated. For instance, their demands seem to have included freedom from serfdom and lordship, the termination of traditional manorial jurisdiction and services as well as of existing lawyers and law, and the abolition of the ecclesiastical hierarchy with the material wealth on which its power rested. Such ideas expressed interests, aspirations and experiences different to those legitimated and sanctified in the leading ideology.[6] Nevertheless, the latter quite precluded notions of chronic conflict of interests and outlook between groups. Similarly, ideas about changing aspirations and increasing social complexity and mobility were quite alien. Yet by Langland's time the dominant ideology had to confront new economic forces, and newly emerging social groups.[7] Like others, however, Langland assumed the total relevance of the chief and traditional social model to his world and his poem, a fact which those critics who call him 'a traditionalist, if not a reactionary' have noted.[8]

In the Prologue to *Piers Plowman* it can be seen in the following passage[9]:

The kyng and knyȝthod and clergie boþe
Casten þat þe commune sholde hire communes fynde.
The commune contreued of kynde wit craftes,
And for profit of al þe peple Plowmen ordeyned
To tilie and to trauaille as trewe lif askeþ.
The kyng and þe commune and kynde wit þe þridde
Shopen lawe and leaute, ech lif to knowe his owene.

(Pr. 116–22)

The peasantry serve the rest of society without any tensions while everybody is certain of his own fixed role. What 'trewe lif' and 'lawe' demand seems quite unequivocal, and in this scheme contemporary crafts all exist without conflict as they simply slot into unambiguous places in the harmonious totality. As late as Passus XIX Langland returns to this model, attributing it to the Holy Spirit (XIX 225–57), and it conveys his wish for the coherent world depicted in the inherited organic ideology. Nevertheless, his Prologue actually shows us something very different, something which goes considerably beyond the criticism of 'deviations' found in the estates satires and sermons mentioned earlier.

Probably all Langland's readers have relished the poetic vitality of the first dream 'Of alle manere of men, þe meene and þe riche,/Werchynge and wandrynge as þe world askeþ' (Pr. 18–19). The vitality is grounded in an outstanding imaginative response to the teeming energies of his society, and these justly famous lines represent the Prologue's impact:

Of alle kynne lybbynge laborers lopen forþ somme,
As dykeres and delueres þat doon hire dede ille
And dryueþ forþ longe day with '*Dieu saue dame Emme*'.
Cokes and hire knaues cryden, 'hote pies, hote!
Goode gees and grys! go we dyne, go we!'
Tauerners til hem tolden þe same:
'Whit wyn of Oseye and wyn of Gascoigne,
Of þe Ryn and of þe Rochel þe roost to defie!'

(Pr. 223–30)

Here, as throughout the Prologue and many of the following passus, we are shown a mass of self-absorbed social practices in which there is no consciousness of any coherent order, organic unity or social *telos*, let alone a divine one. The participants, as in the Meed episode, appear to be discrete members of a mobile, fragmenting society revelling in processes of consumption and production which are an end in themselves. The poetic conviction communicating this state already encourages us to question the applicability of the leading ideological scheme to the culture Langland inhabits and scrutinises – even as a normative paradigm against which deviations may be identified and corrected.

The place of king and clergy in the Prologue may also be early signs in the poem of how extrinsic the major ideology has become. The clergy and religious institutions are immersed in the secular culture. Religion is predominantly another commodity, or an evasion of work, or training for service in secular affairs (Pr. 46–99) its roots and branches quite incompatible with the received model of the clergy's social role. I shall devote the next chapter to the church in *Piers Plowman*, for the degree to which the church is absorbed in the fluid culture Langland depicts is most significant.[10] As for the king, we do not meet him until well into the Prologue (ll. 112 ff.), and no sooner have we noted the image of a harmonious distribution of power and responsibility than Langland relates the fable about belling the cat. While 'þe commune profit' is invoked (Pr. 148, 169), the fable presents the ruler as one acquisitive and violent interest among other similar ones. Neither in theory nor practice is it possible to identify 'commune profit' in the manner envisaged by the presiding social ideology. Whatever Langland's own attitudes to the mouse who advises quietistic resignation in the face of an irresponsible and predatory ruling group, he shows that political power is contended for by autonomous groups and individuals motivated by immediate economic interests. The mouse's acceptance of this state of affairs actually participates in the cool egotism that seems prevalent among both the predators and those thinking about resistance. His own motivation is an unprincipled self-preservation which does not care who else may be destroyed as long as his own carcass is safe (Pr. 185–208).[11]

Struck by the centrality of economic self-interest in the world of the Prologue, Will asks Holy Church who actually has the right to 'þe moneie on þis molde þat men so faste holdeþ' (I. 44–6). The generalised question gets an even more generalised answer. Holy Church quotes from Matthew 22 where Jesus tells the Pharisees' disciples to render the things that are Caesar's to Caesar, and the things that are God's to God, and she rounds this off with her own comment.

> For riȝtfully reson sholde rule yow alle,
> And kynde wit be wardeyn your welþe to kepe
> And tutour of youre tresor, and take it yow at nede;
>
> (I. 54–6)

This brief statement raises issues we shall meet again and in more detail, but it is perhaps already becoming apparent that the instructor's moral language is rather remote from the realities of Langland's world and their visionary creation in his poem. For instance, in the lines just quoted, the abstraction 'welþe' is treated as a static thing, a box of physical treasure, rather than as the symbolic manifestation of social practices and unstable relationships which preoccupied Langland and made Will ask the question about money. Presenting these activities as a manageable fixity disastrously simplifies the problems raised by the mobile, acquisitive society of the Prologue, and Holy Church unhesitatingly puts forward the abstractions 'reson' and 'kynde wit' as agents who can solve the problems. But *Piers Plowman* has begun to make us uneasy with such solutions. We are told that 'kynde wit' is to be warden of wealth, yet we are made to wonder what the case will be if the 'welþe' has been accumulated by, for example, the merchants or tradesmen of the poem. Their occupations are essential in Langland's society, but the poet shows us how their practices transform 'kynde', leaving us to ask whose 'kynde' and 'kynde wit', whose 'reson' is *now* to provide the criteria of reformation.[12] The poem takes these as serious questions, finding that such disembodied and conventional abstractions may actually be controversial and equivocal terms with little obvious application to the world of incarnate beings Langland contemplates. Even Holy Church's confident statement that he who works well and ends in truth will be saved (I. 130–3), is turned by the poem into something profoundly problematic.[13] Doubtless, Langland wished he could simply accept Holy Church's general assertion, for it fits well into the dominant ideology with its depiction of a static social order in which everyone's function is fixed and uncontroversial. But his scrupulous, vital and honest involvement with current developments will not allow him this comfort.

Passus I opened with Holy Church complaining that in Catholic England most people 'Haue þei worship in þis world þei kepe no bettre' (I. 5–9), and Passus II begins with a characteristic act of self-reflexivity. Through his Will the poet acknowledges his own complicity in the life he studies around the figure of Lady Meed: 'Hire array me rauysshed; swich richesse sau3 I neuere' (II. 17). As the marriage of Meed proceeds, Langland's imagination is indeed ravished by the diverse energies of his society exemplified in the numberless 'route þat ran aboute Mede', in their exuberant journey to Westminster and their evasive action under attack which confirms the vigour of their existence.[14] He insists that 'alle manere of men' are involved:

> As of kny3tes and of clerkes and ooþer commune peple,
> As Sisours and Somonours, Sherreues and hire clerkes,
> Bedelles and baillifs and Brocours of chaffare,
> Forgoers and vitaillers and vokettes of þe Arches;

> (II. 58–61)

As in the Prologue, Langland evokes self-absorbed drives and a social matrix so alien to the ideology he favours that any idea of reform within its perspective is coming to seem quite impossible. One may even suspect that the way Theology (II. 115 ff.) remains the personification of an abstraction lacking embodiment or followers in definite social location, unlike Meed's followers who represent particular occupations and groups (e.g. II. 162–77), could be intended to cast doubt on its anchorage in Langland's world.

The poet certainly offers an intense and substantial vision of a world dominated by a money economy, a dynamic Meed dissolving all traditional ties, personal and ethical. He singles out a group of small tradesmen for special attention:

> Brewers and Bakers, Bochiers and Cokes;
> For þise are men on þis molde þat moost harm wercheþ
> To þe pouere peple þat parcelmele buggen. . . .
> Thei richen þoruȝ regratrie and rentes hem biggen
> Of þat þe pouere people sholde putt in hire wombe.
> For toke þei on trewely þei tymbred nouȝt so heiȝe,
> Ne bouȝte none burgages. . . .
>
> (III. 79–86)

He selects such activities at a number of points and this is no mere idiosyncrasy. They represent small-scale commodity production for an impersonal market as it pressed most openly on poorer groups, especially in its control of food and rents.[15] For Langland 'reson' (III. 91–2) was explicitly against developments which absorbed the necessities of life into a system of exchange centred on individual profit. He, like other moralists, assumed an economy where towns and commodity production for a market were peripheral, one governed by unchanging direct relations, just prices and the fixed social order deputed in the chief ideology. This provided no cogent legitimation for a set of practices becoming more and more important,[16] and which the poet attended to with fascination, his imagination filled by their seemingly anarchic energies. Conscience, here expressing Langland's conscious views, tries to resist the energies embodied in Meed's followers. He follows Holy Church by stating that God's eternal Meed will go to those who 'werchen wel' now, those that have 'ywroght werkes wiþ right and wiþ reson', supported the 'riȝtfulle' and eschewed usury (III. 230–45). The passage poses the same difficulties we found in Holy Church's advice, for its pattern of abstractions has no obvious application to the complexities of Langland's milieu. On usury, for instance, reiteration of traditional principles was accompanied by a growing flexibility, an ambiguity in interpretations which accepted 'commercial activity and the irrepressible desire for profit' in a world where there were few philanthropists content to give men capital or loans without considerable interest.[17] Conscience's terms assume a universe of fixed and secure boundaries, between reasonable and unreasonable works, between usurious and non-usurious loans, boundaries which were increasingly hard to detect.

However, Conscience continues by asserting a distinction between just and unjust payment (III. 246–83) which leads to the following judgement:

That laborers and lowe lewede folke taken of hire maistres
It is no manere Mede but a mesurable hire.

(III. 255–6)

The comforting coherence of this statement depends on a body of ideas in which relations between employer and employee are fixed and unproblematic, as they were presented in the dominant ideology Langland favours. Yet despite the many controversies among historians of the later Middle Ages, there is widespread agreement that the fourteenth century was a period of exceptionally fierce social conflicts in the country as well as in towns. R.E. Lerner and G. Leff are representative when respectively they write of the fourteenth century as one including 'some of the most bitter and destructive class warfare to be seen in Europe before the Industrial Revolution', 'perhaps more than any other, a period of class struggles'.[18] Conscience's bland statement about 'mesurable hire' and its straightforward distinction from Meed simply ignores these struggles, despite the manner in which both employers and labourers had reacted to changing circumstances during Langland's own life. It is interesting to contrast the Commons' Petition of 1376, complaining at the failure of the Statute of Labourers (1351) and all attempts to impose a wage-freeze on the working population[19]:

although various ordinances and statutes have been made in several parliaments to punish labourers, artificers and other servants, yet these have continued subtly and by great malice aforethought, to escape the penalty of the said ordinances and statutes. As soon as their masters accuse them of bad service, or wish to pay them for their labour according to the form of the statutes, they take flight and suddenly leave their employment and district . . . they are taken into service immediately in new places, at such dear wages that example is afforded to all servants to depart into fresh places, and from master to master as soon as they are displeased about any matter. For fear of such flights, the commons now dare not challenge or offend their servants, but give them whatever they wish to ask, in spite of the statutes and ordinances to the contrary – and this is chiefly through fear that they will be received elsewhere. . . . But if all such fugitive servants were . . . placed in the stocks or sent to the nearest gaol . . . they would not desire to flee from their districts as they do – to the great impoverishment, destruction and ruin of the commons.

The aggrieved language of the dominant class witnesses to very real conflicts between competing social groups over the whole standard of 'mesurable hire', while the received ideology informing Conscience's argument continues to treat it as straightforward.

Langland, we shall find, was not to settle for Conscience's picture, although he has him develop it further:

In marchaundise is no Mede, I may it wel auowe;
It is a permutacion apertly, a penyworth for anoþer.

(III. 257–8)

Trade is envisaged as a mutual exchange for use; exchange for profits and
their exploitationary consequences (pointed out in Passus III. 79–86), just
disappear. But Langland's own poetry prevents us from believing that the
massive energies of Meed's followers, and the ethos they reflect, can be so
simply contained. His own poetic context makes us suspect that the traditional
ideology he values is either failing to locate new forces and problems or
mastering them with misleading ease.

Langland himself felt the acute tensions between his ideological convictions
and his imagination's insights, and this unhappy experience led him to the
memorable apocalyptic writing at the close of Passus III (284–330). I shall
return to this passage when I consider the overall development and meaning
of the apocalyptic mode in *Piers Plowman* (chapter 3 below), but here I should
note that Langland has chosen to use Isaiah in constructing a messianic age
which not only obliterates social practices and occupations the author found
obnoxious, but also undermines the orthodox social ideology to which he
adhered. For example, the act of abolishing existing legal organisation,
making law a labourer and having 'but oon court' would entail the end of
feudal hierarchy of control and jurisdiction central to his own ideology.[20] As
strikingly, the demilitarisation of the knightly class (III. 305–10, 323–4)
would have removed the main orthodox legitimation of this ruling class, in
the words of Thomas Wimbledon quoted earlier, 'to lette wrongis and þeftis
to be do and to mayntene Goddis Lawe and hem þat ben techeris þereof, and
also to kepe þe lond fro enemyes'.[21] Deprived of its alleged reasons for non-
productive existence and possession of the means of violence in the culture,
the class would also be deprived of the armed power which had always
provided an essential framework for its extraction of labour and produce from
the peasantry. The abandonment of the leading ideology at this point is an
intuitive acknowledgment of its basic strains and inadequacies in the face of
the reality the poet is exploring. The basic paradigm is being subverted,
something that does not happen in conventional complaint and satire, but
although the painful tensions we have been considering made apocalyptic
visions and riddles attractive to Langland, he ultimately denied their
peremptory closure of historical processes. This was not due to the challenge
they offered his conventional social paradigm, but because such closures were
an evasion of his own deepest imaginative preoccupation with the basis of all
spiritual life in history.[22]

Passus IV moves back to power and violence in the poet's culture, but
imposes a successful union between the Ruler (not the apocalyptic king of III.
289), Conscience, Reason, Kynde wit, Love and Leaute (IV. 157–95).[23] This
may have seemed an attractive solution to the difficulties that had been

55

troubling Langland since it avoided the obvious threat to orthodox ideologies posed by the apocalypse in Passus III. Yet it too demands a dissolution of the imaginative texture presenting Meed's permeation of the culture – a *dissolution* rather than an equally realised portrayal of practices and tendencies which might credibly supersede those developments Langland found so offensive. The question as to what social agents will materialise this triumphant union of abstractions is not confronted and this leaves a revealing conceptual and imaginative lacuna.[24] Langland himself, as he does so frequently, immediately indicates his sensitivity to such gaps and his dogged refusal to tolerate their evasions. At the end of Passus IV, Conscience admits that unless 'þe commune' as a whole assents to the overthrow of Meed and the forces she represents, reform is most unlikely (IV. 182–4).

Thus, we are pushed into 'þe feld ful of folk þat I before tolde' (V. 10) as Langland tries to imagine an attempt at reformation in his world. He uses the framework of the seven deadly sins to organise the first part of his return to 'þe feld ful of folk', and a host of readers have testified to the vitality with which he represents practices judged as vicious. One vice is especially relevant to the theme of the present chapter – Covetise (V. 188–95).[25] With this figure he refracts market relationships and values he had contemplated before the apocalyptic passage in Passus III. In the first occupation mentioned, apprentice to 'Symme atte Nok', the characteristic features of present society as Langland experiences it again emerge: the work is considered purely for its 'profit', and in the section as a whole trades seem to exist in a fragmented society where questions of communal needs and well-being are unlikely to be taken very seriously even if they were to be put. Langland's emphasis once more falls on small commodity producers and retailers, and the 'grace of gyle' seems an essential part of the competitive market rather than a corrigible aberration.[26]

When Langland moves on to usury (V. 237 ff.) he has in mind big and small credit financing quite integral to the late medieval economy, and shows his sensitivity to developments which he sees subverting both the dominant ideology and the traditional order it sanctions:

> I haue mo Manoirs þru3 Rerages þan þoru3 *Miseretur et commodat.*
> I haue lent lordes and ladies my chaffare
> And ben hire brocour after and bou3t it myselue.
> Eschaunges and cheuysaunces, wiþ swich chaffare I dele. . . .
>
> (V. 243–6)

The poet believes that the economic difficulties of landowners are being exploited by a social group represented by the voice in the part of the passage just quoted. But the speaker's relish of such practices throughout the overt confession has the effect of evoking the irresistible strength of such psychological and economic forces as they permeate the social fabric, involving all social groups.[27]

Despite this, Langland takes the Vices' revelations as signs of a general urge for a change of behaviour. Accepting the revelations as confessions he shifts into the theological mode (V. 477–512). The ensuing prayer for grace is a powerful, sharply focused poetic meditation on the Christian history of sin and salvation, God's second creation of man, and concentrates on God becoming flesh. This stress on Incarnation is absolutely central to *Piers Plowman*, and the prayer evokes what the dreamer will only grasp by participating in the dramatic process which evolves through the rest of the poem.[28] Langland takes God's Incarnation so seriously that it reinforces his preoccupation with man's fully incarnate existence and encourages him to expect second creation to have affected the whole human being, soul and body growing within and through social relations and institutions – 'A þousand of men þo þrungen togideres . . .'. I suspect that critics do not always appreciate how precisely Langland's particular theological approaches contribute to the characteristic and continual movements of his imagination back to the social world in time present. Piers's directions to the lost pilgrims in Passus V culminate in a marvellous image for the individual's discovery of God and charity within himself (V. 605–8), but the poet does not, certainly not here, use this to initiate a mystical and individualistic search for a way to God 'In þyn herte', placing a cloud of unknowing between self and world.[29] Far from it, Passus VI begins by placing the reader in the world of social labour without which there would be no human spirituality.

It is a world Langland again wants to organise with the traditional dominant ideology, fixing knight, clergy and peasant in static harmony. When discussing Conscience's comfortingly simple distinction between 'mesurable hire' and Meed, with its reconciliation of labourers and employers, I mentioned some actualities in Langland's world which we now need to recall and locate in a slightly wider context. Due to major demographic and economic changes during the period, seigneurial incomes were under severe pressure and after 1349 the knightly class faced a shortage of labour which strengthened the economic positions of peasants still further in relation to landowners. Lords of the manor, as we observed, tried to protect their position by wage freezes and labour legislation, while at the local level they intensified the struggle with assertive peasants over labour services, status, rents and fines. The peasants' rising, it seems, should be seen as the most concentrated and violent episode in a chronic fourteenth-century conflict over the distribution of the social product, a conflict which assumed many forms, non-violent and violent.[30] In this perspective Langland's re-statement of organic estates ideology at the beginning of Passus VI seems so traditional that the historian Rodney Hilton cites it as an example of the dominant ideology and its defence of feudal order.[31] Langland's Ploughman says to the Knight[32]:

I shal swynke and swete and sowe for vs boþe,

And ek laboure for þi loue al my lif tyme,
In couenaunt þat þow kepe holy kirke and myselue
Fro wastours and wikked men. . . .
  Loke ye tene no tenaunt but truþe wole assente,
And þouȝ ye mowe amercy hem, lat mercy be taxour
And mekenesse þi maister maugree Medes chekes; . . .
  And mysbede noȝt þi bondeman, þe bettre shalt þow spede;

(VI. 25–8, 38–40, 45)

The peasants yield up their labour and produce out of love for the landowners
while the latter's jurisdictional and economic rights are unquestioned by
human beings and by divine truth. There seems no possibility of incompatible
versions of rights and truth, no possible irreconcilable disagreements over
what constitutes harming a bondman, no fundamental antagonisms. However,
discussion of the ideology through which Langland perceives his world and
its potential order should not be isolated from the imagination's vision of
social practice.

Throughout the Passus Langland's poetry evokes a sense of extraordinary
vitality among the people committed to the essential work of producing
society's subsistence. For example, threatened by hunger,

Faitours for fere flowen into Bernes
And flapten on wiþ flailes fro morwe til euen . . .
  An heep of heremytes henten hem spades
And kitten hir copes and courtepies hem maked
And wente as werkmen to wedynge and mowynge
And doluen drit and dung to ditte out hunger.

(VI. 183–4, 187–90)

The decisive verbs, the specificity of the work and its materials, the free flow
of the verse, convey the impression of great vigour which characterise the
Passus. Langland's imagination, as so often, is marvellously welcoming to this
secular exuberance. Despite the reiteration of conventional ideology, with
Piers's version of peasants surrendering their labour for love, we find that the
fragmenting of society into self-absorbed groups, investing their energies in
the competitive pursuit of economic interest, has extended to the sphere in
which most people worked and lived – the agrarian.

In this vision frantic work leads to material sufficiency, but with this
opposition to the dominant ideology and its demands on peasants becomes
dramatically evident (VI. 115ff., 310ff.). One appropriate place to celebrate
the exuberance we have been watching is the pub:

Thanne seten somme and songen atte Nale
And holpen ere þe half acre wiþ 'how trolly lolly'.   (VI. 115–16)

Piers resists the drinkers in pragmatic terms (neither religious nor moral) but
his intervention is still fiercely challenged:

> Thanne gan wastour to wraþen hym and wolde haue yfouȝte;
> To Piers þe Plowman he profrede his gloue.
> A Bretoner, a braggere, he bosted Piers als
> And bad hym go pissen with his plowȝ: 'pyuysshe sherewe!
> Wiltow, neltow, we wol haue oure wille
> Of þi flour and þi flessh, fecche whanne vs likeþ,
> And maken vs murye þerwiþ maugree þi chekes.'

> (VI. 152–8)

Given Hilton's commentary on the relatively elevated economic status of
ploughmen in peasant communities,[33] one may well be justified in sensing
that Langland was also registering his consciousness of a stratification among
peasants leading to conflict rather than harmonious hierarchical order within
the village itself. At any rate, the Breton sees the flour and flesh as belonging
to Piers who appeals to a member of the knightly class to reimpose labour-
discipline on those he labels 'wastours' (VI. 159–63).

Langland's imaginative receptivity to conflicts and social movement pushes
the total context beyond the perceptual bounds of his traditional model.[34] He
shows us an extremely powerful peasant resistance, in practice and thought,
to the pressures of the knightly class and the dominant ideology. Like Piers,
the knight and his 'lawe' (VI. 166) are immediately defied:

> 'I was noȝt wont to werche', quod Wastour, 'now wol I noȝt bigynne!'
> And leet liȝt of þe lawe and lasse of þe knyȝte,
> And sette Piers at a pese and his plowȝ boþe,
> And manaced hym and his men if þei mette eftsoone.

> (VI. 167–70)

Of course, the poet's conscious evaluation of this defiance is made obvious in
his naming the knight's opponent as 'Wastour'. But, as I have argued,
Langland's vision is not contained within the framework of the dominant
ideology and estates satire: the poetry carries an energy and conviction in the
'wastour's' defiance which is not matched in the knight's response (VI. 164
ff.), or in any realisation of the normative paradigm. Although the knight has
been invoked by Piers to fulfil his role, he proves unequal to his divinely
ordained task of maintaining a static and hierarchic society. It is not surprising
that neither Piers nor the author adjust their ideas to entertain this
development, for the task of generating new ideologies in changed conditions
is collective and long-drawn. What is arresting is that they do not even
criticise the knight's failure in moral terms. This contributes to an impression

that imaginatively the failure has been accepted as irreversible, beyond the blame of individual knights, or the group as a whole.

The impression is reinforced by the disappearance of the knight from the scene. In the second rising against the established ordering of society (VI. 300 ff.) no one even mentions a knight, although Langland focusses on one of the major areas of conflict – wages. He begins the later passage by figuring the expanded material aspirations of peasants, something reported with great disapproval by many comfortably placed moralists and gentry (VI. 302–11).[35] Even landless labourers who depend entirely on selling their labour for wages – easily the most vulnerable rural group – share these self-absorbed ambitions:

> Laborers þat haue no land to lyue on but hire handes
> Deyneþ noȝt to dyne a day nyȝte olde wortes.
> May no peny ale hem paie, ne no pece of bacoun,
> But if it be fressh flessh ouþer fissh yfryed,
> And þat *chaud* and *plus chaud* for chillynge of hir mawe.
>
> (VI. 307–11)

Langland disapproves, yet his imaginative involvement with the labourers' lives and energies allows him to express their determination, the unabashed material particularity of their aspirations and their independence of the traditional social ideology and ethics he wants them to accept. Their demands for a larger share in the social product, realistic enough in the period, are made through wage claims and what Langland explicitly presents as a total rejection of the dominant ideology and its traditional religious sanctification:

> But he be heiȝliche hyred ellis wole he chide;
> That he was werkman wroȝt warie þe tyme. . . .
>   He greueþ hym ageyn god and gruccheþ ageyn Reson,
> And panne corseþ þe kyng and al þe counseil after
> Swiche lawes to loke laborers to chaste.
>
> (VI. 312–13, 316–18)

The labourers see the connections between God, Reason, existing laws and, in the next two lines, the Statute of Labourers. They see that these all serve the interests of their rulers, clearly opposed to their own, and so they reject them. The social order is experienced and perceived in terms of antagonistic interests which construct their own self-legitimating versions of religion, rationality and law. Hallowed abstractions are brought down to earth and their human constructors and beneficiaries unveiled. Far from notions of a benevolently stratified organic society, theirs is a radically dissenting attitude which could well prove responsive to alternative ideologies such as those attributed to John Ball in 1381.[36]

Be that as it may, after the knight's failure both Piers (VI. 171 ff.) and the author (VI. 319 ff.) invoke Hunger as the only way to confine the challenging energies he has met within the framework provided by the major ideology. Hunger images a reversion to minimal subsistence levels, enforcing a drastic freeze on economic drives whose psychological implications Langland did not welcome. The appeal to Hunger is a desperate and ironically quite amoral wish for nature to reverse processes the poet has shown to be deeply rooted in his world. It also has a further meaning. The social paradigm Langland cherishes, despite its universalising and religious claims, is revealed in a fresh light: it is dependent on material facts like the perpetuation of a minimal subsistence economy, with a peasant population made obedient through living on the brink of starvation. In spite of its own claims, the ideology is disclosed as historical. The poem actually displays to us how, as certain material factors are superseded, the credibility of the orthodox ideology is gravely undermined.

If anyone were to defend and impose this ideology it would be the knightly class, as Piers knew, and the disappearance of the knight at such a crucial point has, I think, a historical significance. It is an example of the way Langland's imaginative integrity fused with a sharp social intuition to give a result incompatible with his own overt ideology. In accepting the logic of his imagination's response to his world, Langland symbolically reflects the gradual disappearance of the feudal knight and lord from the field of history. He seems to reflect what Hilton has described as the 'failing grip of aristocratic domination', the failure of the knightly class to impose a wage freeze successfully, to tighten controls over unfree people and to defend its economic position in the face of internal problems and 'peasant self-assertiveness'. He seems to mediate the fact that 'the long period of the successful and multiform exploitation of peasant labour ended, at any rate in most Western European countries, between the middle and end of the fourteenth century'.[37] The Passus leaves us with a vivid sense of an energetic peasantry in a society where economic and ideological conflict is of the essence. This is distinctly incompatible with the normative ideology used in his perceptual framework, and it illustrates how he was prepared and able to subject cherished patterns of belief to an intense imaginative engagement with realities which were discrediting and destroying those patterns.

Indeed, the strains in received social ideas may be further witnessed as the poet's attitude to the knightly class becomes more explicitly ambivalent. For instance, in Passus X (24–9, 59–89), instead of emphasising the necessary place of upper-class abundance in the feudal order he wants, Langland finds it a cause of economic self-interest, graphically contrasting brotherhood among 'meene men' with lordship's rejection of the needy. Those are 'moost unkynde to þe commune þat moost catel weldeþ' (X. 29); and in that suggestion Langland implies more than the conventional complaints in sermons and estates satire about abuses among what *The Book of Vices and Virtues* depicts

as 'wikkede lordes, þe þei knyӡtes or oþere, þat pilen þe pore folke bi
talyages and gabels borwynge and bi euele customes, and make hem paye
gret amendes for litle trespas, and þretene hem to haue of here good for
feer'.[38] Langland conveys that the very *kynde* of those in the possessing
classes can be changed by their habitual social practices and status, an issue
he has raised before and will return to much later.[39] In Passus XIX he
provides another perspective on the conflicts between landlords and peasants
mentioned in our discussion of Passus VI, for he has a lord express the
attempt to make the peasantry bear the weight of the economic crisis
affecting landowners (XIX. 460–4, quoted pp. 33–4 below). Needless to say,
Langland is not satisfied with such developments and he reminds people able
to give feasts that they should call 'þe carefulle þerto, þe croked and þe
pouere', for Jesus 'In a pouere mannes apparaille pursueþ vs euere' (XI. 185–
94). But the way the poem attends to practice and the historical present
emphasises the incompatibility of such gospel teaching with traditional
aristocratic values and needs, grounded in an order Langland wished to
preserve. The difficulty is not uncommon: a moralist may have wished to
change behaviour which was actually a manifestation of social position and
values that could not be changed without changing the social structure, the
last thing advocated by most moralists.

Langland brings the difficulties well into the open as he appeals to the
notion of Christian equality and brotherhood against the possessing classes.
For instance,

> alle are we cristes creatures and of his cofres riche,
> And breþeren as of oo blood, as wel beggeres as erles.
>
> (XI. 199–200; see 199–211)

Should the idea that all are brethren of one blood, all as 'gentil men' (XI. 203),
have an impact in the present? Or should it be kept as a pious formula
applying only to practices in some safely remote celestial region? Langland
wanted the idea to have an impact, yet he wanted to preserve an order
antagonistic to such ideas. These ideas were part of a radical Christian
tradition which surface in the Peasants' Uprising giving terms for an
alternative ideology, and one may wonder how the poet came to invoke
them at this point.[40]

The answer lies in his frustration at contradictions between his imaginative
presentation of social practice and orthodox ideology. These may have
opened his imagination to sympathise with neo-revolutionary doctrines as
the ones most likely to bring his ethic of love into the sphere that so
preoccupied him – historical practice. Sympathy is evident when he asserts
that 'cristene sholde be in commune riche' (XIV. 201), and has Holy Church
state that necessary clothing, food and drink should be 'in commune' (I. 17–
22).[41] It is not that Langland wanted to change traditional structures, but that

the tensions outlined here turned him towards company he would not have wished to keep, and may suggest the attractiveness the poem held for at least some rebels in 1381.

The tensions I have been discussing and the reading of Passus VI offered above, cast some fresh light on the famously obscure Pardon scene.[42] Passus VII opens with a statement that Truth instructed Piers to plough his fields, and promised him, and all who helped 'a pardoun *a pena et a culpa*' (VII. 1–8). Ninety-seven lines follow, allegedly describing the contents of the Pardon. These lines reimpose the traditional ordering of society which opened Passus VI but was then so drastically undermined. The passage begins by giving Pardon to 'Kynges and kny3tes þat kepen holy chirche/And ri3tfully in Reme rulen þe peple'. This summarises the version of the knightly class's role expressed by Piers and repeats it as though nothing had happened since then to show its supersession. Similarly, the lines on labourers pick up issues raised in Passus VI, offering Pardon to

> Alle libbynge laborers þat lyuen by hir hondes,
> That treweliche taken and treweliche wynnen
> And lyuen in loue and lawe. . . .
>
> (VII. 62–4)

This assumes a straightforward distinction between just and unjust payment reminiscent of Conscience's bland statements in Passus III (255–8), a resolution which ignores Passus VI. There, we recall, the 'Laborers þat haue no land to lyue on but hire handes' joined with others to show that the notion of what constituted 'true' wages was, at least, highly problematic in a conflict-ridden society. Likewise, the lines on merchants ignore key elements in the poem's memorable presentation of merchants' activities, such as that in Passus V (242–53) describing how their trade and financial practices eroded the whole supposedly fixed feudal order. Now, however, the traditional ideology and its world is supposed to absorb and baptise the intense, individualistic and unstable economic energies of the merchants. Truth

> bad hem buggen boldely what hem best liked
> And siþenes selle it ayein and saue þe wynnyng,
> And make Mesondieux þerwiþ myseise to helpe,
> Wikkede weyes wightly amende
> And bynde brugges aboute þat tobroke were,
> Marien maydenes or maken hem Nonnes,
> Pouere peple bedredene and prisons in stokkes
> Fynden swiche hir foode for oure lordes loue of heuene,
> Sette scolers to scole or to som kynnes craftes,
> Releue Religion and renten hem bettre.
>
> (VII. 24–33)

The opening two lines of this quotation approve the qualities of ambition, mobility, and energetic pursuit of markets so abundantly evidenced in modern studies of the merchant class of the later Middle Ages. These Studies show the merchants' thoroughly self-centred drive for political and economic power in towns, together with the aspirations to monopoly. They also document the commitment to accumulate property in town and country from what Langland calls 'þe wynnyng'.[43] In her classic study *The Merchant Class of Medieval London*, Sylvia Thrupp observes some signs that this social group was coming to evolve 'alternative views of the structure of society' to the hierarchical, static and organic ideology which was still dominant, ones which were more in accord with their own practices, 'the opposite of static', fluid and in many ways especially insecure.[44] Committed to the pursuit of economic gain[45]:

> The merchant achieved a very happy justification of his pursuit of wealth as approved by God. The wealthy were fond of texts and mottoes that expressed confidence of divine approval. A fourteenth-century citizen's wife encircled her seal with 'God help þat best man.' A lighthearted letter written by a mayor of Exeter, assuring his friends that an enemy's charge of impurity in his private life was false, adds, 'therefore y . . . sey sadly *si recte vivas*, etc., and am right mery and fare right well, ever thankyng God and myn awne purse.' Late fifteenth-century aldermen displayed such mottoes as 'I trust in God,' 'dextra Domini exaltavit me,' 'A Domine factum est istum.' Wills of the same period, drawn 'of such goodes of fortune as god hath sent me and lent me,' show confidence buoyed up by the doctrine of the stewardship of wealth.

Langland's passage, however, goes on to tell merchants that the justification for their vigorous economic activity is in their use of 'þe wynnyng'. They are to save their profits to invest in charitable works. The dreamer claims that at this prospect merchants were merry and 'manye wepten for ioye' (VII. 38). Given what we see of them in the poem, their weeping at this treatment of their profits seems likely enough – only not for joy.

Yet Langland was in contact with an exceptionally complicated position. For Sylvia Thrupp points out that the merchants she studied were also deeply affected by traditional social ideology and religious attitudes to a life centred on the accumulation of property and material goods. She shows how charitable bequests were indeed an important means of justifying their pursuits and the use of interest which was so hard to distinguish from usury[46]:

> Charity had thus a magic virtue. The only difference of opinion concerned the question whether a man should give alms throughout his life or could safely wait until the division of his estate after death. By long-standing custom it was usual for a man to assign from a third to a half of his

movables to uses that would benefit his soul. It is significant that in London this custom was followed quite strictly and that there was a tendency to extend it to immovables, land often being sold for pious and charitable objects.

This concern reflects their own doubts about the status of their occupation and here Thrupp finds a revealingly mixed attitude to the poor. Merchants believed that 'The better people were the more honest, the wiser, the more prudent, and the more discreet. All these qualities were assumed to be present in maximum strength in the richest of the citizens, the best, the most sufficient, and to be at a low ebb among the poorer citizens.' Nevertheless, she illustrates how they desired the prayers of the poor and arranged for the distribution of many small gifts on their death to ensure this, for there was 'a feeling that the poor were somehow blessed', allied to 'uneasiness as to whether economic relations with the poor were really just'. What Sylvia Thrupp identifies is an increasingly influential social group whose 'curiously mixed' attitudes in these areas are one result of the way traditional social and religious theory could not incorporate the merchants' forms of existence.[47] This was at the heart of Langland's difficulties in the passage under discussion. The significant presence of merchants in Langland's world had been vividly refracted in the poem, yet the traditional ideology the poet wished to affirm could not integrate their practices and basic motivations. The attempts to fuse incompatible outlooks leads to a fantasising reconciliation which the poem itself powerfully discredits.

Indeed, the ninety-seven lines of Pardon themselves have a subtly ambivalent status, one I attempted to acknowledge by stating that they 'allegedly' describe the contents of a divine Pardon. For when Piers unfolds the Pardon it actually contains only two lines from the Athanasian Creed – do well and go to heaven, do ill and go to hell. The long passage is thus presented as a subjective gloss on the lines undoubtedly from Truth, the Creed. It attempts to solve profound contradictions in the worlds of work, social theory, ethics and religion, contradictions dramatically enacted in the poem, by substituting comforting fantasies. Langland himself was sorely tempted to settle for such pseudo-solutions, longing for equilibrium and coherence in the present, but his responsiveness to diverse and conflicting forms of life constantly delivered him from temptation. So in Passus VII his own imagination exploded the ninety-seven line passage which expressed ideological reconciliations his peculiar poetic integrity drove him to reject.[48] Piers's 'pure tene' when challenged by the priest may also be seen more clearly in this light. It was Piers who introduced the orthodox estates ideology in Passus VI, and the alleged content of the Pardon seems to be his gloss, his fantasy.[49] His fragile 'solution' to the problems confronting him and his world-view has been destroyed, leaving him with the vision of antagonistic fragmentation in Passus VI. His 'tene' is very understandable.

It leads to another real and recurrent temptation, for many besides Piers. The temptation is to withdraw from the complex field of social practice to a supposedly transcendent spiritual individualism (VII. 122–35), a retreat which simply abandons the realm of human activity to whatever emerging forces can take possession, and assumes a split between body and soul which many forms of Christianity have resisted.[50] In fact, both Truth and Holy Church stress the primacy of work for man (I. 85–93, 128–33; VII. 1–2), and in the last resort Langland was to remain the poet of *incarnate* man, of the existence of individual spirit in the social and material world.

The relations I have attempted to identify, between the imagination's re-creation of the world and traditional ideology, continue to inform and energize the poem right through to its conclusion. Langland evokes some memorable visions of social love, as in Trajan's speech in Passus XI, replete with sentiments like the following[51]:

And þat alle manere men, enemyes and frendes,
Loue hir eyþer ooþer, and lene hem as hemselue,
Whoso leneþ noȝt, lord woot þe soþe, . . .

And euery man helpe ooþer for hennes shul we alle:
Alter alterius onera portate. [Gal. 6:2]
And be we noȝt vnkynde of oure catel, ne of oure konnyng neiþer. . . .
(XI. 178–80, 211–12)

Langland is completely involved with this vision of brotherhood and love, but his own poetry has made us want to know how such general imperatives could be realized in the concrete activities and social organizations he has displayed. He himself has taught us that in a dynamic, fragmenting society, where markets hold an important place, judgements about 'vnkynde' and 'kynde', about what is natural in social relationships and the handling of 'oure catel', are genuinely problematic.[52] The tensions between Langland's poetic realisation of energies at the root of the problems and his wish to affirm received ideology remains, and with this remains the temptation to dissolve the imaginative insights in favour of the coherence, stability and certainties offered in the traditional model of social order. Rather than trace this recurring movement in detail through the rest of *Piers Plowman*, I will discuss its presence in two major episodes from the second half of the poem, which some readers may have been persuaded by a body of scholarly opinion to treat as a journey inwards simply forsaking the external world of the 'fair feeld ful of folk'.

The first episode concerns Patience and Haukyn, and the ideology in question is a spiritual one, traditional enough, which would sanctify the kind of spiritual transcendence mentioned in connection with Piers's reaction to the priest who read out the 'two lynes' written 'in witnesse of truþe' (VII.

109–35). Near the opening of Passus XIII we are taken to dine with a master of theology, 'goddes gloton' as the dreamer is to call him. This brilliant scene gives an image of the church's institutional reality, and Langland's response shows characteristic movements. One strong tendency is to advocate, like Piers in his 'tene', love and patience which by-pass the essential material mediations of grace and doctrine (XIII. 119–210) – shown by the poem to be distressingly problematic. Patience is so enthusiastic about this path that he claims it does lead back to the social world, a universal elixir transforming all groups (XIII. 164–71). The transformation is expressed in very general terms, lacking any of the specificity we meet in Langland's engagement with both his own world and many aspects of Christian history and doctrine. Such a poetic mode, rather than a more concrete, time-bound one, may well indicate some fallaciousness in Patience's account of the recommended path. It does not take us back to the sphere of active men, and poetic imagination does not sanction this part of Patience's claim. The decadent divine is hardly an endearing witness, but his intervention should not be dismissed as the corrupt comment of despairing worldliness, though it is that too:

> 'It is but a dido', quod þis doctour, 'a disours tale.
> Al þe wit of þis world and wiȝt mennes strengþe
> Kan noȝt parfournen a pees bitwene þe pope and hise enemys,
> Ne bitwene two cristene kynges kan no wiȝt pees make
> Profitable to eiþer peple;' . . .

$$(XIII. 172–6)$$

Patience claims the power to transform social life, and the divine reminds us of actual conflicts he must confront in Langland's world. His check on Patience is salutary and represents decisive aspects of the poet's imagination. Moreover, a certain impatience with Patience's speech is surely justified by his retreat into the much-exegized enigma at lines 151–6:

> Wiþ half a laumpe lyne in latyn, *Ex vi transicionis*,
> I bere þer, in a bouste faste ybounde, dowel,
> In a signe of þe Saterday þat sette first þe kalender,
> And al þe wit of þe wodnesday of þe nexte wike after;
> The myddel of þe Moone is þe myght of boþe.
> And herewith am I welcome þer I haue it wiþ me.

These lines have attracted considerable efforts from scholars assuming that the passage should be interpreted according to some common allegorical and liturgical tradition, treated as an enigma whose shell must be cracked so that an already well-known discursive kernel can be extracted.[53] Yet these efforts ignore at least one real possibility – that the image is not designed to be decoded like a conventional picture model in exegetical and homiletic practice.[54] It may be nearer to the kind of apocalyptic image Conscience used earlier (III. 325–7) where the general sense of urgency and crisis includes areas of deliberately opaque mystery as well as more tangible allusions. Patience breaks into this mode because he tries to carry us over the serious gaps in his account. The image is obscurantist, gesturing at profundities of regeneration which the speaker cannot grasp with any conceptual or imaginative precision. We need not attribute coherence to images which do not have it, especially when there is excellent reason within the particular contexts as to why they cannot have it: the path back to the world of active humanity is harder than Patience realizes, and his obscurity manifests his unresolved difficulties. Conscience is carried away by Patience's self-advocacy to make similar assertions about universal social remedy as he turns to Clergy:

> If Pacience be oure partyng felawe and pryue with vs boþe
> Ther nys wo in þis world þat we ne sholde amende;
> And conformen kynges to pees; and alle kynnes londes,
> Sarsens and Surre, and so forþ alle þe Iewes,
> Turne into þe trewe feiþ and intil oon bileue.
>
> (XIII. 206–10)

Conscience thus still approves and shares Patience's desire to change the historical world, giving his own expression to the poem's orientation to the existence of social man, but he fails to see the inadequacies in the statement of Patience which he echoes.[55]

Nevertheless, Langland does see the lacunae, and he leaves Patience's present remedies at this point because he knows that if Love is to 'dowel' it will be within the field of practices his poem has grasped so concretely, not in some supposedly transcendent realm reached by dissolving the field. So we move to a representative of these practices, Haukyn or *Activa vita* (XII. 220 ff.). In the following passage the poetic mode is very different to the one Patience used. It conveys the need and enjoyment felt for Haukyn's indiscriminate delight in the variety of consumers:

> For alle trewe trauaillours and tiliers of þe erþe
> Fro Mighelmesse to Mighelmesse I fynde hem wiþ wafres.
> Beggeris and bidderis of my breed crauen,
> Faitours and freres and folk wiþ brode crounes.
> I fynde payn for þe pope and prouendre for his palfrey.
>
> (XIII. 239–43)

Patience's spiritual ideology tended to construct a picture of virtuous man in fantastic isolation, and passages like this correct his approach by drawing our attention back to the world of essential human work – 'In the sweat of thy face shalt thou eat bread' (Gen. 3:19):

For er I haue breed of mele ofte moot I swete,
And er þe commune haue corn ynouȝ many a cold morwenyng;
So er my wafres be ywroȝt muche wo I þolye.
Al londoun, I leue, likeþ wel my wafres,
And louren when þei lakken hem; it is noȝt longe ypassed
There was a careful commune whan no cart come to towne
Wiþ bake breed from Stratford; þo gonnen beggeris wepe
And werkmen were agast a lite; þis wole be pouȝt longe:
In þe date of our driȝte, in a drye Aprill,
A thousand and þre hundred, twies þritty and ten,
My wafres were gesene [scarce] when Chichestre was Maire.'

(XIII. 260–70)

One notes the striking specificity of the imagination's loving engagement
with the material conditions under which life had to develop, with daily
responses and drives. These again include areas of work and trade intrinsic to
Langland's culture in which 'vnkynde' (XIII. 355, 378) values and practices
were central. The problem was met earlier, particularly in his treatment of
merchants, and he inevitably reverts to their occupation now[56]:

And if I sente ouer see my seruauntȝ to Brugges,
Or into Prucelond my Prentis my profit to waiten,
To marchaunden wiþ my moneie and maken here eschaunges,
Miȝte neuere me conforte in þe mene tyme
Neiþer masse ne matynes, ne none maner siȝtes;
Ne neuere penaunce parfournede ne Paternoster seide
That my mynde ne was moore on my good in a doute
Than in þe grace of god and his grete helpes:

(XIII. 391–8)

The depiction of psychic obsession symbolizes a transformation of personality,
of 'kynde', caused by an occupation dependent on market practices and
motivation, but necessary to Langland's society. In the way 'my good in a
doute' is shorn of its ethical and self-critical potential by the speaker, we see
how language itself will be reduced to service of the market, commodities
and 'profits'. Langland's first realization of such processes makes it even
harder to accept generalized solutions and abstract moral propositions such as
Patience had put forward, doubtless with the author's sympathy.

For, as I have said, Langland definitely wished to impose such solutions on
the materials he grasped so firmly, and in the next Passus (XIV) he first
moves away from the dynamic world which includes production, zealous
trade and consumption. The movement is by now familiar, but its literary
form deserves comment. Haukyn, image of 'the active life', is to repent and
turn from 'vnkynde' social practices. The setting invites comparison with the

sequence after the general repentance in Passus V. There the poem kept us in the working world, confronting the poet's cherished ideologies with a sharply focussed vision of present energies, conflicts and confusions. Here, however, Patience again takes up his attempt to transcend this densely textured, complicated world:

> 'And I shal purueie þee paast', quod Pacience, 'þouȝ no plouȝ erye,
> And flour to fede folk wiþ as best be for þe soule;
> Thouȝ neuere greyn growed, ne grape vpon vyne,
> All þat lyueþ and lokeþ liflode wolde I fynde
> And þat ynogh; shal noon faille of þyng þat hem nedeþ
>
> (XIV. 29–33)

Once more the form of transcendence is the magic kind – a wave of the wand dissolves the fundamental and essential worlds of work and human relationships, so vividly present in the poem and so perplexing. Certainly man does not live by bread alone (XIV. 46), but his incarnate existence and development as certainly involves labour and community. Patience merely *substitutes* figurative food for material food socially produced (XIV. 30, 47–54). When he does acknowledge the obvious need for material food, he has it met by around-the-clock divine miracles (XIV. 63–70). Through this combination, 'picture-model' allegory and continuous miracle, he thus evaporates historical existence and the complex life-processes the poem habitually engages with.[57] But Langland himself could not rest content with a spiritualism whose foundations rested on the evasory dissolution of major problems he had disclosed as intrinsic to being a human, incarnate individual. With St Augustine he must have often asked himself, 'how could the city of God . . . either take a beginning or be developed, or attain its proper destiny, if the life of the saints were not a social life?'[58]

Certainly, Langland does not allow Patience to follow procedures which dissolved historical existence for long, since his imagination turns again to a fuller version of human living – here, that of the poor:

> Ac beggeris aboute Midsomer bredlees þei soupe,
> And yet is wynter for hem worse, for weetshoed þei gange,
> Afurst soore and afyngred, and foule yrebuked
> And arated of riche men þat ruþe is to here.
>
> Ac poore peple, þi prisoners, lord, in þe put of meschief,
> Conforte þo creatures þat muche care suffren
> Thoruȝ derþe, þoruȝ droghte, alle hir dayes here,
> Wo in wynter tymes for wantynge of cloþes,
> And in somer tyme selde soupen to þe fulle.
>
> (XIV. 160–3, 174–8)

Such writing offers little encouragement to the figurative mode Patience deployed earlier, with its rather jaunty 'spiritual' comments about providing food 'þouȝ no plouȝ erye,/ And flour to fede folk weþ as best for þe soule;/ . . . liflode wolde I fynde/ And þat ynogh'. The speaker is again Patience but Langland has shifted his perspective to take the incarnate nature of human spirituality and suffering seriously.[59] The mode he now creates resists all attempts to dissolve concrete life-processes, whatever respectable ideology such attempts might represent.

The resistance does not, of course, mean the poet stops *trying* to impose traditional schemes on his disturbing materials. His treatment of Charity in Passus XV, for instance, has many elements in common with the shifting handling of Patience. The dreamer's instructor excludes it from trade, war and all concern for rents or riches (XV. 151–78). Despite claims about finding Charity (XV. 216–50) it seems without any possible manifestation in social practice and the speaker resorts to transcendentalizing solutions like Patience's, *substituting* figurative food and divine miracles for the problems of understanding and reforming incarnate man (XV. 179–94, 225–89). There seems no need to analyse these passages as they are close to the parallel ones in Passus XIV discussed above.

But it is worth emphasizing *both* such passages, with the correspondingly extreme internalization of Charity in response to the intractable society (XV. 156–62, 272–87), *and* the characteristic counter-movement back to the poem's dynamic social world and the institutions of incarnate people acting in time present (XV, 307 ff., 546 ff.). For what I have argued is that the poet's commitment to received ideologies *and* to the imagination's engagement with the present, generates creative conflicts which are absolutely vital to the poem's momentum and its genuine exploratory power.

From Passus XV his search for Charity focalizes the theological grounding of the poem in a passionate involvement with Christian history and the Incarnation. Elsewhere I have considered these magnificent Passus with such aspects in mind and here it must suffice to note again how emphatically Langland's theology centres on God's Incarnation, his commitment to human history.[60] He is not interested in detailed meditations on the torn flesh and bleeding wounds of the crucified Christ, a form so popular in the later Middle Ages, and his Christ has perhaps been most remembered as the powerful, triumphant figure who harrows Hell. Yet just as he had stressed the incarnation of Christ in magnificent passages in Passus I (147–62) and V (478–505), so in these Passus it is Christ's immersion in time and the present consequences of his acts that hold his imagination. We see Christ being taught by Piers, becoming man to learn existentially what it is to be a 'creature', to know human sorrow by suffering, and through this we perceive the theological and historical grounds for Langland's own special insistence on the brotherhood of men in Christ and the latter's presence as one of the contemporary poor.[61] The subtle and powerful visionary dramatization of the

Christian version of history, the intersections of time past and time present focussing on the incarnate Christ, the outflow of grace from his acts, these still leave open critical issues about men striving for 'dowel' and Charity in the present society and culture where they gain their being and identity.

To these Langland returns in the final episode I shall now look at, the poem's last two Passus, where Langland concentrated on the human world as he saw it.[62] The dreamer's cry for grace with 'manye hundred' others (XIX. 209–12) includes an allusion to the scene in Passus V where the great passage on incarnation and salvation preceded the search for grace and truth in the world of living, working people (V. 478–516). Now the grace released through Christ's redemptive acts is seen in personal form organizing a Christian world.[63] Grace, the Holy Spirit, explicitly adapts Paul's teaching about the diversity of spiritual gifts in the Church fused in its mystical unity (1 Cor. 12: 4–31), and applies it to society as a whole.[64] Langland thus has him propagate the dominant social ideology we have so often encountered. Society consists of stratified estates, organically related in a divinely established harmony free from flux and change. Perceived like this, the poet can set down vocation after vocation without any sign of the deep antagonism and mobility the poem has mediated so impressively. For example,[65]

And some he kennede craft and knonnynge of sighte,
By sellynge and buggynge hir bilyue [livelihood] to wynne.
And some he lered to laboure on lond and on watre
And lyue, by þat labour, a lele lif and a trewe.
And some he tauȝte to tilie, to coke and to thecche
To wynne wiþ hir liflode bi loore of his techynge

(XIX. 234–9)

We have seen how fully Langland's imagination engaged with traders' activities, showing how deeply problematic they were to his preferred social model; yet in this comfortable statement the grave difficulties of practising anything remotely resembling what Langland would accept as Christian morality in an occupation based on profitable exchange of commodities in a competitive market demanding dedicated energy – difficulties the poem itself has awakened us to – these are simply ignored while the occupational activity persists.[66] Likewise with the labourers: the material and ideological conflicts intrinsic to agrarian relations in Langland's day and so vividly mediated in Passus VI, vanish into bland generalizations about 'a lele lif and a trewe'. Indeed,

alle he lered to be lele, and ech a craft loue ooþer,
Ne no boost ne debat be among hem alle.
'Thouȝ some be clenner þan some, ye se wel', quod Grace,
'That al craft and konnyng come of my ȝifte.

Lokeþ þat noon lakke ooþer, but loueþ as breþeren;
And who þat moost maistries kan be myldest of berynge.

(XIX. 250–5)

The myth of divine institution thus confirms the existing social order in its
orthodox ideological version. However, as with the preceding references to
contemporary vocations, this can only be present in a form which eschews all
imaginative specificity and engagement with the dynamic activities realized
throughout the poem. The absence of particularity, the choice of generalized
repetition ('ech a craft loue ooþer . . . loueþ as breþeren', 'Ne no boost ne
debat be among hem . . . noon lakke ooþer'), these are signs of a reconciliation
which is unconvincing because it only functions at an ideological level.[67]

And, as we have come to expect, Langland's imagination does not rest
here, but re-engages with the social and economic world the poet hoped to
contain within the received ideologies. Instead of the reassuring integration
of merchants' practice with these structures, it now seems that 'pride' is
justified in commenting that Conscience will not be able to judge of any kind
of 'marchaunt þat wiþ moneye deleþ/Wheiþer he wynne wiþ right, wiþ
wrong or wiþ vsure' (XIX. 348–50). Changing and more complex socio-
economic practices are thus undermining received ethical categories and their
received ideological framework. Not for the first time in *Piers Plowman* the
figure who represents the nexus of commitments Langland finds so intractable
is a brewer, one of the determined commodity producers met before:

'Ye? baw!' quod a Brewere, 'I wol noȝt be ruled,
By Iesu! for al youre Ianglynge, with *Spiritus Iusticie*,
Ne after Conscience, by crist! while I kan selle
Boþe dregges and draf and drawe at oon hole
Thikke ale and þynne ale; þat is my kynde,
And noȝt hakke after holynesse; hold þi tonge, Conscience!
Of *Spiritus Iusticie* þow spekest muche on ydel.'

(XIX. 396–402)

This is a stunning contrast to the bland statement made by Spirit in which
buying and selling were uncontentious activities taught by Grace, and it
mediates the market practices of his own world. In its concreteness and
strenuous rhythms the poetic mode once more registers the shift from
ideological assertion to an imaginative grasp of those tremendous cultural
energies so alien to Langland's received world-view but so important in the
history of the later Middle Ages and Renaissance. Like the values of many
groups in *Piers Plowman*, the brewer's are so deeply individualistic and
market-oriented that once more Langland reveals how social practices can
transform human nature, 'my kynde'.[68] He does not explicitly comment on
the relation of this to his own assumption that there is an unchanging human

nature – a universal 'kynde' known to us all and supplying a standard we can all use to asess 'unkynde' attitudes and behaviour, whatever our occupations – but it certainly strengthens our consciousness of cultural fragmentation and relativity. Again, Langland's poetry goes beyond the criticism of deviancy found in conventional satire and sermons, for he discloses how a view of human morality and nature, assumed in traditional paradigms, is in danger of being subverted by actual social practice.

The Passus drives home the fact that the brewer is representative of currents so strong that they include groups who should be defenders of the received ideology Langland wanted to affirm. He shows a knight saying:

> 'I holde it riȝt and reson of my Reue to take
> Al þat myn Auditour or ellis my Styward
> Counseilleþ me bi hir acounte and my clerkes writynge.
> Wiþ *Spiritus Intellectus* þei toke þe reuses rolles
> And wiþ *Spiritus fortitudinis* fecche it, wole he, nel he.'
>
> (XIX. 460–4)

This provides an interesting final perspective on the knightly class appealed to by Piers in Passus VI, and confirms the fundamental place of economic motivation, self-centred acquisitiveness and conflict at all levels in Langland's world. It also shows us how ideal abstractions ('riȝt', 'reson', *Spiritus fortitudinis*', a cardinal virtue) are moulded by the material interests of particular groups and individuals in the culture. We see here how one powerful group's conception of what is desirable for itself is turned into a set of universals which function to generalize and legitimate its daily life and its self-interested goals. Even *Spiritus Intellectus*, Langland suggests, is appropriated and deployed by the leading group in its own interest. Fascinated by these historical processes Langland goes on to expose a classic statement of the organic social hierarchy, in terms of Paul's traditional metaphor, to a damaging image of its function. A king proclaims:

> I am kyng wiþ croune þe comune to rule,
> And holy kirke and clergie fro cursed men to defende.
> And if me lakkeþ to lyue by þe lawe wole I take it
> Ther I may hastilokest it haue, for I am heed of lawe;
> Ye ben but membres and I aboue alle.
> And siþe I am youre aller heed I am youre aller heele
> And holy chirches chief help and Chieftayn of þe comune,
> And what I take of yow two, I take it at þe techynge
> Of *Spiritus Iusticie* for I Iugge yow alle.
>
> (XIX. 466–74)

The corporate metaphor is appropriated by the ruler in defence of interests as

Imagination and Traditional Ideologies in *Piers Plowman*

egotistic and acquisitive as the brewer's or his fellow aristocrat's. Like the latter, he too demonstrates how abstractions supposed to be moral universals ('lawe', '*Spiritus Iusticie*', another cardinal virtue) are shaped by particular social and economic interests. Even Conscience now fails to oppose aristocrat and king, trying instead to use their own abstractions to hint at some vague qualification to their boundless self-interest (XIX. 477–9). As in Passus XX, Langland makes it clear that Conscience too is immersed in specific historical practice, prone to defer before the powerful.[69] The 'Curatour' seems correct when he asserts the 'þe commune' will only use the counsel of Conscience or Cardinal virtues in so far as they tend to visible economic gain, 'somewhat to wynnyng' (XIX. 451–3). And Langland's poetry has just displayed that this will have profound effects on language, ethics, social ideology and 'kynde'. His own poetic vision, in Passus XIX thus mediates a culture evolving in ways which make the inherited ideologies he still cherished seem hopelessly inadequate.

Passus XX keeps us in this dynamic, fluid world, shifting the centre of attention to its absorption of the church, the mediator of Grace and doctrine. The poet abandons hope in his social ideology and constructs a parallel to its disintegration in Passus VI. As before, his vision of social and religious development leads to a call for *natural* disasters (disease, destitutions of age, death) to terrorize a world of people whole-heartedly opposed to Spirit's teachings (XX. 51–89). Jesus may well have told Satan that 'gile is bigiled and in his gile fallen':

Now bigynneþ þi gile ageyn þee to turne
And my grace to growe ay gretter and widder.

(XVIII. 360–2)

But what Langland sees growing is very different:

Antecrist cam þanne, and al þe crop of truþe
Torned it tid vp so down and ouertilte þe roote,
And made fals sprynge and sprede and spede mennes nedes.
In ech a contree þer he cam he kutte awey truþe
And gerte gile growe þere as he a god weere.

(XX. 53–7)

We recall that in Passus II Gyle had been welcomed by merchants, while 'þe False' was embraced by friars (II. 211–17), and in his choice of agricultural imagery Langland obviously invited us to compare this scene with the actions of Piers and Spirit in Passus XIX, of Piers in Passus XVI and the cultivation of the half-acre in Passus VI.[70] Conscience's desperate resort to terror and physical afflictions (XX. 76 ff.) easily shows us the frailty of our lives, but cannot entail any particular set of moral values and social practices.

Langland acknowledges this. Conscience asks Nature to stop torturing men for a while, explicitly echoing Piers's request to Hunger (XX. 106–9; VI. 199 ff.). The result also mirrors the earlier episode, for as soon as the material threat is made less pressing the abundant energies we have got to know so well re-emerge in full vitality, as resistant as ever to the categories within which the poet would have liked to control them (XX. 109–64; see VI. 301 ff.). Conscience's only resort is yet again to summon physical terrors, closing the fruitless circle as Piers had done in Passus VI. Langland's re-enactment of this aspect of the structure of Passus VI invites the reader to draw related implications: there we found that the poet's desired ideological order could only be perpetuated by an economic freeze at subsistence level causing constant hunger (VI. 319–20). Now it becomes clear that the range of secular energies and values explored *negate* the organized Catholic Christianity Langland treasured, that in his culture the only motivation for entering 'into unitee', the church, is terror – at physical and material suffering (XX. 183–206). This is indeed a desperate position for a Catholic poet to reach, but it grows out of the integrity which constantly forced him to expose the solutions offered by inherited social and religious ideologies to his imagination's concrete engagement with alien energies and developments in his own world.

The closing lines of *Piers Plowman* maintain our focus on the consequences of the loss of Grace in the social fabric which has absorbed the church and subverted the poet's social ideal[71]:

Conscience cryed eft Clergie to helpe,
And bad Contricion come to kepe þe yate.
'He lyþ adreynt and dremeþ', said Pees, 'and so do many oþere.
The frere wiþ his phisyk þis folk haþ enchaunted,
And doþ men drynke dwale [opiate]; þei drede no synne.'
'By crist!' quod Conscience þo, 'I wole bicome a pilgrym,
And wenden as wide as þe world renneþ
To seken Piers þe Plowman, þat pryde myȝte destruye,
And þat freres had a fyndyng þat for nede flateren
And countrepledeþ me, Conscience; now kynde me avenge,
And sende me hap and heele til I haue Piers þe Plowman.'
And siþþe he gradde after Grace til I gan awake.

(XX. 375–86)

The poet whose vision consistently returns to the quest for individual salvation in its fully social and institutional context seems compelled, by his own poetic movement, to conclude with an individualistic pilgrimage which perhaps could indicate the total abandonment of the official church to the social and spiritual forces he has grasped so vividly and opposed so strenuously. Deprived of an ideological and institutional framework, the lonely Conscience is left to initiate a search for the lost Ploughman and the Grace he may mediate to the present world. This act of faith is a fitting symbol for the poet's own refusal to short-circuit the central dialectic between inherited ideologies and creative imagination, courageously choosing total engagement with the ambivalence and tensions his culture inspired, and evolving a form of writing brilliantly able to mediate and explore these in all their fluid complexity.

Notes

1. Criticism has characteristically maintained that Langland was quite straightforwardly 'a traditionalist if not a reactionary', E.T. DONALDSON, *Piers Plowman: The C-text and its Poet* (1949), (London: 1966), p. 108. In chapter 3 of his book *Poetry and Crisis in the Age of Chaucer*, University of Notre Dame Press, Notre Dame Ind., 1972, CHARLES MUSCATINE suggests that the poem's 'form and style are symptomatic of some sort of breakdown'. His work points in fruitful directions, seeing art as a 'response to a cultural situation', but the task needs specific analysis of the areas which prove problematic for Langland and this Muscatine does not attempt. His own sketch of both age and poem seem to me misleadingly negative and one-dimensional, for he sees poet and text as 'victims' of an 'age of decline', and of 'economic depression' (p. 16). My differences with his own stimulating work will be clear enough. In thinking about ideologies and their changes I have found the following works equally helpful: T.S. KUHN, *The Structure of Scientific Revolutions* (University of Chicago Press, 1970), 2nd edn, and Kuhn's essays in *Criticism and the Growth of Knowledge*, ed. I. Lakatos and A. Musgrave (Cambridge University Press, 1970), pp. 1–23, 231–78; A.W. GOULDNER, *The Dialectic of Ideology and Technology* (London, Macmillan, 1976).

2. Thomas Wimbledon's sermon is edited by N.H. OWEN in *Medieval Studies*, **28** (1966); 176–97, here quoting from p. 179.

3. *Seriatim* see WIMBLEDON in OWEN, *Medieval Studies*, p. 179; GOWER, *Mirour de l'omme*, II. 27229–30, quoted in J.H. FISHER, *John Gower* (London, Methuen, 1965), p. 170; *Middle English Sermons*, ed. W.O. Ross, EETS, O.S., **209** (1940): 224, 237.

4. On 'estates satire', see R. MOHL, *The Three Estates in Medieval and Renaissance Satire* (1933), (New York, Ungar, 1962) and J. MANN, *Chaucer and Medieval Estates Satire* (Cambridge University Press, 1973). For examples of criticism which does not question the paradigm, see Ross, *Middle English Sermons*, pp. 124, 201–3, 237–9, 255–6, 266, 310–11. For examples in Lollard texts, see *The Lanterne of Lizt*, ed. L.M. Swinburn, EETS, O.S., **151** (1917): 33–4, 117–21; *Select English Works of John Wyclif*, ed. T. Arnold, 3 vols (Oxford University Press, 1869), 1871, II, p. 246. For Wyclif on the theme, see *Dialogus*, ed. A.W. Pollard (Wyclif Society, 1876) pp. 2–5.

5. For a classic example of the 'monstrous' in the perception of Rebellion see JOHN GOWER, *Vox Clamantis*, I, chapters 2–8, trans. E.W. Stockton, *The Major Latin Works of John Gower* (University of Washington Press, 1962).

6. See R. HILTON, *Bond Men Made Free, Medieval Peasant Movements and the English Uprising of 1381* (London, Temple Smith, 1973), p. 229; pp. 221–32 relevant.

7. HILTON, *Bond Men*, p. 233: see too 16 below.

8. DONALDSON, *Piers Plowman*, p. 106 (and chapter 4 *passim*); G.R. OWST, *Literature and Pulpit in Medieval England*, 2nd edn (Oxford, Blackwell, 1966), chapter 9; P. GRADON, *Form and Style in Early English Literature* (London, Methuen, 1971), p. 102.

9. All quotation of *Piers Plowman* is from the B version, eds G. KANE and E.T. DONALDSON (London, Athlone Press, 1975), unless otherwise stated. (References in the text are to passus and line numbers.)

10. The religious whom Langland thinks likely to escape the pervasive practices are those who become genuine 'Ancres and heremites þat holden hem in hire selles' (Pr. 28–30), itself an indication of how alien the emerging world is from the one projected in the traditional ideology he accepts.

11. On the fable see discussion and references in J.A.W. BENNETT, *Piers Plowman: The Prologue and Passus I–VII.* (Oxford University Press, 1972), pp. 100–1.

12. See, for example, X. 29; XIII. 391–8 and XIX. 396–401, discussed later in the chapter; the whole issue is placed in a *theological* context in Passus XVII and XVIII (eg. XVII. 233–80 and XVIII. 396–9).

13. The problems here are also theological – those concerning grace, predestination and free will. Holy Church evades them, but the dreamer and the poet will doggedly confront them.

14. See II. 53–73, 158–88, 211–37.

15. The passage on Covetise is relevant here, V. 188–295 (also XIII. 355–98), as is that concerning Haukyn, XIII. 238–70, discussed in slightly different contexts later in the chapter. Brewing and baking were characteristic of traditional rural economies, but the point here is the role they serve in Langland's poem and in his changing world. In his *English Peasantry* (Oxford University Press, 1975), RODNEY HILTON documents relevant developments in commodity production of the kind Langland had in mind (eg. pp. 43–57, 82–94, 152–3, 167–70, 196–208, 213–14). In a letter replying to my questions on this topic Rodney Hilton comments:

> It is true of course that there were bakers and brewers in the peasant economy before. The assize of bread and ale which attempted to control them goes back (from Langland's day) more than a century and a half. All the same I think there *was* something new which gave life to Langland's bakers and brewers, and to Haukyn. What I think was new was the relaxation of seigneurial pressure not simply on the peasants and agricultural producers but on the retail trade in the villages. . . . In the fourteenth century brewing is . . . a trade which attracts the capital of entrepreneurs.

He also mentions his own recent work on some small town records of the period (Thornbury, South Gloucestershire) where he has apparently found a ruling élite largely composed of traders – bakers, brewers, grain and stock dealers, and retail traders. This seems to me the kind of situation Langland had in mind, but there is certainly room in this area for collaborative work between literary critics and historians.

16. For an introduction to this important subject see the following: S.L. THRUPP, *The Merchant Class of Medieval London* (1948), (Ann Arbor, University of Michigan Press, 1962), pp. 288–99, and *passim*; *Economic Organization and Policies in the Middle Ages*, eds M.M. Postan *et al.*, *Cambridge Economic History of Europe* (Cambridge University Press, 1963), ch. 4 and pp. 287–90, 570; B. GEREMEK, *Le salariat dans l'artisanat parisien du XIIIᵉ s. au XVᵉ s* (The Hague, Mouton, 1968); J.

Le Goff, 'Le temps du travail dans la "crise" du XIVᵉ s.', *Le Moyen Age*, **69** (1963): 597–613; H.A. Miskimin, *The Economy of Early Renaissance Europe, 1300–1460* (Englewood Cliffs, NJ, Prentice-Hall, 1969), chs 2 and 3; F.R.H. Du Boulay, *An Age of Ambition* (London, Nelson, 1970), ch. 3; F. Rorig, *The Medieval Town* (University of California Press, 1969); G.A. Williams, *Medieval London* (London Athlone Press, 1963); R. Bird, *The Turbulent London of Richard II* (London, Longman, 1949); E.M. Veale, *The English Fur Trade in the later Middle Ages* (Oxford University Press, 1966), chs 3 and 6; E. Power, *Medieval English Wool Trade* (1941) (Oxford University Press, 1969), pp. 46–51, 104–23; M. Mollat and P. Wolff, *The Popular Revolutions of the Late Middle Ages* (London, Allen & Unwin, 1973).

17. Here I summarize the findings of G. Le Bras, 'Conceptions of Economy and Society', ch. 8 in Postan *et al.*, *Economic Organization and Policies in the Middle Ages*, especially pp. 560–1, 564–70; see too Thrupp, *Merchant Class*, pp. 174–80 and R. de Roover, *San Bernardino of Siena and Sant 'Antonio of Florence* (Harvard, Baker Library, 1967).

18. R.E. Lerner, *The Age of Adversity* (Ithaca NY, Cornell University Press, 1968), p. 17, and G. Leff, in *The Medieval World*, ed. D. Daiches and A. Thorlby (London, Aldus, 1973), p. 260. For an introduction to this topic, another major one in studying the period, see the following: Mollat and Wolff, *The Popular Revolutions of the Late Middle Ages*; F.R.H. Du Boulay, *An Age of Ambition* (London, Nelson, 1970), pp. 64 ff.; Miskimin, *The Economy of Early Renaissance Europe*, pp. 30–51; Hilton, *Bond Men* and 'Feudalism and the origins of Capitalism', *History Workshop*, **1** (1976): 9–25; G. Duby, *Rural Economy and Country Life in the Medieval West* (London, Arnold, 1968), pp. 277–8, 283–6, 329–36; D. Nicholas, *Town and Countryside* (Bruges, De Tempel, 1971), pp. 63, 77 ff., 333–40.

19. This commons' petition of 1376 is translated in *The Peasants' Revolt of 1381*, ed. R.B. Dobson (London, Macmillan, 1970), p. 73. The Statute of Labourers: see B.H. Putnam, *The Enforcement of the Statute of Labourers* (New York, Columbia University Press, 1908).

20. Compare the attacks on law and lawyers in the uprising of 1381: Hilton, *Bond Men*, pp. 226–7; and for links with *Piers Plowman* see R.B. Dobson, *The Peasants' Revolt of 1381* (London, Macmillan, 1970), p. 380.

21. Wimbledon in Owen, *Medieval Studies*.

22. This topic is developed in chapter 3.

23. For examples of the endemic violence so easily solved by Langland at this point see Hilton, *English Peasantry*, pp. 240–3; J. Barnie, *War in Medieval Society* (London, Weidenfeld & Nicolson, 1974), chs 1–3; H.J. Hewitt, *The Organization of War under Edward II* (Manchester University Press, 1966), chs 2, 5, 7.

24. When Langland came to revise the B version he may have acknowledged this in this addition of a passage claiming that 'Love' will give the king more silver than merchants, ecclesiastics, Lombards and Jews, thus thrusting the difficulties he was tempted to evade into the forefront of the work, re-directing attention to the world where spiritual struggles are waged by economic man. See C. version, ed. W.W. Skeat, *Piers the Plowman in Three Parallel Texts* (Oxford University Press, 1968); V. 191–4, (pp. 115, 117), and the edition by D.A. Pearsall, *Piers Plowman*, (London, Arnold, 1978); IV. 191–4 (p. 96).

25. It is worth recalling that M.W. BLOOMFIELD found later medieval moralists judging covetousness rather than pride as the worst and most prevalent sin: *Seven Deadly Sins* (Michigan State College Press, 1952) pp. 90–1.

26. In the light of the whole poem the 'grace of gyle' so essential to market practices has especially tragic irony, for Langland is actually writing after the victory of Christ over the prince of guile in Passus XVIII: see XVIII. 333–72 and contrast XVI. 154 ff. and II. 214 ff.

27. Explicitly involved are the landed classes, merchants, retailers, financiers and the poor. The religious pilgrimage, product of confession itself has an economic motive – V. 228–9.

28. I have written about this, from a different perspective, in *Piers Plowman and Christian Allegory* (London, Arnold, 1975), ch. 5.

29. On the image here also see XV. 161 ff., and ELIZABETH SALTER [Zeeman], 'Piers Plowman and the pilgrimage to truth', *ES*, **2** (1958): 1–16.

30. The relevant literature here is immense, but I have found the following particularly illuminating in relation to the period's literature: HILTON's *Bond Men* and *English Peasantry*, together with his *Decline of Serfdom in Medieval England* (London, Macmillan, 1969); MISKIMIN, *The Economy of Early Renaissance Europe*, ch. 2; R. BRENNER, 'Agrarian class structure and economic development in pre-industrial Europe', *P and P*, **70** (1976): 30–75; C. HOWELL, 'Stability and change 1300–1700', *Journal of Peasant Studies*, **2** (1975): 468–82; E. MILLER's ch. 6 in *Economic Organization and Policies of the Middle Ages*, ed. Postan *et al.*; G.A. HOLMES, *The Estates of the Higher Nobility in Fourteenth Century England* (Cambridge University Press, 1957), pp. 114–20; DUBY, *Rural Economy*. The picture emerging from these works seems common among historians who differ considerably in accounting for the causes and in emphasis on different factors in describing the situation.

31. *Bond Men*, pp. 221–2, and see role of knights in I. 94–104, VIII. 100–6; and E.T. DONALDSON quoted at opening of n. 1.

32. In quoting lines 38–40 I have rejected two conjectural emendations of their base MS made by Kane and Donaldson: they insert 'þee' in place of 'yow' and 'ye', to accord with their own view of Piers's status, views they do not explicate or defend, understandably enough given their monumental editorial task (p. 170 and critical apparatus, p. 350). I have written at some length on Piers's status here and given my ground for denying a clerical and allegorical role here, *Piers Plowman*, pp. 77–81, 113–24, and a reader could also cast his eyes over the following lines to see how Piers is *not* presented as an image of the clerical estate here: 27, 92–5, 101 ff., 152 ff., 159, 169 ff., 202 ff., 253 ff., 280 ff. See too A.V.C. SCHMIDT's judicious comments in his edition of *The Vision of Piers Plowman*, from the same MS (London, Dent, 1978), p. 272. Also PEARSALL, *Piers Plowman*, pp. 147–8.

33. HILTON's *English Peasantry*, pp. 21–7.

34. The tone of the knight's reply (VI. 164–6) probably itself is a small example of Langland's orthodox ideology imposing itself: his noncoercive courtesy to anarchic peasants and ineffectual ploughmen comprises a brief assertion that the upper and lower estates can still be fixed in a mutually beneficial and respectful order, despite the present events.

35. A shrewd assessment of the uprising in terms of increased aspirations was made by Froissart – text in DOBSON, *The Peasants' Revolt*, p. 370. On literary complaint about the peasantry, B. WHITE 'Poet and peasant', in *The Reign of Richard II*, ed.

F.R.H. Du Boulay and C.M. Barron (London, Athlone Press, 1971), pp. 59–63, 65–7, 73.

36. See texts in DOBSON, *The Peasants' Revolt*, pp. 136–7, 371–83: see especially the egalitarian communism attributed to him by Froissart in Dobson, p. 371, and Hilton, *Bond Men*, ch. 9.

37. In this paragraph I am paraphrasing and quoting Hilton, 'Feudalism and the origins of Capitalism', pp. 20–2; see too references in n. 30 above. Some aspects of the argument here coincide with some views of J.H. FISCHER, 'Wyclif, Langland, Gower and the Pearl poet on the subject of aristocracy', *Studies in Medieval Literature*, ed. M. Leach (Philadelphia, University of Pennsylvania Press, 1961), pp. 139–57.

38. Ed. W.N. FRANCIS, *EETS*, O.S., **217** (1942): 34.

39. See earlier discussion and n. 12 above.

40. On the tradition, n. 36; also, for example, *English Works of Wyclif*, ed. F.D. Matthew, *EETS*, O.S., **74** (revised 1902): 227–8, 233–4.

41. The passage attacking ideas of communal ownership (XX. 273–9) could be taken as Langland's wish to ensure his views are not merged with those of contemporary radical Christians, but it must also be read in its context where it is primarily part of a polemical attack on friars and their concepts of ownership and use.

42. For introduction to the Pardon scene, its problems and the literature on it, J. LAWLOR, *Piers Plowman* (London, Arnold, 1962), pp. 71–84; E. KIRK, *The Dream Thought of Piers Plowman* (Yale University Press, 1972), pp. 80–100; AERS, *Piers Plowman*, pp. 121–3; R.W. FRANK, *Piers Plowman* (Yale University Press, 1957) ch. 3.

43. See works cited in n. 16 above on relevant developments in the period.

44. THRUPP, *Merchant Class*, ch. 7; quoting here from pp. 290, 311.

45. THRUPP, *Merchant Class*, p. 174.

46. On the difficulties of distinguishing usury see the statement at XIX. 348–50; here the quote is from THRUPP, *Merchant Class*, p. 177.

47. THRUPP, *Merchant Class*, 15, pp. 177–80, 313–15. Thrupp sees foreshadowing of 'Puritan culture' in these developments. To her comments should be added the fascinating studies on changing attitudes to poverty during this period collected by M. MOLLAT, *Études sur l'histoire de la pauvreté jusqu'au XVIe s.*, 2 vols (Paris, Sorbonne, 1974). I believe Langland's own text illustrates a shifting and uncertain attitude to poverty which is related to developments outlined in this collection, but this is another area where collaborative work between literary critics and historians could be most fruitful.

48. Doubtless his own social position, as he experienced and represented it, encouraged such critical integrity: a de-classed, wandering intellectual, one of the vagrant types he attacked, he had no place in the social and religious ideology he affirmed. See, e.g. C version, ed. D.A. Pearsall, V. 1–101 (Skeat's VI. 1–101).

49. In my *Piers Plowman*, ch. 5, I tried to show how Piers functions as a lens mediating the fullest spiritual perception available at particular stages of vision in the poem, and here he mediates what the author takes to be the best available social ideas.

50. In the lines referred to I see no reason for rejecting MSS reading 'bely ioye' for Kane and Donaldson's emendation to 'bilye', although the latter too keeps the sense of livelihood (cf. XIX. 235). Langland's own resistance to this split is described in the present and following two chapters.

51. I say Trajan's speech but it is actually often impossible to tell whether it is Trajan or Will or the poet himself to whom the poetry is attributed: e.g. for lines 171–319, 171 says, 'quod Troianus', but for how much further is he the speaker, and how appropriate are lines like 317–18 to him rather than Langland *in propria persona*? The statements, whoever their formal speaker, are very dear and central to Langland's own hopes.

52. See earlier discussions of this and n. 12 above. On Trajan, see J.S. WITTIG's comments in *Traditio*, **28** (1972): 249–63.

53. For a good summary of readings emerging from such approaches, and references, see SCHMIDT, *Piers Plowman*, p. 346.

54. On exegesis and picture models, see AERS, *Piers Plowman*, chs 2–3.

55. Patience's statement at XIII. 164–71; Conscience's enthusiasm here recalling his own earlier messianic vision (III. 284–330) where the period leading to the conversion of the Jews was to be introduced by an apocalyptic king, a very different path to the one envisaged here. Conscience seems rather unstable in the ways he envisages, and he should never be simply identified with a final authoritative-authorial viewpoint (even if there was one final one, which there is not).

56. Besides the earlier discussions referred to here, see n. 12 above.

57. On the dissolution of historical existence in 'picture model' allegory, AERS, *Piers Plowman*, chs 2–3.

58. *City of God*, XIX. 5, trans M. Dods, (New York, Random House, 1950), p. 680.

59. From XIV. 104–273 the speaker is formally Patience: he now speaks with one of the characteristic voices of the poet in his own person – see for example the immensely powerful addition in the C version on the lives of poor people, Skeat's C text, X. 71–97, Pearsall's IX. 71–97.

60. AERS, *Piers Plowman*, ch. 5, *passim*.

61. Respectively see: XVI. 100–7; XVI. 215; XVIII. 212–15 and 222–5: of the many examples of brotherhood in Christ see XI. 199–212; XVIII. 393–9; and V. 384–90, 503: on Christ as one of the contemporary poor, see especially XI. 185–96 (and Luke 14); XI. 232–7; X. 460–81. On Piers teaching Christ, and the powerful dramatization of the Christian version of history in Passus XVI–XX, see AERS, *Piers Plowman*, respectively pp. 107–9, 79–130 *passim*.

62. For some of the major imagistic connections between XIX–XX and VI see M.W. BLOOMFIELD, *Piers Plowman as a Fourteenth Century Apocalypse* (New Brunswick, NJ, Rutgers University Press, 1961), pp. 130, 115, and AERS, *Piers Plowman*, pp. 109–31.

63. For the Holy Spirit as released by Christ's acts, XIX. 199 ff., XVI. 46–52, and John 16:7, Acts 2:1–8.

64. See XIX. 225 ff.: at line 228 he quotes 1 Cor. 12:4. On the changing concepts of the *corpus mysticum* in medieval ideology, the major study is by H. DE LUBAC, *Corpus Mysticum*, 2nd edn (Paris, Aubier-Montaigne, 1949).

65. Kane and Donaldson read 'coke' at line 238 meaning 'to make hay cocks', and they give their reasons for preferring this to 'dyke' or 'dyche' on pp. 174–5.

66. So total is Holy Spirit's evasion here that he does not even attempt to repeat the

ideas: compare the earlier discussion of the treatment of merchants in the gloss to the pardon in Passus VII.

67. Some might feel the vagueness of the generalizations about brotherly love is explained by their reference to a remote past. But in fact the occupations Spirit refers to are not remote from Langland's day and, as we have seen, are essential to the poem's preoccupations and movement. Here Langland wants to fit them into the orthodox ideological framework and stress its divine authority. But what actually happens is that the cherished scheme is exposed as contingent and superseded, as I argue in the following paragraphs. In connection with crafts, love and unity it is worth reminding oneself of the fiercely self-regarding and bitter craft conflicts (see for example the works by Bird, Williams, and Geremek, n. 16 above, and Sylvia Thrupp's chapter on the gilds in Postan *et al.*, *Economic Organization and Policies in the Middle Ages.*

68. Discussed on a number of occasions through the chapter, see references in n. 12.

69. This topic deserves more attention than I can give it here. Conscience does resist Meed earlier in the poem, but his proneness to error is clear enough in the apocalyptic vision (discussed earlier, and at greater length in ch. 3) and in Passus XIII (see n. 55); in Passus XX the physical terrors he invokes seem totally misguided in the task of encouraging real spiritual regeneration, and his acceptance of the glib and typically inadequate friar-confessor is plainly a capitulation to present pressures, which is seen by Langland as a disaster. Aquinas himself emphasizes that Conscience may be erroneous, either through our own fault or through causes for which we are responsible, yet even when it is *wrong* we are morally obliged to follow it: see *Quodlibetum*, 3.27 and *Summa Theologica*, I. 79. 12 and 13. In my view, Langland's attitude to Conscience runs on lines such as these, with particular, and discomforting emphasis on its proneness to err. This itself is an example of his own splendid self-reflexivity, allied to spiritual and intellectual modesty. It is interesting that he has *Jesus* himself acknowledge the potential errancy of Conscience at XVII. 138 ff.

70. XIX. 213–335, fulfilling the images of cultivation and Christian history in XVI. 1–166: Aers, *Piers Plowman*, pp. 79–109, 128–31.

71. At line 379 Kane and Donaldson revise MSS of B version in accord with C version: contrast Schmidt's edition, p. 304. On the friars' 'fynding' see X. 322–30 and XX. 228–35; Langland's rejection of the friar's fiction of collective poverty and freedom from ownership occurs throughout the poem, together with the moral and economic practices he believed the fiction encouraged. On the fierce controversies over theories of ownership and poverty as they concerned the friars, see M.D. Lambert, *Franciscan Poverty* (London, SPCK, 1961); G. Leff, *Heresy in the Later Middle Ages*, 2 vols (Manchester University Press, 1967), I, pp. 51–255.

4 Truth's Treasure: Allegory and Meaning in *Piers Plowman**

LAURIE A. FINKE

Finke compares some medieval and post-modern concepts of allegory, as both analogous to the Incarnation and as a problematic means of representing the ineffable. Where Augustine passes over the problem in the silence of faith, Paul De Man and J. Hillis Miller foreground this aspect of allegory as typical of all writing and representation. *Piers Plowman* can be read as a quest for a transcendental signified which might legitimate all the signs of the mundane world. Yet these signs produce only more signs, more tropes, more glosses: the poem is both an allegory of reading and a demonstration that allegory is a necessary mode of faith.

I

In the *Institutio Oratoria*, Quintilian defines allegory as a trope that 'means one thing in the words, another in the sense.'[1] This definition, the basis of all rhetorical descriptions of allegory in the Middle Ages and Renaissance, presupposes a stable relationship between words and things and assumes that signs reflect unproblematically what they signify. It does so by hierarchically ordering significance and meaning, by promising that allegories will yield up stable meaning if the initiated reader applies the proper 'code' to translate the message. Taken a step further, this definition suggests that allegorical texts produce stable meanings and mirror unequivocal truths. If allegory inserts

---

* Reprinted from LAURIE A. FINKE and MARTIN B. SHICHTMAN (eds), *Medieval Texts and Contemporary Readers* (Ithaca and London: Cornell University Press, 1987), pp. 51–68.

another level of signifiers into the signifying process – the words yield up the sense, which, by virtue of its difference from the words, points to the 'true' meaning – it never seriously questions the existence of a kernel, a truth, at the end of the process. By positing a split between words and what they signify, allegory conceals meaning from the uninitiated while making it visible for those with 'eyes to see and ears to hear'. Hence, for Augustine, figural language exists so that 'by means of corporal and temporal things we may comprehend the eternal and spiritual'.[2]

However, the recent rehabilitation of allegory in the wake of post-structuralist debates about the nature of signs has called into question both its classical definition as a kind of translation and the assumptions about meaning and truth upon which it is based.[3] Paul de Man and J. Hillis Miller, in particular, have suggested that allegory verges on being a self-canceling trope, that it simultaneously holds out the promise of truth and demonstrates the inadequacy of its linguistic formulations. The tension they perceive between the poet's desire to reveal truth and the poet's recognition that stable meaning may be subverted by an equivocating language is central to the genre of allegory. The language of allegory, de Man and Miller argue, is never simple, never simply the transparent means of revealing an unequivocal truth that, almost by definition, it pretends to be. This new interest in allegory as a rhetorical device, as well as a genre, may provide a means of illuminating the interpretive difficulties presented by *Piers Plowman*, certainly among the most intractable of medieval allegories and what Maureen Quilligan has called 'one of the purest examples in the genre'.[4] Before turning to a detailed analysis of this poem's allegories, however, I examine in more detail the interrelations between some medieval and post-modern concepts of allegory.

II

For Augustine, as for most medieval writers, the basis of allegory – the ideal relationship between words and things – is authorized by the Incarnation. In *On Christian Doctrine*, glossing the biblical text 'the Word was made flesh', he defines a characteristic Christian perception of the correspondence of language and thought.

> How did He come except that 'the Word was made flesh and dwelt among us?' It is as when we speak. In order that what we are thinking may reach the mind of the listener through fleshly ears, that which we have in mind is expressed in words and called speech. But our thought is not transformed into sounds; it remains entire in itself and assumes the form of words by means of which it may reach the ears without suffering any deterioration in itself. In the same way the Word of God was made flesh without change that He might dwell among us. (p. 14)

Augustine here argues that the Incarnation grounds the relationship between signifier and signified and guarantees their correspondence: 'our thought is *not* transformed; it remains entire in itself'. Like all logocentric thinkers, Augustine privileges speech over writing; he elevates meaning – content or theme – over the language in which it is conveyed. As the Logos becomes flesh through the mystery of the Incarnation, so, through the mysteries of allegory, divine truths are made accessible to human understanding; and as Christ's divine nature remains unchanged when he takes on human form, so the divine truths conveyed through allegory remain unchanged when they are clothed in words. Language, in this passage, becomes for Augustine a transparent medium in and through which meaning, authorized from above, can be read.

But the theory of representation developed in *On Christian Doctrine* contains within itself the possibility of its own undoing. Almost immediately after Augustine states that 'the invisible things of God' can be understood by 'the things that are made', he questions the basis of representation itself.

> Have we spoken or announced anything worthy of God? Rather I feel that I have done nothing but wish to speak: if I have spoken, I have not said what I wished to say. Whence do I know this except because God is ineffable? If what I said were ineffable, it would not be said. And for this reason God should not be said to be ineffable, for when this is said something is said. And a contradiction in terms is created, since if that is ineffable which cannot be spoken, then that is not ineffable which can be called ineffable. This contradiction is to be passed over in silence rather than resolved verbally. (p. 11)

This passage is a rupture, a seam through which we can read the undoing of Augustine's logocentric concept of representation.[5] Augustine's frustration at the task of representing the divine is evident in the convoluted language of the passage, a language that calls attention to its own hesitancy and cannot say what it means. If God is inconceivable, then we cannot say that he is beyond comprehension, because to say so would be to say something about that of which nothing can be said. Thought cannot assume the form of words, even spoken words, and remain unchanged. Augustine's comparison of the imperfect representations of language to the ideal of the Incarnation can reveal only their irrevocable difference. Because the divine cannot be represented, the contradictions within his theory cannot be verbally – or logically – resolved; they can only be mediated by faith. His silence on this contradiction is finally the silence of faith. For Augustine, this silence becomes the basis of all allegory – faith in the Incarnation and in representation as a means of transmitting unitary meaning and divine truth.

The contradictions and silences within Augustine's theory of allegory are archetypal and hence may illuminate the Yale Critics' interest in allegory.

Hillis Miller suggests that 'the possibility that allegorical representation is a human fancy thrown out toward something which is so beyond human comprehension that there is no way to measure the validity of any picture of it is the permanent shadow within the theory' of allegory.[6] Miller and de Man have recognized this shadow within Augustinian and medieval notions of allegorical representation and used it to argue that allegory rather than symbolism best describes the process of a text's 'coming into being'. Considered by the Romantics and New Critics too prosaic and tendentious to be a conveyor of poetic truth, allegory, in the writings of Miller and de Man, has resurfaced as a critical mode that both confronts and embodies the impenetrability of language and the problematics of interpretation.[7] It is, in this respect, the contradiction that Augustine wishes to pass over in silence that these deconstructive critics wish to foreground.

The concept of allegory that emerges from the critical writings of de Man and Miller destabilizes conventional notions of representation by challenging the one-to-one correspondences between words and things, phenomenon and essence, posited by rhetorical definitions of allegory. Although in this essay I am primarily concerned with allegory's failed attempts to bridge the chasm between human languages and divine presence, the argument can and must be extended to include all human signification. Indeed, the former argument grounds the latter; Logos assures logocentrism. In a passage from *Grammatology* with interesting echoes of Augustine, Jacques Derrida has argued that the history of Western metaphysics documents the search for a transcendental signifier that would legitimate all signs.

> All signifiers, and first and foremost the written signifier, are derivative with regard to what would wed the voice indissolubly to the mind or to the thought of the signified sense, indeed to the thing itself (whether it is done in the Aristotelian manner . . . or in the manner of medieval theology, determining the *res* as a thing created from its *eidos*, from its sense thought in the logos or in the infinite understanding of God).[8]

Allegory, I wish to argue, demonstrates language's inability to guarantee the signified, to wed once and for all word and thing.

In his article 'The Two Allegories', Miller quotes Walter Benjamin's aphorism that 'allegories are in the realm of thoughts, what ruins are in the realm of things'.[9] Allegory, Miller argues, shows the devastating effects of time on thoughts, just as ruins show the devastating effects of time on things. Like ruins, allegories register the gap between past and present, presence and absence. Ruins are the fragments of the past that 'represent' a building's or a civilization's past glory by virtue of their difference from a now lost wholeness. Allegories are also fragments; they too direct our gaze backward across a temporal chasm, representing what can no longer be present because of the nature of language. Representation, as Murray Krieger reminds us, must always stress its prefix *re* over its root *present*. The language we use to represent our world is made up of empty and belated markers. Words 'seek to refer to what is elsewhere and has occurred earlier'.[10] Language, in other words, even as it attempts to recuperate presence, must simultaneously defer it. In this regard, what Coleridge sought to efface by identifying the sign and signified in the symbol, de Man and Miller embrace in allegory – difference, the unbridgeable gap between words and things, between experience and the representation of experience.

This 'ruinous' theory of allegory insinuates itself into Augustinian theory (and theology) by reminding us of allegory's difference from the 'spirit' it purports to recover. The meaning and truth that allegory seeks to represent are, by the deferred nature of representation, present only as fragments. For Miller, as for de Man, meaning and truth are problematic precisely because 'the target toward which signs are turned remains finally unknown':

> Allegory in this view then is quite the opposite of what it often pretends
> to be: the recovery of the pure visibility of the truth, undisguised by the
> local and accidental . . . But its deeper purpose and its actual effect is to
> acknowledge the darkness, the arbitrariness, and the void that underlie, and
> paradoxically make possible, all representations of realms of light, order,
> and presence.[11]

Allegory, as it tries to incarnate the absent signified that would authorize meaning and truth, testifies to their absence. The more language seeks to clarify (literally to illuminate or free from darkness or gloom) meaning, the more it reveals the void, the darkness of its own reflexivity.

III

Piers Plowman, at times, seems almost an allegory of the impossibility of discovering either significance or truth within language whether one searches for divine or merely for human significance. Language in the poem, as I have argued elsewhere, becomes 'a vehicle for classification (of ways of life, of mental powers), a means of imposing order (the law), [and] a means of disorder and deception. More often than not . . . one cannot distinguish between these uses of language . . . Man's language, although created in the image of the Logos, is capable of only an imperfect parody of it.' The more human language strives to represent the world, the more it is trapped and frustrated by its own failure to assure referentiality.[12]

Piers Plowman's resistance to interpretation inheres in its own interpretations of its difficulties. The dreamer's question 'How may I save my soul?' leads him to search for Truth (Passus I–VII), for Dowel (Passus VIII–XIV), and finally for Piers himself (Passus XV–XX). These quests become, in one sense, the search for a transcendental signified that would legitimate all the human signs of the mundane world, the world of the 'fair field' and the 'half acre'. Indeed, the promise of a truth in, behind, or beyond the poem's language, and with it the possibility that Will's dreams actually mean 'something', is from the beginning of the poem both proffered and withheld. The opening tableau of *Piers Plowman* seems simple enough; Will, the poem's narrator, falls asleep and dreams:

> [Ac] as I biheeld into þe Eest, and heiȝ to þe sonne,
> I seiȝ a tour on a toft treiliche ymaked,
> A deep dale byneþe, a dongeon þerInne
> Wiþ depe diches and derke and dredfull of siȝte.
> A fair feeld ful of folk fond I þer bitwene. (Prologue 13–17)[13]

The dreamer's sight here ('biheeld') is figurative rather than literal. What he sees are not things but representations of things. The dreamscape is composed of signifiers – tower, dungeon, and field – that seem to mean more than the poet tells us about them, that seem to point to other signifiers. The simplicity of the physical scene shades into the ambiguity of interpretation. The reader, like the dreamer, is compelled to ask, 'What may it [by] meene?' The scene, in short, demands a gloss, an interpretation, additional text to explain the poetic utterance. The space that exists between the images of the tower, dungeon, and field and what they signify becomes the figural space of interpretation. It can be bridged or filled only by the attempt to understand it, by reading or creating a text that comments upon the text.

In the A and B versions the interpretation of this scene is deferred until Passus I, where the dreamer's first guide, Holi chirche, glosses these images. Of the 'tour on pe toft' she tells the dreamer, 'truþe is þerInne' (I, 8); in the dungeon, 'Wonyeþ a [wye] þat wrong is yhote; /Fader of falsehed' (I, 63–4). The rhetoric of her commentary initially encourages the dreamer to believe that his vision 'means' something, that he can pursue a rational account of the allegorical world in which he finds himself, and that the process of interpretation requires simply a translation or a substitution of one set of terms for another. The tower is Truth, the dungeon is Falsehood or Wrong. Holi chirche encourages the dreamer, in this regard, to believe that Truth is something within his reach, a goal, like the tower, at the end of a journey. Truth can be found simply by avoiding *temporalia* or the 'tresor' of the world: 'þat trusten on his tresor bitraye[d are] sonnest' (I, 70).

The literalness of Will's allegorical thinking, his belief that word and thing can coincide to create meaning, emerges in his request to Holi chirche to 'Teche me to no tresor, but tel me þis ilke, / How I may saue my soule' (I, 83–4). But Holi chirche's answer undermines the dreamer's faith in the precision of allegorical language by troping on the very signifier he has rejected as false: 'Whan alle tresors arn tried treuþe is þe beste' (I, 85).

89

Neither meaning nor truth, it seems, is as unproblematic as Will had thought, nor the relationships between signs and signifieds nearly as simple or stable. In one instance, treasure is equated with the corruption of falsehood; in another, Truth is described as the best of all treasures. Apparently there are two kinds of treasure: one that is earthly and visible to the dreamer, and one that is invisible and not easily circumscribed by language, even the language of allegory. Each signifier – true treasure, false treasure – defines itself in terms of the other; each, therefore, exists only in opposition to its opposite.

The literal-minded dreamer, however, does not understand Holi chirche's explanation. What he wants is to locate a simple means of identifying truth and to pass in silence over the problematics of representation.

> 'Yet haue I no kynde knowying,' quod I, 'ye mote kenne me bettre
> By what craft in my cors it [truth] comseþ and where.' (I, 138–9)

Will is interested in only half of the Augustinian dialectic; for him, allegory is a means of 'comprehending the eternal and spiritual' by means of 'corporal and temporal things' (*On Christian Doctrine*, p. 10). Holi chirche cannot clarify what truth is, and her inability becomes a measure of the difference or the distance between language and what it represents. The dreamer desires a language that can express experience unequivocally and so allow him to dominate it.[14] However, his guide's response generates not certainties, but more commentary, more opportunities for interpretation.

Holi chirche's response is a *dilatio* on truth. A rhetorical trope of amplification often cited in medieval *ars praedicandi, dilatio*, from the Latin *dilatare*, suggests both a deferral and a spreading out.[15] In this respect, Holi chirche's answer simultaneously postpones the dreamer's inquiry and widens its perspective until it encompasses – or attempts to encompass – everything, including the divine.

> For truþe telleþ þat loue is triacle of heuene:
> May no synne be on hym seene þat vseþ þat spice,
> And alle hise werkes he wrouȝte with loue as hym liste;
> And lered it Moyses for þe leueste þyng and moost lik to heuene,
> And [ek] þe pl[ante] of pees, moost precious of vertues.
> For heuene myȝte nat holden it, [so heuy it semed,]
> Til it hadde of þe erþe [y]eten [hitselue].
> And whan it hadde of þis fold flessh and blood taken
> Was neuere leef vpon lynde lighter þerafter,
> And portatif and persaunt as þe point of a nedle
> That myȝte noon Armure it lette ne none heiȝe walles. (I, 148–58)

As this passage suggests, *Piers Plowman*'s poetry is most eloquent – literally, most full of speech – when its language proclaims its own inadequacy. Here it attempts to describe and explain the mysteries of divinity by accumulating a series of highly antithetical images. Yet the allegory circles around the idea of God's highest expression of love and truth – the Incarnation – by calling that love 'heuy' and light as 'leef vpon linde', 'triacle', and 'portatif and persaunt', able to pierce any armor or wall. The same phrase, 'For heuene my3te nat holden it', is used to describe both the Incarnation and Lucifer's fall from heaven. This passage is characteristic of the poem as a whole: language does not progress toward an illumination of truth but falls into the deferral of its own rhetoric. Each sign produces the next sign in a repetitive sequence that never arrives at anything but the next trope. The more the poem's language attempts to describe the divine, the less referential – and the more reflexive – it becomes.

I have quoted extensively from the poem's opening episode because it is typical of Langland's double-edged handling of allegory. The complications inherent in Holi chirche's explanation of the opening tableau are paradigmatic of the poem's repetitive, circular structure, its technique of *dilatio* to defer and expand on the referentiality of its language. Simple, apparently unequivocal figures – Truth and later Dowel and Piers himself – are complicated by the very attempt to define or explicate them. These terms, which de Man might call 'primitive words', cannot be defined because their 'pretended definitions are infinite regresses of accumulated tautologies'[16]; in other words, they can be explained only by recourse to tropes that, like all attempts to represent the unrepresentable, proclaim absence instead of presence, darkness instead of light. Figures – truth is a tower, for instance, or divine love is 'triacle' – offer similitudes in the place of definitions, what Derrida calls identity in difference, not the mystical identity that Coleridge located in the symbol.[17]

The need to dilate – to explain, define, and distinguish – in *Piers Plowman* generates the endless monologues so characteristic of all three versions of the poem. These monologues seem to answer every question but the one that Will has asked precisely because it cannot be answered in human terms. His question is Augustine's: How can one distinguish the true or the divine in a fallen world? Yet the more Will seeks to learn (the more questions he asks, the more answers he seeks), the more text is generated and the more complicated the commentary becomes. Each gloss leads not to definitive answers or interpretations but to more glossing. Passus I ends with Holi chirche's reiterating 'Whan all tresors ben tried treuþe is þe beste' (I, 207). But the dreamer is no more enlightened than he was before he asked his question. At the opening of Passus II he rephrases his inquiry and asks Holi chirche, 'Kenne me by som craft to know þe false' (II, 4). Although the question changes, the rhetorical context does not. Commentary necessitates further commentary. Texts proliferate, but the substance, the thing that Will seeks remains unattainable.

This 'web of words' is the essence of allegory: 'a textual plot of another text's tale, a figure of a figure'.[18] The nature of allegory, as de Man argues in

'The Rhetoric of Temporality', always presents itself as repetition within both the temporal sequence of language – the syntagmatic succession of signs – and the temporal sequence of narrative – the metonymic succession of episodes.[19] The sign always refers to and repeats a previous sign with which it can never coincide. The 'meaning' that the allegorical sign constitutes consists only of repetition, which implies, in the Derridean sense of iterability, both identity and difference: 'the identity of the *selfsame* [must] be repeatable and identifiable *in, through,* and even *in view of* its alteration'.[20] Repetition inscribes in allegory two senses of time: a progression from one manifestation or incident to the next, and a mere iteration of the same. This dual sense of time is what leads Miller to identify the irony of repetition as the trope of all narrative and de Man to privilege allegory as the trope of irony.[21]

The allegorical narrative of *Piers Plowman*, in this respect, operates within two time frames: the temporal narrative of Long Will's quest for Truth (and later for Dowel and Piers), and the atemporal anti-narrative of the dream which frustrates the dreamer's attempts to go forward. Dream visions and journeys are commonplace in medieval allegory precisely because they reflect the disjunction within allegory between sign and signified. In *Piers Plowman* these two allegorical strategies are 'brought together' in such a way that, more often than not, they work at cross-purposes. The journey is metonymic and sequential; it imparts to the poem a sense of forward movement because it suggests that the signified, like the tower in the Prologue or the King at Westminster who arbitrates the marriage of Meed, may be what the dreamer seeks, even as it displaces his goal beyond wherever he happens to be. The dream, on the other hand, is metaphoric and ahistorical; it frustrates progression by making the goal into something else, by offering the endlessly referential web of words that lead only into labyrinthine repetition. The narrative pattern of the poem, then, creates a dialectical tension between the journey and the dream which simultaneously asserts and destroys the narrative's claim to linear progression.

The search for Truth which occupies the *Visio* illustrates this disjunction between the narrative's two displacements, the dream and the journey. After witnessing the confessions of the Seven Deadly Sins, the folk on the field set out, at Reason's urging, to 'seken Seynt Truth, for he may saue yow alle' (V, 57). Their quest repeats Will's earlier quest for Truth, with a difference but with the same results: the forward impetus of the journey stalls as the dream repeats the symbols of desire. On the pilgrimage the folk encounter two guides, who, like Holi chirche, attempt to gloss the signs. The first is a pilgrim, or at least a 'leode' 'apparailled . . . in pilgrymes wise'. His staff, bowl, and bag, his 'Ampulles', 'shelles', and 'vernycle', are the 'signes' of his pilgrimages, his quests for his 'soules hele'. But as signs they point only to other signs and other journeys: 'Syney', the 'Sepulchre', 'Bethlem', 'Alisaundre'. He cannot tell the pilgrims the way to Truth, the way to pure signification, because his understanding does not extend beyond the signs themselves: 'I

[ne] seiȝ neuere Palmere wiþ pyk ne wiþ scrippe / Asken after hym [truth] er now in þis place' (V, 535–6).

The forward progression of the journey is halted; it repeats the sequence with the sudden dreamlike appearance of the second guide Piers the Plowman, who offers to lead the folk to Truth. He conceives of the way to Truth as a series of signposts pointing the way in a moral landscape: a place called 'swere-noȝt-but-it-be-for-nede-and-name-liche-on-idel- þe-name-of-god-almyȝty', for example, or a croft called 'Coueite-noȝt-mennes-catel-ne-hire-wyues-ne-noon-of-hire-seruantȝ-þat-noyen-hem-myȝt'. This allegorical description (V, 561–82) is no doubt long and dull, but its very lack of poetic immediacy – its plodding, one-to-one correspondence between physical place and spiritual state – comments on the failure of the epistemology of the *Visio*, its search for truth and transcendent meaning. The folk's encounters with the pilgrim and Piers again highlight the disjunction between outward signs and the always elusive inner meaning of truth.

In the last two passus of the *Visio*, Piers attempts to redeem the spiritual signification of the pilgrimage, to close the gap between outward forms and spiritual meaning, by transforming this trope into another trope.

> 'And I shal apparaille me' quod Perkyn, 'in pilgrymes wise
> And wende wiþ yow [þe wey] til we fynde truþe,'
> [He caste on] his cloþes, yclouted and hole,
> [His] cokeres and [hise] coffes for cold of his mailes,
> And [heng his] hoper at [his] hals in stede of a Scryppe. (VI, 57–61)

In this passage the image of the quest or journey gives way to the repetitive, circular action of plowing as Piers sets the folk to work. The 'cokeres', 'coffes', and 'hoper', the signs of Piers's life of virtuous labor, replace the traditional signs of the pilgrimage: bowl, bag, and scrip. The simple life of labor, Piers assures the folk and the dreamer, will lead them at last to Truth. But all that this plowing of the fields leads them to is yet another dead end that requires more commentary, yet another textual *dilatio*, another attempt to redefine or resignify the *Visio*'s key terms. When the folk cannot persevere in their labor, Truth sends them a pardon, a document that emphasizes metaphorically the disjunction between temporal words and the allegorical incarnation of the spirit. The allegory of Truth's pardon, as I have shown elsewhere, sets the pardon's spiritual significance as a reflection of God's grace against its debasement as an image of ecclesiastical corruption, a popular target of fourteenth-century satire.[22] Piers's tearing of the pardon and his squabbling with the priest mark the end of the dream before the quest to find Truth has reached a satisfactory conclusion.

The interpretive difficulties that the *Visio* creates inhere, in large measure, in the oppositions between the *Visio*'s principal signs – between true treasure and false treasure, true meed and false meed, true pilgrimage and false pilgrimage, true pardon and false pardon. These dialectical oppositions exist symbiotically; each undermines and reinforces its opposite. The language of the poem's allegory is, to borrow Miller's description of Yeats's prose, 'always forced to say the opposite of what it seems to want to say, as well as the opposite of that opposite'.[23] This 'deconstructive' process of the allegorical text's undoing itself is not, however, nihilistic, nor does it become a simple reversal of dialectical hierarchies that privilege meaninglessness over meaning. The allegory of *Piers Plowman* – its reflexive questioning – is both an attempt to represent what is unrepresentable and an attempt to transcend the mundane world circumscribed by the folk on the field. Its image in the text is the quest, which, precisely because it can never reach a conclusion, must be repeated, for example in the *Vita*'s quest for Dowel and in the quest for Piers with which the poem breaks off. In essence, the rest of the poem unfolds as a repetition of the first two visions, the B and C versions as repetitions with a difference of the A version.

After tearing the pardon and abandoning the life of virtuous labor for that of prayer, Piers all but disappears from the poem until Passus XV, when Anima mentions him as the perfect exemplar of charity. His appearance and transformation at this juncture illuminate the way in which the action of the poem is now generated not by the quest but by language, by puns. This wordplay points to external and material coincidences between signifiers and distorts logocentric fictions about meaning. Piers himself becomes less a 'character' than an instance of what happens to a fallen language in its attempts to define its own limitations. As Maureen Quilligan suggests, language becomes a principal actor in the poem[24] – not simply a medium of expression, however imperfect, but an example of what happens to the spirit, to faith, when it is incarnated in the physical world. The actor in Passus XVI–XIX is not Piers the character but 'Piers' the signifier, a deferral of the linguistic roots – the puns – that comprise its unstable identity.

When Anima mentions Piers in Passus XV, he is no longer the virtuous laborer who set the folk to work in Passus VI, no longer simply a plowman. His name, inscribed in Anima's phrase '*Petrus id est christus*', has become a pun that harks back not only to Piers's namesake St Peter but also to the etymology of Piers's name, from the Old French *pierre* and the Latin *petrus* for rock, also for foundation or support.[25] Anima's phrase, in this regard, becomes a kind of shorthand for Christ's words to Peter (Matt. 16.18): '*Tu es Petrus, et super hanc petram aedificabo ecclesiam meam*' [You are Peter, and upon this rock I will build my church]. The name Piers is embedded both in the logocentric tradition of etymology, of biblical exegesis, and in the nameless incidence of faith. From a description of the mundane rock, *petrus* achieves a figural significance – the foundation or support for the Church – gathering to itself a tradition of meanings that transcend any one interpretation. The allegorical significance of the name, then, goes beyond what language can possibly describe: the phrase *Petrus id est christus* becomes the incarnation of the divine as a pun on the dual nature of man-as-god.

The pun on Piers's name generates the plot of Passus XVI–XVIII by setting in motion biblical history. The dreamer learns that Piers, no longer a plowman, guards the tree of charity (B XVI). In the course of the dream, the tree becomes an elaborate metonymy for the tree of knowledge (the paradisaical *lignum vitae*) and the tree of the cross, both, as Gerhardt Ladner notes, 'part of the metahistorical and historical economy of salvation'.[26] The tree is supported by three 'piles', props or supports that, with Piers, protect the tree and its fruit from assault by the winds and by demons. The tree's 'fruit' is postlapsarian mankind – Adam, Abraham, Isaias, Samson, Samuel, John the Baptist, and the like. When Piers shakes the tree to fetch an 'apple' for the dreamer, this 'fruit' falls and is gathered up by the Devil, initiating the temporal sequence of biblical history from the Fall to Christ's passion, death, and resurrection. The elaborate and bizarre allegory of the tree of charity, with Piers its gardener, is the first of a series of tropes centered on Piers's name which reenact the history of Christianity. These culminate in the allegory of the Christ-knight in which the Incarnation and Passion are figured as Christ jousting in 'Piers armes' (B XVIII, 22) and in the final appearance of Piers in Passus XIX as the Church Militant, the institutional embodiment of faith and spirit as doctrine.

Yet this 'sequence' in the poem is itself figural, a representation not of progression but of progressive revelation. Piers does not begin as one kind of signifier and 'become' another; his name comprehends multiple meanings, none of which – not even *Petrus id est christus* – is definitive. 'Piers' represents not an historical accretion of meaning but the mystery of the unchanging Word that cannot be interpreted, only made manifest. Will's final visions thus unfold in a temporal language that reveals, rather than represents in a more traditional sense, the timeless, ahistorical object of the dreamer's quest for faith. That this revelation can be only obscure and partial, that the essence of what stands behind and gives meaning to the signifier can never be certainly 'known', is suggested by the way in which the poem simply breaks off. There is no conclusion, no end to the quest, but only the dreamlike repetition of Will still searching for the absent Piers.

In one sense, *Piers Plowman* becomes what de Man calls an allegory of reading; it explores the process of coming to terms with its own unreadability. Yet allegory – as the failure of literary language to demonstrate a one-to-one correspondence between signs and signifieds – also becomes the mode of faith. *Piers Plowman* does not fool around with literary language but with the inadequacy of theological language; it is an attempt to explore the generic limitations of allegory not simply as a vehicle for truth but as an epistemological exploration of the mysteries of the Incarnation, which, as Augustine suggests, enables truth. Such a reading of *Piers Plowman* posits an alternative to the authoritative procedure sanctioned by Augustinian hermeneutics:

Medieval English Poetry

Whatever appears in the divine Word that does not literally pertain to
virtuous behavior or to the truth of faith you must take to be figurative. . . .
Scripture teaches nothing but charity, nor condemns anything except
cupidity. (*On Christian Doctrine*, p. 88)

This reading of *Piers Plowman* promotes a knowledge – and a transcendence
– that, far from enlightening the reader, forces him or her to take a 'leap into
darkness', a nearly Kierkegaardian leap of faith. The silence that Augustine
maintains in the face of the divine, and the silence with which *Piers Plowman*
breaks off, may be read as acts of faith as well as the 'stillness of metaphysical
irony'. In this sense, the wandering and the wondering, the quest and the
question, are the poem's mechanisms for trying to recover the signified; and
the word 'recover' suggests paradoxically the hiddenness and the discovery,
the absence and the presence, of what lies behind the word.

Notes

1. QUINTILIAN, *Institutio Oratoria*, Loeb ed. (Cambridge: Harvard University Press,
1953), 8.6.44. Quintilian's definition has passed virtually unquestioned into modern
discussions of allegory. Angus Fletcher, echoing Quintilian, writes that 'allegory
says one thing and means another. It destroys the normal expectations we have
about language that words "mean what they say"'; Northrop Frye argues that 'we
have allegory when the events of a narrative obviously and continuously refer to
another simultaneous structure of events or ideas'; Mary Carruthers, echoing
Augustine, writes that 'all visible things, including language, are signs which point
to something beyond themselves'. See FLETCHER, *Allegory: The Theory of a Symbolic
Mode* (Ithaca: Cornell University Press, 1964), p. 2; FRYE, 'Allegory', in *Encyclopedia
of Poetry and Poetics*, ed. Alex Preminger (Princeton: Princeton University Press,
1965), pp. 12–15; CARRUTHERS, *The Search for St Truth: A Study of Meaning in Piers
Plowman* (Evanston: North-western University Press, 1973), pp. 10–11.

2. AUGUSTINE, *On Christian Doctrine*, trans. D.W. Robertson (Indianapolis:
Bobbs Merrill, 1958), p. 10. All subsequent citations are to this edition and are
noted parenthetically in the text.

3. One recent critic who has rejected the classical definitions of allegory while at the
same time distancing herself from post-structuralist notions of it is MAUREEN
QUILLIGAN. In *The Language of Allegory: Defining the Genre* (Ithaca: Cornell
University Press, 1979), she rejects the 'vertical conception of allegory' (p. 28),
arguing instead that allegories are 'webs of words', pointing to the 'possibility of
an otherness, a polysemy, inherent in the very words on the page' (p. 26).
Quilligan's redefinition of the terms by which we discuss allegory have inspired
my own rethinking of allegory. But although her definition seems closely to
resemble Derrida's notion of dissemination, of signifiers pointing to other signifiers,
endlessly deferring the signified, Quilligan argues explicitly for the logocentrism
of allegory. If deconstruction insists 'on the disjunction between meaning and
word, between sign and signified', she writes elsewhere, 'narrative allegory always
pursues the goal of coherence'. Allegorical texts such as the *Roman de la Rose* insist
upon the 'congruence between word, physical fact, and divine intention'. See her

'Allegory, Allegoresis, and the Deallegorization of Language: The *Roman de la Rose*, the *De planctu naturae*, and the *Parlement of Foules*', in *Allegory, Myth, and Symbol*, ed. Morton Bloomfield (Cambridge: Harvard University Press, 1981), pp. 184–5.

4. QUILLIGAN, *Language of Allegory*, p. 58.

5. For other discussions of Augustine's attitude toward language in *On Christian Doctrine*, see MARCIA COLISH, *The Mirror of Language: A Study in the Medieval Theory of Knowledge* (Lincoln: University of Nebraska Press, 1983), esp. ch. 1; EUGENE VANCE, 'St. Augustine: Language as Temporality', in *Mimesis: From Mirror to Method, Augustine to Descartes*, ed. John D. Lyons and Stephen Nichols, Jr (Hanover, N.H.: University Press of New England, 1982), pp. 20–35. Elsewhere in this volume, Peggy Knapp demonstrates how Augustine's assurance of a logocentric language, grounded in the Incarnation, breaks down when confronted by some of the contradictions inherent in language – contradictions created by multiple meanings, translations, and rhetorical obfuscation.

6. J. HILLIS MILLER, 'The Two Allegories', in Bloomfield, *Allegory, Myth, and Symbol*, p. 360.

7. See MILLER, 'The Two Allegories', pp. 355–70; MILLER, 'Ariadne's Thread: Repetition and the Narrative Line', *Critical Inquiry*, **3** (1976): 57–77; PAUL DE MAN, 'Pascal's Allegory of Persuasion', in *Allegory and Representation*, ed. Stephen J. Greenblatt (Baltimore: Johns Hopkins University Press, 1981), pp. 1–25, and 'The Rhetoric of Temporality,' in *Interpretation: Theory and Practice*, ed. Charles Singleton (Baltimore: John Hopkins University Press, 1969), pp. 173–209. See also de Man, *Allegories of Reading: Figural Language in Rousseau, Nietzsche, Rilke, and Proust* (New Haven: Yale University Press, 1979), and *Blindness and Insight: Essays in the Rhetoric of Contemporary Criticism* (Minneapolis: University of Minnesota Press, 1971).

8. JACQUES DERRIDA, *Of Grammatology*, trans. Gayatri Chakravorty Spivak (Baltimore: Johns Hopkins University Press, 1976), p. 11.

9. MILLER, 'The Two Allegories', pp. 362–3.

10. MURRAY KRIEGER, 'Presentation and Representation in the Renaissance Lyric: The Net of Words and the Escape of the Gods', in Lyons and Nichols, *Mimesis: From Mirror to Method*, p. 118; see also KRIEGER, '"A Waking Dream": The Symbolic Alternative to Allegory', in Bloomfield, *Allegory, Myth, and Symbol*, pp. 1–22.

11. STEPHEN J. GREENBLATT, 'Preface', in Greenblatt, *Allegory and Representation*, p. vii.

12. See my 'Dowel and the Crisis of Faith and Irony in *Piers Plowman*', in *Kierkegaard: Irony, Repetition, and Criticism*, ed. Ronald Schleifer and Robert Markley (Norman: University of Oklahoma Press, 1984), p. 129; there I deal more extensively with the linguistic relativism – the disjunction between human words and earthly things – that infects *Piers Plowman*, particularly in Passus XIX–XX; see pp. 136–7.

13. All quotations from *Piers Plowman* are from *Piers Plowman: The B Version*, ed. George Kane and E. Talbot Donaldson (London: Athlone Press, 1975). All subsequent citations are noted parenthetically in the text.

14. See HILLIS MILLER's discussion of allegory and narrative in 'Ariadne's Thread', p. 72.

15. See LEE PATTERSON's discussion of the *dilatio* in the discourse of La Vieille in JEAN DE MEUN's *Roman de la Rose*, '"For the Wyves love of Bath": Feminine Rhetoric and Poetic Resolution in the *Roman de la Rose* and the *Canterbury Tales*', *Speculum*, **58** (1983): 669–76.

16. DE MAN, 'Pascal's Allegory of Persuasion', p. 6.

17. For Coleridge, the symbol 'always partakes of the reality which it renders intelligible; and while it enunciates the whole, abides itself as a living part in that unity, of which it is representative'. Allegory, on the other hand, 'is but a translation of abstract notions into a picture-language which is itself nothing but an abstraction from objects of the senses; the principle being more worthless even than its phantom proxy, both alike unsubstantial, and the former shapeless to boot'. For a discussion of Coleridge's theory of the symbol and allegory see DE MAN, 'The Rhetoric of Temporality', pp. 177–8, and KRIEGER, 'A Waking Dream', pp. 4–7 (the quotations are from p. 5).

18. VINCENT B. LEITCH, *Deconstructive Criticism: An Advanced Introduction* (New York: Columbia University Press, 1983), p. 184.

19. DE MAN, 'Rhetoric of Temporality', p. 190.

20. JACQUES DERRIDA, 'Limited Inc abc . . .', trans. Samuel Webster, *Glyph* **2** (1977): 190.

21. J. HILLIS MILLER, 'Narrative Middles: A Preliminary Outline', *Genre*, **11** (1978): 386; de Man, 'Pascal's Allegory of Persuasion', p. 12.

22. FINKE, 'Dowel and the Crisis of Faith and Irony', pp. 123–7.

23. MILLER, 'Two Allegories', p. 370. Elsewhere Miller has called this phenomenon the *mise en abyme*; contemporary physicists, I have learned, call it a Strange Loop. But whatever we call it, the existence of signs that refer circularly only to their opposite signs undermines the logocentric promise of all language, including scientific language, that signs can point unproblematically to things in the real world. For an illuminating discussion of this phenomenon in contemporary scientific language, see N. Katherine Hayles, *The Cosmic Web: Scientific Field Models and Literary Strategies in the Twentieth Century* (Ithaca: Cornell University Press, 1984), esp. ch. 1, pp. 31–59.

24. QUILLIGAN, 'Allegory, Allegoresis, and the Deallegorization of Language', p. 180 (see note 3).

25. For a seminal article on this passage and on wordplay in *Piers Plowman*, see BERNARD HUPPÉ, '*Petrus id est Christus*: Word Play in *Piers Plowman*, the B-text', *Journal of English Literary History*, **17** (1950): 163–90.

26. GERHARDT LADNER, 'Medieval and Modern Understanding of Symbolism: A Comparison', *Speculum*, **54** (1979): 236.

5 The Genres of *Piers Plowman**

STEVEN JUSTICE

Cutting across recent readings of *Piers Plowman* as a sequence of narrative
episodes, Steven Justice reads the *Visio* as a narrative of generic
experiments. Langland grapples with the forms of authority implicit in
various poetic and narrative genres; accordingly, poetic form is deeply
implicated with the socio-political and religious critique of institutions,
while genre becomes 'an epistemological and morally accountable tool'.
The dreamer's subjectivity is less engaged than the poet's, in his attempt
to interpret the Prologue according to a range of generic conventions.
Langland progressively abandons authorial control and his claims to
poetic authority as the biblical text comes to dominate the poem.

When Will meets Haukyn in *Piers Plowman* B.13, he meets his double:

> Yhabited as an heremyte, an ordre by hymselue,
> Religion sauȝ rule and resonable obedience;
> Lakkynge lettrede men and lewed men boþe.[1]

(13.284–286)

These lines schematically echo and gloss Will's initial self-characterization: 'I
shoop me into shroudes as I a shep were, / In habite as an heremite unholy
of werkes' (Prol. 2–3). Will's eremitic wandering places him among the
gyrovagi,[2] the wandering monks that Saint Benedict condemns for their failed
obedience, 'never stable, slaves to their own wills'.[3] Haukyn's 'Religion sauȝ
rule and resonable obedience' makes explicit what Will's wandering implies.
But what of the last of those lines? Do we see *Will* 'Lakkynge lettrede men
and lewed men bothe'? We see it at the very beginning of the poem, in the

---

* Reprinted from *Viator*, **19** (1988): 291–306.

Prologue's satirical activity, the comprehensive denunciation – 'lakkynge' – that by generic definition characterizes estates satire. From the perspective of Passus 13, the genre of his prologue is understood as a form of backbiting.[4] I begin with this retrospect to suggest how Langland is conscious of genre as an epistemologically and morally accountable tool, and I will argue that the *Visio*'s pilgrimage to Truth is the search for a genre that will accommodate an authority neither abusive nor idiosyncratic.

I reconsider here two problems suggested by some of the poem's best critics. The first is formulated but never really resolved by Morton W. Bloomfield: *Piers Plowman* displays multiple generic allegiances, while still apparently pursuing some embracing purpose.[5] Bloomfield's own solution – notoriously the least satisfying claim of his important study – is to define the embracing purpose in terms of an embracing genre, the apocalypse. The second is the challenge implicitly offered by John A. Alford and Judson B. Allen, who have outlined the schematic contextual relations of the poem, the pattern of biblical reference that seems to precede and govern any rhetorical strategies or generic characteristics.[6] Their method can explain how *distinctio* and commentary determine the conceptual and even narrative structure of particular episodes, but not how they emerge into the larger rhetorical structures of the poem. Both approaches reach the limit of their explanatory power at the limit of the episode; they can explain the structure, or identify the genre, of any discrete completed action in the poem, but not of the poem as a whole. They are unable not only to locate a structure in the poem, but also to explain the connections between episodes.

Anne Middleton, in an important recent essay, has argued that the poem's episodic quality is crucial to its conception: its most powerful moments are disruptive not only of relations between characters but of narrative continuity.[7] But this raises the question as to whether we can meaningfully interpret the poem as a single structure at all.[8] The recurring image of the pilgrimage has led criticism to seek unity in Will's progress, to read the narrative as his *itinerarium mentis in Deum*. But progress is hard to locate, and Middleton persuasively argues that it is not there at all. Her argument challenges criticism to find in the work a vocabulary that will be both responsive to its episodic quality and capable of describing narrative connections that extend local significance to the whole. I suggest that such a vocabulary is available if we seek continuity in the sequence not of narrated actions, but of narrative genres: Langland's shifting generic commitments form the real plot of the *Visio* and carry the burden of the initial search for Saint Truth. He moves through his genres to an explicit imitation of biblical narrative: the *Visio* progresses by literary ascesis, testing and rejecting generic formulations to approach the literary form that is as little literary, as little dependent upon human authority, as possible. Will thus appears less as a subject with those continuities and dynamic processes that we call character than as a heuristic locus of authorship, a projection of the poet's attempt to configure an integrally authoritative voice — a perspective that will allow us to explain rather than explain away the discrete, discontinuous, and episodic character of the poem. The pilgrimage, and the progress, are Langland's and not Will's, and they approach a solution to problems of institutional authority, not the vision of God.

The problem of authority is initially enacted in the Prologue's ecclesiastical satire (46–111). Its structure describes a hierarchical crescendo unusual in estates satire[9]: first laymen (pilgrims and palmers, lines 46–52), then hermits (unaffiliated religious, 53–7), friars (under formal vows, 58–67), pardoners (not necessarily priests, but licensed by the bishop, 68–82), parish priests (83–6), bishops and *magistri* (87–99), and finally the cardinals and papal court (100–111). This structure mimics the appeals of institutional reform: one looks to higher levels of the hierarchy to contain abuses at the lower levels. But the peak of the hierarchy offers no solution, only cardinalatial presumption that prompts an uneasy silencing of the narrator:

> Ac of þe Cardinals at court þat kauȝte of at name,
> And power presumed in hem a pope to make
> To han þe power þat Peter hadde — impugnen I nelle —
> For in loue and lettrure þe eleccion bilongeþ;
> Forþi I kan & kan nauȝht of court speke moore.
>
> (Prol. 107–11)

The narrator's stammering unwillingness to commit himself indicates the strain of a judgment to which his competence does not extend. He has run out of institutional authority, and is left with only his own.

This, in small, is the epistemological problem of the *Visio*: how does the writer locate authority when the institution to which it has been entrusted has compromised its own moral credit? The problem ends the *Visio* even as it initiates it, with the dispute between Piers and the priest. Like that dispute, this passage in the Prologue addresses the relation of learning to authority: 'in loue and lettrure þe eleccion bilongeþ' (Prol. 110). The angular metrics of these lines ease into a certain confidence and resolution here. 'Loue and lettrure': he preempts institutional definitions of authority in favor of a definition that negotiates between traditional textual authorities ('lettrure') and the active embodiment of their teachings ('loue'). In Langland's literary enterprise, the deployment of learning is weighted with the responsibility of becoming authoritative, healing the deficiencies of ecclesiastical authority by embodying 'loue' in writing.

The late medieval spirituality of suffering defines that love and, for Langland, its literary consequences. Mâle says of the fifteenth century, 'S'associer à la Passion devint l'acte principale de la piété chrétienne.'[10] It is a love defined and enabled by the self-abnegation that finds for the Christian a place with Christ on the cross,[11] and it is the love in which *Piers Plowman* finds its normative vision of the Passion (17–18).[12] But the ascetic character of this love is formally and not just thematically determinative. Will, the projected image of the poet's self-definition, suffers the reduction of self in suffering less as a character than as a narrator; he is stripped of those formal and generic elements that assert his own authority rather than submit his authority to God's. And this takes the form of a generic ascesis.

Will has two doubles in the Prologue, two groups who are at once targets of his satire and models of his own behavior. As a wandering hermit he is at one with those he denounces, the 'Heremites on an heep', who 'Cloþed hem in copes, to ben knowen fram oþere; / Shopen hem heremytes hire ese to haue' (Prol. 53, 56–7). But there is also his relation, insisted upon throughout the poem,[13] with the 'mynstralles', a connection that enforces at once the doubt as to whether he is one of those who 'geten gold with here glee giltles' (35), or of those 'laperes and langleres, ludas children' honored with a suggeston of Will's own name when they 'Fonden hem fantasies and fooles hem makeþ, / And han wit *at wille* to werken, if hem liste' (36–7).

In uniting these roles, minstrel and wandering hermit, Langland infects authorship with the *gyrovagus's* threat of divisive autonomy. The centuries between Saint Benedict and Langland had refined the suggestions of the term, already resonant in the *Regula* with suggestions of spiritual as well as geographical wandering. It retained a literal currency[14]; but Peter Damian better illustrates its metaphorical development. He uses the term to rebuke the canons at Fano: 'But those whom we see owning property, wandering without purpose here and there, freed from law by the decision of their own will, we judge worthy to be called, not monks, but *gyrovagi*, or *sarabaiti*.'[15] Their self-willed independence is a threat to the church and its unity:

> We should call 'schismatics' not only those who split the unity of the faith, but also those who separate themselves from fraternal love through the vice of pride or avarice . . . . One who falls from love is no less culpable than one who wanders from the faith.[16]

Fissuring 'fraterna charitas', the gyrovague's self-aggrandisement threatens the disciplined unanimity that would enable reform. One of Langland's own masters, Guillaume de Saint-Amour, adopts the term to describe those who damage ecclesiastical discipline by arrogating authority: 'And concerning the slothful, the *gyrovagi* . . . they too are often false, and therefore dangerous to the whole church, living in opposition to the teaching of the apostles.'[17]

If I am correct in reading 'lakkynge lettred men and lewed men boþe' as a reference to Will's satire in the Prologue, then he does just what Peter Damian says that *gyrovagi* do ('a fraterna charitate [se] divellunt'), and is implicated in what the Middle Ages could see as the malice of satire: 'odio non vacet', Petrarch says of the genre.[18] The union of satirist and *gyrovagus* suggests that satire, the hereditary occupation of Langland's alliterative predecessors (the first fit of *Winner and Waster* and, if we accept an early judgment of Elizabeth Salter's, *The Simonie*),[19] is an abuse, a sterile form of writing that signals a sterile, unspiritual understanding of contemporary history. The satirist assumes his own habit, criticizes in his own voice; his observations are authorised only by himself; he becomes what he criticizes, an abusive authority; and reform is routed into a circle where literary authority is appropriated by those most in need of reform. When reform comes provisionally to the poem, it comes not through satire but through penance – the confession of Passus 5 – and in contrast to this sacramental reconciliation, satire is mere carping.

This is why Will, though an accomplished satirist, is treated by Lady Holy Church in Passus 1 as an illiterate: 'To litel latyn þow lernedest, leode, in þi youþe' (1.141). Will's is the illiteracy of the too literal, of one who lacks the language of glossing ('latyn'); Holy Church is unneeded and uninvoked until he tries to interpret. The estates satire is only a prologue, barred from the logic of progress implicit in the very term 'passus'. The passus, and the progress they aim at, begin only when Will turns to exegesis, to describing 'What þe mountaigne bymeneþ and þe merke dale / And þe feld ful of folk' (1.1–2). 'Bimeneþ' signifies signification[20]: the beginning of Passus 1 promises exegetical definitions. But what immediately follows the promise is not an explanation but an authority:

> A louely lady of leere in lynnen yclopþed
> Cam doun from þe Castel and called me faire.
> And seide, 'sone, slepestow? . . .'
>
> (1.3–5)

The details of her entrance and appearance recall those of Boethius's Philosophy,[21] and they place this passus within the genre of the *consolatio*. This generic affiliation has long been recognised; but I want to argue that the passus looks directly to Boethius. Although Holy Church's question, 'sone, slepestow?' does issue a Pauline summons from moral torpor,[22] it does so in Boethian terms: 'Why silent? . . . I wish it were from shame, but I see that oblivion [*stupor*] oppresses you.'[23] The *stupor* is a moral somnolence, and its precise symptoms explain why Langland alludes to Boethius here: the latter's self-indulgent sorrow has driven him to the solace of a meretricious literary activity, rather than to Philosophy's severer melodies. Philosophy's first act of consolation is to banish those literary consolations: 'When she saw the poetic muses by my bed, dictating to my tears, she was angered a little, and her eyes flamed, and she said, "Who has allowed these theater whores to approach the bed of this sick man?"'[24] Just as Philosophy banishes poetry in favor of dialectic, Holy Church banishes satire in favor of interpretation. When Will asks, 'Mercy, madame, what may this be to mene?' (11), she disciplines his exegetical innocence by directing his attention away from the field itself – the scene of satire – to the landscape surrounding it:

'The tour on þe toft,' quod she, 'truþe is þerlnne,
And wolde þat ye wrouȝte as his word techeþ.'

(1.12–13)

Her exegesis of the tower and the dungeon is basic, obvious, and new to
Will as it cannot be to the reader. Will's impulse to satire exercises itself in
his ignorance of the spiritual context of human life; as a merely human
attempt at reform, it is a form of illiteracy.

Holy Church suffers her own generic limitations, however. She cures Will
of satire, but her constructive functions are oddly circumscribed. As R.E.
Kaske has shown, her instruction contains the poem in miniature, embraces
the whole didactic range of the following nineteen passus.[25] But that
observation only exposes her quick obsolescence: if Holy Church wields such
comprehensive authority, we must ask why the rest of the poem is there,
why it cannot rest in the quiet plentitude of her exegesis. The reason is
located in the limitations of her literary genre; she is evacuated under the
same rules by which she banishes Will's estates satire. The character of Holy
Church is merely a more sophisticated version of that same individual literary
authority that her arrival has banished, and she turns out to be
incommensurate with the narrative world that, as a consequence of her own
pedagogy, interrupts her dialogue with Will. For medieval commentators
recognised the Boethian pedagogue as a faculty of the narrator's soul or of
his literary activity. A ninth-century commentary on the *De consolatione*
identifies the entrance of Philosophia as the initiation of authorship:
'"Philosophy stood by me", that is, I decided to write philosophically.'[26]
Abelard says that Boethius speaks to Philosophy 'as someone speaking to
himself'.[27] She represents interpretive authority, but only that authority
possessed by the reflective individual author.

This Boethian filiation emphasizes Holy Church's inability to fulfill the
promise of her own name. The patristic and medieval etymology of 'church'
is unvarying: 'Ecclesia id est convocatio.'[28] The name implies the power of
social convocation, the creation of community belied precisely by the Boethian
solitude of Lady Holy Church. The historical world cannot be understood
without the authority of the church, but at the same time, 'church' has no
meaning outside the *convocatio*, outside its incorporation in history.[29]

In this, she is no match for Lady Mede, although she defines their relation
as a rivalry: 'I ouȝte ben hyere þan she – I kam of a bettre' (2.28). What
motivates her resentment – what makes Mede in fact 'hyere' – is Mede's
fuller incarnation in the social world. She wields the convocative powers that
Holy Church lacks, and her wedding reassembles the crowded cast that Holy
Church has edged out of the narrative:

To marien þis mayde was many man assembled,
As of knyȝtes and of clerkes and ooþer commune peple,

As Sisours and Somonours, Sherreues and hire clerkes,
Bedelles and baillifs and Brocours of chaffare,
Forgoers and vitaillers and vokettes of þe Arches;
I kan noȝt rekene þe route þat ran about Mede.

(2.54–62)

The ordering of the folk of the field is the initial challenge of the poem; their
periodic reentries into the poem test the ability of each genre to better the
ordering that satire was not able to perform.[30] Like the Prologue, Passus 2 is
satire, but satire with an interpretive dimension, conducted by means of those
conceptual doubles we call personifications. When the vices ease their trip to
London by riding on the backs of their human victims –

Thanne fette Fauel foles of þe beste
Sette Mede vpon a Sherreue shoed al newe,
And Fals sat on a Sisour þat softeli trotted,
And Fauel on ⟨a Flaterere fetisly⟩ atired . . .

(2.162–6)

– the control of human agents by the vices that in fact drive them forms a
narrative exegesis of the corruptions presented in the Prologue.[31] The genre,
that is to say, is one that profits from Holy Church's lesson of interpretation.

What is the genre? The action of the Mede passus (2–4) describes a
familiar trajectory: disorder is arrested by the intervention of civil authority,
and is resolved by pleading before the king. The trajectory belongs to the
influential English adaptation of the *débat*, and particularly that of *Winner and
Waster*.[32] The genius of that poem is the implicit revisionist etiology of its
own form: it imagines the debate not as the grandchild of Virgilian pastoral
contests but as the poetic extension of public deliberation.[33] The central
element of Langland's episode is the antiphonal, judicial pleading of
Conscience and Mede.[34] The pleading exhibits the recurrent gestures of its
genre: mutual abuse, citation of opposing authorities, appeals to the judge's
sense of political expediency.

If the Boethian solitude and impassibility of Holy Church mirror the
inherently private and literary character of her genre, the deliberative genre
of the Mede passus commits the poet at once to a public responsibility and
to the impersonation of social voices. This is without question progress, but
it happens simply by the author's autonomous generic decision; it does not
arise through narrative logic. *Within* each of these episodes, the action
progresses by the logic of narrative and dialectic – Holy Church educates
Will on the tower and the dale and on the right use of treasure, Reason
educates the king on the nature of Mede – but *between* the episodes progress
obtains simply by the discontinuities of authorial choice. Langland drops a
genre when its resources are depleted; Holy Church disappears when she has

no more to say, has trammeled up progress in the privacy of the merely internal dialogue. The suddenness of authorial decision leaves Will baffled; his immediate attraction to Lady Mede signals his inability to interpret correctly in this new genre.

The debate of the Mede passus applies the exegetical lessons of Passus 1 to the social world of the Prologue. But it finds itself trapped as well within its own terms when resolution of the debate is abdicated to an apocalyptic that is alien to the logic of the genre: 'And Dauid shal be diademed and daunten hem alle, / And oon cristene kyng kepen vs echone' (3.288–9). This speech by Conscience (3.284–330) promises order to the secular world only through the intervention of the sacred. The celebratory closure with which the episode ends – Reason, Conscience, and the King agree to rule together (4.192–5) – is unstable and provisional: the order it imposes quickly loses its equilibrium. For the conceptual vocabulary that the genre offers is incommensurate with its promise of finality. This tableau of hierarchical concord seems to fulfill the prophecy Reason makes fifty lines earlier:

> And if þow werche it in werk I wedde myne eris
> That lawe shal ben a laborer and lede afeld donge,
> And loue shal lede þi lond as þe leef likeþ.
>
> (4.146–8)

But the crucial moment of decision in the passus, the decision referred to the King whom the genre conventionally commissions as judge, can only come in the terms that such a genre and judge can provide. The King recalls Reason's caution that Mede should not control the law, and reasons his way to her condemnation: 'þoruȝ youre lawe, as I leue,' he addresses Mede, 'I lese manye escheetes; / Mede ouermaistreþ lawe and muche truþe letteþ' (4.175–6). This is true, on the evidence of the preceding discussion. But the terms of Mede's condemnation reestablish her social position even as they condemn it: the King's motive is his loss of reversions, his loss of the rewards – the meed – of his position. Political reform is, by its nature, the slave of policy; the political world cannot choreograph its own apocalypse. Such political efforts are mortgaged to, and eventually foreclosed by, political interests.

What is omitted in this moment of reform is the first element in Reason's advice to the King: 'þi confessour' (4.145). Passus 5 supplies the lack, reconvening both the folk of the field and the *dramatis personae* of 4 under the supervision of sacramental confession and its attendant genre. I will argue elsewhere the scene's close relation to, and insistent querying of, the reforms of the Fourth Lateran Council; here I want simply to insist that this identification yields a clear generic affiliation. The consequence of the Lateran reforms and their enthusiastic pursuit by the English hierarchy was the circulation of episcopal letters outlining and explaining the main themes of vernacular preaching: the seven deadly sins, the ten commandments, the sacraments, the parts of confession. The growth, translation, and diffusion of these instructions for both clerical and lay use produced a new and identifiable genre, the confession manual, of which the central and longest part was the treatise on the deadly sins.[35] The literature of reform, aimed at educating the laity for participation in sacramental life, enforced a powerfully pedagogic image of church and society. The ordering of the folk, at the beginning of 5 – the most successful ordering so far – reproduces the lineaments of this thirteenth-century image:

> For I seiȝ þe feld ful of folk þat I before tolde,
> And how Reson gan arayen hym al þe Reaume to preche;
> And wiþ a cros afore þe kyng comsede þus to techen.
>
> (5.10–12)

Although the identity of the preacher prepares for instabilities to come, the configuration of the scene – preaching *ad populum* in a penitential context – reproduces in narrative tableau the procedures of the Lateran reforms. The dependence of the confessions on the deadly sins treatises is clear. The larger structure of the passus betrays Langland's self-consciousness about the genetics of his genre. For the second major structural element of the passus is Piers's oddly elaborated topography of the pilgrimage to Truth. The Latin tag attached to one of the locations – 'a ford, your-fadres-honourep: / *Honora patrem & matrem &c.*' (567–7a) – identifies the scheme as a tour of the ten commandments: the passus invokes both the negative and positive standards of regenerate behavior (the deadly sins and the commandments) that structure the confession manuals.

Will's progressive detachment from the action of the *Visio*, both as an interlocutor and as source of its voices, signals the progressive relinquishing of authority. The genre of Passus 5 purports to elide the individual author altogether in favor of the therapeutic pedagogy of institutional authority. The passus discovers a genre with a credible claim to escape the assertiveness and the limitations of human authorship. The church's double aspect – a human and historical community of divine origin – and the institutional authorization and sacramental context of the genre offer the possibility of such escape. But that double aspect is precisely the source of uncertainty about the church in the Prologue, the uncertainty that surrounds the attempt to find an unambiguous incarnation of divine authority at any level of the church; and this same uncertainty hobbles the ability of this genre to finish what it starts. The initial gathering is supervised by Reson, who shares the same structural character as the church itself. It is not quite accurate to say, as Elizabeth Kirk does, that Reson's appearance here indicates the unambiguously human character of the penitential enterprise.[36] For reason is, in one aspect, the image of God in humanity, identified exegetically with the sapiential Christ,[37] but it is also, in its other aspect, the bounded and fallible instrument of historical humanity. The cast of the Mede passus – Conscience and Reson, Waryn Wisdom and Witty – has already established the distinctive aspects of reason, and the camouflages that make it necessary to draw those distinctions. Similarly, the human aspect of the church is what causes the initial problem in the Prologue. The reform of 5 is poised in uncertainty about its own source and authority just as it proclaims the poverty of human projects. The force of the confession of Roberd the robber, unable to make satisfaction (461–76), of Repentance's sermon on the *felix culpa* (477–505), of the palmer whose appurtenances form a physical encumbrance (515–24), is to establish the gravitational effect of human limitations on human reforms.

While Passus I offered an authority without a social convocation, Passus 5 does just the opposite: the folk who 'prungen togideres' (510) lack direction, lack the authority that Holy Church could provide: they 'Cride vpward to Crist and to his clene moder / To haue grace to go to truþe' (511–12). The incipient dispersion that threatens even the *convocatio* threatens also the literary continuation: with narrative continuity hanging on the possibility of pilgrimage, the pilgrims must know where to direct their *passus* before Langland can direct his. The most significant fact about Langland's solution of the problem is its sheer willfullness: ' "Peter!" quod a Plowman, and putte forþ his hed' (537). He invents the character made to order, a character who both convenes and directs. Piers's authority is established precisely by that discontinuity; his ability to arrest the incipient dispersion of the characters establishes his relation both to the authority of Holy Church and to the historical world that she was unable to direct. The initial expletive establishes his entrance as an irruptive moment, but the expletive itself, as many have noted, at once names Piers and recalls the authority of the disciple-primate Peter. The resonance of the identification, the informal typology that obtains between Piers and the leader of the new Israel, signals the appearance of the next and final genre of the *Visio*.

To establish that genre, it will help to look at the most familiar moment of these passus. The resemblance of Piers's tearing of the pardon in 7 to Moses's breaking of the tablets has been most fully described by Mary Carruthers.[38] She notes particularly that Piers's 'pure tene' makes specific textual reference: *'iratus valde* proiecit de manu tabulas' (Exodus 32.19). What has gone unnoticed is the fact that an earlier, less celebrated appearance of Piers's anger makes reference no less specific to the same moment:

> Thanne seten somme and songen atte Nale
> And holpen ere þis half acre wiþ 'how trolly lolly.'
> 'Now, by þe peril of my soule!' quod Piers al in pure tene.
>
> (6.115–17)

In Exodus, Moses's anger is ignited when he descends Mount Sinai to hear 'the voice of singers. And when he came nigh to the camp, he saw the calf, and the dances: and being very angry, he threw the tables out of his hand' (Exodus 32.18–19).[39] Piers plays a Mosaic role not just in the tableau of the pardon scene, but throughout the sequence of Passus 6 and 7.

He plays this role consistently, and indicates the larger conformity of the narrative action to the action of the Mosaic books. Passus 6 reproduces in the half-acre the process of wandering and defection that characterizes Israel's forty years in the desert. Its genre is Bible; more specifically, it is exodus. The question of what happens to the pilgrimage to Saint Truth – does the plowing of the half-acre supplant it, or is the plowing itself the pilgrimage? – may argue pedantry on the part of the poem's critics, but not inattention. The text supports both claims, and in doing so recapitulates a similar ambiguity from the exodus story. Piers promises to dress 'in pilgrymes wise / And wende wiþ yow þe wey til we fynde truþe' (6.57–8), having hung by his side 'his hoper . . . in stede of a Scryppe' (61). But less than ten lines later, he asks for seed: 'For I wole sowe it myself, and *sipenes* wol I wende / To pilgrymage . . .' (63–4). A linear pilgrimage with a definite goal is delayed in favor of a penitential pilgrimage without one. Israel's forty years of wandering form just such a pattern; they must delay their entry into (their pilgrimage *to*) Canaan to wander through (their pilgrimage *in*) the desert: 'Your children shall wander in the desert forty years, and shall bear your fornication, until the carcasses of their fathers be consumed in the desert' (Numbers 14.33). The sin that calls forth this punishment is Israel's pusillanimity before the promised land: 'And they said to one another: Let us appoint a captain, and let us return into Egypt' (Numbers 14.3–4). A similar pusillanimity afflicts the folk of *Piers's* field at the end of Passus 5:

> 'Bi seint Poul!' quod a pardoner, 'parauenture I be nou3t knowe þere,
> I wol go fecche my box wiþ my breuettes & a bulle with bis-shopes lettres.'
> 'By crist!' quod a comune womman, 'þi compaignie wol I folwe.
> Thow shalt seye I am þi Suster.' I ne woot where þei bicome.
>
> (639–40)

And just as these two embody Israel's pusillanimity, the folk of the field reproduce an almost formulaic biblical expression of Israel's impatience with the discipline of the desert, 'et murmurati sunt': 'þus þis folk hem mened' (6.2).

A hymn at the end of Deuteronomy defines retrospectively the experience of the desert: 'The beloved grew fat and kicked: he grew fat, and thick and gross, he forsook God who made him' (Deuteronomy 32.15). One of God's responses has particular cogency for Passus 6. They suffer famine because they murmur about their food: 'Our soul is dry, our eyes behold nothing else but manna' (Numbers 11.6), 'There is no bread, nor have we any waters: our soul now loatheth this very light food' (Numbers 21.5). The folk of the field are struck from the same mold:

'Wiltow, neltow, we wol haue oure will
Of þi flour and þi flessh, fecche whan vs likeþ,
And maken vs murye þerwiþ, maugree þi chekes.'

(156–8)

Laborers þat haue no land to lyue on but hire handes
Deyneþ noȝt to dyne a day nyȝt olde wortes.
May no peny ale hem paie, ne no pece of bacoun,
But if it be fressh flessh ouþer fissh 〈fryed ouþur ybake,〉
And þat *chaud* and *plus chaud* for chillynge of hire mawe.

(307–11)

Langland's Hunger can teach Piers and quote Scripture. Like the plagues, serpents, and famine of the exodus, Hunger is a divine emissary that imposes unwelcome penance on a recalcitrant folk.[40]

Passus 6 has been taken as an empirical and literal reflection of fourteenth-century England's painful economic experience.[41] It is in fact, as I hope I have shown, deeply typological. But it wears its typology with a difference; it is easy to miss or mistake, because it hangs on a precision of narrative imitation uncommon in the traditional typological readings of the exodus. In Rabanus Maurus's commentary on Exodus, Israel figures the church.[42] But it is an oblique identification: while he equates allegorically the *mirabilia* of the journey with the sacraments of the church,[43] he dissociates the church from Israel's murmuring and backsliding.[44] Israel's experience of the desert, in this tradition, figured either (*in bono*, so to speak) the monastic *community's* virtuous asceticism or (*in malo*) the *individual's* alternation of backsliding and reform; not, in any case, the community's backsliding.[45] Franciscan exegesis, too, though its interest in Israel's sufferings were more central to the order's self-definition, made it the willingly accepted suffering of the Zephanian 'remnant'.[46] But Langland takes the inconstant Israel of the exodus to figure the inconstant church in fourteenth-century England, and thus erects a typology that is also a narrative imitation and a generic appropriation; although it inscribes a typological interpretation into the exodus story, it leaves the shape of the story intact, leaves it recognizable as a kind of narrative.[47]

The imitation continues through Passus 7. The queer behavior of the pardon – a summary of its contents takes 102 lines, but 'In two lynes it lay and noȝt a lettre moote' (109) – merely imitates the law that takes chapters to summarise, while on two tablets it lay, and not a verse more. Piers's resolve after tearing the pardon – 'I shal cessen of my sowyng . . . & swynke noȝ so harde, / Ne aboute my 〈bely ioye〉 so bisy be na moore' (121–3) – reproduces Moses's: 'I cast the tables out of my hands and broke them in your sight. And I fell down before the Lord as before, forty days and nights neither eating bread nor drinking water, for all your sins' (Deuteronomy 9.17–18). But at the same time, Langland's enterprise reaches a sort of crisis. I eschew the temptation to heap new exegetical weight on the pardon scene, and simply add to the most pertinent critical tradition some remarks on its consequences for Langland's self-negating authorship.

When the priest declares himself unable to locate a pardon in the pardon, he displays a literal and literal-minded understanding both of 'pardon' and of interpretation.[48] The typological resonances of their stalemate in Piers's tearing of the pardon recalls the idolatry of Aaron, priest and calf-smith, that motivates Moses's breaking of the tablets.[49] The literal-mindedness of Aaron's levitical descendant, then, is an idolatry of the text, a dogged attachment to authoritative verbal expressions and their most proximate significance. D.W. Robertson has taught us suspicion of literal interpreters. But Langland here directs suspicion onto his own project, for the progressive abandonment of authorial control in favor of control by the biblical text, and his rejection of more traditional exodus typologies in favor of one that is closer to the letter of the narrative, risks a summons to the same court. The assertion of the scriptures against the authority of the human author and independent of traditional exegesis itself risks textual idolatry. The project of generic ascesis has sought an escape from authoritative self-assertion, but Piers's gesture of verbal iconoclasm is at least on the surface a self-assertive and idiosyncratic gesture.[50] In the terms of the Prologue, the cession to Scripture risks becoming 'lettrure' without 'loue'.

This, in fact, is the focus of the disputation that follows the tearing of the pardon. I say 'disputation' because *apposen* ('þe preest and Perkyn apposeden eiþer ooþer', 144) appears usually as a quasi-technical term for formal theological debate.[51] Their debate, strikingly, focuses not on the exegesis of the pardon — that has been left to us — but on the sources of exegetical authorization. The priest mocks Piers's scriptural citations: 'Peter! as me þynkeþ / Thow art lettred a litel; who lerned þee on boke?' (136–7). His taunt recalls the linguistic and textual authority that brought him to the poem in the first place, by which the first estate translates and construes for the third. Piers's response formulates a different ideal of lettered authority: 'Abystynence þe Abesse myn a b c me tauȝte' (137).[52] What is curious is not the assertion of the priority of penance over learning (a well-roasted chestnut of ascetical literature) but the assertion that penance is the most reliable *source* of learning.[53] That this is the burden of Piers's response is clear from his rejection of the priest as 'lewed' (142) and from his accusation, 'On Salamons sawes selden þow biholdest: / *Eice derisores . . .*' (143–3a).

Two issues pertinent to Langland's strategy in the *Visio* emerge from this debate. One is the idolatrous risk that threatens Langland's poem as seriously as it does Truth's pardon. Although the choice of biblical narrative provisionally resolves the problem of authority in human writing, the resolution is only provisional: to stop with the authoritative text is idolatry, and that idolatry, the temptation to rest in the discovery of the text, is the refusal to interpret. The poem needs to continue, and the imperative is adumbrated, before the *Visio* ends, by that avatar of authorship, Will:

Many tyme þis metels haþ maked me to studie
Of þat I sei3 slepynge; if it so be my3te,
And for Piers loue the plou3man wel pencif in herte,
And which a pardon Piers hadde þe peple to conforte,
And how þe preest inpugned it wiþ two propre wordes.

(149–53)

The end of the second vision has brought an exegetical imperative. It ends with an emphatic irresolution – 'þe preest and Perkyn apposeden eiþer ooþer' – but an irresolution on a different plane: it is not the location of the authority that is now in question, but its meaning, and this fact determines the form of what follows. What we call the *Vita* is in fact largely concerned with narrowly epistemological issues. It is banal but necessary to remark again that when Will goes in search of Dowel, he is in fact tracking the meaning of the pardon's *'qui bona egerunt'* – is seeking the interpretation of an authoritative text – and therefore the literary quest I have described ends here. I have called this article 'The Genres of *Piers Plowman*', despite its specific concentration on the *Visio*, because the *Visio* has all the genres. Traditional literary genres disappear after Passus 7; the rest is enacted interpretation.[54]

This invites the second point. Piers asserts the principle that action must precede and validate interpretation; in assigning to Will the interpretation of *'qui bona egerunt'*, Langland puts a point to the issue: seeking the interpretation and enacting it are simply one and the same. As Mary Carruthers has argued, Will must learn not *what* or *where* Dowel is, but *to do well*.[55] So the resolution of the poem is doubly deferred, first by the necessity of interpreting the injunction to do well, and second by the necessity of doing well before speaking with authority. And, notoriously, the poem never reaches resolution: the long interpretive pilgrimage of the *Vita* ends on a moment of emphatic deferral. But this is only the logical conclusion of the phrase that, I have argued, contains Langland's program: 'loue and lettrure'. The text cannot make final claims for itself.

A schematic summary is in order. Problems of authority are also problems of form, of which Will is the narrative subject. Langland enables narrative progress and approaches religious authority by discontinuous choices of genre that progressively abandon claims to poetic authority. The resolution enacts a plenary abdication of authorship in favor of biblical narrative, but the resolution only generates the questions of interpretation – coextensive with the challenge of reform – that motivate the *Vita*. Precipitated into summary, these arguments assign an odd status to the text. The Prologue presses questions of *institutional* authority, an authority obscured but not despaired of; the self-effacing author that the poem proposes in response (along with the biblical text his self-effacement trails) is only an interim, a substitute that lives provisionally. His self-evacuation must be directed eventually to a reformed and restored community. And so the *Vita*'s double task of interpretation and reform becomes also the task of institutional reconciliation. Will there is less the figure of authorship than the occasion around which conflicting ideologies – scholastic and Augustinian, 'pelagian' and Augustinian, fraternal and antifraternal, all those opponents prefigured by Piers and the priest – are voiced and reconciled.

The poem seeks its provisionality. It stands in for a fractured communal authority, and enacts in its own procedures the reforms that would heal the fracture. If these reforms were effected in the institution, the poem would not need to exist: everything following Holy Church's imperatives for individual reform *would* be obsolete if Holy Church were unmistakably embodied in history. And this indicates yet another programmatic provisionality in the text. Proxying for an institution is a job tied to the moment; since the failure of the church is a failure to incorporate an ideal form into the specific configurations of history, its proxy must change with the shifting contours of the historical world. Elizabeth Salter is only the most recent critic to sense that Langland's revisions were inevitable.[56] His successive rewritings are consequent on his project and prefigured within it. The halts and restarts of the *Visio*, playing out one literary form to its limits and then reforming it in a fresh start, only show the process of revision at its most visibly premeditated. The poem solicits revision.[57] Just as it keeps us from following a narrative logic in its narrated actions, and forces us to trace that logic in its own process of configuring itself, the fact of the revisions should keep us from locating *Piers Plowman* in the A, B, or C text, or in an imaginative amalgamation of them. There is not a whit of evidence to suggest that Langland sought a definitive version of the poem; *Piers Plowman* is the insistently provisional enterprise that he pursued over two or three decades. I have joined a long and distinguished tradition in discussing the B-text as if it were the poem itself, but I have done so to show that even within a single text, the poem itself insists on a process of stalling and restarting, dismissal and reformation. A text laying claims to a final integrity would not stand in for, but supplant, the absent authority: it would propose itself as a textual idol. A 'loue' that negotiates with history offers 'lettrure' no rest.

Notes

1. Quotations from the B-text are from the Kane and Donaldson edition, *Piers Plowman: The B Version* (London, 1975). I have occasionally restored manuscript readings emended by Kane and Donaldson; these are marked with pointed brackets.

2. MORTON W. BLOOMFIELD, *Piers Plowman as a Fourteenth-Century Apocalypse* (New Brunswick, 1962), pp. 24–5.

3. 'Numquam stabiles et propriis uoluntatibus . . . seruientes,' *La règle de saint Benoît*, ed. Jean Neufville and Adalbert de Vogüé, 1 (Paris, 1972), p. 440.

4. Haukyn elsewhere enforces the comparison with Will's poetic activity; he defines himself as 'a Mynstrall', 13.224.

5. BLOOMFIELD (n. 2 above), pp. 7–34.

6. JOHN A. ALFORD, 'The Role of the Quotations in *Piers Plowman*', *Speculum*, **52** (1977): 80–99; JUDSON BOYCE ALLEN, *The Ethical Poetics of the Later Middle Ages* (Toronto, 1982); pp. 275–81, and idem, 'Langland's Reading and Writing: *Detractor* and the Pardon Passus', *Speculum*, **59** (1984): 342–62.

7. ANNE MIDDLETON, 'Narration and the Invention of Experience: Episodic Form in *Piers Plowman*', in *The Wisdom of Poetry: Essays in Early English Literature in Honor of Morton W. Bloomfield*, ed. Larry D. Benson and Siegfried Wenzel (Kalamazoo, 1982), pp. 91–122.

8. The importance of narrative unity is less an aesthetic problem for the poem – Langland shows little interest in a polished aesthetics – than it is a problem of understanding. The convergence of phenomenological and analytic philosophy on the importance of narrative in the act of understanding makes this point particularly visible now. For phenomenology, the central representative is of course Paul Ricoeur; for a recent statement, see *Time and Narrative*, trans. Kathleen McLaughlin and David Pellauer (Chicago, 1984), esp. ch. 3; for analytic philosophy, see ALASDAIR MACINTYRE, *After Virtue: A Study in Moral Theory* (Notre Dame, 1981).

9. JILL MANN's tabular summary shows that those satires which treat the ecclesiastical hierarchy tend to start at the top, with the pope, and work toward the local clergy; *Chaucer and Medieval Estates Satire* (Cambridge, 1972), pp. 203–6.

10. EMILE MÂLE, *L'Art religieux de la fin du moyen-âge en France* (Paris, 1925), pp. 90–1.

11. Starting from Mâle's work, F.J.E. RABY described the literary dynamics of this devotion: *A History of Christian Latin Poetry from the Beginnings to the Close of the Middle Ages*, ed. 2 (Oxford, 1953), pp. 417–43.

12. At the entrance of Piers, 'peynted al blody' (19.6), this normative vision is most nearly appropriated into the poem's narrative; the subsequent building of Unity Holy Church from the wood of the cross identifies Christ's Passion as the principle of ecclesiastical reform.

13. Imaginatif rebukes Will for wasting his time with poetry (12.10–19); as I noted before, Haukyn, in so many ways Will's double, first announces himself 'I am a Mynstrall' (13.224).

14. St Bernard writes to another abbot that he has received a monk at Clairvaux, because '. . . semper apud vos gyrovagus fuisset', ep. 68 in his *Opera*, ed. J. Leclercq, O.S.B., and H. Rochais (Rome, 1974), 1.168.

15. 'Quos autem proprium possidere, indifferentes huc illucque discurrere, solutos legibus juxta propriae voluntatis arbitrium diffluere cernimus, non monachorum, sed gyrovagorum potius, vel sarabaitorum dignos vocabulo judicamus'; PETER DAMIAN, Opusculum 27, PL 145.507.

16. 'Porro non illi soli schismatici sunt dicendi, qui fidei unitatem dividunt; sed ii etiam, qui se per elationis vel avaritiae vitium a fraterna charitate divellunt. . . . Non minus improbandus est, qui excidit a charitate, quam qui errat a fide'; PL 145. 507–8.

17. 'De otiosis autem, Gyrovagi . . . et ipsi frequenter Pseudo sunt, et ideo periculosi sunt toti Ecclesiae, et contra doctrinam Apostoli vivunt'; G. de St Amour. *De periculis novissimorum temporum*, in his *Opera* ('Constance', 1633), p. 47. The term

also appears in a *catena* of abuse, 'per Hypocritas, Pseudo-Praedicatores, et Penetrantes Domos ac Otiosos et Gyrovagos . . .'; *Collectiones*, ibid., p. 117.

18. PETRARCH, *Familiares* 23.11; *Le familiari*, ed. Umberto Bosco (Florence, 1942), 13.181.

19. ELIZABETH SALTER, 'Piers Plowman and the Simonie', *Archiv für das Studium der neuern Sprachen und Literaturen*, **203** (1967): 241–54. A. C. SPEARING takes the A-text, unlike the later versions, as an orthodox entry in this tradition of alliterative satire: see *Medieval Dream-Poetry* (Cambridge, 1976), p. 140.

20. MED s.v. 'bimenen', which shows that the word has a much more specific range of meanings than the root 'menen'.

21. 'Mulier reverendi admodum vultus' becomes 'lovely lady of leere'; 'vestes . . . tenuissimis filiis subtili artificio' is the obvious suggestion for 'in lynnen ycloþed'. BOETHIUS *Philosophiae consolatio*, ed. Ludwig Bieler (Turnhout, 1957), p. 2.

22. D.W. ROBERTSON, JR and B.F. HUPPÉ, *Piers Plowman and Scriptural Tradition* (Princeton, 1951), p. 37.

23. 'Quid taces? . . . Mallem pudore, sed te, ut uideo, stupor oppressit'; BOETHIUS (n. 21 above), p. 4.

24. 'Quae ubi poeticas Musas uidit nostro adsistentes toro fletibusque meis uerba dictantes, commota paulisper ac toruis inflammata luminibus,'Quis,' inquit, 'has scenicas meretriculas ad hunc aegrum permisit accedere . . .?'; ibid., p. 2.

25. R.E. KASKE, 'Holy Church's Speech and the Structure of *Piers Plowman*', in Beryl Rowland (ed.), *Chaucer and Middle English Studies in Honour of Rossell Hope Robbins* (London, 1974), pp. 320–37.

26. 'Adstitit mihi Philosophia, id est cogitaui philosophice scribere'; *Saeculi noni auctoris in Boetii Consolationem philosophiae commentarius*, ed. E.T. Silk (Rome, 1935), p. 12.

27. 'Quasi . . . aliquis secum loquens'; PETER ABELARD, *Expositio in hexaemeron*, PL 178.760.

28. YVES M.-J. CONGAR, *L'ecclésiologie du haut moyen âge* (Paris, 1968), p. 61.

29. Or rather the only such meaning it has cannot be available to Will: she is the celestial Church, a church by definition unavailable within history except as hypothesis. On the 'celestial church' imagined as a royal woman, see EMILIEN LAMIRANDE, *Etudes sur l'ecclésiologie de saint Augustin* (Ottawa, 1969), pp. 21–4.

30. The most important such reprises are here in Passus 2, the beginning of 5, their naming in the pardon of 7, their summary in Haukyn in 13–14, and the apocalyptic events of the field in 19–20.

31. MARY CARRUTHERS, *The Search for St Truth* (Evanston, Ill., 1973), p. 45.

32. On the influence of *Winner and Waster* on Langland, see S. S. HUSSEY, 'Langland's Reading of Alliterative Poetry', *Modern Language Review*, **60** (1965): 163–70. I accept, despite Elizabeth Salter's final reconsideration, the traditional chronology of the poems, which puts *Winner and Waster* ca. 1353, and the A-text of *Piers* in the 1360s: Salter's argument appears in 'The Timeliness of *Wynnere and Wastoure*', *Medium aevum*, **47** (1978): 40–65. Forthcoming work by CARTER REVARD offers powerful arguments in favor of the traditional dating of *Winner and Waster*.

33. At the same time, the poet does situate his efforts in the lingering pastoral tradition; the rustic/oneiric frame in which he hangs the poem claims its place in

the diffusive debate tradition. And the descent of the *débat* is itself a complex issue: see BETTY NYE HEDBERG, 'The *Bucolics* and the Medieval Poetic Debate', *Transactions of the American Philological Society*, **75** (1944): 47–67.

34. ELIZABETH D. KIRK, alone among the poem's commentators, has identified this episode as a formal debate: see her *The Dream Thought of Piers Plowman* (New Haven, 1972), p. 41.

35. On the direct relation of the extremely popular vernacular manuals (like MANNYNG's *Handlyng Synne*) to the reform movement, see D.W. ROBERTSON, JR., 'The *Manuel des Péchés* and an English Episcopal Decree', *Modern Language Notes*, **60** (1945): 439–47. See LEONARD E. BOYLE, O.P., 'The *Oculus sacerdotis* and Some Other Works of William of Pagula', *Transactions of the Royal Historical Society*, ser. **5**. **5** (1955): 92 for the manual's status as a genre, and John V. Fleming, *An Introduction to the Franciscan Literature of the Middle Ages* (Chicago, 1977), for a discussion of the 'literary' confession manual. Their continuing popularity through the early sixteenth century is documented in THOMAS N. TENTLER, *Sin and Confession on the Eve of the Reformation* (Princeton, 1977), pp. 28–53. As an example of the proportions within a confession manual, nearly half of MANNYNG's *Handlyng Synne* (lines 2991–8586) is devoted to the deadly sins: the other traditional elements – the ten commandments, the explanation of the sacrament, the parts of sacramental repentance – are squeezed into the remainder.

36. KIRK (n. 34 above), pp. 51–2.

37. D.B. BOTTE describes the retroactive interpretations by which, in post-biblical theology, the Old Testament figure of Wisdom became attached to the mediating christology of St Paul; 'La sagesse et les origines de la christologie', *Revue des sciences philosophiques et théologiques*, **21** (1932), esp. 66–7. The *Roman de la rose* has been the focus of literary studies of this topic; see P. BADEL, 'Raison "Fille de Dieu" et le rationalisme de Jean de Meun', in *Mélanges de langue et de littérature du moyen-âge et de la renaissance offerts à Jean Frappier* (Geneva, 1970), pp. 41–52, and JOHN V. FLEMING, *Reason and the Lover* (Princeton, 1984), ch. 2.

38. MARY C. SCHROEDER, '*Piers Plowman*: The Tearing of the Pardon', *Philological Quarterly*, (1970): 8–18, and CARRUTHERS (n. 31 above), pp. 68–80.

39. English biblical citations are taken from the Douay-Reims version.

40. The pedagogic function of Hunger is discussed by KATHERINE TROWER, 'The Figure of Hunger', *American Benedictine Review*, **24** (1973): 238–60.

41. GUY BOURQUIN, *Piers Plowman: Etudes sur la génèse littéraire des trois versions* 1 (Paris, 1978), p. 19; DAVID AERS, *Chaucer, Langland, and the Creative Imagination* (London, 1980), pp. 13–24.

42. I take Rabanus as my representative exegete because of his frankly representative character. BERYL SMALLEY characterizes his period of exegesis as one of vastly learned, vastly productive, and thoroughly unimaginative consolidation of tradition: *The Study of the Bible in the Middle Ages* (Oxford, 1952), pp. 37–8.

43. 'Inter caeteras Scripturas quas Pentateuchas legis continet, merito liber Exodi eminet, in quo pene omnia sacramenta quibus praesens Ecclesia instituitur, nutritur et regitur, figuraliter exprimuntur'; RABANUS *In Exodum*, PL 108.9.

44. See, for example, 'Manifesto autem lumine fidei, datur manna populo, manna utique quod est Christus. . . . Qui per nubes evangelicas universo orbe pluitur, non

jam murmuranti et tentanti Synagogae, sed credenti et in illo spem ponenti Ecclesiae'; ibid., 108.80.

45. GREGORIO PENCO, 'Il tema dell'Esodo nella spiritualità monastica', in Cipriano Vagaggini *et al., Bibia e spiritualità* (Rome, 1967), pp. 333–77.

46. I follow here AUSPICIUS VAN CORSTANJE, *Un peuple de pèlerins* (Paris, 1964), pp. 37–73, and JOHN V. FLEMING, *From Bonaventure to Bellini: An Essay in Franciscan Exegesis* (Princeton, 1982), pp. 46–65.

47. 'For a person, an event, a body of laws, a rite, etc., to be both itself and real in its own right, and yet stand for something else later in time and equally real which is to fulfill it, imposes a strain especially on the earlier moment'; HANS W. FREI, *The Eclipse of Biblical Narrative: A Study in Eighteenth and Nineteenth Century Hermeneutics* (New Haven, 1974), p. 29. Frei's argument usefully sets apart the distinctiveness of Langland's activity in appropriating a biblical narrative for typological purposes while still retaining the narrative quality of the exodus story.

48. ROBERTSON and HUPPÉ (n. 22 above), pp. 93–4.

49. CARRUTHERS (n. 31 above), pp. 70–1.

50. This, in fact, is how R.W. CHAMBERS understands the tearing of the pardon; 'Long Will, Dante, and the Righteous Heathen', *Essays and Studies by Members of the English Association,* **9** (1924): 50–69.

51. MED s.v. 'apposen' la.

52. I reluctantly reject ALLEN's ingenious and fetching reading of this line, which takes 'Abstynence' as referring to the first entry of an alphabetical *distinctio* collection, and thereby to the collection itself; ALLEN, 'Langland's Reading' (n. 6 above), p. 355. I reject it because a more literal understanding of the line shows that the scene recapitulates an episode from John 7 that juxtaposes literacy, the giving of the law to Moses, and suffering. Jesus, teaching on the Feast of the Tabernacles, is wondered at by the crowds: 'How doth this man know letters [*litteras scit*], having never learned?' (John 7.15). He answers, 'If any man will do the will of him, he shall know of the doctrine. . . . Did not Moses give you the law, and yet none of you keepeth the law?' (17, 19), and notes their resentment: 'Are you angry at me because I have healed the whole man on the sabbath day?' (23).

53. To be sure, this claim has its own tradition; I trace its proximate origins to Franciscan attributions of exegetical authority to the self-styled *idiota,* FRANCIS:'Quamvis homo iste beatus nullis fuerit scientiae studiis innutritus, tamen quae de sursum est a Deo sapientiam discens et aeternae lucis irradiatus fulgoribus de Scripturis non infime sentiebat'; THOMAS OF CELANO, *Vita secunda sancti Francisci,* ed. Quarrachi fathers, *Analecta Franciscana,* 10.190.

54. Arguably, this overstates the case. If one were willing to refer to liturgy as a literary genre, it would clearly be untrue; if Bloomfield is correct anywhere in identifying *Piers Plowman* as an apocalypse, it is in 19–20. But (for the former) the enacted quality of liturgy distinguishes it precisely from literature's textuality. As to the latter, although I would be willing – more willing, actually, than Bloomfield – to define 'apocalypse' at least loosely as a genre (as a conventional theme with conventional forms of treatment), these conventions in the late Middle Ages take an exegelical/prophetic form, not the narrative/dramatic form of these passus. More challenging is the argument of MACKLIN SMITH's '*Piers Plowman* and the Tradition of the Medieval Life of Christ', PhD Diss. (Princeton, 1975), which

asserts that the poem finds resolution when it eases into the genre of the *vita Christi*. But Langland displaces the elements of this genre into visionary narrative and liturgical enactment.

55. CARRUTHERS (n. 31 above), pp. 81–2.

56. She speaks of a quality of 'disturbance' that 'is . . . a driving force, insisting to Langland that *Piers Plowman* should always be re-made, re-written, and that creation should be fresh and continuous': ELIZABETH SALTER, *Fourteenth-Century English Poetry: Contexts and Readings* (Oxford, 1983), p. 106.

57. Langland's versification – not precisely an exhausted topic in *Piers Plowman* studies – may confirm the assertion. The most remarkable fact about his prosody is its resistance to the isochrony and multiplication of accents, and (conversely) to the shortening of the long line, that are evident in Middle English alliterative verse; the effect is that he maintains the long line's openness to change of syllable count. Slightly less remarkable is his resistance to consistent or intermittent rhyme schemes. In the larger structures of his art, the willfulness of the shifts in landscape and *dramatis personae* resists the establishment of an inviolable narrative continuity. At the level of words within the line, of lines, and of episodes, he leaves his structures open to deletion, insertion, and transposition.

6 Price and Value in *Sir Gawain and the Green Knight**

JILL MANN

Jill Mann has published widely on Chaucer, with attention to both the socio-cultural contexts, and later feminist readings of his work. In this essay she explores the significance of the mercantile vocabulary and narrative structures of *Sir Gawain and the Green Knight*. Like many readers, she focuses on the exchanges within the poem, but insists that the poet is aware of the importance of market forces in determining both material and ethical value, in addition to the theological and philosophical traditions he invokes. Far from contaminating the courtly milieu, however, the commercial world is seen as equally important and dignified, and the poem thus attempts to synthesise mercantile with knightly values.

At the end of *Sir Gawain and the Green Knight*, the Green Knight reveals his complicity in the attempted seduction of Gawain by the lady of the castle (his wife), and voices his whole-hearted admiration for Gawain's resistance to it:

'I sende hir to asay þe, and sothly me þynkkez
On þe fautlest freke þat euer on fote ʒede;
As perle bi þe quite pese is of prys more,
So is Gawayn, in god fayth, bi oþer gay knyʒtez.'

(2362–5)[1]

The pearl is a fitting image for the spotless purity of 'the most faultless of men'. But this idea remains latent; the quality of the pearl on which the Green Knight explicitly bases his comparison is not its purity but its value. 'As a pearl is of greater value than a white pea, so is Gawain by comparison with

---

* Reprinted from *Essays in Criticism*, **36** (1986): 294–318.

other fair knights.' The subject of value in general, and Gawain's value in particular, is central to the poem. I wish to show first, that the poet posed himself the questions 'what does value consist in? how is value to be determined?', and second, that it is against the background of medieval economic thought, as it developed within the tradition of Aristotelian commentary, that we can best appreciate the intensity, precision and witty ingenuity with which the poet conducts his own exploration into the difficulties involved in answering them.

The word 'pris' is itself an ideal base from which to launch such an exploration. Its radical meaning is 'price' (from Latin *pretium* via Old French *pris*) – the only meaning it retains in modern English. In the medieval period it meant 'value' or 'worth' in a more general, non-monetary sense as well, and it also had a range of functions now taken over by the later formations 'praise' and 'prize'. That is, it denoted the applause or esteem which is accorded to excellence, 'fame, renown or good reputation' (OED 9, 10; MED 9), and also 'preeminence, superiority', the 'prize' of coming first in an imaginary contest of excellence (OED 11–13; MED 7–8). In the chivalric context of *Sir Gawain and the Green Knight*, where moral excellence and knightly renown are of obvious importance, we are not surprised to find the word used in all these transferred senses; what *is* surprising is to find how alive the poem is to the basic, commercial sense of the word, and how this awareness of its economic centre animates the inter-relations between its other meanings.

It is obvious from the first that the *Gawain*-poet uses 'pris' to denote both monetary and non-monetary value, and that in doing so he makes the one the mirror of the other. Material splendour and moral worth share a common vocabulary, as a glance at the entries for 'dear' and 'rich' in the Concordance immediately makes clear.[2] The description of Gawain's arming provides a formal illustration of this paralleling of the material and the moral. Gawain's armour and accoutrements glitter with gold (569, 577, 587, 591, 598, 600, 603); the pentangle on his shield is 'of pure golde hwez' (620), and his helmet is crowned with diamonds 'o prys' (615). The jewels and precious metals externalise and communicate his intangible inner worth, the links between the two being suggested by metaphor and simile:

> For ay faythful in fyue and sere fyue syþez
> Gawan watz for gode knawen, and *as golde pured*,
> Voyded of vche vylany, wyth vertuez *ennourned* . . .

> (632–5)

When the poet later says of Gawain that '. . . alle prys and prowes and pured þewes/Apendes to hys persoun' (912–13), this earlier description of jewels and precious metals hovers behind the word 'pured' like a concealed metaphor. The 'pured þewes' match the 'pured gold'; inward 'prys' and outward value are in perfect harmony. And it is not only in being 'highly prized' that gold and knightly worth are analogous. The evolution of the 'pured' of line 620 into the 'pure' of line 634 combines with the surrounding emphasis on the demonstration of Gawain's qualities in action ('watz for gode knawen', 'watz funden fautlez': 633, 640), to suggest that knightly worth, like precious metals, can be subjected to a process of 'refining', accomplished by the trials of knightly adventure. This suggested analogy gives a punning quality to the Green Knight's use of the word 'assay' – the process by which the value of precious metals is ascertained – in referring both to his own challenge to Arthur's court and to his wife's temptation of Gawain:

> ... 'to *assay* þe surquidré, ʒif hit soth were
> þat rennes of þe grete renoun of þe Rounde Table.'
>
> (2457–8)
>
> 'I sende hir to *asay* þe . . .'
>
> (2362)

The trial both tests and enhances value. It functions as refining to gold or polishing to a jewel; the past participles used by the Green Knight of Gawain's confession are again pregnant with metaphor:

> I halde þe *polysed* of þat plyʒt, and *pured* as clene
> As þou hadez neuer forfeted syþen þou watz fyrst borne.
>
> (2393–4)

If this were all, however, it would still leave us with a very romantic conception of 'prys' – would leave it, that is, in the glamorous world of jewels and precious metals, forming a flattering parallel to and appropriate focus of interest for an aristocratic class secluded and sheltered from the less dignified aspects of economic life. Yet the very first use of the word 'prys' in the poem reminds us of these aspects in a quite unembarrassed way. The tapestries adorning the dais on which Guinevere sits are said to be set with 'þe best gemmes/þat my ʒt be preued of prys wyth penyes to bye' (78–9). 'Preued', like 'assay', suggests a process of testing, the expert establishment of value by a method resembling an ordeal. But the added phrase 'wyth penyes to bye' takes us away from the solitary, respectful confrontation of expert and valuable material, and into the world of the market. What 'proves' the value of these jewels is purely and simply the amount of cash that has to be paid for them.

This early mention of market realities prepares the way for the much more prominent role to be assumed by the language and practices of the market later on, in Fitt Three of the poem. The presence of a consistent strain of mercantile or commercial vocabulary, running throughout the poem but especially prominent in this Fitt, has been noted several times before, and has recently had a whole monograph devoted to it.[3] By their bantering use of words like 'bargayn', 'chaffare', 'chepe' and 'chevisaunce',[4] Gawain and the lord of the castle turn their daily exchange of winnings into a mock-barter, in which profit and loss are reckoned up on each side. This mercantile language can be most succinctly illustrated by the conversation following Gawain's proffer of the three kisses in the third and final exchange:

'Bi Kryst,' quoþ þat oþer knyȝt, 'ȝe cach much sele
In cheuisaunce of þis chaffer, ȝif ȝe hade goud chepez.'
'ȝe, of þe chepe no charg,' quoþ chefly þat oþer,
As is pertly payed þe chepez þat I aȝte.'

(1938–41)

Most critics have linked this mercantile language in one way or another with Gawain's failings in his test – as representing his 'spiritual penury',[5] for example, or as a sign that he is sinking into 'consumerism and merchandising' to such an extent that 'he comes to resemble the archetypal shady dealer'.[6] In my view, the mercantile language is not a mere stratagem, a means of tarring Gawain with the brush of anti-commercial snobbery, but a subject in its own right; it takes the exchange of winnings out of the world of party games and into the real world of barter and bargaining. Within the playful banter, serious questions about the establishment of market-value can be raised and reflected on.

The events of Fitt Three are utterly appropriate to the exploration of these questions. For it is exchange, and not 'assay', that is the crucial process in determining value. 'Assay' can locate a precious metal on a scale of values, but cannot determine that precious metals will be *per se* valuable. Medieval thought on the questions of price and value was in no doubt that the process in which value is determined, both relatively and absolutely, is exchange. The fact that *both* Gawain's tests take the form of an exchange (exchange of winnings, exchange of blows) thus assumes a startling significance.[7] The reader's interest is directed not just towards the moral quality of Gawain's performance in these exchanges, but also towards what they can tell us about 'prys' and its determination.

Medieval thinkers learned that value is essentially exchange value from their study of Book V, Chapter 5 of Aristotle's *Nicomachaean Ethics*. The *Ethics* was translated into Latin by Robert Grosseteste in the mid-thirteenth century,[8] and commentaries on the work began to appear almost immediately, continuing unabated until the end of the Middle Ages. The analyses of *Ethics* V, 5 in these commentaries constitute the most important line of development in medieval economic thought.[9] Aristotle's main interest in this section of the *Ethics* is not in economic questions *per se*, but in commutative justice, of which justice in exchange is a sub-category; his discussion is in consequence brief. It is also occasionally obscure, but from our point of view the meaning of the original text is less important than the way the medieval commentators interpreted it. Aristotle's concern is to show that justice in exchange is not a matter of 'tit-for-tat' equivalence (simple *contrapassum*), but rather of 'proportionate requital' (*contrafacere proportionale*). Since men need to exchange objects of different kinds for their mutual benefit, the kind of exchange which cements the bonds of human society is not a matter of identical return (a blow for a blow, for example), but of maintaining a *proportionate* equivalence between non-identical things – Aristotle cites shoes and a house. In order to effect a just exchange, the builder and the shoemaker must be able by some means to establish the 'proportionate equivalence' between the shoes and the house – i.e. their relative worth – and this means that despite their disparity as objects, they must be capable of being referred to a common measure of value: 'all things that are exchanged must be somehow comparable'. In practical terms, this end is achieved by the use of money: 'it is for this purpose', Aristotle says, 'that money is introduced, and it becomes in a sense an intermediary; for it measures all things, and therefore both surplus and deficiency – that is, how many shoes are equal to a house, or to food'. But money is an index of value, not its source: the real creator of value is not money, but need. 'All goods must therefore be measured by some one thing . . . Now this unit is in truth need (*chreia*), which holds all things together . . . but money was invented by convention, for the sake of the exchange of need.' What exactly Aristotle meant by 'chreia' is a matter of debate, but its medieval meaning was fixed by the translators and commentators of the *Ethics*, who rendered it variously as 'opus', 'necessitas' or 'indigentia'.[10] Need makes things 'commensurable' for purposes of exchange – that is, establishes their relative value.

The medieval commentary tradition developed different aspects of this theory in turn. Albertus Magnus, whose first commentary on the *Ethics* followed hard on the heels of Grosseteste's translation, introduced a new element into the explanation of the relative value of shoes and a house by referring it to the difference in 'labour and costs' (*in labore et expensis*) expended by the shoemaker and the builder in producing them.[11] Later commentators saw the role of the consumer as more important than the role of the producer in fixing value, and turned their attention to elucidating the nature of *indigentia*.[12] The most important advance on this front found expression in the influential commentary of the fourteenth-century philosopher John Buridan, who answered the potential objection that many (indeed most) objects exchanged are not 'needed' in the sense of being necessary for basic survival, by glossing *indigentia* in Stoic terms as *any* felt lack or consciousness of insufficiency.[13] In this sense, rich men show their 'need' of luxuries simply by their willingness to exchange other goods for them. As interpreted by Buridan, the term comes very close to the modern English 'demand'; the emphasis is on the subjective desires of the consumer, rather than the objective utility of the commodity. Medieval canon lawyers expressed a similarly hard-headed perception of the role of the consumer in creating value in the maxim 'Res valet quantum vendi potest' ('a thing is worth what it can be sold for').[14] Scarcity, whose role was acknowledged in maxims such as 'omne rarum est carum',[15] is not enough to create value in itself; it must be combined with demand – as is well understood by Chaucer's Wife of Bath:

> Great prees at market maketh deere ware
> And to greet cheep is holde at litel prys.

> (Wife of Bath's Prologue 522–3)

Buridan also introduced into general circulation another important refinement of the Aristotelian theory – namely, the explanation that the need in question is not a merely individual need (otherwise starving men would have to pay more for bread than well-fed ones), but the generalised demand for a particular commodity felt by a whole community, considered in the aggregate[16]; the importance of this definition for *Gawain* will become clear later.

The Aristotelian commentary tradition was quite clear about the fact that the scale of market-values established by *indigentia* is completely independent of other, more idealistic, types of value-hierarchy. Aquinas, borrowing from St Augustine, pointed out that in economic terms a pearl is more valuable than a mouse, but in the scale of being the mouse must be rated higher, as living creatures are superior to insensate minerals.[17] In a chivalric romance such as *Gawain*, we might expect that value would be established by an appeal to idealistic hierarchies of just this sort – that the analogous 'prys' of the knight and gold depends on their analogous positions at the top of their respective ontological categories. But the exchange of winnings sequence pushes beyond such abstract schematisations, and brings us uncompromisingly up against the recognition that it is in the operations of the market – in exchange – and not in the tidy classifications of moralists or theologians, that value is determined.

A closer look at this section of the narrative will illustrate the point. On the first day of the exchange, Gawain offers a kiss as his 'winnings' for the day. In return the lord produces the mounds of venison he has brought home from the hunting-field. The lord's excited demand for an assessment of the relative worth of the two contributions – 'How payez you þis play? Haf I prys wonnen?/Haue I þryuandely þonk þurჳ my craft serued?' (1379–80) – insists on their commensurability. But how is the lord's question to be answered? The market-imagery with which the whole exchange of winnings is permeated rules out any recourse to idealistic value-hierarchies in pondering the question; we are not encouraged to answer, for example, that the kiss is superior to the venison since it is food for the spirit rather than the body – or that the venison is better than the kiss because it represents a communal rather than an individual good. We have to turn to other possible means of defining value, more appropriate to the rules of everyday bargaining.

The wit and ingenuity with which the poet has constructed the exchange of winnings in such a way as to dramatise this central problem now becomes clear. In the first place, he has made the disparity between the objects exchanged far more extreme in nature than Aristotle's comparison of shoes and a house. The substantial is matched with the insubstantial, the corporeal with the incorporeal. Only Buridan's hypothetical example of the exchange of verbal thanks for a gift of £10 comes close to it.[18] The poet has also created an extreme contrast between the methods by which the respective winnings are acquired: the lord's hunting spoils are won by dint of long and energetic physical effort, while Gawain's kisses are accumulated as he lies comfortably in bed. Yet this difference is not allowed to determine their worth. When the question of cost is raised by the lord on the third day (Gawain's three kisses represent an impressive profit '3if 3e hade goud chepez': 1939) – Gawain evades the question ('of þe chepe no charg': 1940). The 'labour and costs' theory of comparative value is invoked only to be serenely (and wisely, according to the lights of modern economists) dismissed. The question of value is kept within the confines of the exchange itself.

Turning our attention to the objects themselves, it seems at first that the venison is obviously the more valuable, since it has what can be called an 'objective' utility, accessible and beneficial to the majority of potential consumers, while the kiss has only a 'subjective' value in the sense that it is dependent on the attitude of the individual receiver.[19] The value of the venison appears to be more stable in that it appears to inhere in the object itself, rather than in the unpredictable responses of the consumer. Moreover, a kiss does not remain constant through a series of exchanges; when given by Gawain to the lord it is a very different thing from a kiss offered by a lady to Gawain. This point is comically and paradoxically emphasised by Gawain's scrupulous efforts to reproduce as exactly as possible the kiss he has received:

He hasppez his fayre hals his armez wythinne,
And kysses hym as comlyly as he couþe awyse . . .

(1388–9)

The harder Gawain tries, the more it becomes apparent that the value of the kiss he bestows cannot be intrinsically the same as that of the one he received. One could say that it has a purely 'notional' value, such as is possessed by paper money; its value is referential, guaranteed by the original it represents as paper money is guaranteed by gold.[20] However, even the value of the original kiss would have depended on the identity of its bestower, as the lord points out:

'Hit is god,' quoþ þe godmon, 'grant mercy þerfore.
Hit may be such hit is þe better, and 3e me breue wolde
Where 3e wan þis ilk wele bi wytte of yorseluen.'

(1392–4)

A kiss from a serving-wench is not as valuable as a kiss from a lady; a kiss from an ugly woman not as valuable as a kiss from a pretty one; a kiss from a stranger not as valuable as a kiss from a woman one loves . . .[21] But, as modern economists point out, a distinction between 'objective' and 'subjective' value is both naive and misleading – and their opinion was shared by the *Gawain*-poet. The desiderated commodity and the desiderating consumer are inseparable elements in the attribution of value; one cannot say that it is the desire in the consumer that creates desirability in the object, or the desirability in the object that arouses desire in the consumer. The *Gawain*-poet uses the freedom offered by the world of romance to construct an artificial situation which wittily opposes the two kinds of value – but which collapses the opposition as soon as it is perceived. For if the kiss has no 'objective' value for the lord (as it might have if passed on by a woman), the venison has no 'subjective' value for Gawain; he cannot eat it, store it, take it away. Despite its solid substantiality, his 'profit' remains purely notional.[22] And despite the apparent disadvantages of 'subjective' value, illustrated in the uncertain and elusive worth of the kiss, the exchange of winnings demonstrates how indispensable is the role of the subjective element. For even the 'objective' utility of the hunting-spoils needs to be realised in Gawain's subjective 'appreciation' of them. It is here that the connection between 'prys' and 'prayse' assumes significance, emerging in the alliterating cluster of words expressing Gawain's admiration for the boar killed by the lord on the second day:

> þat oþer knyȝt ful comly comended his dedez,
> And praysed hit as gret prys þat he proued hade . . .
> þenne hondeled þay þe hoge hed, þe hende mon hit praysed,
> And let lodly þerat þe lorde for to here.
>
> (1629–30, 1633–4)

The lord's 'prys' is 'proued' first in the boar itself, and then in Gawain's praise of it; they are the external manifestations of, and testimonies to, the lord's worth. Gawain's praise establishes the value of the lord's offering, despite the fact that it is of no objective utility to him. And similarly, the lord's admiration for the kisses is sufficient to establish their value as equal and in his view superior to that of his own offerings. On the third and last day he proclaims himself vanquished; his 'foule fox felle' is 'ful pore for to pay for suche prys þinges/ . . . suche þre cosses/so gode' (1945–7). This time it is his own gift which is redeemed by the function of the exchange that makes it equal in worth to such treasures.

It is the exchange alone, which makes the different types of 'winnings' commensurable in value, creates a 'proportionate equivalence' between the two – as Gawain implies when on the second day he gives the lord his two kisses with the comment 'Now ar we euen' (1641). It is the exchange which

guarantees the equivalence of the worth *attributed to*, not inherent in, the
respective winnings, since it implies a judgement of such equivalence in the
minds of the consenting parties. So far, the exchange conforms impeccably
to the classic model, on the basis of which the poet must have worked
out his own bizarre demonstration of the magic power of the exchange to
realise a commensurable value in commodities of the most heterogeneous
sort.

Yet the more we see the exchange as the only means by which the relative
value of kisses and venison can be established, the more we become aware
that it diverges from the classical model in one crucial aspect – that is, in the
absence of *indigentia* as its motivating force. The agreement to exchange is
not instigated by the need of either party (even if we take the term in
Buridan's extended sense). It *could* not be, for at the time the bargain is made,
neither of the parties to it knows what the next day's winnings will be, and is
thus not in a position to calculate the level of his own desire for the objects
to be exchanged. We cannot therefore explain or justify the 'proportionate
equivalence' of the exchange by reference to the role of *indigentia*. There are
important strategic reasons behind the creation of this non-realistic, 'pure'
exchange: to remove the unifying force of *indigentia* revives our sense of the
heterogeneity of the goods which that unifying force can hold on the same
scale, and brings the central problem of defining the nature of value into
focus. The 'exchange of winnings' sequence thus equips us with some ideas –
albeit doubtful and conflicting ones – about the different ways of defining
value, and in particular about the double nature of 'prys' – subjective and
objective, internal and external. It is these ideas which we are to carry with
us into the rest of the poem.

The question of 'prys' looms large in the bedroom conversations between
Gawain and the lady of the castle, where the word itself becomes a weapon
in a duel of wits. It is first used by Gawain in a conventional formula of
politeness: he calls the lady 'youre prys' ('your excellence': 1247). The lady
immediately seizes on the word, and insists that the 'prys' is not hers but his:

> 'In god fayth, Sir Gawayn,' quoþ þe gay lady,
> 'þe prys and þe prowes þat plesez al oþer,
> If I hit lakked oþer set at lyȝt, hit were littel daynté;
> Bot hit ar ladyes innoȝe þat leuer wer nowþe
> Haf þe, hende, in hor holde, as I þe habbe here,
> To daly with derely your daynté wordez,
> Keuer hem comfort and colen her carez,
> þen much of þe garysoun oþer golde þat þay hauen.
> Bot I louue þat ilk lorde þat þe lyfte haldez,
> I haf hit holly in my honde þat al desyres, purȝe grace.'

(1247–58)

The lady's speech brings to the forefront of the poem the question it is designed to raise and to answer: what is Gawain's 'prys', and how is it established? The lady is aware that exchange measures value, and invents a hypothetical exchange by which to evaluate the worth of Gawain's company (as in the exchange of winnings, the insubstantial – 'daynté wordez' – is held to outweigh in value objects of a more solidly material sort – 'garysoun oþer golde'). The lady also shows herself a good medieval economist in her consiousness that 'prys' is established by *indigentia* in the sense of 'demand'; the value of Gawain's company is determined by the simple fact that all women desire it. As in the exchange of winnings, 'prys' is guaranteed by praise – the connection between the two having already been established by the description of the enthusiastic response to Gawain's first rival at the castle:

> . . . alle *prys* and prowes and pured þewes
> Apendes to hys persoun, and *praysed* is euer;
> Byfore alle men vpon molde his mensk is þe most.
>
> (912–14)

The praise follows on the 'prys' (in the sense of 'worth'), but it also *is* the 'prys' (in the sense of 'renown'). The lady's first remarks to Gawain put a similar emphasis on universal praise as the basis of his reputation:

> 'For I wene wel, iwysse, Sir Wowen ȝe are,
> þat alle þe worlde worchipez quere-so ȝe ride;
> Your honour, your hendelayk is hendely praysed
> With lordez, wyth ladyes, with alle at lyf bere.'
>
> (1226–9)

Gawain's response to the lady's flattery is to protest that the honour bestowed on him by the world in general and the lady in particular reflects not so much his own intrinsic value, as the honourable worth of the lady (in the terms used earlier, he protests that it is purely 'subjective'). His own merits are 'no match for' their praise, and the exchange is therefore 'uneuen':

> '. . . þe daynté þat þay delen, for my disert nys euen,
> Hit is þe worchyp of yourself, þat noȝt bot wel connez.'
>
> (1266–7)

The lady rejects this emphatically, asserting that her own experience has shown that the valued qualities are inherent in the admired object, and not just in the imagination of the admirer:

> 'Bi Mary', quoþ þe menskful, 'me þynk hit an oþer;
> For were I worth al þe wone of wymmen alyue,

And al þe wele of þe worlde were in my honde,
And I schulde chepen and chose to cheue me a lorde,
For þe costes þat I haf knowen vpon þe, kny3t, here,
Of bewté and debonerté and blyþe semblaunt,
And þat I haf er herkkened and halde hit here trwee,
þer schulde no freke vpon folde bifore yow be chosen.'

(1268–75)

She inverts another hypothetical market exchange to establish Gawain's value
– were she in herself worth all the women alive, and the possessor of all the
world's wealth besides, she could not 'barter' herself for a better husband than
him. Gawain repeats his insistence that this high valuation is a mere subjective
whim on her part – while delicately reminding her that so far as she is
concerned, the marital bartering process is over:

'Iwysse, worþy,' quoþ þe wy3e, '3e haf waled wel better,
Bot I am proude of þe prys þat 3e put on me . . .'

(1276–7)

I do not think that this reply reveals Gawain falling prey to the temptation
to value himself at the flatteringly high rate the lady attributes to him, or that
'he finally believes that value is subjective only and takes thus the making of
his life into his own hands'.[23] On the contrary, his remark constitutes a
humble acknowledgement that his 'prys' is not his to determine; it is for
others to furnish the 'proof' of his value by their praise. But his clear-sighted
insistence on the importance of the subjective response in establishing value
opens up a gap between 'prys' as inner worth and 'prys' as outer reputation;
he refuses to identify himself with the Gawain who figures in the gossip
picked up by the lady. He needs to do this because the lady is herself
opening up such a gap for her own ends. In the conversations that follow,
she projects his 'prys' as a reputation for philandering and ubiquitous
gallantries, rather than a renown for 'clannes' and 'trawþe' (1512–29). And so
far from resulting from Gawain's behaviour, this reputation is used to
determine it: at the end of the first interview, she doubts whether he is, in
fact, Gawain ('Bot þat 3e be Gawan, hit gotz in mynde': 1293), since 'So god
as Gawayn gaynly is halden' could not have failed to beg a kiss from her
(1297–1301). Gawain's insistence that his 'prys' has its source in others, not
himself, is to a large extent motivated by his desire to dissociate himself from
this false definition of what constitutes his 'worth'.

The problem posed by this scene is thus more complex than the question
of whether Gawain will be able to resist the lady's demands. It is the problem
of the relative roles played by Gawain's inward quality and his outward
reputation in defining his 'prys'. Modern high-mindedness might incline to

disregard reputation altogether, but the market-imagery of the poem
forestalls this hasty conclusion. Desire is as necessary an element in the
creation of value as desirability; what people think of Gawain, and
what they consider desirable in him, are not irrelevant to his 'prys'. If
Gawain were universally scorned and belittled, could he be said to have
'prys' at all? 'What's aught but as 'tis valued?' – as Shakespeare's Troilus puts
it (in a play which also shows the influence of the *Ethics*). If gold were
universally scorned, it would be of no value. On the other hand, if there
is a generalised 'demand' for skill in 'luf-talkyng' and flirtatious gallantries,
do not these qualities become *ipso facto* valuable? If we argue that
Gawain's 'prys' is *simply* his inward worth, as he himself defines it, we
appear to be insisting on a naive theory of 'objective' value which ignores
the realities of the market in favour of an idealistic belief in inherent
worth.

Gawain, however, resists the lady's suggestions that he adapt his sense of
his own worth in terms of a prevailing demand. He clings desperately to his
own sense of his 'prys', both in the bedroom scenes and also when he is
faced with the guide's suggestion that he run away from the encounter with
the Green Knight. 'If I ran away' he says 'I *would be* a coward' ('I were a
knyȝt kowarde': 2131) – even if no-one ever knew about it. It seems that the
irrelevance of reputation to fundamental worth could hardly be more
uncompromisingly expressed. And the definition of this worth also seems to
be developed in isolation from the rest of the community; the comments of
the other knights at Gawain's departure from Arthur's court suggests that
they see the exploit as folly rather than heroism (674–83). If this were all, we
could conclude that the poet was endorsing Gawain's faith in his own
private, individual definition of 'prys', in eccentric defiance of market demand
– that outward reputation was being discarded as irrelevant and unimportant.
But matters are not so simple. For what is being defended in this solitary
quest *is* reputation – the 'renoun' or 'los' of the Round Table (258, 313; cf.
2457–8), which the Green Knight wished to have substantiated. Gawain's
acceptance of the Green Knight's challenge makes it clear that renown is not
merely derivative of prowess; it is an external standard against which the
knight may measure his worth, an outer mould within which knightly
endeavour may shape itself. A knight's 'prys' is the result of a collaboration
between inward worth and outward renown[24]; his 'trawþe' – the integrity or
'wholeness' imaged in the pentangle – commits him to the attempt to keep
the two in matching harmony. The values expressed in the device of the
pentangle are externalised in order that Gawain may match himself to their
high standards, even more than to show that in the past he has done so.
Gawain is thus not only concerned that his reputation should accurately
match his inward state (as with his final confessions), he is also concerned
that he should match his reputation: he is sensitive to any suggestion that he
is falling short of it – such as the lady's reproach 'Bot þat ȝe be Gawan, hit

gotz in mynde' (1293), or the Green Knight's taunt 'þou art not Gawayn . . . þat is so goud halden' (2270).

This concern for 'prys' in both senses explains the complicated shifts in the re-definitions of the value of the girdle as the poem moves to its close. At its first appearance, Gawain prizes it very highly as a 'juel' (1856). He is persuaded to think his motives for taking it honourable by his previous rejection of the 'objectively' valuable ring, thus succumbing to the suggestion that subjective value is unimportant. It is only 'þe jopardé þat hym jugged were' (1856) that gives the girdle the value of a 'juel' *for him*; others have no need of its protection so no-one will suffer loss if he takes it. 'Need' raises its head for the first and last time – and paradoxically it motivates the only unfair exchange in the poem; Gawain takes the girdle knowing that he will not render it to the lord at the end of the day. Gawain is not to know, of course, that the girdle is the poem's most glaring example of 'subjective value' in the sense that its life-saving powers appear to exist entirely in Gawain's mind; they are attributed to and not inherent in it. Since the value of the girdle is subjective, it can shift dramatically when the Green Knight makes his revelation, and Gawain's private decision to default on the exchange of winnings is brought into the public domain. Gawain is first made conscious of his fault through its externalisation; while his inner conscience acts as its own imaginary 'audience' in respect of the exchange of blows, it is less vigilant in the apparently more frivolous context of the exchange of winnings. But as soon as he sees himself reflected in the Green Knight's gaze, Gawain acknowledges the stain on his inward worth. The girdle thus becomes the visible sign of his invisible loss of 'prys'; he declares he will wear it as a corrective of 'renoun' (2434). For the Green Knight, however, Gawain's flaw disappears, paradoxically, as soon as it is externalised – first, in the nick on his neck, and second, in his frank 'confession':

> 'I halde it hardily hole, þe harme þat I hade.
> þou art confessed so clene, beknowen of þy mysses,
> And hatz þe penaunce apert of þe poynt of myn egge,
> I halde þe polysed of þat plyȝt, and pured as clene
> As þou hadez neuer forfeted syþen þou watz fyrst borne.'
>
> (2390–4)

These outward manifestations mend the rupture between inner state and external appearance, make them once again 'match' each other. The integrity of Gawain's 'prys' is recreated – as is confirmed by the symbolic healing of the nick on his neck during his journey home ('þe hurt watz hole þat he hade hent in his nek': 2484). But Gawain's inner state must then be externalised once again for the benefit of his fellow knights, and he uses both the scar and the girdle as means to this externalisation.

'þis is þe token of vntrawþe·þat I am tan inne,
And I mot nedez hit were wyle I may last;
For mon may hyden his harme, bot vnhap ne may hit,
For þer hit onez is tachched twynne wil hit neuer.'

(2509–12)

The second confession, like the first, re-creates a continuum between inner
state and outward reputation; Gawain's 'prys' is redefined for the court. And
so the value attached to the girdle can be altered yet again. The court's
brilliantly imaginative and tactful reaction empties it of its significance as a
badge of shame; they wear such a girdle as an *honour* –

For þat watz acorded þe renoun of þe Rounde Table.

(2519)

What Gawain considers 'blame' the other knights consider 'renoun'; the
discrepancy is not cynical but reflects an awareness of the role of the valuer
in creating value. Gawain's 'prys' is not to be established by himself alone; it
is by the community as a whole that it is to be fixed. And for them, to have
only so small a fault is a state to be desired. As the nick on Gawain's neck
heals, so the 'wounding' significance of the girdle disappears as it is absorbed
into the wholeness of the Round Table. There is no attempt to conceal or to
dismiss Gawain's one failure, but its significance shifts as it is evaluated by
the outside world. And it is only in this communal context – in the fixing of
'prys' as 'renoun' – that Gawain's value is externalised and stabilised. The end
of the poem re-affirms the importance of renown as the external definition of
'prys' – as the beginning and end of a long and subtle commerce between the
internal and the external through which value is not merely recognised but is
realised.

Gawain's 'prys' is identified with his 'trawþe', its worth imaged in the 'pure
golde hwez' of the pentangle. When he takes the girdle, he 'exchanges' for it
his 'trawþe'. In the privacy of his own thoughts, he counts the cost a small
one; it is only when the watching gaze of a concealed audience is revealed to
him – when his inner state is mirrored in outward fame – that he takes the
true measure of his 'losse' (2507). I should now like to make some more
speculative suggestions about the role of 'trawþe' in the exchanges of the
poem.

Truth cannot be the object of exchange, since it is one of the 'goods of the
soul' which, Buridan argues, are by nature insusceptible of valuation in terms
of external goods, because they are 'ends in themselves' ('fines ipsorum')[25] – a
definition nicely matched in the self-enclosed impenetrability of the pentangle.
How, then, is its value to be established? Only, I think, by the negative route
taken in its exchange for the girdle – that is, by estimating the cost of its *loss*.

The method has some similarities with that by which medieval commentators argued for the 'value' of items such as air and water, which were not scarce, were not sold for a high price, and yet were of the greatest value for human existence. The value of such goods, it was said, can be measured by the value that men would place on them if they lacked them; it depends on imagining a 'demand which might have been'.[26] The *Gawain*-poet, we may say, imagines something like a 'demand which might have been' for 'trawþe'. The exchange of blows makes it quite clear that had Gawain abandoned 'trawþe' entirely, he would have lost his head. Its 'worth' is thus realised in the preservation of his life.

The explanation usually given for Gawain's acceptance of the girdle and surrendering his 'trawþe' for so poor a return is that he succumbs to a desire for life; this interpretation is supported by the Green Knight's comments at 2367–8. But as a knight, Gawain risks his life daily, against human and non-human foes. Why should he give way to cowardice in this particular instance? (The fact that he flinches at the first swing of the axe suggests that his faith in the girdle has evaporated by the time he confronts the Green Knight, so that he is proved both to possess and to exercise the courage necessary for the ordeal.) I would suggest that in this particular instance Gawain is under pressure not merely from his physical fear – which he can and does master – but also from an intellectual rebelliousness. That is, he is driven to take the girdle by his consciousness that the initial agreement is unfair, and is tempted to *equalise the exchange* – to match the magic powers of the Green Knight with his own. For the exchange of blows is unlike the exchange of winnings in that it involves an exact (rather than a 'proportionately equivalent') return – the return of one blow for another being the classic example of simple *contrapassum* in both the *Ethics* and the medieval commentaries on it.[27] In *Gawain*, however, the ostensible fairness of the exact exchange conceals an underlying imbalance: the Green Knight can replace his head if cut off, but Gawain cannot. That Gawain himself is only too conscious of this monstrous inequality in the exchange becomes clear when the Green Knight tauntingly contrasts his own steady endurance of the axe-blow with Gawain's flinching, and receives the tight-lipped rejoinder:

'. . . þaȝ my hede falle on þe stonez,
I con not hit restore.'

(2282–3)

So that when Gawain takes the girdle, it seems to even up the exchange, to create the 'tit-for-tat' correspondence which the Green Knight infuriatingly pretends that it represents.

The exchange of blows is thus not only an excellent illustration of simple *contrapassum*, but also of Aristotle's argument that simple *contrapassum* is not *ipso facto* just. Aristotle himself gives as an example the difference between a

ruler striking one of his subjects (in his official capacity) and a subject striking
his ruler (in an unofficial capacity) – an example which seems to have been
translated into extreme and melodramatic terms by the *Gawain*-poet, so that
the point is made in the absolute way which only the romance allows.[28]
Gawain is held to the exchange of blows not because its terms are (as the
Green Knight pretends) just, but because he has agreed to it; as with the
exchange of winnings, the agreement to exchange of itself creates an
equivalence between the two sides. 'Trawþe' takes over the role of need as
the regulator of exchange; it is the matching honesty on both sides that
makes the exchange 'euen' (1641). This balancing role of truth creates a
contrapassum which *is* just, expressed in the Green Knight's words to Gawain:

> Trwe mon trwe restore
> þenne þar mon drede no waþe.
>
> (2354–5)

Truth cannot be exchanged for external goods, but it *can* be exchanged for
itself. Like the kiss, it 'returns itself, pays its own debt, and keeps its own
balance'.[29] The exchange of winnings lies behind the exchange of blows,
controlling and determining its outcome by an invisible power. To perceive
the shadowy presence of the one behind the other teaches us to perceive yet
another shadow beyond both – the exchange of 'trawþe' which fills the
apparently futile or frivolous bargaining with serious meaning. The 'need' in
the exchange is not a need for the goods exchanged; it is a need for 'trawþe',
and 'trawþe' alone.

It is therefore in the form, not the content, of the bargain that its
equilibrium is to be found. In the exchange of blows as in the exchange of
winnings, punctiliousness in keeping to the terms of the bargain must be
accompanied by insouciance as to the inequality in their realisation. When
Gawain reproaches himself, at the end of the poem, with having abandoned
'larges and lewté þat longez to knyȝtez' (2381), he puts his finger on the
twin qualities that the exchange calls for – 'lewté' in the scrupulous fulfilment
of exchange, 'larges' in the uncalculating nature of the initial agreement.
Profit and loss are to be determined by chance; acceptance of the riskiness of
the enterprise is a condition of the bargain.

Thus if the poet removes the role of need in stimulating exchange, it is to
get nearer to the fundamental realities of mercantile life, not to negate them.
For the merchant sending his argosies to the sea commits himself, like the
knight, to the vagaries of chance, allowing it to determine his final balance of
profit and loss, to make him 'even now worth this,/And now worth nothing'.[30]
The line describing the second agreement to exchange winnings – 'Wat
chaunce so bytydez hor cheuysaunce to chaunge' (1406) – is a beautiful
embodiment of this overlap between the mercantile and the knightly; the
knightly bravado of the first half of the line informs the mercantile

phraseology of the second, so that we feel both 'larges' and 'lewté' in it, and feel them to be characteristic of both classes. The merchant values 'trawþe' as highly as the knight – for him too, his word is his bond. He too treasures his reputation, as the source of his credit, his 'worth'. He understands as well as the knight does the intangible and elusive nature of 'prys', and shares a reverence for the gold and jewels which are mysteriously agreed to possess it, though they minister to no bodily comforts. If the merchant of the parable is so well able to understand the value of the 'pearl of great price' that he surrenders all he has in order to possess it, then the real-life merchant will well understand Gawain's willingness to sacrifice everything for the sake of the 'trawþe' that gives him the value of a pearl.

This overlay of knightly and mercantile values suggests that the audience for which the poem was intended was not an exclusively courtly one – that the poet was speaking to both classes, and attempting to create an ideal to which both could aspire. The obvious location for such an audience of sophisticated and wealthy merchants and knights in the late fourteenth century is London – and the last twenty years of that century saw indeed the creation of merchant-knights who in themselves embodied the fusion adumbrated in the poem. My analysis of the poem may therefore lend literary support (though not of course proof) to the theory, originally advanced on historical grounds, that London is the likeliest location for its audience.[31] If the *Gawain*-poet was acquainted with Aristotle's theory of value and the medieval commentaries on it – as I believe we must conclude he was – then it is most probable that he himself was a cleric and a scholar. But if so, he put his clerkly learning to good use in the imaginative creation of a romance world which could act as a model for both knights and merchants and harmonise the potential conflict between them. So far from seeing the commercial world as contaminating knightly values, he accords it an equal dignity, and takes its realities as the firm basis on which to build his ideal of knightly 'prys'.

Notes

1. All quotations from the poem are taken from the edition by J.R.R. Tolkien and E.V. Gordon, revised by Norman Davis (Oxford, 1967).

2. *A Concordance to Five Middle English Poems*, ed. Barnet Kottler and Alan M. Markman (Pittsburgh, 1966).

3. R.A. Shoaf, *The Poem as Green Girdle: Commercium in Sir Gawain and the Green Knight* (Gainesville, Florida, 1984); for earlier discussions of the commercial imagery in the poem, see note 2 to Shoaf's Introduction, p. 81.

4. A full list of words belonging to the linguistic register of trade and commerce is provided in Shoaf's Appendix, pp. 77–80. I agree with Shoaf (pp. 55–6) that the word 'cost' is drawn into this linguistic field although technically it is a different word from 'cost' meaning 'expense' (see MED, s.v. cost, n. [1] and [2]); it suggests

its homonym by a quasi-pun. Cf. also P.B. TAYLOR, 'Commerce and Comedy in *Sir Gawain'*, *Philological Quarterly*, **50** (1971): 1–15, at pp. 10–12.

5. TAYLOR, 'Commerce and Comedy', p. 3.

6. SHOAF, *The Poem as Green Girdle*, p. 59.

7. As does the fact that the *Gawain*-poet seems to have been the first to bring these two motifs together; see the Introduction to Tolkien and Gordon's edition, pp. xix–xx.

8. GROSSETESTE's translation exists in a 'pure' and a 'revised' version, both of which are edited by René Antoine Gauthier, *Ethica Nicomachea. Translatio Roberti Grosseteste Lincolniensis sive 'Liber Ethicorum', A. Recensio Pura; B. Recensio Recognita, Aristoteles Latinus* XXVI. 1–3, fasc. 3–4 (Leiden/Brussels, 1972–3).

9. An excellent and scholarly account of this commentary tradition is given in ODD LANGHOLM, *Price and Value in the Aristotelian Tradition* (Bergen/Oslo/Tromsø, 1979); see Langholm also for further bibliography. Langholm provides in an appendix the Latin translation of the crucial passage of *Ethics* V, 5 in Grosseteste's 'pure' version, with interlinear variants of revision. My exposition is based on this composite text; translations are my own.

10. See LANGHOLM, *Price and Value*, pp. 37–50.

11. Ibid., pp. 61–84.

12. The emphasis on *indigentia* characterises the *Ethics* commentary of Thomas Aquinas (see LANGHOLM, *Price and Value*, pp. 85–95); it was Thomas who clarified another of Aristotle's obscurities by developing the theory of the 'double measure' of value, in which the true measure, need, is reflected in terms of money, the practical measure.

13. LANGHOLM, *Price and Value*, pp. 123–7. BURIDAN's contribution to economic theory is contained in Quaestiones xiv–xvii of his commentary on *Ethics* Book V (*Quaestiones super Decem Libros Ethicorum Aristotelis ad Nicomachum*); I have consulted the Paris editions of 1513 and 1518 and the Oxford edition of 1637. For the earlier sources of these four Quaestiones, see LANGHOLM, pp. 107, 118, 125. The Stoic influence appears in Buridan's quotation of Seneca's second letter to Lucilius (*Epistulae Morales* II): 'Non qui parum habet, sed qui plus cupit, pauper est' (*Quaestiones* V. xv) – one among several Senecan quotations in the *Quaestiones*.

14. LANGHOLM, *Price and Value*, pp. 130–1.

15. Ibid., p. 155; cf. pp. 113–17.

16. Ibid., pp. 109, 125; BURIDAN, *Quaestiones* V. xvi.

17. LANGHOLM, *Price and Value*, p. 87; cf. AUGUSTINE, *De Civitate Dei* XI. 16.

18. *Quaestiones* V. xiv; Buridan explains that a rich man would need 'honour', and would therefore regard £10 as a fair exchange for it.

19. A distinction between 'objective' and 'subjective' value (termed respectively *virtuositas* and *complacibilitas*) is a feature of the value-theory of the Franciscan San Bernardino of Siena (1380–1444); see RAYMOND DE ROOVER, *San Bernardino of Siena and Sant' Antonino of Florence: The Two Great Economic Thinkers of the Middle Ages* (Boston, Mass., 1967), pp. 16–23; the terms originated with the thirteenth-century Franciscan Petrus Olivi, of Sérignan in Languedoc (LANGHOLM, *Price and Value*, pp. 115, 153–4), but his association with heresy impeded the circulation of

his ideas until they were taken over by Bernardino. It is unlikely that either could be considered a source for the *Gawain*-poet, but they show that this line of thinking was a perfectly possible development within medieval economic thought.

20. Cf. the notion of 'ascribed value' discussed in WILLIAM J. COURTENAY, 'The King and the Leaden Coin: The Economic Background of "Sine Qua Non" Causality', *Traditio*, **28** (1972): 185–209.

21. 'What is a kiss worth? It depends who has given it' (J.A. BURROW, *A Reading of Sir Gawain and the Green Knight* [London, 1965], p. 88). Burrow contrasts the kiss with the 'solid winnings' represented by the venison, and adds 'The kisses are like merchandise ('cheuicaunce'), their value conditional upon the state of the market' (ibid., pp. 88–9).

22. Cf. the comments of THOMAS D. HILL, 'Gawain's Jesting Lie: Towards an Interpretation of the Confessional Scene in *Gawain and the Green Knight*', *Studia Neophilologica*, **52** (1980): 283.

23. SHOAF, *The Poem as Green Girdle*, pp. 40–1, 42; cf. p. 63.

24. Cf. DEREK BREWER's comments in 'Honour in Chaucer', *Tradition and Innovation in Chaucer* (London/Basingstoke, 1982), p. 90.

25. *Quaestiones* V. xv.

26. LANGHOLM, *Price and Value*, pp. 138–9; the commentators in question belong to the late fourteenth and early fifteenth century, so that the *Gawain*-poet could not have known them, but he seems to have followed an analogous line of thought.

27. See, for example, BURIDAN, *Quaestiones* V. xiv.

28. An interesting hint for such an 'impossible exchange' is given in Buridan's passing reference to the theory that death is not commensurable with external goods, 'for no-one of sane mind would agree for all the money in the world that his head should be cut off' (*Quaestiones* V. xv).

29. TAYLOR, 'Commerce and Comedy', p. 5.

30. *Merchant of Venice*, I. i, 35–6.

31. MICHAEL J. BENNETT, '*Sir Gawain and the Green Knight* and the Literary Achievement of the North-West Midlands: The Historical Background', *Journal of Medieval History*, **5** (1979): 63–88; *Community, Class and Careerism: Cheshire and Lancashire Society in the Age of Sir Gawain and the Green Knight* (Cambridge, 1983), pp. 231–5. It is important to distinguish here between the *author* (who certainly, as the dialect of the poem shows, came from the north-west Midlands) and the *audience*; Bennett's case rests on the absence of any local courts important enough to have exercised literary patronage on the one hand, and on the substantial numbers of men from Cheshire and Lancashire gathered in London in the king's service on the other.

7   Leaving Morgan Aside: Women, History and Revisionism in *Sir Gawain and the Green Knight**

SHEILA FISHER

In this confident exercise in feminist revisionary critique, Fisher demonstrates the different ways in which female characters, especially Guenevere, are marginalised or silenced in *Sir Gawain and the Green Knight* as the poet tries to provide a 'proleptic cure' for Arthurian society and its eventual downfall. Moving beyond the simple study of the representation of women, Fisher uses these patterns to analyse the poem's relation to Arthurian ideology and its nostalgic displacement of women from their central place within that tradition.

The anonymous author of *Sir Gawain and the Green Knight* knew how the story would end, both the story of Arthurian history and the story of his own romance. In the end is the beginning, because the end of Arthurian legend in the collapse of the Round Table accounts for the beginning of this poem, for its motivation, its selected and selective emphases, and its design. With a knowledge of the end, the romance focuses on the beginning and on one adventure of one young knight, for this is essentially a poem about beginnings: about the New Year and the first youth of King Arthur; about the young court's solidarity and the first assumption of the pentangle by Gawain.[1] Through its emphasis on beginnings, *Sir Gawain and the Green Knight*, as I will argue in this essay, tries to revise Arthurian history in order to make it come out right. The purpose of this revisionary agenda is nothing less than to demonstrate how the Round Table might have averted its own destruction by adhering to the expectations of masculine behavior inherent in Christian chivalry.

---

* Reprinted from CHRISTOPHER BASWELL and WILLIAM SHARPE (eds), *The Passing of Arthur: New Essays in Arthurian Tradition* (New York and London: Garland Publishing, Inc., 1988), pp. 129–51.

If the end is the beginning, it also serves as the means, the poem's
directive for its revisionism. The poem alerts us to the connections between
beginnings and ends through the cyclical emphases of its narrative and
specifically through the articulations of historical betrayal and of the loss of a
civilization that frame the romance: 'þe segge and þe asaute watz sesed at
Troye' ['Since the siege and the assault was ceased at Troy'] (lines 1 and
2525).[2] Projected onto the Arthurian past, these references to historical gain,
loss, and betrayal forecast the Arthurian future. Given these narrative
emphases, it is significant that, at the end of the poem, about a hundred lines
from the closing reiteration of historical betrayal, we find Morgan le Fay,
who is here not only named for the first (and last) time, but also designated
as the generator of the romance, of the complex narrative of Gawain's
testing. For Gawain's edification, Bertilak finally reveals Morgan's presence in
the plot (and even then, once he has introduced her, it takes him ten lines
[2446–55] to get to the point):

> Ho wayned me vpon þis wyse to your wynne halle
> For to assay þe surquidré, ȝif hit soth were
> þat rennes of þe grete renoun of þe Rounde Table;
> Ho wayned me þis wonder your wyttez to reve,
> For to haf greued Gaynour and gart hir to dyȝe
> With glopnyng of þat ilke gome þat gostlych speked
> With his hede in his honde bifore þe hyȝe table.
>
> (2456–21)

> [She guided me in this guise to your glorious hall,
> To assay, if such it were, the surfeit of pride
> That is rumored of the retinue of the Round Table.
> She put this shape upon me to puzzle your wits,
> To afflict the fair queen, and frighten her to death
> With awe of that elvish man that eerily spoke
> With his head in his hand before the high table.]

Morgan's placement is not, as some critics have argued, a flaw in this
carefully constructed narrative; it is neither an accident nor an authorial
mistake.[3] The poem, as I will argue in this essay, deliberately leaves Morgan
aside, positioning her at the end of the narrative when she is, in fact, its
means: the agent of Gawain's testing.

Sir Gawain and the Green Knight marginalizes Morgan le Fay because her
marginalization is central to its own revision of Arthurian history. If, however,
we take our cue from *Sir Gawain and the Green Knight* and reread the
narrative backwards from the perspective of Morgan's agency, we can define
the trajectory and the ideology of the poem's revisionism. Morgan and her
marginalization are the means to the poem's end, because women are centrally

implicated in the collapse of the Round Table and the end of the Arthurian
Age. If women could be placed on the periphery, as Morgan is in this poem,
then the Round Table might not have fallen. To deny the female would be to
save the kingdom, and, in its revisionary agenda, that is precisely what *Sir
Gawain and the Green Knight* attempts to do. In the name of a lost but
presumably worthy cause, it attempts an uneasy, because necessarily
incomplete, erasure of women from the poem. It should not be surprising,
after all, that the poet who wrote a Christian dream-vision allegory to offer
consolation for the death of a child could write what is, in essence, a political
allegory of women's displacement to offer nostalgic consolation for the death
of Britain's greatest king.

If Pearl has gone to a New Jerusalem far removed from the transience and
decay associated with her death, Arthur and his court, in Fitt I of *Sir Gawain
and the Green Knight*, have gone to an old Camelot far removed from the later
struggles associated with its own decay and ultimate transience. As one strategy
of its revisionism, the poem focuses on a conspicuously youthful court.

> With all þe wele of þe worlde þay woned þer samen,
> þe most kyd knyȝtez vnder Krystes seluen,
> And þe louelokkest ladies þat euer lif haden,
> And he þe comlokest kyng þat þe court haldes;
> For al watz þis fayre folk in hir first age,
> > on sille,
> > þe hapnest vnder heuen,
> > Kyng hyȝest mon of wylle;
> > Hit were now gret nye to neuen
> > So hardy a here on hille.

(50–9)

> [In peerless pleasures passed they their days,
> The most noble knights known under Christ,
> And the loveliest ladies that lived on earth ever,
> And the comeliest king, that that court holds,
> For all this fair folk in their first age
> > were still,
> > Happiest of mortal kind,
> > King noblest famed of will;
> > You would now go far to find
> > So hardy a host on hill.]

Although some readers of the romance find Arthur and his retinue more
youthful, more 'childgered' (86), more 'wylde' of 'brayn' (89) than they ought
to be, still, this is, as other readers have pointed out, a court in its first blush
of youth, as green, one might say, as the giant who comes to test its pride.[4]
As such, this court is conspicuously removed from later tensions and egoisms,

from later intrigue and infighting.[5] It is thus, in the context of its own history, a prelapsarian court. And we see it, significantly enough, in the midst of its celebrations to inaugurate Christmas and the New Year: 'Wyle Nw ȝer watz so ȝep þat hit watz nwe cummen' ['While the New Year was new, but yesternight come'] (60). The triple repetition of newness in this one line (that opens the stanza immediately following the long passage quoted above) emphasizes not only the birth of Christ and the rebirth of the year, but the poem's own revisionary regeneration of Arthurian legend.

This revisionary regeneration is a central strategy in the poem's characterization – in what is essentially its rewriting – of Gawain himself. According to one well-known branch of Arthurian legend, the king's nephew is something of a womanizer. Some critics, in fact, have suggested that *Sir Gawain and the Green Knight* actually plays with this aspect of its hero's reputation by making him confront it at Morgan's castle.[6] Another way of putting this would be to say that there the sins that Gawain has not yet committed come back to haunt him. In Fitt III, Gawain stands accused of being someone he knows nothing about, to the point that both he and the Lady will agree, with some justice, that he is not Gawain (1292–3).[7] For the poem does not want its audience to believe that this is the old Gawain either. Were the hero of this romance the womanizer of legend, the problem of the pentangle's appropriateness to him and the challenge in the bedroom would both be, quite obviously, somewhat beside the point, mysteries resolved for the audience by Gawain's reputation before Gawain ever mounts Gringolet or the Lady ever mounts her assault.

If the poem's revisionary agenda is evident in the initial description of Arthur's court, the portrait of Guenevere in Fitt I both emphasizes this agenda and indicates the ways in which the positionings of women are central to it. Indeed, one of the most conspicuous signals of the work's agenda is its rehabilitation of Guenevere. Guenevere and her betrayals of her king are, of course, notorious in the dissolution of the Round Table; she is most famous, in other words, for her association with the end. In *Sir Gawain and the Green Knight*, however, Guenevere is most prominent at the beginning. There are, in fact, few subsequent references to her in the poem: we are told that she sits near (the similarly rehabilitated) Gawain at the New Year's feast (109); Arthur bids her not to be bothered by the Green Knight's talking head (470–3); we later learn that she is not so beautiful as the Lady (945). The last reference to her in the poem is the most telling, for, as Bertilak informs Gawain, the third of Morgan's motives for sending him on his mission as the Green Knight was

> For to haf greued Gaynour and gart hir to dyȝe
> With glopnyng of þat ilke gome þat gostlych speked
> With his hede in his honde bifore þe hyȝe table.

> (2460–2)

[To afflict the fair queen, and frighten her to death
With awe of that elvish man that eerily spoke
With his head in his hand before the high table.]

If Morgan had had her way, then, the beginning of the poem would be the
end of the queen. Yet, by the time this plot against Guenevere has been
revealed, it has been delayed so long, both within the narrative and within
Bertilak's list of Morgan's motivations, that it seems somewhat beside the
point. Had Morgan been successful, however, she might, some would argue,
have done her half-brother something of a favor.

With the end of its story and of Arthurian history in view, the poem can
figuratively if not literally accomplish Morgan's wishes. As she is portrayed
in Fitt I, Guenevere, in one sense, could not be more dead than she already is.
In her most detailed appearance in *Sir Gawain and the Green Knight*, she is
utterly static. She does not speak (here or elsewhere in the poem). She simply
sits and looks, and, perhaps more importantly, she is looked upon.

> Whene Guenore, fulgay, grayþed in þe myddes,
> Dressed on þe dere des, dubbed al aboute,
> Smal sendal bisides, a selure hir ouer
> Of tryed tolouse, of tars tapites innoghe,
> þat were enbrawded and beten wyth þe best gemmes
> þat myȝ be preued of prys wyth penyes to bye,
> > in daye.
> > þe comlokest to discrye
> > þer glent with ȝen gray,
> > A semloker þat euer he syȝe
> > Soth moȝt no man say.   (74–84)

[Guenevere the goodly queen gay in the midst
On a dais well-decked and duly arrayed
With costly silk curtains, a canopy over,
Of Toulouse and Turkestan tapestries rich,
All broidered and bordered with the best gems
Ever brought into Britain, with bright pennies
> to pay.
> Fair queen, without a flaw,
> She glanced with eyes of gray.
> A seemlier that once he saw,
> In truth no man could say.]

As the syntactical circlings of this passage show, it is difficult to distinguish
Guenevere and her worth from that of her splendid accoutrements. This is
Guenevere fresh from the marriage settlement in which she, like most
historical medieval women of her class, has been bought.[8] This is Guenevere

set at the high table for all to admire, a token of Arthur's wealth, still the chaste queen who is the sign and symbol of the king to whom she refers. Her rehabilitation according to the revisionist directive of *Sir Gawain and the Green Knight* is inscribed in her stasis, in her function as the emblem of Arthur. Because she seems incapable of movement, she seems incapable of the specific movement that would lead her to a treacherous union with Lancelot.

Not moving or speaking, Guenevere is here marginalized to such an extent that she is buried in the plot of the poem.[9] For, if there is never just one margin, there is never just one way to be marginalized. Morgan le Fay is marginalized within the narrative by being placed at the end of the poem. But the poem marginalizes and thereby rehabilitates Guenevere by displaying her at the beginning of its own story, as a token of Arthur, and dissociating her from the end, where, as Morgan le Fay attempts to do in this romance, she will become the agent of his destruction. It is significant, however, that the initial description of Guenevere is placed as close to the opening mention of historical betrayal as Morgan's agency is placed to the closing repetition of 'þe segge and þe asaute . . . at Troye'. And it is significant, too, that when Guenevere *is* mentioned at the end of *Sir Gawain and the Green Knight*, a desire for her death as well as her own capacity for destruction are projected on to the single figure of Morgan le Fay.

Guenevere and Morgan may be marginalized in very different ways at the beginning and end of the poem, but there is always, of course, the Lady in the middle. In a romance that makes much of beginnings and ends because it is concerned with the end of beginnings, the Lady's placement squarely at the poem's center is significant for many reasons. If Morgan is the means to the end of trying young Gawain (and, by extension, the pride of the Round Table), then the Lady is a stand-in for Morgan, in the middle, literally and figuratively, as Morgan's intermediary, despite Bertilak's rather suspicious attempt in Fitt IV to claim her as *his* agent.[10] Bertilak tells Gawain:

> Now know I wel þy cosses, and þy costes als,
> And þe wowyng of my wyf; I wroȝt hit myseluen.
> I sende hir to asay þe. . . .   (2360–2)

> [I know well the tale,
> And the count of your kisses and your conduct too,
> And the wooing of my wife – it was all my scheme!]

Although sex with her may temporarily seem an end in itself, it is, or would be, a means to the end of trying young Gawain. Moreover, it is no accident that one of the few references to Guenevere comes when Gawain sees the Lady for the first time:

> Ho watz þe fayrest in felle, of flesche and of lyre,
> And of compas and colour and costes, of alle o þer,

And wener þen Wenore, as þe wyȝe þoȝt.
He ches þurȝ þe chaunsel to cheryche þat hende.
An oþer lady hir lad bi þe lyft honde,
þat watz alder þen ho, an auncian hit semed . . . .

(943–8)

[The fair hues of her flesh, her face and her hair
And her body and her bearing were beyond praise,
And excelled the queen herself, as Sir Gawain thought.
He goes forth to greet her with gracious intent;
Another lady led her by the left hand
That was older than she – an ancient, it seemed. . . .]

This reference to Guenevere is not simply a conventional aesthetic observation.[11] As the construction of this passage shows, it serves to underline the Lady's placement between two marginalized females, Morgan and Guenevere, because she, the woman textually and sexually in the middle, is the common denominator between them.

If the Lady is the common denominator between these two female characters, what she denominates is, in essence, femaleness itself. Nor is this definition of the Lady so obvious, nor so reductive, as it would at first seem. And while it may seem strange to make much of Morgan's marginalization when the Lady is at the center of the poem, it is the nature of the femaleness ascribed to and designated by the Lady, and shared by both Guenevere and Morgan, that needs marginalizing if *Sir Gawain and the Green Knight* is to succeed in its Christian chivalric revision of Arthurian history. For, rather than contradicting the poem's agenda of leaving the female aside, the centrality of the Lady works to underline the poem's purpose. Situated as she is between Guenevere in Fitt I and Morgan in Fitt IV, the Lady is, as Gilbert and Gubar would define it, 'framed' within the poem.[12] That is, she is both enclosed and 'set up', as it were, in the poem's effort to contain and delimit her meaning. The Lady is contained and redefined in the text so that Gawain can be reintegrated, green girdle and all, into the reconstituted court at Camelot.

Indeed, containment, it seems, is the essence of the Lady who is always situated within and associated with enclosed and private spaces. We see the Lady first entering the closet in which she hears Mass on the first day of Gawain's stay in the castle: 'þe lorde loutes þerto, and þe lady als, / Into a cumly closet coyntly ho entrez' ['The lord attends alone: his fair lady sits / In a comely closet, secluded from sight'] (933–4). The poet's choice of the adverb 'coyntly' to describe her entrance into the private space of the closet suggests to readers of Chaucer the famous pun on 'queynte' as female genitalia, which marks the Wife of Bath's characterization of herself in her prologue.[13] Interestingly, Gawain repeats this adverb again at the beginning of his anti-feminist diatribe: 'þus hor knyȝt wyth hor kest han *koyntly* bigyled' ['They have trapped their true knight in their trammels so quaint'] (2412; emphasis mine). When the Lady emerges from the closet, with her retinue of ladies and with Morgan le Fay some eight lines later, one hardly needs to invoke Freud to catch the associations with female sexuality that the poem is making. And, of course, the Lady's most famous activities within private enclosed spaces occur not merely in Gawain's bedroom, but inside the curtains of Gawain's bed: 'and ho stepped stilly and stel to his bedde, / Kest up þe cortyn and creped withinne' ['And she stepped stealthily, and stole to his bed, / Cast aside the curtain and came within'] (1191–2).

The Lady, it might seem, can exercise considerable power even within such containment. But the containment of the Lady within the castle or the closet or the bedroom echoes her containment within the text, a containment that, while it places the Lady at the center, simultaneously underlines her marginalization. She is, as we will see, placed at the center in order to be displaced from it. And it is here that, in order to accomplish its revision of Arthurian legend, the poem takes as its model late medieval social and legal history. For, like her historical counterpart, the medieval noblewoman, the Lady is contained within the castle in order, finally, to be marginalized within aristocratic society.[14] She is so marginalized, in fact, that a poem that names everything, including Gawain's horse Gringolet, never names her. She has no ostensible existence outside the castle walls unless a man chooses to name her (Bertilak generally calls her 'myn owen wyf' [2359] or 'my wyf' [2361] as if to underline his ownership; Gawain mentions her as little as he can [2497]). She is simply the Lady. That is all there is to know and all we need to know.[15]

Contained as she is within the castle and the poem, the Lady and the femaleness she shares with Guenevere and Morgan become fundamentally associated with privateness. The Lady is associated with privateness because that is the realm she inhabits. But she is so thoroughly associated with privateness, that privateness itself becomes feminized in *Sir Gawain and the Green Knight*. Certainly, her privateness is linked to female sexuality, as the possible pun on 'coyntly' suggests. The dangers associated with the Lady, the threat she poses to Gawain's life, may ultimately derive from this source and from the poem's inscription of the otherness of female sexuality according to the time-honored tradition of medieval misogyny.[16] But *Sir Gawain and the Green Knight* goes even farther, I believe, in order to suggest the political and social implications of the female's privateness and the fundamental disruptiveness attributed to the female and to the values associated with her in this poem. For it is through the redefinition of this privateness and of the emblematic girdle that the poem accomplishes its revision of Arthurian legend and provides a model of masculine behavior by which the Round Table might have been saved.

As the course of Arthurian history and of chivalric literature makes clear, trouble arises when the knight withdraws from public life to fulfill private desire, when the knight yields to private desire at the expense of public function. And Gawain, with his pentangle and armor locked away somewhere in one of this castle's many private rooms, is in such a precarious situation from the moment that he enters Morgan's castle in Fitt II. The plot of the romance has relegated him to privateness to test how he fares there, for the temptations posed by private desire are essentially the ones that Gawain must overcome both to save his life and to ensure the preservation and continuation of the Arthurian world.[17]

Gawain, in assuming the Green Knight's challenge at Camelot, has ceased to be a private individual. He has assumed the responsibility of acting as a token of Arthur's fame and reputation. In this capacity, he has no room for private desires, or at the very least, his private desires must be trained to the service of the public good. Indeed, when Gawain claims the test, he does so on the basis of relationship to Arthur, who is both his uncle and his king: 'Bot for as much as ʒe ar myn em I am only to prayse, / No bounté bot your blod in my bodé knowe' ['That I have you for my uncle is my only praise; / My body, but for your blood, is barren of worth'] (356–7). There can be no more concise statement of the alignment of public and private in the worthy knight than Gawain articulates here. Arthur is in him; he stands for Arthur; and thus he publicizes his king and kingdom in the testings he undertakes. And this, then, is also the meaning of the pentangle, each of whose five interlocked points refers to the way the individual male's private virtues are inextricably interwoven with the public systems of belief, the ideologies, of Christianity and chivalry. The pentangle is a sign of the private male's conscription into the public order. The interconnectedness of these virtues underlines, then, the religious and political stability that would result from adherence to the values encoded in the pentangle.[18]

For Gawain to yield to the Lady would, in fact, involve more than yielding to the otherness of her sexuality. Implied in that yielding to otherness would be the Round Table knight's capitulation to privateness, to private desire, and to the feminization of the private that has been inscribed in this poem. But this romance's rehabilitated Gawain will not yield to mere sexual desire, despite his attraction to the Lady. Certainly, the confrontation at the Green Chapel preoccupies him, perhaps more than his agreement to exchange winnings with his host, and in its own terms, this preoccupation is understandable enough. At this point, however, the poem's revision of Gawain's often spotted past is especially telling. Unlike the Gawain of legend, and even more significantly, unlike Lancelot, this Gawain will not give in to the temptation of mere female flesh, even when, as we have been told, it is lovelier than Guenevere's. At this early stage of the Round Table's career, Gawain is a stronger knight than Lancelot will turn out to be. Gawain is too publically committed to take his private pleasure and to betray his vows to men, that is, to his king or to his unnamed host, until, indeed, he thinks that his life depends on it.[19]

And then Gawain fails and falls, but not so badly nor so far that the poem cannot reinstate him in its attempt to restore a prelapsarian Camelot. Gawain does not err because of desire for the Lady's body or because of the temptation of her or his sexuality. Rather, he falls because he yields to the desire to save his life, once he has learned of the magical properties inherent in the girdle:

þen kest þe kny3t, and hit come to his hert
Hit were a juel for þe jopardé þat hym iugged were:
When he acheued to þe chapel his chek for to fech,
My3t he haf slypped to be vnslayn, þe sle3t were noble.

(1855–81)

[Then the man began to muse, and mainly he thought
It was a pearl for his plight, the peril to come
When he gains the Green Chapel to get his reward:
Could he escape unscathed, the scheme were noble!]

This is, we might think, a natural enough desire, just as Gawain does at the moment and as Bertilak does later at the Green Chapel, when he judges Gawain:

Bot here yow lakked a lyttel, sir, and lewté yow wonted;
Bot þat watz for no wylyde werke, ne wowyng nau þer,
Bot for 3e lufed your lyf; þe lasse I yow blame.

(2366–8)

[Yet you lacked, sir, a little in loyalty there,
But the cause was not cunning, nor courtship either,
But that you loved your own life; the less, then, to blame.]

But this yielding is particularly dangerous because the desire for life might well be the most natural and instinctive of all. As such, it is the private desire that includes all others within it. To yield to this desire might be only the beginning.

What is more, in political terms, to yield to this desire would spell the end of Arthur's kingdom, of its famous prowess, of its military strength. What would happen, after all, if members of the Round Table, individually and collectively, succumbed repeatedly to the desire to preserve their lives? Gawain may be over-reacting when he speaks later of his 'cowarddyse and couetyse' (2374), but he is not entirely wrong. To assume the girdle, as the poem states, 'for gode of hymseluen' (2031) is to think primarily of himself. It is to think not of the kingdom's reputation, of its security and solidarity, but of his private desire; it is, in essence, an act of cowardice in which Gawain also shows himself

147

more greedy than he ought to be to save his own private neck.[20] In the feudal and chivalric world of this romance, a man's desire to save his life might be understandable, but wanting 'lewte' is no minor political transgression.

The girdle initially signifies life, and specifically Gawain's desire to save his own. Because this private desire is linked in *Sir Gawain and the Green Knight* to the privateness that is the Lady, Gawain's action implicitly betrays the masculine codes of Christian chivalry affirmed as the central values of this poem. When Bertilak has revealed the shape of the testing to Gawain, Gawain's response shows his understanding of the political, ethical, and sexual consequences of his action. Flinging the girdle back at Bertilak, he admits that desire for his life caused him 'to acorde me with couetyse, my kynde to forsake, / þat is larges and lewté þat longez to kny3tez' ['And coveting came after, contrary both / To largesse and loyalty belonging to knights'] (2379–80). His belief that he has betrayed his 'kynde' cuts many ways; he has betrayed his nature, which is not only the virtues signified by the pentangle. It is also Arthur, and Arthur's blood, and the values of the Round Table's knighthood. In these terms, to betray his 'kynde' is also to betray his masculinity, that is, his fundamental identity, for, in this poem, knighthood and masculinity are in the end the same thing. Without the synonymity of masculinity and knighthood, we are left in a romance world in which masculinity and masculine behavior become synonymous with courtliness, with love dalliance in the bedroom, with the world of ladies and Lancelot, with the world that is contained in Morgan's castle and contained by the narrative. And this is the world from which Gawain has just made a well-timed escape.

After the woman in the middle has compromised Gawain's manhood with her privateness, the poem provides for him, in Fitt IV, a father-confessor to conduct the process of marginalizing the woman and reintegrating Gawain into the court at Camelot. This father-confessor is none other than the Green Knight/Bertilak, whose words to Gawain should carry special weight because he has experienced the dangers of enclosure within the private world of women.[21] Bertilak, after all, can rapidly change color at Morgan's whim.

It is his father-confessor that Gawain has betrayed by failing to return the girdle in the exchange of winnings game. And it is from this father-confessor that Gawain receives an axiom that he should never forget and that will restore his knighthood and his masculinity. In two highly condensed and elliptical lines, Bertilak tells Gawain that 'Trwe mon trwe restore, / þenne þar mon drede no waþe' ['True men pay what they owe; / No danger then in sight'] (2354–5). One need not fear harm if the true man truly restores, that is, if he maintains the essential social contracts between men.[22] Then the true man will truly be a man, because he has not yielded to private and thus feminized desires. These lines might well serve as a motto for a poetic, political, and ethical program that would, in effect, save Arthur's kingdom. By following Bertilak's advice, Gawain in his completed confession and analysis of his motives is a redeemed man, here bought back from the woman with whom he has bargained for his life.[23]

But it is not that easy for Gawain, for the court of Arthur, or for the poem that knows the end of its own story and the end of the story of the Arthurian world. For if Arthur's blood is in Gawain, we learn, when we learn of Morgan's agency, that her blood is in him, too. Bertilak, the great revealer, finally reveals Morgan, at the end of the poem, but not until Gawain has shown himself ready for this revelation. By now, Gawain has sufficiently distanced himself from association with the Lady to guarantee his public reintegration into Arthur's court. By now, in an anti-feminist diatribe that has given many critics pause,[24] he has successfully completed this distancing by claiming that, since all great men fall to women's wiles, he might be excused for following suit:

Bot hit is no ferly þaʒ a fole madde,
And þurʒ wyles of wymmen be wonen to sorʒe,
. . . .
. . . hit were a wynne huge
To luf hom wel, and leue hem not, a leude þat couþe.

(2414–21)

[But if a dullard should dote, deem it no wonder,
And through the wiles of a woman be wooed into sorrow,
. . . .
. . . 'twere a very joy
Could one but learn to love, and believe them not.]

He can learn, then, that not only did Morgan concoct this adventure, but that she is also 'þyn aunt, Ar þurez half-suster' ['Your own aunt . . ., Arthur's half-sister'] (2464). Throughout the poem, the woman Morgan has been assigned to a privateness so complete that she cannot be admitted until this point, when Gawain has proven himself protected from the influence of her blood. And yet, by Bertilak's admission, she is always simultaneously lurking at the fringes and inescapably at dead center, related to Arthur and to Gawain, just as her influence is at the narrative center of the romance. The poem forcefully leaves her aside because that is all it can do, but to do that, if it could be done, would be plenty.

And thus the fate of the green girdle, the love token that the Lady wove and wore and gave to Gawain as a sign not only of her, but of his life and his desire to save it. By the time Gawain rides back into Arthur's hall bedecked with the girdle, the Lady has vanished from the realm of its signification. She has been marginalized so that Gawain and the girdle can be publicized. Along the route of the girdle's redefinition and Gawain's return home, Bertilak has claimed that it is his, just as he claims to have pimped for his wife in order to test Gawain's virtue: 'For hit is my wede þat þou werez, þat ilke wouen girdel' ['For that is my belt about you, that same braided girdle'] (2358). The girdle has gone from being a sign of Gawain's life and his desire to save it to a sign of his threatened death, his sin and his unkindness, his unnaturalness, all so that it can be, as Bertilak claims, a 'pure token / Of þe chaunce of þe grene chapel at cheualrous knyghteʒ' ['token / How it chanced at the Green Chapel, to chivalrous knights'] (2398–9). The green girdle is a sign now not of the woman, but of the tested man, who has not been found so wanting after all.[25] The woman in the middle has effectively been displaced from the center, to become as marginalized as Guenevere and Morgan. And thus the token is pure, cleansed of female signification, and particularly of male alliance with the female at the expense of bonding with the male. 'Trwe mon trwe restore.'

But Gawain cannot accept the girdle back so easily. He himself must redefine it in order to associate it directly with his sins, and only marginally with the Lady. And yet the Lady is signified in the specific sin that Gawain links to the girdle: 'þe faut and þe fayntyse of þe flesche crabbed, / How tender hit is to entyse teches of fylþe' ['The faults and the frailty of the flesh perverse, / How its tenderness entices the foul taint of sin'] (2435–6). At this point, the Lady's marginalization and the placement of the female in the poem are complete. The Lady of the girdle is reduced to the corruption of the flesh, in an image that specifically evokes withered, old Morgan, the 'auncian', as she has been described in Fitt II (947–69). The Lady, through this rapid deterioration, has been revised. Or perhaps we see here signs of the specific revision that this poem has worked on Morgan herself, because I, for one, find it difficult to understand how Arthur's half-sister could have become so old so soon, unless it were to link her with the corruption of the flesh, that, in this poem, becomes linked to the corruption that is women in the center of Arthur's court.[26]

The court, however, is ready to forgive and forget, just as, I would argue, the poem would like to forgive and forget, but primarily to forget as it nears the end of a revisionary agenda that it knows must fail. As a sign of its forgiveness, the court assumes the sign of Gawain's self-defined sin.

> þe kyng comfortez the knyʒt, and alle þe court als
> Laʒen loude þerat, and lufly acorden
> þat lordes and ladis þat longed to þe Table,
> Uche burne of þe broþerhede, a bauderyk schulde haue . . .
>
> (2513–16)

[The king comforts the knight, and the court all together
Agree with gay laughter and gracious intent
That the lords and the ladies belonging to the Table,
Each brother of that band, a baldric should have. . . .]

In the process, the court collectively rehabilitates the girdle by making it a public sign of honor.[27] Interestingly enough, the rehabilitation of the girdle follows the same model as does the rehabilitation of Guenevere in Fitt I. Through this sign, the woman is safely placed within the court, safely placed specifically because she is removed from the dangerous realm of the private and the feminine and published as a token within a masculine world. If Guenevere in Fitt I is rehabilitated because she so surely refers to Arthur, then the publicized girdle is rehabilitated specifically because it now refers to the honor of Arthur's court.

The poem knows, however, that the end is not so easy and that its own means are insufficient to the end. The woman may have been marginalized by leaving Morgan aside, but the process of her marginalization involves her naming. In other words, it involves her publication, her removal from her own sphere of the private so that she can become the public sign of the male. But, as such, the woman as token becomes dangerously current within the court, just as the green girdle, redefined though it might be, is dangerously current in the closing scene at Camelot. For, among the male gazes directed at the static Guenevere in Fitt I is, we can assume, that of Lancelot (who is mentioned only once in the poem [553], included in the brotherhood of knights advising Gawain before his departure in Fitt II). And, unless Guenevere is blind as well as mute, she can, of course, look back.

In its marginalization of women, then, the poem provides a proleptic cure for Arthurian history. If Guenevere had been the static and silent queen, then the Round Table would not have fallen. If men could redefine and thereby control experience for other men, as Bertilak does for Gawain, and, indeed, as the poet does for his audience, then Morgan's power would be diffused. But the poem and its poet know better, because they know the story of Arthur and because women, in the legend and in life, cannot be effectively marginalized. The poem tries to suggest that the life-giving girdle and its giver are ultimately lifethreatening. In the historical world of feudal chivalry, however, the bearers of death are not generally women. If our end comes from our beginning, we still know where that beginning starts. If women were legally and politically marginalized within feudal society, they were nonetheless central, biologically, economically, *and* politically, to its continuation. Guenevere's barrenness may thus discount her within this world. But Morgan is, as Bertilak admits, 'þe goddes'. Although Bertilak makes her magic secondary by attributing it to Merlin, that magic, as Morgan practices it, is powerful stuff. Bertilak may be bent out of shape by it, but he can still grow a new head. It is this regenerative capacity that enables the Green Knight to make his reappearance in Fitt IV.[28] His end, then, is only his beginning and the beginning of the narrative, thanks to Morgan le Fay.

It is no wonder then that the poem's erasure of women, of Guenevere, of the Lady, and of Morgan, is uneasy and incomplete. The odds of Arthurian legend and of human history are against it. Could the female be marginalized, then the

Round Table would not have ended. But she cannot be, and it will. Nonetheless, the meaning of this end is not the end of the meaning, not of the 'rex quondam rexque futurus' and not of his queen. And not, for that matter, of Morgan le Fay.

Notes

1. See, for example, LARRY D. BENSON, *Art and Tradition in Sir Gawain and the Green Knight* (New Brunswick: Rutgers University Press, 1965), pp. 97–8; A.C. SPEARING, *The Gawain-Poet: A Critical Study* (Cambridge: Cambridge University Press, 1970), pp. 181 and 222; JOHN EADIE: 'Morgain la Fée and the Conclusion of *Sir Gawain and the Green Knight*', *Neophilologus*, **52** (1968): 300–1; ROBERT W. HANNING, 'Sir Gawain and the Red Herring: The Perils of Interpretation', in Mary J. Carruthers and Elizabeth D. Kirk (eds), *Acts of Interpretation: The Text in its Contexts 700–1600: Essays on Medieval and Renaissance Literature in Honor of E. Talbot Donaldson* (Norman: Pilgrim Books, 1982), p. 11. In 'Myth and Medieval Literature: *Sir Gawain and the Green Knight*' (*Speculum*, **18** [1956]:172), CHARLES MOORMAN argues that the poem is 'a highly compressed allegorical commentary on the entire Arthurian history' and that 'the seeds of [its] tragedy were present even in the "first age" of the youthful and joyous court at Christmas time'. Moorman does not argue, as I do, that the poem valorizes the youthful court as part of its revisionist project. In a chapter on *Sir Gawain and the Green Knight* in her thesis, 'Mordred's Hidden Presence: The Skeleton in the Arthurian Closet' (PhD, Yale, 1985), M. Victoria Guerin offers a thorough analysis of the ways in which the poem follows a revisionist program in its relation to the unnamed Mordred. I am grateful to Professor Guerin for sharing the manuscript of her chapter with me.

2. *Sir Gawain and the Green Knight*, ed. J.R.R. Tolkien and E.V. Gordon, 2nd edn, rev. Norman Davis (Oxford: Oxford University Press, 1967). All quotations of the poem are taken from this edition and are cited by line number. The translation cited is that of Marie Borroff (New York: Norton, 1967). On these lines, cf. MOORMAN, 164 and 171.

3. See BENSON, for example, pp. 32–35. Morgan's traditional enmity toward the Round Table stands as the most frequent justification for her presence in the poem. Most book-length studies of the poem, however, give relatively little emphasis to Morgan's significance to the poem. The exception to the general neglect of Morgan occurs primarily in the articles published on her in the 1950's and 1960's: DENVER EWING BAUGHAN: 'The Role of Morgan la Faye in *Sir Gawain and the Green Knight*', *ELH*, **17** (1950): 241–51; ALBERT B. FRIEDMAN, 'Morgan la Faye in *Sir Gawain and the Green Knight*', *Speculum*, **35** (1960): 260–74; MOTHER ANGELA CARSON, OSU, 'Morgain la Fée as the Principle of Unity in Gawain and the Green Knight', *MLQ*, **23** (1962): 3–16; DOUGLAS MOON, 'The Role of Morgan la Faye in *Gawain and the Green Knight*', *NM*, **67** (1966): 31–57. The most recent study of Morgan is EDITH WHITEHURST WILLIAMS' 'Morgan la Fée as Trickster in *Sir Gawain and the Green Knight*', *Folklore*, **96** (1985): 38–56. To date, there has been no comprehensive feminist study of the placement of women in the poem.

4. In addition to the sources cited in footnote 1, see also MOORMAN, 167–72; BAUGHAN, 244–47; and FRIEDMAN, 269.

5. VICTORIA GUERIN's chapter on *Sir Gawain and the Green Knight* offers a comprehensive analysis of this issue in relation to the poem's themes and purposes.

6. For discussion of Gawain's traditional reputation as a 'lady's man', see FRIEDMAN, 265; BENSON, pp. 95 and 103; SPEARING, pp. 198–99; W.R.J. BARRON, *Trawthe and Treason: The Sin of Sir Gawain Reconsidered* (Manchester: Manchester University Press, 1980), p. 21. Guerin's chapter on *Sir Gawain and the Green Knight* offers a comprehensive discussion of this issue.

7. For a thorough and perceptive discussion of the fluctuation of Gawain's value and identity, see R.A. SHOAF's *The Poem as Green Girdle: 'Commercium' in 'Sir Gawain and the Green Knight'* (Gainesville: University Presses of Florida, 1984), especially the section, 'What *Prys* Gawain?', pp. 34–6. Throughout my discussion of Gawain's activities in the bedroom and of the girdle's meaning, I am particularly indebted to Professor Shoaf's analysis as well as to the bibliography that he generously shared with me before his monograph appeared in print.

8. For a discussion of medieval women's legal, political, and marital rights, see SHULAMITH SHAHAR, *The Fourth Estate: A History of Women in the Middle Ages*, trans. Chaya Galai (New York: Methuen, 1983), pp. 11–21, and the chapter on aristocratic women, pp. 126–73.

9. In this essay, my thinking about the placement of women in narrative has been influenced by SANDRA M. GILBERT and SUSAN GUBAR's chapter, 'The Queen's Looking Glass', in *Madwoman in the Attic: The Woman Writer and the Nineteenth-Century Literary Imagination* (New Haven: Yale University Press, 1984), pp. 3–44, esp. pp. 20–7.

10. BENSON, for example, writes that the Lady was 'following Bertilak's orders', although he acknowledges Morgan as the source of Bertilak's activities (p. 55). PETER L. RUDNYTSKY takes the same approach to the Lady in '*Sir Gawain and the Green Knight*: Oedipal Temptation', *AI*, **40** (1983): 377. Carson was the first to stress Morgan's responsibility for the plot *and* Bertilak's role as *her* agent (13).

11. MOORMAN, 167. Moorman's arguments resemble my own here, but he does not associate the Lady, Guenevere, and Morgan, as I believe the poem does, on the basis of the femaleness that they share.

12. I take this idea of 'framing women in art' from GILBERT and GUBAR, *Madwoman in the Attic*, pp. 13 and 42. My thinking about the significance of Guenevere's placement at Arthur's table was influenced by Susan Gubar's discussion of the dual meaning of Judy Chicago's *Dinner Party*: 'But *The Dinner Party* plates also imply that women, who have served, have been served up and consumed.' See ' "The Blank Page" and the Issues of Female Creativity', reprinted in Elaine Showalter (ed.), *The New Feminist Criticism: Essays on Women, Literature, and Theory* (New York: Pantheon Books, 1985), p. 300 (originally printed in *Critical Inquiry*, **8** [Winter 1981]). Hanning also notes that Guenevere in this scene is an 'elegant courtly artifact' (11).

13. Speaking of her inexplicable love for Jankyn, the Wife of Bath says: 'We wommen han, if that I shal nat lye, / In this matere a queynte fantasye', *The Riverside Chaucer*, ed. Larry D. Benson (Boston: Houghton Mifflin, 1987), III [D], 515–16. The pun on *queynte* as female genitalia occurs frequently enough in Chaucer that it does not seem too much to assume that its possibility would have been familiar to the *Gawain*-poet.

14. For a discussion of medieval women's marital position and rights, see SHAHAR, pp. 65–125. Throughout my analysis of women's placement within marital, political, and economic systems, I am indebted to Gayle Rubin's important feminist revision of Claude Lévi-Strauss' *The Elementary Structures of Kinship* in 'The Traffic in

Women: Notes on the "Political Economy" of Sex', in Rayna R. Reiter (ed.), *Toward an Anthropology of Women* (New York: Monthly Review Press, 1975), pp. 157–210.

15. For representative interpretations of the Lady as seductress, see BENSON, pp. 38–40, and W.A. DAVENPORT, *The Art of the Gawain-Poet* (London: Athlone Press, 1978), pp. 137, 167–8, and 187. Taking a much different approach, VICTOR Y. HAINES, in *The Fortunate Fall of Sir Gawain: The Typology of Sir Gawain and the Green Knight* (Washington: University Press of America, 1982), argues that while the Lady seems to 'corrupt' Gawain in a first reading of the poem, 'in the redeemed history of [a] second reading, the lady is benevolent', because she wants to save Gawain's life (p. 145). According to Haines, the Lady operates as an emissary of Mary (not of Morgan) because her love for Gawain is charitable, not concupiscent (pp. 131, 138–42, and 148).

16. Two important feminist contributions to the study of women's relationship to medieval literature include JOAN M. FERRANTE, *Woman as Image in Medieval Literature: From the Twelfth Century Through Dante* (New York: Columbia University Press, 1975), and E. JANE BURNS' and ROBERTA L. KRUEGER's 'Introduction' to *Courtly Ideology and Women's Place in Medieval French Literature*, *Romance Notes*, **25** (Spring 1985): 205–19.

17. Cf. SHOAF's discussion, pp. 31–46. While Shoaf concludes, 'Bertilak's Lady manipulates Gawain until he insists on private value exclusively' (p. 46), he studies Gawain's yielding to privacy in the context of medieval Christian sacramentality and not in the context of the inscription of the female in the narrative.

18. SPEARING (pp. 175 and 196–8) and BURROW (pp. 50 and 105) offer representative interpretations of the criticism on the pentangle. In his monograph, Shoaf gives a new reading of the pentangle, which is based in medieval and post-modern sign theory and which gives full weight to the problematics of referentiality in the poem. See, especially, pp. 71–5.

19. Many of my ideas about the configurations of male homosociality in literary texts and the (dis)placement of women within these configurations are indebted to the introduction and first two chapters of EVE KOSOFSKY SEDGWICK, *Between Men: English Literature and Male Homosocial Desire* (New York: Columbia University Press, 1985). While Sedgwick's book primarily discusses later literature, these opening sections are relevant to the study of medieval and early modern texts.

20. Critical disagreement about the poem is sharpest in the divergent interpretations of the seriousness of Gawain's sin. For three recent examples of this divergence of opinion, compare THOMAS D. HILL, 'Gawain's Jesting Lie: Towards an Interpretation of the Confessional Scene in *Sir Gawain and the Green Knight*', *Studia Neophilologia*, **52** (1980): 279–86; SHOAF, pp. 15–30; and WILLIAMS, 51.

21. For representative interpretations of Bertilak's role in Fitt IV, see MOORMAN, 166; BURROW, pp. 137 and 169; DAVENPORT, pp. 168–73; SPEARING, pp. 31 and 221; and BARRON, p. 132.

22. Cf. SHOAF, pp. 15–30.

23. See Shoaf's appendix (pp. 77–80) for an indication of the density of commercial images in this poem. For earlier discussions of the implications of the poem's commercial idiom, see BURROW, pp. 76–7 and 88–9, and PAUL B. TAYLOR, 'Commerce and Comedy in *Sir Gawain and the Green Knight*', *Phil Q*, **50** (1971): 1–15.

24. The conflicting reaction to Gawain's anti-feminist diatribe is one of the most interesting interludes in the history of the critical tradition on this poem.

25. Shoaf's monograph stands as the most comprehensive discussion of the complex significations of the girdle and of its thematic function within the poem.

26. Tolkien's footnote on Morgan's advanced age (p. 130) has been consistently accepted by most critics who have raised this issue. Others, like Benson (p. 32), associate Morgan's aging with the filth of the flesh whose presence within him Gawain must acknowledge as the wages of his sin. Carson argues, on the basis of the poem's sources, that Morgan and the Lady are one and the same because of the dual nature of Morgan. In Carson's reading, Bertilak is Uriens, and Morgan's traditional characterization becomes attributed to the two central women in the poem (5 and 13). While Carson's reading engages Morgan's centrality in the poem, it does not sufficiently engage the marginalization of Morgan that the poem accomplishes by substituting the Lady for her. Williams offers an analysis similar to Carson's, but bases her discussion on Jungian archetypes (41 and 49).

27. For a representative sampling of the disagreement over the poem's ending, see MOORMAN, 170; BURROW, pp. 158–59; SPEARING, pp. 222 and 230; BENSON, pp. 241–2; EDWARD WILSON, *The Gawain-Poet* (Leiden: Brill, 1976), pp. 130–1. Williams' discussion of the concluding presentation of the girdle comes close to my own, but she does not discuss the significance of the erasure of the Lady in the final scene (52).

28. See, for example, BENSON, p. 94, and HANNING, pp. 6–7, on the meaning of the natural landscape. The complex meanings that circulate around the natural world in this poem align themselves in interesting ways with what Elaine Showalter has designated as 'the wild zone' of female culture, that is, the private world of women's culture that men never see. See 'Feminist Criticism in the Wilderness', in *The New Feminist Criticism*, p. 262 (originally published in *Critical Inquiry*, **8** [1981]).

8 The Narrator in *The Owl and the Nightingale*: A Reader in the Text *

R. BARTON PALMER

Unusual in its invocation of modernist self-reflexiveness to read an early medieval poem, this essay analyses the metafictional and dialogic structure of *The Owl and the Nightingale*. Barton Palmer draws attention to the widely conflicting interpretations offered of this poem, and suggests that this diversity is a failure of hermeneutics already foreshadowed by the text. The narrator functions as a surrogate for the reader, in that he can never succeed in fully writing out, or representing either the debate between the birds, or the final conclusion of their appointed judge. The poem's dialectic is thus narrative, rather than didactic, and works primarily to interrogate the very process – the debate – which forms its structural core.

The appearance of Kathryn Hume's full-length study of the difficulties of interpretation posed by the Middle English *The Owl and the Nightingale* has effectively silenced what had been, for the last three decades or so, a lively (if chaotic) debate over the meaning of the poem. Since Hume's persuasive debunking of a wide variety of previous hermeneutic claims in 1975, no new thoroughgoing reading, in fact, has been proposed. Thus her own view that this literary debate is a burlesque-satire which takes as its object 'human contentiousness' has been unchallenged.[1] Though I agree with Constance Hieatt that Hume has performed a 'much-needed job of house-cleaning' by pointing out the inadequacies of previous interpretative efforts, I do believe that Hume's reading of the poem is likewise seriously flawed.[2]

Hieatt has suggested that, mindful of the failure of past scholarship, we should go back to the poem itself, and that is what I intend to do here. In

---

* Reprinted from *Chaucer Review*, **22** (1988): 305–21.

particular, I hope to demonstrate that *The Owl and the Nightingale* is self-reflexive, that it is a poem which transforms the task of its own reading into an aspect of content. Metafictional structures in the poem deliberately undermine, by establishing different stances to the understanding of the birds' debate, any attempt at a transcendent interpretation, at a reading that would take us beyond the boundaries of literary experience as the text defines them. In short, I will argue that the poem is not the serio-comic treatment of any theme, as Hume would have it, but rather a playful exploration, based on the expectations aroused by certain genres and by medieval literary tradition in general, of the processes by which texts, in collaboration with the reader, either construct or (more blatantly) offer up their own meaning. Central to my argument is a full-scale analysis of the poem's narrator, who, in tradition of the *exemplum* and fable, functions as the reader's surrogate in the text, as an intelligence who attempts to (but never succeeds in) writing out the meaning of the avian debate he witnesses. Before turning to the poem itself, however, we can usefully begin with a brief survey of critical opinion, for these various readings, when placed in the context of certain larger structural features of the work, have much to tell us about the contradictory stances that the narrator adopts toward the discussion he witnesses.

In reviewing briefly critical work on the poem I do not intend to follow Hume in testing the adequacy of different readings; instead I would like to examine the significance of the fact that such readings have been wildly conflicting, much more so than those occasioned by most other medieval texts. Beyond an extensive body of scholarship that has sought answers to the historical questions of authorship, date, and provenance, critical treatment of the poem uniformly falls into the category of what Tzvetan Todorov would term 'interpretation' (or the filling in of the gaps in the text's consciousness of its own message) rather than 'analysis' (or the structural description of the ways that the text works to produce meaning).[3] We might say that the gaps in *The Owl and the Nightingale* are particularly troubling to the hermeneutic enterprise: the debate raises the issue of outside judgement but the poem does not represent the scene of decision; the issues debated range from the serious (and human) to the trivial (and largely avian); the disputants, though they are advocates of differing views on a range of important matters, are never identified chiefly with one question, be it political, artistic, social, or characterological. The underlying assumption of the poem's critics, however, has been, as Hume puts it, 'that valid interpretation is possible', a hermeneutic expectation that, as many have maintained, is essentially a modern notion.[4]

In *Critical Practice*, for example, Catherine Belsey argues persuasively that works from the older periods of English literature do not always set up to be read like the realist fiction of Eliot and Dickens. In particular, she challenges the notion that the poems of Donne or the plays of Shakespeare, for example, uniformly contain an ordering of discourses which, through the devices of closure and disclosure, reveals the 'truth' about the represented world within. If in *Middlemarch* a narrative metalanguage recuperates the differences among the characters' separate points of view and renders up an unchallengeable 'presence' of meaning, such a device is lacking in a play like *Coriolanus*, which instead foregrounds the paradox 'that heroic individualism is both necessary to and destructive of a militaristic society'.[5] Expanding on the views of Roland Barthes, Belsey suggests that literary texts fall into three general categories. The declarative text works diligently toward the suppression of any contradiction between its overt thematic project and the challenges posed to that project by the work's constitutive discourses; it generates some form of metalanguage to contain these contradictions. Like the declarative, the imperative text reconciles conflict in the name of 'readerliness', but does so with a view toward engaging the reader's partisanship. Interrogative texts, however, work toward the display of paradox and irresolution, for they emphasise the differences of the claims for meaning and attention made by their constituent discourses.

My point is this: the Hirschian expectation of Hume (and of course others) that a singular and valid interpretation of the poem is possible may well be historically inappropriate. Like other works from the Middle Ages and Renaissance, *The Owl and the Nightingale* might be an interrogative text whose 'meaning' resides precisely in an unwillingness to provide final answers and resolve contradictions.

Such a view of the poem goes against established opinion, but, it seems to me, criticism devoted to medieval texts has in large measure failed to grapple with the historical limitations of its underlying assumptions and methods of analysis. Nineteenth-century canons of *vraisemblance* can hardly account for literary practices (and expectations) which are based on radically different notions of the relationship between 'text' and 'world', as the recently burgeoning attention to intertextuality as a determining principle of medieval literary production demonstrates.[6] Likewise, modern notions of closure (and of the structural functions such as narrative metalanguage which are designed to achieve it) are clearly derived from the practice of classic realist writers, yet these notions have obviously influenced even 'historical' approaches to medieval works, notably Robertsonianism. While the fourfold method of Biblical exegesis produces an open and plural text resistant to closure (as readers of Gregory's *Moralia in Job* will agree and as Fredric Jameson demonstrates in his radical co-optation of this critical theory[7]), Robertsonianism has assumed a univocal text in which elements of the dialogic tend to be interpreted away.[8]

Closer attention to the ways medieval works produce meaning will, I believe, lead to a more historical understanding of their literariness; in *Troilus and Criseyde*, for example, the narrator's concept of the 'story' as equally something fixed which pre-exists his discourse and yet also a dynamic process or a structuration of meaning reveals more about the poem's

construction of its (and I would argue necessarily ambiguous) interpretation
than any extratextually-derived 'code of reading'.[9] Like Chaucer's poem, *The
Owl and the Nightingale* is a work which repays this kind of analysis, for its
discursive structures aim at an interrogation rather than a declaration of
'meaning', as we will see below.

The fact that the readings occasioned by the poem fall largely into two
opposed categories gives further weight to this supposition. Calling attention
to whimsical literary debates in Latin and the various vernaculars as well as to
the comic uses of animal characters in the fable and beast epic, some scholars
have maintained that the poem is a farcical *sic et non* that depends for its
humor, in large measure, on the incongruous juxtaposition of avian debaters
and questions with human relevance. Others, on the contrary, have suggested
that the poem is an attempt to propound some serious issue (which has been
variously identified) and that the birds, in the manner of medieval allegory,
are therefore used as ciphers for opposing views.[10] Because it involves the
rewriting of the poem in political, aesthetic, philosophical, or religious terms,
this second approach has been the most productive of variant interpretations.

The diversity of critical opinion, however, is interesting not only because it
seems to index the poem's resistance to interpretative closure; the two
categories of readings produced by the poem also correspond roughly to
medieval methods for reading this kind of literature. As a hermeneutic
procedure, allegoresis bears a close similarity to an important structural
feature of the *exemplum* and fable: both of these story types customarily (but
not always) end with a *moralitas* delivered by the narrator that rewrites the
letter of the narrative as a 'lesson'. Content with an immanent interpretation
(and hence with the elucidation of the various mechanisms of humour such as
invective, irony, and burlesque), the critics who argue for the comic view also
have their medieval counterparts: the reader (and indeed the text) satisfied
with the pleasures of literary mimesis and narrative.

The twelfth-century French *Isopet*, for example, a translation into verse of a
Latin fable collection, points out to its prospective reader both these different
strategies of enjoyment/intellectual nourishment:

Me voil traveillier et pener
D'un petit jardin ahener
Ou chascuns porra, si me samble,
Cuillir et fruit et fleur ensemble:
Fleur, que a òir est delitables,
Fruis, quar en fait est profitables.
Qui la fleur plaira, la fleur prengne,
Et qui le fruit, le fruit retiegne;
Qui voudra le fruit et la fleur,
Prengne les deus, c'est le meilleur.

(7–16)

[I intend to take pains in and apply myself to constructing a tiny garden where everyone might, so it seems to me, gather fruit and flowers together: flowers, which are delightful to hear, and fruit, because it's undoubtedly advantageous. Let him who likes the flower, take the flower, and let him who likes the fruit keep it for himself; whoever would like the fruit and the flowers, let him take both, for that's the very best.][11]

Modern readers of the Middle English poem fall neatly into all three categories, with those moralists desirous of fruit alone undoubtedly the dominant party. In attempting to reconcile the poem's comedy (burlesque) with a serious rhetorical purpose (satire), Hume obviously aligns herself with what, at least in the *Isopet*, is praised as the best strategy for reading a text whose surface (and easily appreciated) pleasures might lead to the consumption of more solid, moral nourishment. Modern criticism, in short, has responded to *The Owl and the Nightingale* in ways recognised within the tradition of such learned genres as the debate and the fable, genres that, controlled by the notion of *translatio studii*, demand a 'serious' attention to their *significatio* and yet an enjoyment of their *littera*. Furthermore, we should remark that the author of the *Isopet*, though producing a text with explicitly drawn moral lessons, recognises a variety of reading strategies that his audience might adopt. What is written as *dulce et utile* might be understood *dulce aut utile*. We should, moreover, not fail to notice that the narrator's own project of rewriting the fable with the *topos* of the garden pleasantly (and probably intentionally) breaks down in favor of the special circumstances of storytelling pleasure. The flowers he has to offer are indeed delectable to hear.

Returning to the Middle English poem, we see that *dulce* and *utile* constructions of the text find an obvious reflection (and to a large measure a source) in the two debaters themselves. The Nightingale, a bird who prizes the aesthetic and the sensuous, defines her service to mankind as an enhancement of human enjoyment, while the Owl, as Hume puts it, 'represents all that is conservative, ascetic, and solemn', discovering her own usefulness to man in her baleful warnings and exhortations to reform.[12] Furthermore the debate itself, inevitably reflecting the natures and *weltanschauungen* of the disputants, moves back and forth from moments that can only be called humorous (these involve not only name-calling but obvious failures on the parts of the birds to be consistent, perceptive, or to the point) to moments which, because they deal with human questions such as the struggle for salvation and the gravity of mortal sin, necessarily evoke a serious response, at least in part. As Hume suggests, both the oscillating tone of the argument and the fact that neither bird receives the endorsement of a judgement in her favor mean that strictly humorous and strictly serious approaches to the poem are equally unable to incorporate or explain the poem's nature as a whole. Any decision in favor of the flower of pleasure or the fruit of morality is further militated against by the inconclusiveness of the debate's finale, which is not characterised by any inherent resistance of the argument to settlement but rather by the narrator's decision not to represent the scene of judgement.

With this in mind, Hume's view of the poem becomes both attractive (because it is a more comprehensive explanation of the work's various features) and, in a sense, authorised (genres such as the literary debate belong to the tradition of *dulce et utile* consumption). There are, however, serious objections to Hume's interpretation. Beyond some general considerations of the poem as a literary debate, Hume is unable to account for *The Owl and the Nightingale*'s satiric rhetoric in terms of either specific models or types. Medieval literature, we must remember, is tightly structured by a network of intertextual relationships. These involve not only an omnipresent sense of literary history (those *auctores* peering over the writer's shoulder) but the unshakable conception of literary production as a series of categories or genres. The second flaw, I think, is a more damaging one: the reading off of 'human contentiousness' as the subject of the satire. Human contentiousness is not one of the issues debated by the birds, nor does the debate itself, which with its humor and good will argues for the pleasures involved in the witnessing of quarreling, demonstrate that contentiousness is to be condemned. At the end of their argument the birds fly off together, and it is the narrator's expectation that somehow they will be reconciled. Hume suggests that because both birds raise the issue of the deaths suffered by owls and nightingales at the hands of men this proves the disastrous consequences of contention. But, as Hieatt has pointed out, 'the men who crucify owls or dismember nightingales are not "quarreling" with the birds'.[13] We are, in short, no more authorised by the text to name 'human contentiousness' as the theme of the debate than other commentators have been to rewrite it in other ways.

The failure of the hermeneutic enterprise seems to me rather strong evidence that the poem deliberately resists efforts at interpretation, that it is, in fact, an interrogative text designed to foil such attempts. Examining the narrator's role, however, we can come to a more specific conclusion. For, as we will see, the function of this structure in the poem is to keep the reader off balance about the way the text should be read.

Traditionally, critics have treated *The Owl and the Nightingale* as if it were a dramatic dialogue; the poem, however, is *diegesis*, not *mimesis*, the argument between the birds reported (and to a large extent) mediated by the presence of a narrator. Hume's characterization of the poem's form is typical. She acknowledges that a narrator establishes the tone at the outset, but errs in observing that 'once the birds start to exchange acidulous comments, the narrator effaces himself'.[14] This is simply not true, for the narrator, though he does disappear during some of the longer exchanges, is present in the poem from beginning to end. His often long comments on the different stages of the discussion have not entirely escaped critical notice. In *Criticism and Medieval Poetry*, A.C. Spearing, for example, calls attention to one such passage (lines 669–706) as an example of the rhetorical figure of *amplificatio*. Not only, he states, does it provide 'some sort of interlude' for an audience perhaps tiring from the debate's fast pace. It also marks a 'turning-point in the development of the poem's meaning', when the poet's sympathies shift from the attractive Nightingale to the solemn Owl.[15] Spearing's commentary on this passage is, I think, essentially correct. The interpretation of the poem he bases upon it, however, misses the mark, because, like other critics, he pays no attention to the narrator's other and frequent interventions.

The narrator's role in the poem, however, is easily defined, since he interests himself from the beginning not only in the reportage of an unusual event at which he is accidentally present, but also in its interpretation/analysis. In so doing he functions in some of the same ways as the narrator of the fable. But if the author of the poem has utilised a convention of the fable literature with which he was so obviously well acquainted (for embodied in the text are several short versions of fables), he has made it serve quite different ends. The narrator in this poem, in fact, renders 'correct' interpretation quite impossible, because his view of the action is inconsistent. At times he is detached and ironic, while at others he is involved and serious. In the beginning he makes us believe that the proceeding at which we are imaginatively present is humorously incongruous. Later, however, he suggests that the debate is a search for truth and justice. His initial attitude, moreover, suits the Nightingale's demand for sensuous pleasure and her adamant rejection of solemnity. But a change of heart puts the narrator on the side of the moralistic Owl.

Like the birds, the narrator thus sees the discussion from two irreconciled viewpoints. When he is sympathetic to the Nightingale, he makes us believe that the poem is something of which that somewhat frivolous creature would approve: a charming *divertissement*. Agreeing with the Owl, however, he finds a different rationale for song, namely that it benefits (or at least should benefit) those who hear it. Near the debate's end, however, the narrator withdraws into an unexplained neutrality. The judge agreed upon by the disputants, however, has divided sympathies, much like the narrator. A misspent youth, we are told, found him enamored of the Nightingale's delightful music, though in maturity he has listened more intently to the Owl's message. We never discover, of course, if this Master Nicholas of Guildford has truly been converted to the Owl's point of view. Similarly the claims of the disputants are left unadjudicated by the text.

The narrator begins by announcing the strange experience that forms the subject of his poem, an experience which he frames lightheartedly in the inappropriate language of the law:

Iherde ich holde grete tale

An Hule and one Niȝtingale.
þat plait was stif & starc & strong,
Sum wile softe & lud among.
An aiþer aȝen oþer sval
& let þat vvole mod ut al;
& eiþer seide of oþeres custe
þat alre worste þat hi wuste.
& hure & hure of oþere[s] songe
Hi holde plaiding suþe stronge.[16]

(3–12)

With its playful directness, its avoidance of pious invocation and any reference
to literary tradition, this opening signals humorous intent to any reader
familiar with the customary moralising of the serious prose and verse of the
period.[17] The narrator, we learn, is no clerk feeling the burden of *translatio
studii*, but rather a chance observer, who, avoiding any interference in the
birds' dispute, chooses to relate it. His motive is thus narrative, not didactic,
the inventive 'fictionality' of the text an index of its desire to entertain.
Present at an event only imaginatively possible, the narrator, moreover, is
strictly fictional himself; he asks to be read as an element of the work's
structure and not as an intradiegetic representative of the author. In the fable,
on the contrary, the narrator is set apart from the realm of the story in the
metafictional – but still textual – area of its interpretation.

Yet the narrator at this point is more than a character whose witnessing of
the birds' debate places him in much the same role as the reader (or listener)
of the poem. For his misappropriation of legal jargon – words like *tale*, *speche*,
and *plait* are legalisms – suggests his complicity in what, in the beginning,
promises to be one of the poem's main effects: the juxtaposition of human
and human *manqué* for their comic effect, a humorous device which, although
it has its roots in the anthropomorphism of the fable, is more obvious a
product of the beast epic. In the *Roman de Renart*, which during the likely
period of the Middle English poem's composition (c. 1180–1250) was at the
height of its international popularity, the animal figures of the fable are
removed from that genre's somewhat abstract *mise-en-scène* and placed in a
setting more similar to everyday reality, a setting in which the society of
animals is formed on the analogy of that of men.[18] Like the Owl and the
Nightingale, the Fox and the Wolf of the beast epic move in a 'realistic'
world, a world in which they are, incongruously, still beasts, but beasts with
human desires, failings, and institutions.

Because at this stage the narrator of the poem, like the narrator of the
beast epic, serves the essentially comic purpose of underlining the
impossibility (and hence the fictionality) of the experience he relates, it is also
fitting that his sympathies (hardly, however, real partisanship) lie with the
nightingale who finds sensuous pleasure in song. And, appropriately enough,

he reacts favorably to the harmony of her singing because of the analogy
with human music that the sound forces upon him:

> Ho was þe gladur uor þe rise,
> & song a uele cunne wise.
> Bet þuȝte þe dreim þat he were
> Of harpe & pipe þan he nere.

> (19–22)

Silent throughout the Nightingale's initial attack, the owl affords no pleasure;
she therefore receives no compliments from the narrator. Detached at first, he
has become a superficial critic of the proceeding. And as long as the
argument concerns the birds' natures alone, the Nightingale, because of her
obvious appeal, will remain the narrator's favorite.

After the birds decide on a proper debate, however, the narrator's attitude
shifts dramatically. The Owl defends her nature (lines 269–308) as that
proper to 'hauekes cunne', slyly introducing into the argument a point based
on the human notion of the chain of being here applied analogically to avian
society (an idea, of course, that is presented more dramatically in Chaucer's
Parlement of Fowles). This rationale is intellectual and shifts the discussion, at
least for the moment, away from simple flyting. The Owl further suggests a
new standard according to which different songs should be judged. Pure
delight in 'harpe & pipe & fuȝeles song' (343) can, she maintains, be
overdone. A superfluity of any good, except that of God's kingdom, soon
becomes objectionable. And discussion of benefit, as necessarily limited by
moderation, leads almost inevitably into the Owl's claim about the importance
of serving mankind:

> Ich do god mid mine þrote
> & warni men to hore note.

> Ich folȝi þan aȝte manne,
> An flo bi niȝte in hore banne.

> (329–30, 389–90)

No matter that this second point, in particular, is a dubious construction
of the owl's nighttime activity and interests, the Nightingale is befuddled
by a different tack in the discussion. Her plight engages the narrator's
attention:

> þe Niȝtingale in hire þoȝte
> Athold al þis, & longe þoȝte
> Wat ho þarafter miȝte segge;
> Vor ho ne miȝte noȝte alegge

þat þe Hule hadde hire ised,
Vor he spac boþe riȝt an red.

(391–96)

Here the narrator has obviously adopted the Owl's point of view, though it is uncertain, because formulated in something resembling indirect free discourse, whether it is the narrator's, the Nightingale's, or the narrator and nightingale's shared view that the owl has said what is true and right. In any case, the narrator's comment here suggests to the reader that song can not only speak the truth, but it can also urge good counsel. The Owl's sharply conceived defense of her nature and abilities, in other words, has caused the narrator (like the Nightingale) to reconsider the relationship between the world of birds and that of men or, analogically, the relationship between the text and the reader.

The narrator's earlier attitude was that the juxtaposition of the birds and a human observer was the occasion for comic dismissal, to be accomplished by his characterization of avian argument in terms of human discourse (that of the law). Following the Owl's call for the human relevance of the birds' various activities, the narrator begins to view the debate as an experience which can be interpreted in the light of human wisdom. The narrator, in short, functions here in the mode of the fable narrator, rewriting the Nightingale's behavior as an instance illustrating a proverb:

Ac noþeles he spac boldeliche;
Vor he is wis þat hardeliche
Wiþ is uo berþ grete ilete,
þat he uor areȝþe hit ne forlete:
Vor suich worþ bold ȝif þu fliȝst
þat wle flo ȝif þu (n)isvicst;
ȝif he isiþ þat þu nart areȝ
He wile of bore wrchen bareȝ.

(401–08)

This short quotation hardly does justice to the tone and style of the narrator's intervention. The commentary lasts some twenty lines (lines 390–410) and is characterized by a homely didacticism which bears no trace of the comic sense revealed in the narrator's opening remarks. Since a pleasant song is no longer sufficient in itself as a criterion of judgement, he has begun, like the Owl, to seek the fruit of moral nourishment concealed by the pretty flowers of the debate's humorous surface.

After this radical shift in attitude, the narrator continues to move us from the world of animals (embodied truth) to the world of men (its moral application) and then back again. The truths he gleans, however, are strictly psychological, as when he remarks (lines 665–74) about the difficulty involved in putting up a brave front in the absence of inner conviction. Certainly he never explicitly supports any of the Owl's intellectual positions beyond a general endorsement of her valid argumentation. He never addresses himself to the issues debated, but he does adopt a stylistic level very similar to that used by the Owl, a stylistic level which, with its repetitions and circular reasoning, often resembles homiletic prose. The narrator's sententiousness appears genuine, as when he remarks:

> For Aluered seide of olde quide –
> An ȝut hit nis of horte islide:
> 'Wone þe bale is alre hecst
> þonne is þe bote alre necst.'

> (685–88)

The movement of such commentary suggests an allegorising of the text; but the fact is that the proverb, once enunciated, has more application to the progress of the debate itself than to the more generalised, humanised realm of morality that the fable's *significatio* trades in. In the fable, the *moralitas* is less a comment on the narrative which engenders it than a replacement for it. This means that the *moralitas* often maintains only a tenuous connection with the narrative; as Albert Pauphilet has said, the closing moral 'dévie souvent, interprète tout de travers l'exemple où il s'appuie, et se peine pour en tirer un enseignement qui n'est pas celui qu'on attendait, and qui souvent vaut moins'.[19] In the Middle English poem, on the contrary, the narrator's moralising expends itself in extended commentary, such as the passage (lines 659–700) where the proverb above is quoted twice and where many lines are devoted to a painstaking and finally tedious attempt to make a rather obvious point about human resilience *in extremis*.

The effect of the narrator's remarks, however, is to make the reader return to the text, his critical attention focused more on the letter than the lesson of the proceedings. The narrator, in short, becomes another version of the Owl, who tries but signally fails to raise the horizon of the debate beyond the fact of different natures. The narrator's didactic tone does hint that the poem has some serious intent (and seems, in fact, to have been responsible in some measure for the view of many modern readers that it does). If they were familiar at all with learned genres such as the fable and the literary debate, medieval readers, it seems to me, would not have been so easily taken in. They would likely have read the narrator as the straw man he is, a structure designed to provoke interest in the kind of reading the poem demands for itself. The hermeneutic circle of his commentary shows that the reading strategy recommended plays with the notion of *allegoresis* but finally returns us directly to the pleasant surfaces of the debate. Notoriously silent about the larger aspects of literary structure, medieval critical theory offers, at least to my knowledge, no support for this 'interrogative' analysis of the poem's manner of presentation. Schooled in the open pluralism of biblical exegesis, however, the educated reader for whom this poem was obviously destined would have experienced little difficulty in recognising the English author's separation of the levels of meaning represented by the discourses of his two debaters, a separation that he fails to recuperate with the narrator's metalanguage. For like the narrator in *Troilus and Criseyde*, the teller of this tale reflects a 'process' of meaning beyond his ability to unify and simplify.

The clearest signal of this rhetorical intent is the fact that the narrator's attitude shifts once again. After another extended comment replete with proverb (lines 940–54), he reassumes his initial ironic detachment. When describing the Nightingale's reaction to the news that one of her fellows had been murdered by a cuckolded husband, the narrator observes:

> þe Niʒtingale at þisse worde
> Mid sworde an mid speres orde,
> 3if ho mon were, wolde fiʒte;
> Ac þo ho bet do ne miʒte
> Ho uaʒt mid hire wise tunge.
> 'Wel fiʒt þat wel specþ,' seiþ in þe songe.
> Of hire tunge ho nom red:
> 'Wel fiʒt þat wel specþ,' seide Alured.

(1067–74)

Here the simple wisdom of the old saw underlines a humorous comment. Angry enough to 'fight like a man', the Nightingale, after all, is only a bird. And possessing neither arms nor martial vigor, she decides on the next best course – talking, one which, however, is itself hardly avian. Here the narrator, as at the poem's beginning, calls attention to the birds' incongruous burlesque of human action. The tongue is indeed often mightier than the sword, but the narrator is not seriously offering this lesson. He uses it instead to underline the fictionality of the debate's playful surface.

His ironic tone, moreover, serves to deflate the importance of the issues raised at this point. The Owl maintains that even dead she continues to help man, hanging on a hayrick to scare off magpies and crows from newly planted fields. The Nightingale, however, boasts that she has won because the Owl speaks of her own shame. Making no claims about either the Nightingale's or the owl's 'riʒt' or 'red', the narrator turns his attention instead to the birds who assemble happily, thinking the Nightingale victorious. All argument is at this point abandoned as the Owl must respond to *ad baculum* persuasion. As the dialogue sinks again to threats and invective, the narrator's role becomes the underlining of the scene's absurd disorder:

> þeos Hule spac wel baldeliche,
> For þah heo nadde swo hwatliche

Ifare after hire here,
Heo walde neoþeles ȝefe answere
þe Niȝtegale mide swucche worde.
For moni man mid speres orde
Haueþ lutle strencþe, & mid his chelde,
Ah neoþeles in one felde
þurh belde worde and mid ilete
Deþ his iuo for arehþe swete.

(1707–16)

A squawking crowd of birds is no true analogy for the grim encounter of war. Thus the narrator's juxtaposition of images does not teach, but amuse. The Owl's feistiness is merely a comic distortion of human bravery.

The arrival of the Wren, however, threatens this comic scene with interpretation. To decide which of the debaters has the upper hand would be to suggest that her outlook on life is correct and, correspondingly, which way of reading the text is appropriate. With a represented judgement, the poem would fulfill the traditional didactic purpose of fable literature, a purpose that is obviously incarnated in the wisdom of the Wren as the narrator describes her:

þe Wranne was wel wis iholde,
For þeȝ heo nere ibred a wolde,
Ho was itoȝen among mankenne
An hire wisdom brohte þenne.
Heo miȝte speke hwar heo walde,
Touore þe king þah heo scholde.

(1723–28)

Even though she is wise, the Wren cannot resolve the dispute judiciously because she is the Nightingale's friend.

The birds then decide to take their case to Master Nicholas, but he would be a judge with hopelessly divided sympathies, someone very much like the poem's narrator, in fact. As the Nightingale tells us at the very beginning (lines 192–8), Master Nicholas is a moralist and music critic *par excellence*. The Owl adds that, in passing from youth to maturity, he has moreover learned to appreciate not only the Nightingale's pleasant harmony but the Owl's serious message:

Vor þeȝ he were wile breme,
& lof him were niȝtingale
& oþer wiȝte gente & smale,
Ich wot he is nu suþe acoled.

(202–5)

Because of the Nightingale's enthusiasm for Nicholas, however, we cannot be certain that the Owl is correct in assuming he will judge in her favor. More important, the narrator in effect decides that the reader will never learn the result of Nicholas's deliberations. The poem ends with the birds flying off to seek a resolution of their dispute. The narrator, however, must remain behind, for, like the reader himself, his search for correct understanding is limited by his role as witness to an extraordinary event. Nicholas, the poem's exemplar of human nature, resolves within himself the attraction to pleasure and the need for instruction. But any account of a judgement that would settle the contradictions of human nature (or the contradictions of a human 'song' such as the poem itself) would exceed the boundaries of fiction as the narrator wisely defines them:

Au hu heo spedde of heore dome
Ne can ich eu na more telle.
Her nis na more of þis spelle.

(1792–94)

This ultimate refusal of closure, however, hardly comes as a surprise to the attentive and responsive reader of *The Owl and the Nightingale*. For through the agency of the narrator strategies of interpretation are indentified through the poem with the opposed positions/natures of the two birds, and neither strategy is endorsed as sufficient to the nature of the debate. The narrator quickly realises, once the Owl raises the issue of the birds' relationship to man, that the simple comic view of the animals, derived from the tradition of beast epic, is clearly inadequate because it can only underline the incongruity of birds functioning as characters in human discourse. Sympathising with the Owl, he then attempts, in the manner of the fable, to write out the meaning of the proceedings according to those elements of proverbial wisdom which ordinarily constitute the content of the fable's *moralitas*. This interpretative move, however, also fails, as the narrator's commentary moves us not beyond the narrative into some realm of moral deliberation with only a tenuous connection to the story but rather leads us inexorably back to the unfinished debate itself. The poem's end balances off both *dulce* and *utile* constructions of the text. On the one hand, the narrator himself resumes a comic view of the proceedings, once again emphasising the lack of fit between animal characters and human concerns/language. On the other hand, the debate projects itself toward judgement, toward the prospect of interpretation and rewriting which the Owl herself, in introducing the notion that the bird's natures are not so important in themselves as they are to mankind, has offered us as a means of understanding their dispute.

The Owl and the Nightingale, in short, presents itself as an interrogative text resistant to hermeneutic criticism in the sense that it does not permit the horizon of meaning to be raised beyond the limits of the fiction itself; like the narrator, the reader must be satisfied with not knowing and with not being able to produce the fictional experience of the debate as something final or closed. The poem does not authorize us either to name its subject or its conclusions, but rather forces us to experience partial and unsatisfactory attempts to do so. Earlier I suggested that one of the problems with Hume's reading of the poem is that it does not offer a firm connection to the contemporary world of texts into which *The Owl and the Nightingale* was inserted. Focusing on the narrator figure, however, we can see that one of his primary functions is to recall to the reader a repertoire of reading strategies gleaned from the consumption of similar kinds of literary works. In that sense the Middle English poem is 'about' the tradition of which it has become a part.

It is precisely this aspect of the poem which further, hermeneutically oriented work needs to probe, especially with a view toward rewriting its intent and effects within the larger social and literary horizons of the Middle Ages. The metafictional structures and yet socio-intellectual content of the work suggest a connection with what Bakhtin has termed the 'dialogically imagined' works of the late Middle Ages and early Renaissance, the primary example of which are the texts of Rabelais.[20] In Rabelais, as Bakhtin points out, social contradictions are displayed by a literary representation that parodies the mechanisms of literary discourse. Much the same can be said of this early Middle English poem, as I hope to have indicated here.

Notes

1. *The Owl and the Nightingale: The Poem and Its Critics* (Toronto, 1975).

2. 'A Full-Length Study of *The Owl and the Nightingale*', *Mosaic*, **10** (1976): 149.

3. 'How to Read?' in *The Poetics of Prose*, trans. Richard Howard (Ithaca, 1977), pp. 234–46.

4. HUME, p. ix.

5. (London, 1980), p. 96.

6. The criterion of *vraisemblance* has produced a particularly distorted view of medieval literary production when applied to writers who felt most strongly the burdens of – but also the opportunities made possible by – tradition. For discussion of this question with specific reference to Guillaume de Machaut see R. BARTON PALMER (ed. and trans.), *The Judgment of the King of Bohemia* (*Le Jugement dou Roy de Behaingue*), Garland Library of Medieval Literature 9 (New York, 1984), pp. xvi-xxvii, and also KEVIN BROWNLEE's important study, *Poetic Identity in Guillaume de Machaut* (Madison, 1984).

7. *The Political Unconscious: Narrative as a Socially Symbolic Act* (Ithaca, 1981), pp. 17–102.

8. This is not to say, of course, that the Robertsonian critique of other 'closed' approaches to medieval texts does not continue to furnish valuable insights about

the historical nature of this literature. See, in particular, ROBERTSON's analysis of
doctrinaire views about 'amour courtois' in *A Preface to Chaucer* (Princeton, 1962),
pp. 391–503.

9. I would agree wholeheartedly with JOHN GANIM's view that 'the gist of the best
recent criticism of the poem has been to show how the narrator, the hero, and the
philosophical background of the poem all change before our very eyes'. See his
Style and Consciousness in Middle English Narrative (Princeton, 1983), p. 79.

10. For a full-scale discussion of these different critical approaches see HUME, pp. 51–
83, and 101–18.

11. The text is from ALBERT PAUPHILET (ed.) *Jeux ex sapience du moyen age* (Paris, 1951),
p. 452. The translation is my own.

12. HUME, p. 55.

13. HIEATT, p. 149.

14. HUME, p. 98.

15. 2nd edn (New York, 1972), p. 73.

16. All quotations from the poem are from E.G. STANLEY (ed.), *The Owl and the
Nightingale* (London, 1960).

17. For a most enlightening discussion of the uses of the narrator in poetry of this
period see KARL D. UITTI, 'The Clerkly Narrator Figure in Old French Hagiography
and Romance', *Medioevo Romanza*, **2** (1975): 394–408, many of the conclusions of
which have some application to early Middle English literary structures.

18. See ROBERT BOSSUAT, *Le Roman de Renard* (Paris, 1967), pp. 90–121.

19. PAUPHILET, p. 448.

20. MIKHAIL BAKHTIN, *Rabelais and his World* (Cambridge, Mass., 1968).

9 The Romance of Kingship: *Havelok the Dane**

SHEILA DELANY

Sheila Delany's work is characterised by its rigorous insistence on the complex relations between the material and cultural contexts of literary production, and her refusal to privilege questions of gender above other forms of political – often specifically Marxist – critique. Her reading of *Havelok the Dane* is grounded in thirteenth-century theories of kingship, and traces the ways in which the poem's action, its omissions and silences, articulate not simply traditional mythical structures of romance and the divine rights of monarchy, but also contractual theories of social mobility and government by consent.

In claiming romance for the 'mythos of summer', Northrop Frye associates the genre with 'wish-fulfillment dream'. At the same time, Frye introduces an important qualification to the utopian or fantastic dimension of romance: the quest-romance 'is the search of the libido or desiring self for a fulfillment that will deliver it from the anxieties of reality but will still contain that reality' (p. 193). The Middle English verse romance *Havelok the Dane* exemplifies this double perspective in the two dimensions in which it explores the nature of kingship – a topic of the first importance in English public life of the thirteenth century, when *Havelok* was composed. The poem operates simultaneously on mythic and political levels, defining kingship in the same terms as were used in contemporary discussions of kingship: a compromise between the royal prerogative conferred by divine ordination, and the practical limitations imposed on royal power by social structure. That compromise is incarnated in the person of Havelok, who rules in two registers: as theologically ordained monarch and figural hero, saviour of the

* Reprinted from SHEILA DELANY, *Medieval Literary Politics: Shapes of Ideology* (Manchester: Manchester University Press, 1990), pp. 61–73.

kingdom; and as socially responsible leader of a multi-class nation united under law.

A brief resumé of the historical background must precede my reading of the poem.

By the late thirteenth century, the Norman and Angevin effort to centralise government had produced in England a strong sense of national unity. It had also engendered significant baronial resistance to royal power. And, especially with the thirteenth-century boom in the wool trade, a powerful bourgeoisie was clamouring – or, more accurately, manoeuvring – for extended influence in local governments and in Parliament.[1] The net result of these social forces was neither an outright rejection of absolute monarchy, nor thorough repression of dissidence and ambition. Instead, a balance was eventually achieved between royal power and the rights of subjects of various classes, which some scholars have called a 'partnership' of the interested parties: king, barons, wealthy merchants and burgesses (Tout, p. 135; Wilkinson). From a modern point of view this balance remains a conservative one, in which theocratic notions were not fully replaced but were rather tempered by the exigencies of English class structure.

Such an adjustment appears, for example, in the Great Charter of 1215. John, 'by the grace of God king of England', acting 'by the will of God, . . . to the honour of God and for the exalting of the holy church and the bettering of our realm', is forced nonetheless to limit the power of the Crown, to specify the rights of barons and other classes, and, in article 61, to reassert the legal right of resistance.[2]

But Magna Carta is a programmatic and not a theoretical document. A more fully developed statement of limited monarchy appears in the work of the jurist Henry Bracton (d. 1268), *De Legibus et Consuetudinibus Angliae*. So finely balanced is Bracton's treatise that it was quoted during the seventeenth century by royalists and parliamentarians alike. Bracton conceives the king both above and below the law, divinely appointed but, just because of this, obliged to govern properly:

The king himself must be, not under Man, but under God and the Law, because the Law makes the king. . . . For there is no king where arbitrary will dominates, and not the Law. And that he should be under the law because he is God's vicar, becomes evident through the similitude with Jesus Christ in whose stead he governs on earth. For He, God's true Mercy, though having at His disposal many means to recuperate ineffably the human race, chose before all other expedients the one which applied for the destruction of the devil's work; that is, not the strength of power, but the maxim of Justice, and therefore he wished to be under the Law in order to redeem those under the Law. For he did not wish to apply force, but reason and judgment.[3]

The success of Bracton's book (it became the basis of legal literature in the reign of Edward I) reflected the attempts being made in historical practice to redefine the nature, rights and obligations of kingship. Those attempts were evident throughout the century in several ways: the constant claims of barons and burgesses to participate in government, the baronial crisis of 1298 and the subsequent Confirmation of Charters, the development of Parliament as a legislative organ.

The concern with the nature of kingship that dominated English public life in the thirteenth century was given literary expression in *Havelok the Dane*. In its Middle English version, *Havelok* was probably composed during the reign of Edward I (1272–1307), though the precise date is uncertain.[4] The stylistic simplicity of *Havelok*, its humor and energy, and its attention to physical detail have caused many critics to call it 'bourgeois romance'. Yet since the medieval bourgeoisie included a very wide range of wealth and social status, from great banking families and mercantile magnates down to the local brewer and baker, the adjective 'bourgeois' does little to pinpoint the actual politics of a given work. My view of *Havelok* is that the main purpose of the poem is to define the nature of kingship in the person of its eponymous hero. What emerges is the characteristically English resolution, familiar from thirteenth-century theory and practice: Havelok reigns by divine right and also by consensus; he is born to rule, but, unaware of this, he earns the right to rule. In this chapter, therefore, I want first to show that Havelok is established as theocratic king, and then to indicate how that status is qualified and limited by contractual notions.

The single extant copy of *Havelok* is found in a collection of saints' lives (MS. Laud Misc. 108, Bodleian), and its imposing title seems more appropriate to a religious story than to romance: *Incipit Vita Havelok Quondam Rex Angliae et Danemarchie.* This placement need not be coincidental, for the romance presents Havelok as a worker of miracles. As rightful king, moreover – king by heredity and divine right – he is not only protected by God but becomes the instrument of divine justice. In this sense, Havelok is a figural hero: not a Christ-figure, but one whose literal or historical role in the narrative duplicates the archetypal victory of good over evil

After an invocation to Christ (15–22), the story opens with a description of the idyllic reign of Athelwold, the English king whose daughter Havelok will marry and whose ideal government he will duplicate. The description is a conventional one, with many antecedents and analogues in medieval literature and historiography.[5] Yet the convention serves a special literary purpose here, and is tailored to show particular virtues. Athelwold's piety takes the form of justice, as it ought to do when the king is God's representative on earth; in Bracton's phrase *'Dum facit justiciam, vicarius est Regis Eterni, minister autem diaboli dum declinat ad iniuriam'* (f. 107b). As we will see, the story includes both types. Athelwold, however, administers the strait retributive justice expected of *'vicarius Regis Eterni'*:

He lovede God with all his might,
And holy kirke and soth and right.
Right-wise men he lovede alle,
And overall made hem forto calle.
Wreyeres and wrobberes made he falle
And hated hem so man doth galle; . . .   (35–40)

Friend to the fatherless, protector of widows and maidens (71–97), Athelwold
practises the primary Christian virtue of *caritas*, feeding the poor and winning
Christ's reward in duplicating Christ's goodness (98–105). Loved by all,
Athelwold is mourned by all in his fatal illness. He entrusts his small daughter
Goldeboru to the wardship of Earl Godrich of Cornwall. It is a sacred trust,
and the ceremony is a religious one which includes

      the messebook,
The caliz, and the pateyn ok,
The corporaus, the messe-gere . . .   (186–8)

Thereupon the king takes to his deathbed; his preparation is that of a saint
and includes prayer, confession and self-flagellation. Then Athelwold
distributes all his goods and money (218–25), an act which reminds us that 'it
is easier for a camel to go through the eye of the needle than for a rich man
to enter the kingdom of God' (Mark 10:25). Athelwold dies calling on Christ
and repeating Christ's dying words (from Luke 23:46; lines 228–31).

After the sorrow of the populace is somewhat abated, bells are rung and
masses sung,

That God self shulde his soule leden
Into hevene biforn his Sone
And ther withuten ende wone.   (245–7)

The extended portrait of Athelwold and his reign has thus set a standard for
godly rule which will not be easily met.

The idyllic condition of England ends abruptly, less by Athelwold's death
than by the treachery of the evil Earl Godrich. Despite his holy vow to guard
both Goldeboru and England, Godrich establishes a strict and oppressive
bureaucracy (248–79), and when Goldeboru comes of age withholds the
kingdom from her. As Athelwold was linked with Christ and the saints,
Godrich is compared with Judas and Satan (319, 1100–1, 1133–4). Like Judas,
Godrich betrays God and his leader for material gain: he has broken a
religious vow and usurped the throne from its divinely ordained occupant.
The author calls for miraculous intervention to restore Goldeboru (and, by
implication, England), like Lazarus, to her former condition (331–3).

Godrich's usurpation figurally re-enacts the archetypal Christian conflict of good and evil; plainly the hero who can perform the prayed-for feat of liberation must be Christ's agent.

The narrative turns now to Denmark, where the preceding story of betrayal is repeated (though it is told less amply). Birkabein, the good and holy king, entrusts his heirs to Earl Godard. Godard kills the two girls in a particularly bloody way (465–75), and arranges to have Havelok killed by his serf, Grim. Godard's momentary pity on the boy is called 'miracle fair and good' (500), and Godard, like his English counterpart, is compared to Judas and to Satan (422–5, 482, 496, 506, 1409, 1411, 2229, 2512). Christ's curses are heaped on him (426–46), and another miracle is prayed for so that Havelok may avenge himself (542–4). In fact a sequence of 'miracles' has already begun, as noted above. The first of them (not explicitly labelled as such) was that which caused 'the dumb to speak': the seven-year-old Havelok's extraordinary access of rhetoric which had prompted Godard's pity. Another providential miracle occurs immediately after the prayer: in the dimness of their cottage, Grim and his wife see a light shining from Havelok's mouth 'als it were a sunnebem'; they also notice the 'kine-merk' on his shoulder (later we discover that it is a golden cross: 1262–3, 2139–40). These signs of divine appointment cause Grim to commit himself to Havelok rather than to the diabolical Godard. He does so in a prayer-like passage which deliberately exploits the ambiguity of the words 'lord' and 'freedom':

> 'Loverd, have mercy
> Of me and Leve, that is me by!
> Loverd, we aren bothe thine,
> Thine cherles, thine hine . . .
> Thoru other man, loverd, than thoru thee
> Shal I nevere freeman be.
> Thou shalt me, loverd, free maken.
> For I shall yemen thee and waken;
> Thoru thee wile I freedom have.'   (617–31)

The theological dimension of this speech is intensified by the resemblance of Grim's repentance to that of Peter after he denies Christ; as Peter 'broke down and wept' (Mark 14:72) so Grim 'sore gret' (615). We may add that Grim, like Peter, is a fisherman; that he is Havelok's first subject, as Peter was the first apostle; and that his role as founder of the town of Grimsby parallels Peter's as founder of the Church (Matthew 16:18). Again the symbolism is a deft and unobtrusive reminder of Havelok's theocratic role.

With his family and Havelok, Grim sails to England, settles at Grimsby, and becomes a prosperous fisherman and merchant. Havelok finds work in nearby Lincoln, where his good qualities endear him to all (945–88). So well-known is Havelok that Godrich, attending Parliament in Lincoln, decides to use him in order to rid himself of Goldeboru. Having promised to wed

Goldeboru to the 'hexte' (highest) man in the land, Godrich thinks he will observe only the literal meaning of that promise (the tallest man), unaware that in so doing he providentially fulfills its moral and social meanings as well (the best man, the most exalted) and prepares his own downfall. The forced marriage is performed by the Archbishop of York, who 'cam to the parlement / Als God him havede thider sent' (1179–80). Thus the marriage is consecrated by the highest ecclesiastical authority.

Havelok now returns with his royal bride to Grimsby, where the holy marks of kingship are revealed for the second time. Goldeboru does not understand their full significance until an angel's voice interprets them and reveals Havelok's destiny. With this heavenly communication Goldeboru is able to interpret Havelok's prophetic dream and to help him plan a strategy for winning the throne of Denmark. Havelok consecrates his project at church, and sets sail for Denmark.

In Denmark Havelok does battle with a group of thieves who, as 'Caimes kin and Eves' (2045) participate in the nature of archetypal Biblical sinners. After this victory the holy king-marks are again revealed, this time to the royal justice Ubbe. Recognised at last as rightful heir in his own land, Havelok is able to bring Godard to the hideous death he deserves. Returning to England, Havelok engages in climactic single combat with Godrich. He shows his mercy by offering to forgive if Godrich will renounce all claim to the throne. When mercy is rejected, justice must be done, and Godrich meets as painful a death as Godard had done. Havelok is made king, rewards are distributed, fealty is taken 'on the bok'. A new golden age begins for England under a divinely appointed king who equals Athelwold in strength, virtue and piety.

To read *Havelok* from a religious point of view reveals a king who is virtually a saviour-figure: he defeats diabolical opponents, avenges those who have been wronged, and brings a new reign of harmony, love and peace. But the poem also develops another aspect of Havelok's rule, simultaneously with the theocratic. That is the political or contractual side of his rule, to which I now turn.

Reviewing the beginning of *Havelok*, we find that England's golden age under Athelwold is defined in political as well as in religious terms. The king is distinguished by his ability to make and enforce good laws (27–9), and his reign by a remarkable consensus among all social classes:

Him lovede yung, him lovede olde,
Erl and barun, dreng and thain,
Knight, bondeman, and swain,
Widwes, maidnes, prestes and clerkes,
And alle for hise gode werkes.   (30–4)

The theme of consensus is constant in the story, and it is as important a key to judgement as the religious symbols discussed above. Again and again the author emphasises that the good ruler governs on behalf of and with the approval of his population, at least the middle and upper classes. Thus when Athelwold falls ill,

> He sende writes sone anon
> After his erles evereich on:
> And after hise baruns, riche and povre,
> Fro Rokesburw all into Dovere . . .   (136–9)

This council of earls and barons chooses Godrich as ward of Athelwold's daughter, just as Godard is chosen ward of Birkabein's children by a similar council of Danish barons and knights (364–82).

Havelok's influence when he works as a cook's helper in Lincoln transcends class lines (955–8), a trait which anticipates the contractual character of his rule. When Goldeboru interprets Havelok's prophetic dream, she is careful to include among his future loyal subjects 'Erl and baroun, dreng and thain, / Knightes and burgeys and swain' (1327–8). When Ubbe discovers Havelok's holy light, he summons his entire retinue of 'knightes and sergaunz'. The formulaic list is repeated when Ubbe promises that Havelok shall take fealty of the entire population (2138–85), when he summons them (2194–5) and when the oath is sworn (2258–65). When the ceremony is done, Ubbe sends out an even more general writ throughout the entire country to castles, boroughs and towns, knights, constables and sheriffs (2274–89). When Godard is caught, his sentence is decided by a popular assembly which includes knights and burgesses (2465–73). Godrich is judged by a more limited but still representative jury of his peers (761–5).

In contrast to Athelwold and Havelok, the usurpers Godrich and Godard govern autocratically. Godard makes decisions solely on the basis of personal will (249–59). He demands a loyalty oath from all subjects without admitting any to partnership in government (260–2), and Godard does the same in Denmark (437–42). Godrich rules by fear alone, creating an oppressive bureaucracy in order to enforce his ambitious schemes (266–79). When Godrich rallies his barons for battle with Havelok, not only does he fail to seek their advice, but he coerces by threatening to reduce them to thralls (2564–5) – a flagrant and unheard-of violation of custom and law.[6]

Although consensus is an important feature of kingship in *Havelok*, the poem puts forth nothing like what we would now call a 'democratic' social ideal – nor did political and legal theory of the time. The 'partnership' mentioned earlier included barons, smaller landholders (knights) and the upper bourgeoisie. Peasants and labourers were not considered to have legitimate class interests other than what was defined for them by their lords or employers: this was to remain generally true in England well into the seventeenth century, and even through the Civil War (MacPherson, Part 3). The interests represented in *Havelok* are those of the newly powerful propertied classes: they hoped to share the privilege of government, but had no intention of extending that privilege beyond themselves.

Among Athelwold's virtues is his prompt attention to crimes against property. Thieves are the particular object of his hatred (39–43), and his zeal against them makes England a safe place for wealthy people and travelling merchants (45–58).[7] Indeed the prosperity accruing from commercial activity seems to constitute a large part of England's 'ease' in praise of which the author concludes this passage (59–61).

Acquisition of wealth and property appears in the poem as an honourable pursuit and one requiring virtuous character. Grim's loyalty to Havelok, as well as his industry, is rewarded by prosperity, which, by the time he dies, amounts to a large family fortune in money, goods and livestock (1221–8). Even as Godard's thrall, Grim had not been badly off; he owned substantial livestock (699–702) and a well-equipped ship sturdy enough to sail to England (706–13). Still, Grim is not free, and he acknowledges that only Havelok can make him free (618–31). This would seem at first to infringe contemporary feudal law, for a serf could be directly manumitted only by his overlord (in this case Godard), not by the king. The only way in which the king could be said to confer freedom was through the law of year and day. This privilege, included in many borough charters, provided that any person who lived peacefully in the borough in his own house for the stipulated period, would automatically become free.[8] What Grim seems to anticipate, then, is that his path to freedom lies through the borough privileges which were the essence of the alliance between king and upper bourgeoisie.

As a youth, Havelok heartily adopts the middle-class work ethic; he helps Grim to sell fish, for

> It is no shame forto swinken;
> The man that may well eten and drinken
> That nought he have but on swink long;
> To liggen at hom it is full strong.   (799–802)

But a shortage ('dere') of grain forces Havelok to seek full-time work in Lincoln instead. The situation there is grim. Havelok remains unemployed and hungry for two days, until

> The thridde day herde he calle;
> 'Bermen, bermen, hider forth alle!'
> Povre that on fote yede
> Sprongen forth so sparke of glede,
> Havelok shof dune nine or ten

> Right amidewarde the fen,
> And stirte forth to the cook,
> Ther the erles mete he took
> That he boughte at the bridge;
> The bermen let he alle lidge,
> And bar the mete to the castel,
> And gat him there a ferthing wastel.   (867–78)

Noteworthy in this passage are, first, the large number of unemployed who, at the cook's call, 'spring forth like sparks from a coal'; and, second, Havelok's brutal fervour in shoving his hungry competitors into the mud. The incident is repeated the next day. So impressed is the earl's cook with this eagerness that he offers Havelok a steady job. Havelok accepts, stipulating no other wages than enough to eat (901–20). Havelok is as conscientious a worker as we might expect from his behaviour so far: he does everything (931–42) and afterward does more:

> Wolde he nevere haven rest
> More than he were a best.
> Of alle men was he mest meke,
> Lauhwinde ay and blithe of speke;
> Ever he was glad and blithe;
> His sorwe he couthe full well mithe.   (943–8)

In short, Havelok is presented as an ideal worker. Yet we must acknowledge that he is an ideal worker only from the point of view of an employer. He is extremely competitive with other workers, works for nothing, gladly works to the point of exhaustion, and never complains but always smiles. None of this behaviour could be considered either realistic or admirable by an audience of ordinary workers, though it would suit the taste of their urban employers or manorial supervisors.

With Havelok's experience in Lincoln we see that his movement through the story, after Godard's usurpation, is to be a progression from lowest to highest social class. He begins as the foster-child of a serf, at Grimsby becomes a free fisherman's assistant, and at Lincoln an employee in the earl's household. That progression continues when, after marrying Goldeboru, Havelok returns to Denmark as a merchant, is knighted by Ubbe in token of his victory over the thieves, and finally achieves the throne. Presumably Havelok's experience of all classes will enlarge his political sympathies when he is king, and teach him the needs of his entire population. At the same time Havelok's social ascent permits him to display, in each condition, the noblest side of his nature and the one most appropriate to the particular class, whether cheerful acquiescence or valiant self-defense.

Nearly two hundred lines are lost from that portion of the poem which narrates the crossing to Denmark, a project supported and financed by Grim's (now wealthy) sons. When the text resumes we find Havelok conversing with Ubbe. It is Ubbe's function, as justice, to grant foreign merchants permission to sell their goods, and to receive for that privilege a toll or hanse: in this case a very valuable gold ring (1632–4). Ubbe invites Havelok and Goldeboru to dine with him, guaranteeing, with an elegant play on her name the safety of Havelok's most valuable property':

> 'And have thou of hire no drede;
> Shall hire no man shame bede.
> By the fey I owe to thee,
> Thereof shall I myself boru be.'   (1664–7)

Despite this assurance, Havelok worries lest someone abduct his wife (1668–73), and Ubbe himself, acknowledging the possibility, sends a special guard to Havelok's lodging. When the attack occurs, its motive is unclear. Huwe Raven is sure that *raptus* is the aim of the sixty armed invaders (868–70); but Havelok's wealthy host Bernard Brun thinks it is robbery (1955–9). Though the local burgesses agree with Bernard, rejoicing that he has lost no property ('tinte no catel', 2023), Ubbe continues to emphasise the protection of Goldeboru.

Beside letting the poet display some of his most vigorous verse, and Havelok his formidable courage and strength, the battle episode underscores the need for a strong just king and a centralised administration. Again this point of view coincides with the interests of the upper bourgeoisie, whose property and fortunes could be protected, whose liberties and privileges could be granted and maintained, only by a strong centralised government. When we recall that under Athelwold no merchant travelling in England would have encountered the least trouble (45–8), the entire episode shows Godard's abysmal failure to sustain the moral tone of Denmark and to make it safe for the middle classes. Since Godrich has been unable to establish a judicial system or a public police force, Ubbe, fearing retaliation from friends of the slaughtered thieves, removes Havelok to his own well-protected house – where of course the recognition scene occurs.

A curious feature of Havelok's accession to kingship is its complete secularity. In Denmark, Ubbe summons the population, who confer the kingdom upon Havelok (2316–19). Of the English accession we hear only that the feast lasted more than forty days (2948–50). The Danish accession emphasises the ancient electoral principle, and conspicuously absent from both accounts is any mention of a traditional coronation ceremony. There is no reference to a crown; no bishops or other ecclesiastical figures are present; Havelok is neither consecrated nor anointed with holy oil; he wears no coronation robes, so closely resembling sacerdotal vestments; nor does he take anything resembling the traditional English coronation oath with its promise to safeguard the Church.

My argument is admittedly *ex silentio*: nonetheless the omission of a coronation ceremony, with its heavy ecclesiastical overtones, is significant. First, such a ceremony could have provided the author with an ideal opportunity for ceremonial description, an opportunity most medieval authors welcomed in such events as weddings, dubbings, battles, and so on. Indeed we have already seen that our author enjoys and excels at physical description and detail: the death of Athelwold, the battle at Bernard's, and other *loci* prove that. Second, even more surprising than the poet's bypassing a splendid literary opportunity is his ignoring an event which in his own time was an extremely important one in English public life, and which had been important for generations.[9] Both literary and social tradition, then, suggest that a coronation scene would be an obvious climax in the poem. Its omission, however, is neither accidental nor inconsistent.

In part the secularity of Havelok's accession may reflect the nationalistic sentiment that infused thirteenth-century English public life, for that sentiment was largely a product of England's assertion of sovereignty against papal intervention to emphasise the rights of *regnum* over those of *sacerdotium*. It stresses the inviolable unity of the nation.

But beyond this, the secular coronation rounds out the new definition of kingship offered in *Havelok*, and here a historical analogue cannot be ignored. Like Havelok, Edward I became king in an unusual manner. Since he was abroad when his father died in 1272, Edward's succession was proclaimed immediately by hereditary right and will of the magnates. This was confirmed by oath of fealty from knights and burgesses, and Edward began to reign from the date of his election. It was the first time that full legal recognition had been extended to an heir before coronation, for Edward was formally crowned – that is, he received ecclesiastical approval – only two years later, on his return to England. Thus Edward's accession itself showed that the English notion of kingship had already moved well away from the theocratic extreme, and that the will of those governed had become as significant a factor as the will of God. 'The double note, of conservatism and experiment, which was to sound throughout his reign, seemed already struck before he began it' (Johnstone, p. 393). It is the same double note that *Havelok* strikes.

At the end of the romance, the theme of social mobility emerges again. The rise of Grim and Havelok has already validated social mobility, while the villainy of Earls Godard and Godrich indicates that rank cannot guarantee character. Havelok himself underlines the importance of moral, rather than social, superiority when he refers to Godard as a 'thrall' (1408); later the author calls Godrich a 'mixed [filthy] cherl' (2533), rhyming 'cherl' with 'erl' to intensify the paradox.[10] Now, social mobility is extended to Havelok's supporters. Grim's three sons are elevated to knights and barons (2346–53), and Grim's daughters are raised even higher. One of them is given in marriage to the Earl of Chester, the other to Havelok's former employer, the cook, who is now by Havelok's grant Earl of Cornwall. These rewards, especially the last, may seem extravagant, and Halvorsen has called this scene 'a peasant fantasy'.[11] But the scene is neither fantastic, nor expressive of peasant aspirations; it represents the social reality and realistic ambitions of the upper bourgeoisie and knighthood.

I would point out, first, that a post in a noble household was often a prestigious sinecure. The Earl's 'cook' may have been himself a wealthy tenant-knight with merely supervisory duties. Though the exact duty of a nobleman's 'cook' is not known, it is known that William the Conqueror gave his 'cook' half a hide of land, and that the Count of Boulogne conferred on his 'cook' the estate of Wilmiton (Pollock and Maitland, pp. 262–71). Moreover, the period was one of rapid and often dramatic social change. Serfs left the manor to become free labourers or artisans; artisans might amass sufficient capital and property to become burgesses; recently wealthy merchants and financiers bought estates and titles, intermarried with nobility, adopted an aristocratic life-style, and aspired to participate in government. In 1307, perhaps only a few years after *Havelok* was composed, the young Edward II created Piers Gavaston, a knight's son, Earl of Cornwall – a title whose two previous holders had been king's sons. Joan, daughter of Edward I and widow of the Earl of Gloucester, in 1295 married a knight, to whom Edward eventually entrusted the Gloucester inheritance. However it was not only in Edward's private life that he confirmed social mobility, but also in his deliberate expansion of 'the community of the realm' to include the upper middle classes, as in the 'Model Parliament' of 1295. For Edward recognised that the upper bourgeoisie was both a valuable financial resource, and a reliable ally against the barons. Thus the reward scene in *Havelok* represents little that had not been, or would not soon be, accomplished in reality.

The idea of theocratic monarchy in England would long outlive the thirteenth century, though the history of Richard II shows that Tudor and Stuart monarchs could assert with impunity what their predecessors could not. Still, the origins of its demise in the Civil War of 1642 lay precisely, and paradoxically, in the 'partnership' – the gradual institutional adjustments – by which monarchy survived in the thirteenth century. To the beginning of that fruitful change *Havelok the Dane* bears witness.

Notes

1. See POWER and, for a convenient summary of scholarship on medieval English government and social structure, WICKSON.

2. Text in McKECHNIE. Article 61, McKechnie notes, was 'nothing more nor less than legalised rebellion' (p. 153); and though it was scarcely a feasible concession, it is nonetheless a significant one.

3. Bracton, *De Leg.*, f. 5b, in the edition of Woodbine, vol. 2, p. 33; quoted in KANTOROWIZ, p. 156. See also SCHULZ, POLLOCK and MAITLAND, vol. I; and McILWAIN, Chapter 4.

4. The later limit is generally taken to be 1303, the date of composition of Robert Mannyng's *Handlyng Synne*, which seems to imitate parts of *Havelok*. Skeat's discussion of final -e suggests that the poem was originally written before 1300, and other internal evidence points to a date after 1296. See 'Introduction' (revised by K. Sisam) to W. Skeat's edition (Oxford, 2nd ed. 1915). All quotations in my text are from the edition of Sands. The two earlier versions of the Havelok story are Geoffrey Gaimer's Anglo-Norman *Estorie des engles*, and the Old French *Lai d'Havelok*, both twelfth century.

5. Thus Bede's *History* (2:16) praises the great peace in Britain under King Edwin, commenting on the king's special care for travellers. The *Anglo-Saxon Chronicle* for 1087 commends the righteousness and piety of William the Conqueror, his mildness to good men and severity to bad; his reign is described as a time when 'a man might go over the kingdom unhurt, with his bosom full of gold'. The Peterborough continuation of the *Chronicle* claims that under Henry I a man could carry treasure anywhere without being molested. For some details in my account of the religious theme, I am indebted to a paper by V. Ishkanian, my graduate student at Simon Fraser University.

6. The reduction of free men to servile status was not in itself unheard of in the later thirteenth century, for it was a widely debated legal question whether performance of base services over several generations could make free stock servile (POLLOCK and MAITLAND, p. 410). Opinion generally ran that it could not. As applied to magnates the threat can have had no real social analogue, and is meant to show the hyperbolic viciousness of Godrich's nature, as well as his contempt for the law of the land.

7. This may allude to Edward's special campaign against robbery, embodied in the Statute of Winchester (1285). The Statute specifies the duties of towns and hundreds, lords, sheriffs and bailiffs in expanding roads, cutting forests, guarding estates, and general surveillance against strangers: see *Records of the Borough of Northampton* (Northampton, 1889) vol. I, pp. 416–19. This was only one of Edward's many attempts to investigate and correct the bureaucratic abuses of the previous regime and his own; the results of his official inquiries appear in the Hundred Rolls and in various county assize rolls.

8. POLLOCK and MAITLAND add that the same law applied to serfs who escaped to the king's domain. As a borough privilege, the law of year and day helped to create a pool of free labour required by the bourgeoisie. Encouraged partly by this law, serfs and villeins deserted the manors in considerable numbers; see DOBB, Chapter 2.

9. See RICHARDSON. A convenient guide to scholarship on the coronation ceremonies and oaths is the bibliography in HOYT. SCHRAMM provides a full study of the ceremony and its tradition.

10. The relation of rank and character is a familiar theme in the literature of the twelfth through fourteenth centuries. It is debated in *De Arte Honesti Amandi* of Andreas Capellanus (Dialogues two and three). In Jean de Meun's continuation of the *Roman de la Rose*, Reason shows that the nobleman who seeks only pleasure becomes Satan's serf (4396–8). Chaucer, following Jean, would take up the question of true 'gentilesse' in his *Wife of Bath's Tale*, and it would be illustrated (through from a different angle) by Langland in the person of Piers Plowman.

11. While I admire Halvorsen's wish to place *Havelok* in its social context, his concept of class is vague and inaccurate. He suggests, for instance, that 'middle class' is

preferable to 'bourgeois' as a designation for this type of literature, because the former term is more inclusive, ranging from 'the villager and peasant at one end [of the social spectrum] and powerful burgher and even petty nobility at the other'. But it is just this inclusiveness that produces imprecision: witness Halvoren's inclusion of peasants in the middle class with no specification as to rich or poor peasant, servile or free, etc. My argument is that *Havelok* is by no means as diffuse in its ideology as Halvorsen implies: its range of social consciousness does not include that of villagers and peasants but is limited to that of burgesses and barons. One would be surprised to find a work of literature so false to social reality that it could claim identity of values among classes so divergent in their interests.

Such, however, appears to be the vision of David Staines, whose discussion of *Havelok* is hopelessly confused as far as class and class ideology are concerned. For Staines, the poem expresses social ideas suitable to royalty and 'the lower classes' alike. This would be quite a juggling act, even if Staines had enlightened us as to the referent of 'lower classes' and explained what they are lower than: lower than the king? lower than the bourgeoisie? lower than the artisanate? The article beautifully illustrates the need for precision in class terminology.

References

DOBB, MAURICE, *Studies in the Development of Capitalism* (New York, 1947).

HALVORSEN, JOHN, '*Havelok the Dane* and Society', *Chaucer Review* **6** (1971), pp. 142–51.

HOYT, ROBERT S., 'The Coronation oath of 1308', *Traditio* **77** (1955), pp. 235–7.

JOHNSTONE, H., Chapter 14, vol. 7 in *The Cambridge Medieval History*, 8 vols. (Cambridge, repr. 1964–7).

KANTOROWICZ, ERNST, *The King's Two Bodies* (Princeton, 1957).

MCILWAIN, C.H., *Constitutionalism Ancient and Modern* (Ithaca, rev. ed. 1947).

POLLOCK, F. and F.W. MAITLAND, 'The Age of Bracton' in *The History of English Law* (Cambridge, 1895).

POWER, EILEEN, *The Wool Trade in Medieval English History* (Oxford, 1941).

RICHARDSON, H.G., 'The Coronation of Edward I', *Bulletin of the Institute for Historical Research* **15** (1937–8).

SANDS, DONALD B., *Middle English Verse Romances* (New York, 1966).

SCHRAMM, P.E., *A History of the English Coronation* (Oxford, 1937).

SCHULZ, F., 'Bracton on Kingship', *English Historical Review* **60** (1945), pp. 136–75.

STAINES, DAVID, '*Havelock the Dane*: A Thirteenth-Century Handbook for Princes', *Speculum*, **51** (1976), pp. 602–23.

WICKSON, ROGER, *The Community of the Realm in Thirteenth Century England* (London, 1970).

10 The Rhetoric of Excess in *Winner and Waster**

STEPHANIE TRIGG

Many interpretations have been offered for this difficult and incomplete text. My essay uses deconstructive strategies to examine the binary opposition around which the poem seems to be structured, and suggests that the poet uses competing literary, historical and rhetorical traditions to continually redefine and indeed, conflate, the opposing figures of Winner and Waster. Working in a period of radical social and political change, the poet attempts to contain his economic and ethical critiques within traditional formulations, but he is not always able to produce the impartial, authoritative voice on which such poetry conventionally depends.

It has sometimes seemed that we might be able to chart our way more securely through the complex networks of fourteenth-century alliterative poetry if we listened carefully to the voices of its poets. In the absence of much external evidence about the identities, location, or dates of these authors, we must make do with internal hints, however indirect or uncertain they may be, as in the cases of Langland and the *Gawain*-poet. In our desire for information about the circumstances in which these poems were composed and performed, we have, so to speak, asked them a series of questions, inviting a series of fairly literal answers. As a result, our ideas of poetic voicing in alliterative poetry are comparatively straightforward, especially when set beside the complexity allowed to Chaucer's speaking voices by critics such as Donaldson, and more recently, Nolan and Leicester. In the light of these more sophisticated models, we may need to reconsider the conditions which produce the effect of authorial voice in alliterative poetry, rather than using voice to reconstruct its original contexts.

---

* Reprinted from *Yearbook of Langland Studies*, **3** (1989): 91–108.

The prologue of *Winner and Waster* is usually read as an autobiographical narrative which not only yields up information about the author and his presumed location in the West Midlands, but also, by implication, serves as an interpretive key to the poem as a whole. Once we identify an authorial voice in the prologue, it is easy to read *Winner and Waster* as a highly motivated expression of conservative distrust and resentment of change.[1] The speaker here seems to be an old man, hostile to the influences of the towns and courts of the south, presumably London:

Dare neuer no westren wy   while this werlde lasteth
Send his sone southewarde   to see ne to here
That he ne schall holden byhynde   when he hore eldes.

(7–9)[2]

Yet this is itself a voice created by the tradition of complaint literature: it has been well remarked by Turville-Petre that *Winner and Waster* anthologises some of the most popular commonplaces of vernacular poetry (20). This miniature *compilatio* appeals to a number of familiar topoi: the claims about Britain's origins in Brutus's treachery at Troy; the current state of the kingdom as the site of more and more frequent marvels; dire warnings about change and corruption; apocalyptic prophecies; and laments about the disfavor into which good poetry has fallen, finishing with the poet's advertisement for his own skills in the poem which follows. These topoi and the typical speaking voices which express them – or indeed, which help us to identify them as conventions – are similar enough to produce the illusion of a consistent speaking-voice, but it is important to acknowledge the range of voices at play here and elsewhere in the poem, drawn from or produced by specific literary, ethical, and rhetorical traditions. The prologue represents only one such voice.

   That this voice is inadequate to contain or ground an interpretation of the text is evident from the widespread disagreement and uncertainty over the meaning of *Winner and Waster*. The poem can show us no clear solution to the many problems raised by the debate, and readers disagree as to whether they think Winner or Waster is the victor; whether the poet is praising or satirizing the current economic policies of the king and his court. Jacobs suggests that the debate is intended to be of the balanced or resolved type, arguing for the conceptual interdependence of the two positions: winning and wasting, or saving and spending (485). But as he points out, the terms and presentation of the debate favor Waster, contrary to the semantic associations of the key words, according to which Winner should enjoy the moral approval of the poem and its readers.[3] Harrington recommends Iser's textual indeterminacy as an interpretive model for reading *Winner and Waster*, but his conclusion, that 'a poet succeeds if he stimulates us to respond more intelligently than his characters do' (256), is based on a formalist reading of the text which ignores its economic, social, and political contexts.

The chief point of contention is the relationship between winning and wasting, whether the conjunction in the title denies or conceals a hierarchic distribution of value between these terms. There are at least three configurations of the opposition, corresponding to the three theoretical possibilities for the outcome of the debate: a victory for Winner, a victory for Waster, or reconciliation in some kind of ethical synthesis or resolution of the two positions. When we first meet them, Winner and Waster are presented very formally as the leaders of two armies representing two sides of an allegorical dispute to be judged by the king. However, there is also an important sense in which Winner occupies the privileged position – as the ant is victorious over the grasshopper – representing providence and social responsibility, and seeming to echo the conservative voice of the prologue by arguing in favor of restraint and stability. It is all the more surprising, then, that a number of readers have found narratorial favor in the poem ultimately residing with Waster (Jacobs 495–6; James 253–7). He is generally agreed to be the more attractive character; and his readiness to spend money on entertainment and pleasure is linked with a greater expansiveness of spirit and humor which makes Winner appear a parsimonious miser, a bourgeois merchant concerned only with personal profit. As we will see, the poem marks out the conflict between these different value systems by constantly altering the representations of its two personifications, attempting to flesh out a formal opposition in contemporary social terms. At different times, Waster is the leader of a mercenary army, a knight of the king's household, a disaffected aristocrat who squanders his inheritance, a laborer who refuses to work, a wealthy man with due concern for the poor, a glutton, and a courtly lover.

These competing representations of both characters generate a number of contradictions, and the situation is further compounded by the text's appeal to a variety of different historical contexts and material conditions. It is impossible for the king (and us) to resolve the debate, not because the claims of Winner and Waster are equal, or so badly presented (Bestul 31; Harrington 252), but because they cannot be weighed against one another: the rhetorical, literary, and historical contexts which would give content and meaning to their abuse, insults, and claims keep shifting. The following section traces some of these different senses of winning and wasting. Instead of the stable perspective offered by the prologue, or the static economy of antithesis suggested by the alliterative title, we find the generous production of meanings and voices, and the progressive undermining of the initial opposition, through what I shall call the rhetoric of excess. Finally, I will propose a different way of reading the poet's own engagement with these ideas, suggesting that his own circumstances might have been such as to render him unable to maintain the objective, authoritative perspective to which the genre of debate and the tradition of complaint would encourage him to aspire.

Curiously, we meet the two named disputants, Winner and Waster, only in the second half of the poem, though the title, or at least the manuscript *incipit*, gives us some clues about the identity of the leaders of the two armies. There is only one manuscript of the poem, British Library Additional MS. 31042, and the scribe, Robert Thornton, has copied the following words at the head of the poem: *Here begynnes a tretys and god schorte refreyte bytwixe Wynnere and Wastoure.* The poem is thus introduced as a very formal debate; and the two armies that march towards one another in the poet's dream landscape are, at first glance, of equal strength:

> In aythere holte was ane here   in hawberkes full brighte,
> Harde hattes appon hedes   and helmys with crestys;
> Brayden owte thaire baners   bown for to mete;
> Schowen owte of the schawes   in schiltrons þay felle
> And bot the lengthe of a launde   thies lordes bytwene.
>
> (50–4)

The dreamer describes the clothes of the king who sits, like a tournament judge, above the clearing; the *wodwyse* who attends him; then the herald, who arms himself and descends to address the assembled troops, forbidding them to fight. He blazons the charges carried by the armies, and here the first major interpretive difficulty arises. Several lines (138–42) describe foreigners assembled from France, Italy, Spain, Ireland, and various parts of Germany, though it is not clear on whose side they are fighting: their presence presumably underlines the seriousness of the event. Then the combined forces of the Pope, a company of lawyers, the four orders of friars, and representatives of merchant towns are described in great detail, while the other side, consisting of more warlike archers, is presented in four lines. We soon guess that these are led by Winner and Waster respectively. Moreover, there is a confusion of registers, for to group Pope, lawyers, and friars together as winners is to invoke the traditional attitudes of estates satire, yet the herald describes the friars' banners in terms of warm praise. At the same time, he identifies the Franciscans as fighting for profit:

> I wote wele for wynnynge   thay wentten fro home,
> His purse weghethe full wele   that wanne thaym all hedire.
>
> (161–2)

And if there is a tone of disapproval in the herald's speech, it does not take the form of traditional anti-mendicant satire (this is reserved for Waster's attack on his opponent): rather, he expresses his surprise, several times, at seeing the representatives of religious orders arrayed in such warlike guise.

On his bidding, the two leaders ride out and approach the king, but they are not described in any way that might identify them with their respective armies: they are praised as 'Knyghtis full comly one coursers attyred', retainers of the king, who 'clothes vs bothe / And hase vs fosterde and fedde this fyve and twenty wyntere' (205–6). We thus witness a complete reversal of the situation invoked in line 134, where the herald addresses the assembled forces as foreigners who are not familiar with the laws governing private armies. The ground is shifting very quickly, and we need to be alert to these changes. Still unnamed, Winner and Waster kneel before the king, in the formal ritual of homage and obedience, and share his wine. As this first fitt closes, the scene is transformed: the armies, the herald, the pageantry virtually disappear, and the debate becomes more domestic and personal though there are further transformations to come. And while the two knights occasionally refer back to their armies and their desire to fight, the formal alternation of speeches – four each – is undisturbed.

In this framing of the debate, the poem relies structurally on a model of simple, balanced opposition. We might anticipate its distribution between the two ethical poles of avarice and prodigality; and the poet does indeed invoke and return to this scheme as the debate develops. It is by no means a universal medieval pattern, of course: in some ethical treatises, prodigality is classed as a branch of pride. However, the most important conceptual influence on the poem, that of the *Nicomachean Ethics*, posits these two as extreme vices, and generosity as the golden mean between them (Bestul 5–7). This is the tradition which seems to generate the debate form, both at a structural level and also in the rhetorical patterns of abuse and contrast which recur in the speeches of both disputants. Winner and Waster rarely answer each other's accusations with anything more than counter-accusations; and Bestul draws a parallel with a passage from the *Inferno*, which 'provides an illuminating instance of how the abstractions of theology pass into concrete literary representation'(16). As the avaricious and the prodigal meet, they cry to one another: '"Perchè tiene?", e "Perchè burli?"' These personifications are also found in an example of antithesis in Matthew of Vendôme's *Ars Versificatoria*:

Prandeo, jejunas; do, quaeris; gaudeo, maeres;
Poto, sitis; retines, erogo; spero, times.

I lunch, you fast; I give, you ask; I rejoice, you lament;
I drink, you thirst; I spend, you save; I hope, you fear.

This material opposition between those who would preserve and those who would consume lends itself easily to the dramatic representation of struggle over the same goods; and the *Winner*-poet takes up this idea in his suggestion that Winner and Waster represent two departments of the king's household. He similarly combines rhetoric, syntax, and the two halves of the alliterative long line to confirm the opposition. This is part of Winner's opening speech:

Alle þat I wynn thurgh witt   he wastes thurgh pryde,
I gedir, I glene   and he lattys goo sone,
I pryke and I pryne   and he the purse opynes.

(230–2)

At line 390, Waster's appeal to proverbial wisdom is structured in the same way, when he argues for the interdependence of the two positions:

Whoso wele schal wyn   a wastour mo[st]e he fynde
For if it greues one gome   it gladdes anoþer.

On a closer reading, though, it seems that the poet is not content with such a simple opposition, and the debate is far more complex than these examples would suggest. Having started with this kind of antithesis, the poet could easily use it to resolve the issues raised; but even though the king's final speech remains incomplete, he clearly does not accept the Aristotelian model of moderation between the two extremes. That is, he does not read tropologically, to deduce an ethical model for his own behavior. Nor does he try to effect any kind of reconciliation between the two plaintiffs. He does seem to accept that each is necessary to his kingdom, then subordinates their rival claims to his own political expediency, to ensure that Winner can still finance his overseas wars (Stillwell). Now what has happened in the debate to render a moral, personal resolution impossible? These strong linguistic oppositions have been continually tested and undermined, and the poem concludes, not with a new synthesis, but with the collapse of some of the most familiar, and most consoling, medieval fictions.

One of these, explored by Langland in *Piers Plowman*, would accord the superior position to Winner. In this tradition, winning bears no taint of avarice, but signifies the virtuous acquisition of goods and supplies for the community; and more specifically, manual labor as the third of the three divisions of responsibility in medieval political theory (Le Goff 53–7; Duby). Accordingly, Piers Plowman is a winner, especially when represented as the plowman whose task is hampered by the wasters who will not work. Langland is unambiguous in his representation of the latter as destroying the fabric of society.[4] We recall the covenant Piers makes in B.6 with the knight who is keen to learn how to plow. Piers says he will work for them both, provided the knight will fulfill his traditional duty of protection, and

        . . . kepe holy kirke and myselue
Fro wastours and wikked men þat wolde me destruye.

(27–8)

The wasters, however, have no respect for the knight's authority, and Piers must call on Hunger, or sheer necessity, to frighten them into work. Aers illuminatingly discusses this episode as a failure of traditional ideologies, and

191

we can draw a number of parallels with his reading of *Piers Plowman* as an imaginative engagement with the contradictions between these ideologies and perceived social and political realities (*Chaucer, Langland*, 1–37).

Langland's reading of the winning and wasting opposition is firmly inscribed, on the literal level, within the tightly constructed social and economic context of the manorial farm. He seems especially concerned with the impact of higher wages and greater geographical and social mobility on the traditional organization of labor on the estate, and his wasters are denounced as vagrant workers who have wandered away from the home demesne: 'And þo [n]olde Wastour noȝt werche, but wandre[d] aboute' (B.6.302). Langland seems to refer here to the labor shortages which followed the Black Death in 1348 and the consequent demands for higher wages. The 1349 Labor Ordinance, which attempted to restrict the movements of workers in search of better conditions, and to keep wages at pre-plague levels, was followed in 1351 by the Statute of Laborers, and other versions followed, although historians disagree about the effectiveness of this legislation and, indeed, the seriousness of the problems it was designed to alleviate.[5] In particular, recent research suggests that the more extreme labor shortages and higher wages, commonly argued to be a direct, almost immediate effect of the plague, did not really arise until the 1360s or 1370s (Bolton 62, 72; Thomson 13). But in the repressive mid-century legislation, the symptoms of anxiety about these changes are clearly legible. At the very least, this is a powerful indication of the sensitivity of medieval English culture to any perceived disparities between established ideologies and material realities. As Putnam writes: 'The statutes of labourers must be regarded not as having created a new system or a new set of economic relations, but as affording proof that radical changes had occurred, ushering in a new era' (223).

Thus, although Langland's prologue begins with a fairly balanced opposition between winning and wasting, in which the plowmen 'Wonnen þat þise wastours with glotonye destruyeþ' (B. Prol. 22), he quickly dramatises them in distinctive fashion, whereby Waster is consistently depicted as a pugnacious vagrant, while the winner is given a distinctive name, Piers, and is represented as the means of salvation, the way to Truth. Langland thus reveals his conservatism, in associating virtue, peace, and authoritative control over the means of production with the traditionally conceived figure of the plowman, but threat, anxiety, and breakdown of the social order with his more socially relevant realization of the waster as unwilling laborer.[6] The plowing scene closes with the language of apocalypse:

Ac I warne yow werkmen, wynneþ whil ye mowe
For hunger hiderward hasteþ hym faste.
He shal awake þoruȝ water wastoures to chaste.

(B.6.321–3)

The *Winner and Waster*-poet draws heavily on this understanding of winning, primarily in Winner's initial characterization of himself: here he claims to be able to assist the world as a whole by teaching lords (reminiscent of Piers's compact with the knight); his partner is Witt, and his enemy is Waster:

> . . . this felle false thefe   þat byfore ʒowe standes
> Thynkes to strike or he styntt   and stroye me for euer.
>
> (228–9)

In the remainder of the poem, however, Waster is represented less as a reluctant laborer than as a disaffected aristocrat who takes no care for the maintenance of his estate. Still, the apocalyptic tone recurs in Winner's abuse:

> This wikkede weryed thefe   that Wastoure men calles,
> That if he life may longe   this lande will he stroye.
>
> (242–3)

The scene in which Waster is depicted drinking in the tavern has a number of close affinities with Langland's picture of itinerant beggars (B.7.91–5), though the passage it resembles most closely is Glutton's confession, reminding us that avarice is not the only sin associated with wasting: gluttony and lechery are closely allied. The strongest piece of evidence for Waster's affinity with vagrant laborers is his own abuse of Sir William Shareshull at line 317. This passage is not unambiguous, and probably refers to Judge Shareshull's legislation for the Statute of Treasons, not the Statute of Laborers (Salter 41–4). Even so, the reference actually links two of the different pictures of Waster in the poem: first, as laborer; and second, as the leader of a private army.

To consider the third possible reading of the opposition between Winner and Waster is, in a way, to return to the first Aristotelian model, but in a version which has become politicised, and indeed, updated to accommodate particular aspects of later medieval economic theory. Here, the ethical contrast between avarice and prodigality is transmuted – not without a certain tension – into a dispute between the rival economic policies of providence and expenditure. Similarly, the desirable mean is not the more abstract virtue, generosity, but rather the attractive secular reputation for magnanimity, Aristotle's *megalopsychia*. Importantly, the context of debate undergoes a radical shift from that of personal ethics to political expediency: here we are less concerned with the disposition of private wealth and labor than with the organization of resources in a royal court, or more generally, the household, as the most important economic unit. Recent research on late medieval economic theory by writers as diverse as Gurevich, Le Goff, Bloch, and Shoaf reveals a strong theoretical interest in the relations between economics and ethics, especially in the later medieval period. In particular, an important essay by David Starkey studies the household ordinances, the *Black Book* of Edward IV, and relates this text to late medieval and early Tudor domestic practice and other literary discussions of the household, including *Winner and Waster*.

Regarded in this light, the opposition between winning and wasting subordinates the former to the latter, in ethical terms. In this secular, political sense, providence – the careful and responsible economic management of resources – is simply the means to the more desirable end of magnificence, the prince's capacity to outdo his rivals in the display of personal and public wealth, to present generous gifts to his servants, family, friends, and foreign guests as an unambiguous indication of the wealth and consequent power of his kingdom. In this form of exchange, to give is to exert political power, and such giving depends in a very obvious fashion on the less ostentatious work of increasing funds and resources. 'The supreme embodiment of prudential ostentation', writes Starkey, 'was Henry VII. Simultaneously, he made Burgundians wonder at the splendour of his court and Venetians marvel at the endless hours he devoted to bookkeeping' (256). Essentially, though, the winners must serve the wasters in this scheme: hence the dramatic tensions of our poem's simultaneous appeals to more traditional ethical models. We are less concerned at this level with personal ethics, for as the financial stakes increase, we move further away from a tropological reading to a concern with public policy.

Winner and Waster, we remember, pictures the two heroes kneeling before the king as knights, servants of his household; and a comparison with Edward IV's *Black Book* is illuminating. Starkey summarizes its account, stressing the importance of the clerical posts in the royal household, held by 'relatively large numbers of educated clerks and officials', who theorised and defined their tasks quite precisely. The *Black Book*, he says, 'takes the two main divisions of the royal household – the lord chamberlain's department and the lord steward's department – and moralises them. Both are given a characteristic virtue: the lord chamberlain's department is the "Household of Magnificence": the lord steward's department is the "Household of Providence"' (255). While we are admittedly dealing with a slightly earlier period, this household theory is an important context for our poem. McKisack notes, for example, that during the reign of Edward III there was a substantial reorganization of the household finances, directed towards increasing the power and independence of the exchequer. It was from this department that gifts were given, and from which funds were drawn to support Edward's campaigns in France (215–18). We may thus regard Winner and Waster as heads of rival departments, fighting for control over the same resources; hence the bitter resentment of each other's practices. Starkey, for example, confidently predicts the king's final judgement:

that magnificence needs both Wynnere and Wastoure: it is characterized essentially by lavishness, but lavishness in turn must be disciplined and regulated by providence so that expenditure does not exceed income. (257)

Yet if matters were this simple, we would not find such disagreement about the poem; besides, the poet's characterizations of Winner and Waster are, as we have seen, far from consistent. He does not refer directly to the household in the debate proper, although Waster's self-definitions do rely implicitly on its ideology of conspicuous consumption. Winner accuses him, for example, of spoiling his retainers, who wear golden belts whose value is comparable to that of his inherited lands. In reply, Waster defends his feasting, and his clothes in terms of a courtly ethic of expenditure for greater personal honor:

> And if my peple ben prode   me payes alle þe better
> To [s]ee þam faire and free   tofore with myn eghne.
>
> (433–4)

But there is a negative side to this kind of consumption and this picture of Waster. To complicate things further, the poet has introduced another kind of class dialectic, which contrasts strongly with that of the *Piers Plowman* tradition. Waster is transformed from a reluctant laborer to an aristocrat who has failed in his duties and responsibilities; Winner is less the conscientious supervisor than the envious merchant who claims to know better how to make use of Waster's land. Winner is angry at the neglect of Waster's inherited properties, his lack of style, at his insouciant attitude to the future:

> 3e folowe noghte 3oure fadirs   þat fosterde 3ow alle
> A kynde herueste to cache   and cornes to wynn
> For þe colde wyntter and þe kene   with gleterand frostes.
>
> (274–6)

Rodney Hilton describes Waster as representative of the many landowners who spent 'up to the hilt on personal display, on extravagant living, on the maintenance of a numerous retinue, and on war'. Conversely, he also suggests that Winner's failure to re-invest capital in his land is equally culpable under medieval theories of estate management. Neither practice, he suggests, would 'promote capital formation' (177–8). The most severe charge in some respects is Winner's accusation that Waster's aristocratic companions no longer preserve the dignity of their class:

> That are had [ben] lordes in londe   and ladyes riche
> Now are þay nysottes of the new gett   so nysely attyred
> With [sy]de slabbande sleues   sleght to þe grounde.
>
> (409–11)

195

While the manuscript text of this passage is corrupt and obscure, the reconstructed complaint would be consistent with Winner's other criticisms of Waster. To make better sense of these accusations, though, we need to build into our discussion one final context to which the poet implicitly appeals – this time a more local one. When Winner accuses Waster of riding out with a few friends (238–41) whom he entertains with lavish feasts (327–63), we may suspect that Waster is establishing his own power network, independent of the emperors, kings, knights, barons, bachelors, and lords whom Winner finds missing from his company (327–8). That is, Waster is depicted as a practitioner of 'bastard feudalism', the term used by McFarlane 'to describe the society which was emerging from feudalism in the early part of the fourteenth century, when most if not all of its ancient features survived, . . . but when the tenurial bond between lord and vassal had been superseded as the primary social tie by the personal contract between master and man' (McFarlane 161). McFarlane further comments that 'these knights of a late though not decadent chivalry seemed more anxious to see service than to care whether it was always under the same banner' (176), and we recall the disproportionately short account of Waster's professional-looking army:

> And sekere one þat other syde   are sadde men of armes,
> Bolde sqwyeres of blode,   bowmen many,
> þat if thay strike one stroke   stynt þay ne thynken
> Till owthir here appon hethe   be hewen to dethe.
>
> (193–6)

Given the poem's own appeals to a western context, there are strong grounds for associating these troops with the soldiers and archers of Cheshire and Lancashire, so powerful in the French wars, in battles such as Crécy and Poitiers. Their return to England, rich and restless, has been documented most recently by Bennett, who traces the subsequent career of many of these provincial men – as both soldiers and clerics – in the courts of Edward III and, more particularly, Richard II. Richard gathered these western men around him virtually as a private army, and provides a good example of the manner in which bastard feudalism could cut across more conservative and traditional power structures. The badges which replaced familial coats of arms as the indicator of political allegiance – Richard's badge of the White Hart, for instance – were often greatly resented. There was not such a big difference, either, between such private armies and the armed bands which were the subject of so many complaints around the mid-century. The Statute of Treasons of 1352, which aimed to regulate their activities, distinguished between treason and felony. To ride under someone else's banner was felonous if the object of attack was another man's army; but it was treasonable to ride against the king (Salter 41–2). The *Winner and Waster*-poet seems to imply that Waster is one such knight who has neglected his pastoral role in favor of short-term political and personal power. And if this is so, then aspects of this charge might also apply to the king, who displays his wealth most conspicuously, in his own beautiful clothes and the elaborate accoutrements of his court – and who provides so generously for his two retainers, Winner and Waster. And, as we will see, the king bypasses the ethical implications of the debate in favor of a short-term plan to fund his overseas wars.

It seems, then, that the poet experiments with these competing senses and representations of winning and wasting – an experiment which is facilitated by the virtual absence of any authorial voice during the debate. As the poem concludes, there are a number of points where the opposition seems hopelessly, almost deliberately confused; and the text itself is incomplete. (The manuscript is also badly damaged on its last leaf, and the sense is not always easy to reconstruct.) We should examine these moments carefully, for it has been argued by Speirs, Jacobs, and others that they are part of the poet's demonstration of the interdependence of winning and wasting, that we can translate the conceptual debate into a coherent economic theory. It seems to me, however, that the poet cannot collapse his two characters back into the simple allegorical abstractions that would permit such a resolution.

After Winner's long complaint about Waster's extraordinary feast (at least twenty-five separate dishes, for four or five men), Waster, who has earlier argued that such entertainment pleases God by providing employment for the poor, now argues from a somewhat different premise. Lords, he asserts, must live in lordly fashion, must consume the produce of their fields and rivers. If they did not, if fish, fowl, and flesh were freely and cheaply available, servants would no longer need to serve lords. 'þis wate þou full wele witterly þiseluen', he adds, 'Whoso wele schal wyn a wastour mo[st]e he fynde' (389–90). If winners are to make profit, there must be wasters to buy from them. This might look like the interdependence of the two positions, but in his final speech, Waster accuses Winner of putting off improvements to his estate – Winner's own complaint against Waster – and then cursing himself when the harvest is good and he has nowhere to store excess grain. In what seems like a very perverse accusation, he concludes: 'Forthi, Wynnere with wronge þou wastes þi tyme', thus conflating the terms of the opposition. At the same time, he admits the truth of Winner's accusations: he agrees that he consumes his own wood without replanting, because he has no care for the future ('take þe coppe as it comes, þe case as it falles'), and acknowledges that the longer he lives, the further he'll need to travel to get wood. Finally, he asks the king to tell them where each should dwell, because he cannot bear the sight of his enemy.

The king looks on them affectionately, and sends each to live where he is most loved: Winner to the papal court at Rome (at this time, in fact, at Avignon[7]), to be pampered by the cardinals, who will give him silk sheets, and rush to obey his every whim. This seems an obscure decision, as we have come to associate such pleasures with Waster; and indeed, it has been argued that 'Wynner' in line 460 is a scribal error for 'Wastoure'. Jacobs argues that the cardinals are wasters who need the services of a winner, forgetting that the papal court is already well represented in Winner's army. There was, we remember, considerable resentment during this period at the amount of revenue collected for the Church in England, exacerbated by the Hundred Years' War. As Hewitt explains, 'the papacy and a French pope being at Avignon, moneys received by alien churchmen of whatever status went – it was believed – to enrich the enemy, France' (168). So it is more likely that the cardinals consider Winner as their champion, and the reader must negotiate an apparent conflict between what Winner preaches and what he desires. We will return to this shortly.

Waster is to go where there is already 'most waste'; that is, to London, close to Cheapside, the 'Pultrie' and Bread Street, to look out for any passersby, to encourage or trick them into spending all their money on food and drink. The king echoes Waster's words: 'þe more þou wastis þi wele þe better þe Wynner lykes' (495). As a merchant, Winner stands to profit from Waster's activity, though this in turn runs counter to the king's earlier warning to Winner that he'll enjoy no success while he stays in the same country as Waster. On the king's command, Waster will leave England and Winner will return, to accompany the king to war. He will be dubbed a knight in Paris, and help the king reward his followers with 'giftes full grete of golde and of sil[uer]'. Again, the decision seems strange: we are reminded of the huge army Winner has been able to command, yet asked to forget he has already been described as a knight.

In this conclusion, then, we find a rapid interchange between the two concepts, inhibiting the emergence of any coherent economic policy from this debate. There can be no interdependence where the two terms are so unstable: winners may well need wasters, an attractive alliterative formula, but we have become increasingly unsure how to distinguish winners and wasters from each other. The poem can offer no closure; its signifying systems clash. Instead, we find an excess of signification which seems almost to devalue the poem's key terms.

Recent discussions of medieval linguistic and literary theory emphasise the relationship between economic value and linguistic signification, and we might speculate on the ways in which *Winner and Waster* enacts the split that Bloch articulates between an economic realism and nominalism; that is, the increasing recognition that coins, like linguistic or conceptual terms, have a value or buying power, agreed on by the community, by demand, not fixed by crown or parliament (159–74). In this way, 'winner' and 'waster' can change in value and signification according to the context in which they are used. Similarly, in negotiating these exchanges, we can take up Starkey's suggestion that the later medieval emphasis in economic theory on conspicuous consumption finds parallels in the art, architecture, and literature of the period. For example, rhetorical theory concerned with the economy of expression contrasts *abbreviatio* and *amplificatio*: 'but in fact abbreviation had only a formal interest for them; amplification was their true goal, and to this was all their ingenious armoury of language devoted' (259). The *Winner and Waster*-poet is no exception, as his poetic practice and, indeed, his advertisement for his own skills in the prologue bear witness. Included in Geoffrey of Vinsauf's list of figures associated with *amplificatio* are repetition, periphrasis, comparison, and description; and *Winner and Waster* excels in these techniques, presenting and re-presenting 'winning' and 'wasting' in different guises. Curiously, the most outstanding example of *descriptio* is Winner's twenty-eight line account of Waster's feast, in which he indulges in the characteristic rhetorical trope of Wasting. As Starkey comments, 'adjectives and figures of speech come cheap in comparision with gold plate (or even with well-carved stone)', and Winner's excesses in this area would confirm Starkey's thesis that extravagance is perceived as the most desirable end (260). Where there is nothing to be lost, there is everything to be gained. This would explain Winner's jealous description of the feast from which he is excluded, and indeed, his reward of a life of luxury, for which he does not have to pay, in the cardinals' court.

Let us return to the poet, and the question of where he stands in relation to the debate. If we concede that the speaking-voice of the prologue is simply one of the many voices and rhetorical traditions woven into the poem, we may look elsewhere in the text for traces of the poet, if not to determine his own attitude to the issues raised, then in search of some explanation of the uncertainties of his text. At the very least, it is possible to trace an uneasy contradiction between his claims to the status of truth-teller in the prologue, with its complaint about the duplicity of language at court, and the textual complexity of the debate proper. Far from declaring the truth to the king, the poet allows him the last word, in his short-term solution which solves none of the problems raised. And as we have seen, the text shifts its ground constantly, demonstrating an elaborate rhetorical and linguistic generosity in the license it allows its key terms to generate meaning, to play and bounce off each other.

Perhaps the poet's idea of his poem has shifted. Perhaps it has taken him in unexpected directions. Given the mixed dialect of the poem, and its author's apparent knowledge of London, it is quite likely that he was himself one of the West Midlands clerks who received employment at Edward III's court, one of Bennett's careerists. Perhaps he saw action or clerical service in France, and was not content to return to the provinces. Perhaps he resisted the voice of the old man of the prologue (which we might hear as the voice of his own father), and came to London himself, perhaps in turn to be duped of his money by a 'waster'. This is a speculative, though not implausible scenario: it may be that the poet profited directly from some of the practices Waster seems to defend or exemplify (for example, a life of glamor under the protection of a powerful lord), while having been trained, like Langland, in a clerical tradition which rejects them. Having begun with an apparently orthodox topic and straightforward dialectic form, the poet may have unwittingly opened up a profound challenge to his own career; namely, identifying himself as a waster. We should not be surprised, in this case, at the uncertainty and anxiety displayed by the poem and its representations of its two central figures, if it hesitates to crystallise a distinction whose implications are so profoundly disturbing.

Notes

1. This tradition of reading originates with Gollancz, the poem's first editor and most influential critic (TRIGG, 'Israel Gollancz's *Wynnere and Wastoure*').

2. All quotations from *Winner and Waster* are taken from my edition of the poem. References to *Piers Plowman* will be to the Kane-Donaldson B-text.

3. Cf. *OED Win* v. 1 and *Waste* v. The only exception is the morally neutral sense of *Waste* 3, 'To consume, use up, wear away'.

4. We find the same idea in the lyric which appears in the same manuscript as *Wynnere and Wastoure*, 'Waste makes a kyngdome in nede'. The text of this poem is printed by BRUNNER, pp. 193–9; and the lyric is discussed by TURVILLE-PETRE, pp. 21–2.

5. DOBSON comments that contemporary responses to the Statutes were very skeptical as to their efficacy. However, as he acknowledges, PUTNAM lists a number of successful prosecutions in the 1350s. BOLTON finds that enforcement was stricter during the 1370s.

6. See AERS, 'Representations of the "Third Estate"'. In 'The Good Shepherds of Medieval Criticism', Aers also reminds us of the significance of reclassifying mobile workers as 'vagrants', as an important ideological strategy in the interests of maintaining constant labor supplies (p. 177). SCHMIDT discusses Langland's use of 'win' and 'waste' (pp. 311–25). The Meed episode in *Piers Plowman* can be read in similar terms as a discussion of the various significations ascribed to 'Mede', and the conflicts between ethics and politics.

7. I have argued elsewhere that the commonly accepted date for this poem, 1352, is based on a very literal interpretation of the internal evidence: a more reasonable estimate is c. 1352–70 ('Israel Gollancz's *Wynnere and Wastoure*').

Works Cited

Primary

BRUNNER, KARL 'Spätme. Lehrgedicht'. *Archiv*, **164** (1933): 178–99.
GEOFFREY OF VINSAUF *Poetria Nova*, trans. Margaret F. Nims (Toronto, 1967).
GOLLANCZ, ISRAEL (ed.) *A Good Short Debate Between Winner and Waster: An Alliterative*

Poem on Social and Economic Problems in England in the Year 1352, with Modern English Rendering (1920; rpt Cambridge and Totowa, NJ, 1974).

LANGLAND, WILLIAM *Piers Plowman: The B Version*, ed. George Kane and E. Talbot Donaldson (London, 1975).

MATTHEW OF VENDÔME *Ars Versificatoria*, ed. E. Faral. *Les Arts poétiques du XII*^e *et du XIII*^e siècle: Recherches et documents sur la technique littéraire du moyen âge (Paris, 1924).

——*The Art of Versification*, trans. Aubrey E. Galyon (Ames, IA, 1980).

TRIGG, STEPHANIE (ed.) *Wynnere and Wastoure*, EETS, **297** (Oxford, 1990).

Secondary

AERS, DAVID *Chaucer, Langland and the Creative Imagination* (London, 1980).

——'Representations of the "Third Estate": Social Conflict and Its Milieu around 1381', *Southern Review* (Adelaide), **16** (1983): 35–49.

——'The Good Shepherds of Medieval Criticism', *Southern Review* (Adelaide), **20** (1987): 168–85.

BENNETT, MICHAEL J. *Community, Class and Careerism: Cheshire and Lancashire Society in the Age of Sir Gawain and the Green Knight* (Cambridge, 1983).

BESTUL, THOMAS *Satire and Allegory in Wynnere and Wastoure* (Lincoln, NE, 1974).

BLOCH, HOWARD *Etymologies and Genealogies: A Literary Anthropology of the French Middle Ages* (Chicago, 1983).

BOLTON, J.L. *The Medieval English Economy 1150–1500.* (London, 1980).

DOBSON, R.B. (ed.) *The Peasants' Revolt of 1381* (London, 1970).

DONALDSON, E. TALBOT 'Chaucer the Pilgrim', *PMLA*, **69** (1954): 928–36.

DUBY, GEORGES *The Three Orders: Feudal Society Imagined*, trans. Arthur Goldhammer; Foreword by Thomas N. Bisson (Chicago, 1980).

GUREVICH, A.J. *Categories of Medieval Culture*, trans. G.L. Campbell (London, 1985).

HARRINGTON, DAVID V. 'Indeterminacy in *Winner and Waster* and *The Parliament of the Three Ages*'. *ChauR*, **20** (1986): 246–57.

HEWITT, H.J. *The Organisation of War under Edward III, 1338–62* (Manchester, 1960).

HILTON, RODNEY *The English Peasantry in the Later Middle Ages* (Oxford, 1975).

JACOBS, NICOLAS 'The Typology of Debate and the Interpretation of *Wynnere and Wastoure*'. *RES*, n.s. **36** (1985): 481–500.

JAMES, JERRY D. 'The Undercutting of Conventions in *Wynnere and Wastoure*', *MLQ*, **25** (1964): 243–58.

LE GOFF, JACQUES *Time, Work and Culture in the Middle Ages*, trans. Arthur Goldhammer, Chicago, 1980.

LEICESTER, H. MARSHALL 'The Art of Impersonation: A General Prologue to *The Canterbury Tales*'. *PMLA*, **95** (1980): 213–24.

McFARLANE, K.B. ' "Bastard Feudalism" '. *Bulletin of the Institute of Historical Research*, **20** (1945): 161–80.

McKISACK, MAY *The Fourteenth Century: 1307–1399* (Oxford, 1959).

NOLAN, BARBARA ' "A Poet Ther Was": Chaucer's Voices in the General Prologue to *The Canterbury Tales*', *PMLA*, **101** (1986): 154–64.

PUTNAM, BERTHA *The Enforcement of the Statutes of Labourers During the First Decade after the Black Death 1349–59* (1908; New York, 1970).

SALTER, ELIZABETH 'The Timeliness of *Wynnere and Wastoure*', *MÆ*, **47** (1978): 40–65.

SCHMIDT, A.V.C. 'Langland's Structural Imagery', *EIC*, **30** (1980): 311–25.

SHOAF, R.A. *Dante, Chaucer and the Currency of the Word: Money, Images and Reference in Late Medieval Poetry* (Norman, OK, 1983).

SPEIRS, J. '*Wynnere and Wastoure* and *The Parlement of the Thre Ages*'. *Scrutiny*, **17** (1950): 241–49; rpt in *Medieval English Poetry: The Non-Chaucerian Tradition* (London, 1957).

STARKEY, DAVID 'The Age of the Household: Politics, Society and the Arts, c. 1350–c. 1550', *The Later Middle Ages*, ed. Stephen Medcalf. (London, 1981), pp. 225–90.

STILLWELL, GARDINER '*Wynnere and Wastoure* and the Hundred Years' War', *ELH*, **8** (1941): 241–47.

THOMSON, JOHN A.F. *The Transformation of Medieval England 1370–1529*. (London, 1983).

TRIGG, STEPHANIE 'Israel Gollancz's *Wynnere and Wastoure*: Political Satire or Editorial Politics?' *Medieval English Religious and Ethical Literature: Essays in Honour of G.H. Russell*, ed. Gregory Kratzmann and James Simpson. (Cambridge, 1986), pp. 115–27.

TURVILLE-PETRE, THORLAC 'The Prologue of *Wynnere and Wastoure*', *LSE*, n.s. **18** (1987): 19–29.

11 English, Latin, and the Text as 'Other': The Page as Sign in the Work of John Gower*

ROBERT F. YEAGER

In this suggestive essay, Yeager explores the visual semiotics of the manuscripts of the *Confessio Amantis*. Starting from the marginal glosses in Latin, which he argues may be Gower's own, Yeager draws attention to their neutral narrative voice, in contrast with the play of voices and personae in the poem itself. The reader's focus is dispersed across English text, Latin hexameter verses and Latin prose glosses, as the manuscript pages demand a polysemous reading. Accordingly, the manuscript organisation seems to indicate a semiotic intention analogous to Jacques Derrida's concern with the dissolution of textual boundaries and his critique of the hierarchic organisation of meaning.

For most readers, the *Confessio Amantis* is John Gower's 'English' poem. Certainly the *Confessio*'s more than thirty thousand middle English lines do justify this general classification, the more so when we recall that the remaining two-thirds of Gower's work – like the *Mirour de l'Omme* and the *Vox Clamantis* – were written in Anglo-Norman and Latin. Yet it is important to notice, for a number of reasons, that the *Confessio Amantis* is neither all English nor all poetry. Interspersed throughout are Latin hexameter headings which introduce, albeit often in a somewhat oblique fashion, the activity described in the English sections to follow [See Figure 1]; and in the margins of many manuscripts there are to be found at various intervals Latin prose lines which also comment on the English text, in the manner of glosses [See Figures 2 and 3].[1]

The mere fact that such verse and descriptive commentary appear in *Confessio* manuscripts is, in itself, scarcely worth remarking. Many poems

* Reprinted from *Text: Transactions of the Society for Textual Scholarship*, **3** (1987): 251–67.

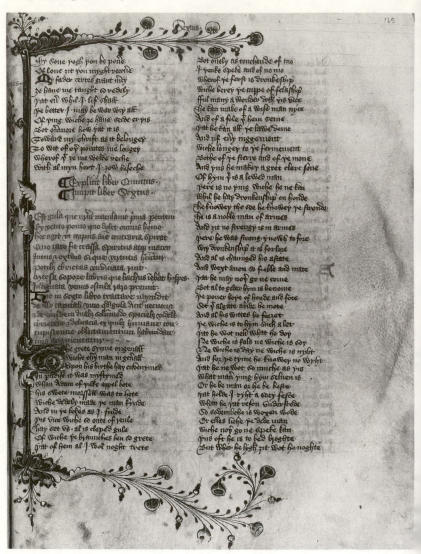

Figure 1   Beinecke Library, Yale University, MS. Osborn fa. 1, fol. 125ʳ.

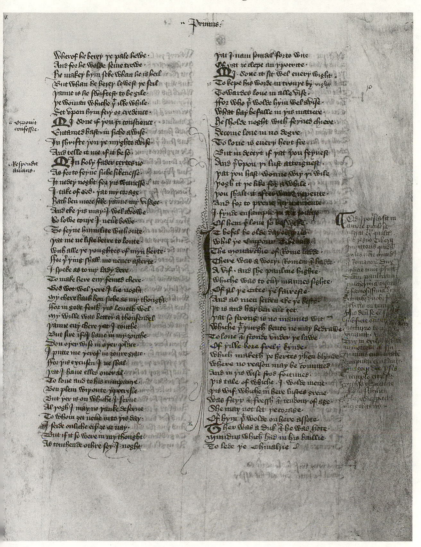

Figure 2 Beinecke Library, Yale University, MS. Osborn fa. 1, fol. 4ʳ.

205

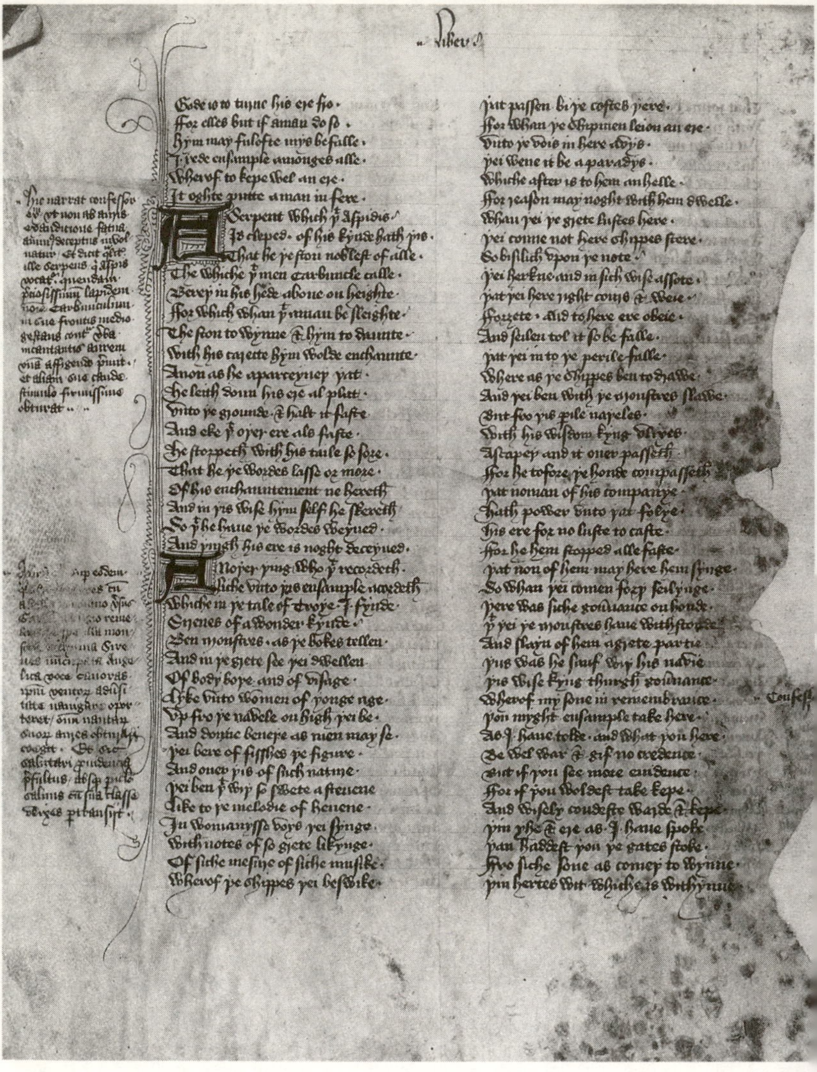

Liber I

Gade is to tune his ere fro.
ffor elles but if a man do so.
hym may fulofte mys befalle.
I rede ensample amonges alle.
Wherof to kepe wel an eye.
It oghte gutte a man in fere.
A Serpent which yt Aspidis
Is cleped. of his kynde hath yis.
That he ye ston noblest of alle.
The whiche yt men carbuncle calle.
Berey in his hede above on heighte.
ffor which whan yt a man be sleighte.
The ston to wynne & hym to daunte.
With his carecte hym wolde enchaunte.
Anon as he aparceyneþ yat.
He leith doun his ere al platt.
Vnto ye grounde & halt it faste
And eke yt oyer ere als faste.
He stoppeth with his taile so sore.
That he ye wordes lasse or more.
Of his enchauntement ne hereth
And in yis wise hym self he skereth
So yt he haue ye wordes weyned.
And myght his ere is noght deceyned.
A Noyer ying who yt recordeth.
liche vnto yis ensample accordeth
Which in ye tale of Troye I fynde
Syrenes of a wonder kynde.
Ben monstres. as ye bokes tellen.
And in ye grete see yei dwellen.
Of body boye and of visage.
Lyke vnto women of yonge age.
Vp fro ye navele on high yei be.
And doune beneye as men may se.
yei bere of fisshes ye figure.
And ouer yis of such nature.
yei ben yt wiy so swete a stevene
Like to ye melodie of hevene.
In womannysshe voys yei synge.
With notes of so grete likynge.
Of suche mesure of suche musike.
Wherof ye shippes yei beswike.

yat passen bi ye costes yere.
ffor whan ye shipmen leion an ere.
Vnto ye vois in here avys.
yei wene it be a paradys.
Which after is to hem an helle.
ffor reason may noght with hem dwelle.
Whan yei ye grete lustes here.
yei conne not here shippes stere.
So bisiliche vpon ye note.
yei herkne and in such wise assote.
yat yei here right cours & weie.
fforzete. and to here ere obeie.
And seilen til it so be falle.
yat yei in to ye perile falle.
Where as ye shippes ben to drawe.
And yei ben with ye monstres slawe.
But fro yis peril naþeles.
With his wisdom kyng vlixes.
Ascapeþ and it over passeth
ffor he tofore ye honde compasseth
yat noman of his companye.
hath power vnto yat folye.
His ere for no luste to caste.
ffor he hem stopped alle faste.
yat non of hem may here hem synge.
So whan yei comen forþ seilynge.
yere was suche gouernance on honde.
yt yei ye monstres haue withstonde.
And slayn of hem a grete partie.
yus was he sauf wiy his navie
yis wise kyng thurgh gouernance.
Wherof my sone in remembrance.
you myght ensample take here.
As I haue tolde. and what you here
Be wel war & gif no credence.
But if you se more evidence.
ffor if you woldest take kepe.
And wisely coudeste warde & kepe
yin yhe & ere as I haue spoke
yan haddest you ye gates stoke.
ffro suche sone as comeþ to wynne.
yin hertes witt which is withynne.

Figure 3 Beinecke Library, Yale University, MS. Osborn fa. 1, fol. 2^{v}.

contain Latin tags or short sections of introductory verse, and glossed texts
are of course common in the Middle Ages. What is unusual about the Latin
glosses in Gower's manuscripts, however, is that they seem very likely to
have been his own creation. This, as I shall argue, privileges the Latin work in
a noteworthy way. G.C. Macaulay, who edited the full corpus of Gower's
writings, was the first to suspect that emendations in several of the best
copies of both the *Confessio* and the *Vox Clamantis* gave evidence of authorial
correction.[2] John Fisher's subsequent review of the materials substantially
corroborated Macaulay. Although the recent work of Peter Nicholson, as well
as the thorough-going re-examination of all manuscripts, full and fragmentary,
being carried out now by the team of Jeremy Griffiths, Kate Harris, and
Derek Pearsall pointedly disagree with Macaulay and Fisher about how
responsible Gower might have been for specific variations, they too appear
content that Gower composed marginal glosses for his own poem.[3]

Such glossing of one's own text is indeed unusual, raising the question
why might Gower have wished to create commentary, in Latin prose, for his
major English work?[4] And, one might ask in conjunction, what prompted him
to include the Latin hexameters as he did? Two very different lines of inquiry,
leading to equally different but oddly related answers to both of these
questions, suggest themselves.

One – the more purely aesthetic, perhaps – I have pursued in print
already.[5] Gower, I believe, wished to make a point with his use of both Latin
and English in the *Confessio*. In the Prologue and in the opening lines of Book
I, he acknowledges his didactic intentions for the poem and evinces an
awareness of how choices of subject matter, language, and style may affect
his success. Reading devoted only to morally instructive things 'dulleth ofte a
mannes wit', Gower remarks, and therefore in this, perhaps his last poem, he
will turn from the loftier topics he has chosen in the past to write instead of
love. The 'mateere' of the book will thus present 'the middel weie', including:

> Somwhat of lust, somwhat of lore,
> That of the lasse or of the more
> Som man mai lyke of that I wryte . . .

(CA Pro. 19–20)

Language too is an issue of importance and requires decision. We receive an
illuminating glimpse of the thoroughness of Gower's poetic planning when
he continues, describing his choices:

> And for that fewe men endite
> In oure englissh, I thenke make
> A bok for Engelondes sake . . .

(CA Pro. 22–4)

Later on, in Book I, Gower once more calls attention to the problem of a proper style, with a further reference to his notion of the 'middel weie':

> Forthi the Stile of my writinges
> Fro this day forth I thenke change
> And speke of thing is noght so strange,
> Which every kinde hath upon honde. . . .

(*CA.* 8–11)

Of course, by 'stile' here Gower can be understood to mean several things. Primarily he was calling attention to that plainness of speech for which he has been often praised.[6]

What is less frequently noticed, however, is Gower's decision to write in 'oure englissh', located among the lines above. The development of thought there seems to indicate Gower's sense of his native language as appropriately a 'median tongue', neither as lofty as Latin nor as courtly as French – the mode rather of frank parlance and consequently well suited for a poem ostensibly a secular confession. Similarly, from the reticulation of ideas in these lines, we might conclude as well that English in Gower's mind was also a somewhat novel vehicle for major poetry.

In the 1380s, when Gower was composing the *Confessio Amantis*, Chaucer had probably finished *Troilus and Criseyde*, but may not have begun the *Canterbury Tales*, and Gower himself had written two lengthy poems and a sequence of ballades, but nothing, as far as we know, in English.[7] The decade of the *Confessio*'s writing is, then, best thought of as the infancy – albeit glorious – of Middle English poetry. Such an English poem might well be counted on to bring with it a desirable newness requiring and focussing attention.

If these inferences are correct, they have several things to tell us about Gower's poetics. First and simplest, they suggest that Gower included the Latin verses and commentary in his 'low' English poem to give it credentials, to provide the learned polish that, judging from the style of both the *Mirour de l'Omme* and the *Vox Clamantis*, Gower so clearly admired. If, as the passages from the *Confessio* imply, Gower deliberately chose to write it in English, so did he choose to embellish his text with Latin verse and prose, which claim for their author a sophistication greater than the major language of the composition; on this level, the bilinguality of the *Confessio Amantis* is there to bulwark the reputation of a learned and sensitive man.

The second observation evoked by Gower's languages in the *Confessio*, however, brings us closer to our present topic. Primary among the 'special effects' produced by the presence of the Latin verse and marginalia – and indeed by the appended French ballade sequences as well, in a particular manner[8] – is the multiplication of authoritative point of view, or what we might call authoritative 'voice'. By this I do not mean the points of view or voices of characters, either in the many narratives or in the larger *personae* of the frame story, Genius and Amans/John Gower. What indeed prevents the crowd of speakers in the total *Confessio* from raising an uninterpretable cacophony is precisely this absence of the authoritative voice from any of the fictional multitude. Not even the confessor figure Genius, the priest of Venus, has the credibility requisite to anchor the poem's direction. Genius is too carefully compromised for this, first because, despite the elaborate cosmetics, the confession we are overhearing is no true one, but a lover's. While Gower's audience accepted some overlap of the behavior proper to a good lover and to a good man, we ought to harbor no confusion about the stakes at the *fictive* level in Gower's poem: the salvation Amans seeks, like the absolution Genius may at last provide, is wholly limited to a secular attachment.[9] Amans confesses in order to purify himself sufficiently that a prayer to Venus to further his suit will stand a chance of success and bring his lady to his arms. Repentance and moral regeneration, while they occur, ultimately transforming Amans to aged John Gower praying 'for the pes', are not the original goal of the Lover's confession.

In this limitation of viewpoint – and hence of the ultimate credibility of the directing voice – Genius shares certain important characteristics with the Pilgrim Dante of the *Inferno*, for there, hampered by his as yet unenlightened point of view, the Pilgrim must be reprimanded on several occasions by the guiding Virgil who, in this milieu at least, can be trusted as one who has achieved the requisite degree of detachment from earthly prejudices and misplaced sympathies. Like the Pilgrim, Genius is not a voice we can trust: the canto depicting Paolo and Francesca and the special character of Genius's catechism unfold to present the same messages.[10]

Nor is Genius helped in this regard by Gower's portrayal of his personality. Again the comparison with the *Divine Comedy* is a helpful contrast. Genius should be, after all, a guide figure, as is Dante's Virgil; but, rather than offering us the impression of knowledgeability and control, Genius seems at times argumentative, unprepared, even uncertain in the face of some of Amans' questions. Virgil, on the other hand, is aware of his failings of understanding and knows the reasons for them.[11] We are comfortable with Virgil because Virgil understands his place in a larger scheme of things; we trust him to guide us as far as he can. Yet Genius's uncertainties reduce the priest's authority in our eyes, render him but one voice among a number of characters' voices in the many minor narratives of the *Confessio*, who sometimes tell the truth and sometimes only the truth as they each know it, with no help for us to sort out the differences. In the end, we are left with a Genius who must be interpreted, neither interpreter nor key.

If, then, there is no directive voice emergent among the *personae* of the *Confessio*, where *do* we find it in the poem? Given Gower's clear didactic purposes, outlined in the Prologue and Book I and reiterated in the epilogue passages following Book VIII, it seems most unlikely that he would have risked leaving the body of the poem to indiscriminate interpretation. The answer, I believe, is to be found in a closer look at the Latin verses and marginalia, for what they have to tell us about Gower's reading of the text itself as sign. For if we are to comprehend what Gower thought possible for the *Confessio* as a poetic and didactic artifact, we must recognise the full dimensions of his plan. These included an attitude toward the entire page which, while it has more recent analogues, is arguably unique in medieval English literature. There *are* authoritative voices in the *Confessio Amantis*, but Gower's direction of them becomes apparent only if we step back from the fiction of the poem to consider the text in terms of the process by which it must be read.

So doing, we see that there are actually three 'voices' requiring reading in the *Confessio*. The first is the fiction – the frame story of Amans and Genius, along with the many exempla told by Genius. To 'read' this voice, we must interpret the fictional events one by one, finding and employing moments of irony, points of special information derived from allusions to sources, passages weighted to generate sympathy, laughter, repulsion, and scorn. Because we are concerned at this level with an overall reading, derived from the fitting-in of every element available, including all events and characters, we are able to find a 'voice' for the work which requires no spokesman from within – no guide, in short. This is Chaucer's method in the *Canterbury Tales* and to some degree in the *Troilus*. Specific attention paid to its application in the *Confessio* has already yielded useful, specific results in the form of most standard interpretations of the poem.[12] This 'voice' need not concern us here.

The second 'voice' with both artistry and authority is heard through the Latin verses. Their function in the *Confessio* is to divide sections of narrative into wieldy size, to announce shifts in mood and speaker. Again the similarity to the *Canterbury Tales* is worth notice, if only to note the differences. In Chaucer's poem, the so-called headlinks and endlinks carry many of the same responsibilites as Gower's Latin verses do in the *Confessio*. The contrasts, however, are significant. Gower was a strong, if idiosyncratic, Latinist and the meaning of the 'links' he wrote is frequently as problematic as his treatment of the hexameter line is skillfully musical. Aesthetically, the intent of the Latin verses is clear from their complexity: they are there to be read by a clerical audience whose Latin was sufficient to parse and appreciate their elegant, knotty beauty.[13]

In this, Gower's Latin 'links' differ from Chaucer's Middle English ones, which are not ornamental but integral to the narrative flow of his poem, miniature dramas, joining together the otherwise unrelated tales. The voices we find in them are those of specific pilgrims, bantering, bickering, developing a context out of which the ensuing tale will grow. By contrast, Gower provides no dramatic or fictive involvement of the 'voice' of his Latin verses. He does not, so to speak, *embody* it into the *Confessio*. No character, no fictive or even omniscient narrator, speaks these Latin lines; they appear as devices only, looking ahead for us to the unfolding of the larger narrative in English, providing a glimpse of what will be said and done. The result is a kind of unusual displacement of the Latin poetry, describable perhaps as a 'present non-presence': what Blanchot has distinguished in *L'entretien infini* as the 'narrative' voice which, unlike what he calls the 'narratorial' voice of a character recounting any given story, is 'neutral', and 'utters [*dit*] the work from the placeless place where the work is silent'.[14]

Such a 'neutral' voice creates a special fiction about itself – about whether it should be 'heard' as 'present' or not. On one hand, in order to enjoy the narrative drama by entering into it with suspended disbelief (an effect Gower obviously strove to bring about for his readers through careful attention to establish the verisimilitude of his frame-story) we must forget that the Latin verses are there. On the other hand (and contrarily), as we read the Latin verses, we learn from them about the narrative. Thus, more contrarily still, they insist upon reminding us of the textuality of the experience, of its *un*reality, of its craftedness, even as we join in it, not as acknowledged participants simply in the fiction, but as *readers*, self-conscious of our distance from the text and its 'voices'. The effect is increased participation in an increasingly complex association of self and multiplicitous 'other'.

This 'voice', then, of the Latin verses fulfills several loose purposes: aesthetically, in line with the argument advanced in the first half of this paper, it balances the 'plain style' English of the larger poem, demonstrating to sophisticated audiences that their author John Gower can sing as well at the top as at the bottom of the scale. Moreover, it speaks up strongly for the recognition of the reading experience as the primary engagement between self and 'other' – in this case, not a guide figure or a particularly imposing fictive character to whom we owe emotional allegiance (Dante's Virgil and Beatrice garner this, as does his Pilgrim; Chaucer's Troilus has taken on another shade of it by that poem's close); instead it is a *text* we are asked to consider and address, even be addressed *by*. And, finally, the 'voice' of the Latin verses permits entry into the fictional world of frame and exempla an authoritative, directing presence which is also authorial. By reminding us continually that the fiction is text, neither self-productive nor uncrafted, the Latin verses bring us back to the source of such crafting. Partly in this way, the *Confessio* earns for itself its palinode: predictably vigorous Amans, we find, has been hoary John Gower all along. Thus the dream-tale told by a made-up character is transformed into that 'prayer for the pes' commanded the character Amans/Gower by Venus, a prayer which is also the text in our hands, the work of the human being John Gower, connected consequently with his otherwise-perimetrical life as a lawyer and land speculator, as Geoffrey Chaucer's friend, and yet unconnected too, 'narrative' in Blanchot's sense, speaking from beyond place and biographical isolation in time. Fiction is thereby grafted onto/transmuted into 'fact' in a most unusual way, simultaneously being and pressed to bypass itself, to set up independently and remove itself from the poet (both as man and as mechanic act) altogether. Thus Amans/Gower, in writing an amorous poem as a prayer for peace, succeeds in stepping out of all roles by the *Confessio*'s end, transforming himself from narratorial lover to narratorial poet to 'real' old man to – finally – 'narrative' text unrelated to *persona* or personality.

This certainly is not Chaucer's method in *Troilus and Criseyde*, where the *persona* Troilus looks back to deny the world even as the narrator/poet/ 'voice' asserts itself and its powers over its creation most fully, to conclude with the 'litel bok' sent off to do the poet's will, bringing him fame and salvation. Nor is it the method of the *Canterbury Tales*. There the 'narratorial' voice is fictively enformed and located in 'Geoffrey' the Pilgrim and in the individual Canterbury travellers. What results is humor, irony, and a necessary blurring, even loss, of any single lesson or point for the work as a whole. Nonetheless, a comparison of Chaucer's authorial presence in the *Canterbury Tales* with Gower's Latin verses is instructive. *Strategically* the attempt of both poets is analogous: for, through their respective means each poet has contrived to include a 'voice' of his 'own'. This similarity of *strategy* is obscured by the differences in purpose. Gower's Latin hexameters attempt to enforce a single meaning on their context, while Chaucer's fictive narrators insist upon the opposite, offering instead a rich multiplicity of voices that denies unified effect, almost to the broadest extension of reading. Yet each poet succeeds at his task: we are required to read the text itself as 'other', as autonomous presence, actual and active – as sign, in short – rather than as transparent conduit or medium beyond, or through, which the fictive world potentially unfolds. Chaucer's reminders of this, in the *Canterbury Tales*, are instructions slipped into the head- and endlinks, such as the Pilgrim/narrator's warning to the 'gentils' before the 'Miller's Tale' to 'Turne over the leef and chese another' if we mind a little bawdy talk.[15] These links thus remind us that, first, Chaucer the poet has (had) power over his text and that we too, as readers with the volume now on our knees, have similar decisive control. Gower's Latin verses, which also serve his text as links, enforce similar demands by denying us the possibility of forgetting how fully and uniquely, in fact, we are engaged in an act of reading. In so doing, they provide us with a second 'voice' in the *Confessio Amantis*.

There is also a third such 'voice' active in the poem, the result of Gower's inclusion of Latin. Just as do the hexameter verses, so do the Latin prose marginalia bring us into touch with the text as significant 'other'. Their primary purpose, as I have elaborated elsewhere, is to 'glosse' this poem of a first-person narrator by referring to the events from a third-person point of view, as for example in the following, taken from the margin in Book III, beside lines 2362 ff.: *Hic declarat per exemplum contra istos Principes seu alios quoscumque illicite guerre motores.*[16] The prose Latin 'glosses' tell us what will happen, but more often what it means, and they further make reference to source texts from which a figure or a line is borrowed.[17]

Assuming these Latin marginalia to be Gower's own product, the nature of his intentions and their effects become especially interesting from the theoretical point of view. One may argue that the marginal 'glosses' represent Gower's solution to the problem of didactic precision which confronts all moralists who trust important lessons to unavoidably misreadable fictions: Gower seeks to limit polysemy and avoid misunderstanding by directing the act of comprehension through an expansion of the poetic text to include the margins of his page.[18] Here meaning may be presented in a 'distilled' state, exclusive of the demands of Blanchot's 'narratorial' voices. The similarity of Gower's marginalia to the *Glossa Ordinaria*, and to a lesser degree the *Fasciculus Morum*, suggests Gower's model for the practice at the structural, though of course not at the theoretical, level.[19]

Yet if this explains some portion of what Gower may have hoped to accomplish with the Latin prose commentary in the margins, it does little to express the unusual quality of the decision. Composing marginal glosses for one's own poem, leaving the impression that they are the work of an unnamed 'other' reader, is not common in the Middle Ages or any period. Indeed, we must go as far forward as Coleridge and 'The Rime of the Ancient Mariner' to find a suitable parallel. The practice may well be a device of Gower's own invention, and as such it should be of interest in helping us categorise the boundaries of what was possible for a late medieval writer thinking about texts.

One certainty is that, for a man of his time, Gower was unusually concerned with the production and correction of his manuscripts. Although it now seems unlikely that the priory at St Mary Overeys in Southwark, where Gower lived while writing the *Confessio*, had a scriptorium (as Fisher and others once surmised) in which his poems were copied under his oversight,[20] nevertheless, from the uniformity of many manuscripts, the consistent orthography showing the same mixture of Kentish and East Midland features, from certain additions and deletions of a type best explained as authorial, it seems Gower took a direct hand in bringing his work to the public.[21] In so doing he stands apart from Chaucer and other contemporaries, whose conceptualization of the book as an idea was quite different.[22]

This evidence is important for present purposes because it renders more credible a suggestive line of inquiry. From Gower's other practices, it is apparent that he put much thought into the *look* of the page. Consistent orthography, such as we find in the many manuscripts of the three recensions of the *Confessio*, does not often appear where such concern is lacking. But to conceive of the page as a totality, an *environment* – that is, as a space to be inhabited poetically and spoken *from* – involves a shift of semiotic awareness we seldom grant medieval authors other than Dante. The question is one Jacques Derrida has recently attempted to define in terms of the 'edge' ('le bord') of the text, in his doubled essay, 'Living On: *Border Lines*' (p. 77). Significantly, Derrida here conjoins two texts, one printed in the margins of the page, one commenting freely (we would be correct to say 'marginally', in two senses) upon the other. His purpose is 'to create an effect of *superimposing*, of superimprinting one text on the other' (p. 83), to demonstrate graphically that 'the text overruns all the limits assigned to it so far . . . everything that was to be set up in opposition to writing (speech, life, the world, the real, history, and what not, every field of reference . . .)', so that in the end we may 'work out the theoretical and practical system of these margins, these borders, once more, from the ground up' (p. 84). He is, he says, 'seeking merely [!] to establish the necessity of this whole problematic of judicial framing and of the jurisdiction of frames' (p. 88). His experiment brings him to conclude that in so encumbered[23] a case as a work with a 'doubled' text, the narratives ('récits') become 'synonymous, homonymous, anonymous', and the narrator innominate because 'there is no guarantee that he does not have two [names] . . .' (p. 163).

This concern of Derrida's for the dissolution of jurisdictions – over margins, pages, books, and even authors' names themselves – is, I contend, John Gower's also, in his handling of the Latin marginalia in the manuscripts of the *Confessio Amantis*: that is, with what manner of vision did Gower perceive the possibilities of the page *qua sign* that allowed him to see it capable of such spatial signification? In the end, that is what he has produced, or come closest to producing, by stretching the limits of the meaningful in graphic ways. The noteworthy elements here are Gower's apparent recognitions that the page itself can embody the message, can become clearly a sign – in Derrida's phrase, 'synonymous, homonymous, anonymous'; and that the text is, *must be*, an element actively making meaning, regardless of specific literary approach. We can see this clearly if we refer to the plates. Pages such as these, with their multiple cognitive foci, unfold toward the reader unwaveringly; indeed, they insist upon layered interpretation, one might say 'conversational', or even choric, interpretation, given the several 'voices' present in the marginalia, the poetic narrative in middle English, and the Latin verses. (In many manuscripts of the *Confessio* these Latin sections are highlighted further by being written in red ink.) The act of reading the text thus becomes also an act of variable recreation of it, since the 'voices' will be encountered in different orders by different readers or by the same reader on different readings. Thus, in Gower's hands the blank sheet of vellum, which eventually becomes the manuscript page with the addition of writing, has also a 'being', autonomous of the lines of text but relatable as a subsidiary, or 'con-text', if pressed correctly to reveal the supporting mechanics of 'voices'. The result is an unusually rich field on which issues commonly considered *either* paleographic *or* theoretical may be seen to link, the one playing into, and informing analysis of, the other necessarily, through an inextricable association of the visual format and the comprehensible, or argumentative, poetic text. To 'read' this text, the *Confessio Amantis*, is to recognise the page as sign, apparently with the full intent of the author, to draw meaning from its layout – its tactile surface, the very page one turns, to view another, 'read', and turn again in a motion simultaneously distancing and enclosing. Such elements of poetic mechanics have long been advanced to favor the idea that Gower (for all his failures in not being Chaucer) was in possession of a breadth of vision which permitted him to look beyond the comparative security of tradition and to draw his own conclusions. If I am correct, and John Gower *was* responsive to the unique multiplication of the 'voices' in his last poem and that he exploited and directed them, enforcing meaning through the physicality of the manuscript page itself, then something extraordinary has happened in the sophistication of how men envisioned, and perceived, manuscripts. In Gower's hands at least, they could join an enfolding realm of the meaningful; they could, in short, become signs.

Notes

1. The arrangement of Latin verse headnotes and prose marginalia is reproduced in the primary modern edition of the *Confessio Amantis*: see G.C. MACAULAY, (ed.), *The Complete Works of John Gower* (Oxford: Clarendon Press, 1901) II–III; rpt as *The English Works of John Gower*, EETS, e.s., 81–2 (London: Oxford University Press, 1969). All references to the works of John Gower are to this edition.

2. See, for example, MACAULAY's comments on the emendations in the manuscripts of the *Vox Clamantis*; *Complete Works*, IV, lix–lx; on the *Confessio* as evident in MS. Fairfax 3, see II, clvii–cix.

3. See JOHN H. FISHER, *John Gower: Moral Philosopher and Friend of Chaucer* (New York: New York University Press, 1964), p. 117; PETER NICHOLSON, 'Gower's Revisions in the *Confessio Amantis*', *Chaucer Review*, **19** (1984): 123–43; the work of GRIFFITHS, HARRIS, and PEARSALL is forthcoming from Garland Publishing, Inc.

4. I am grateful to Professor Sandra L. Hindman of the Department of Art History, Northwestern University, for calling my attention to the *Epistre Othéa* (MS. Paris fr. 848, produced ca. 1400), in which Christine de Pizan appears also to be glossing her own poem. Whether she was influenced by Gower is not known. For a detailed discussion of this manuscript, see Professor HINDMAN's forthcoming study, *Christine de Pizan's Epistre Othéa: Painting and Politics at the Court of Charles VI* (Toronto: Pontifical Institute, 1986).

5. R.F. YEAGER, '"òure englisshe" and Everyone's Latin: The *Fasciculus Morum* and Gower's *Confessio Amantis*', *South Atlantic Review*, **46** (1981): 40–53.

6. The 'middel weie' as Gower applies it in the *Confessio* has been studied extensively. The most complete recent study is by GOETZ SCHMITZ, '*The Middel Weie': Stil- und Aufbauformen in John Gowers Confessio Amantis* (Bonn: Gründman, 1974).

7. FISHER, *John Gower*, p. x, provides a helpful comparative chronology of the works of Gower and Chaucer.

8. The better manuscripts of the *Confessio* have appended to them the so-called 'Traitié pour essampler les amants marietz', a collection of eighteen ballades with amorous themes composed in Anglo-Norman sometime after 1385. From the Latin prose headnote, it is clear that Gower intended to have them read as the last portion of his poem.

9. For example, see *CA*, I, 148–97.

10. The Pilgrim Dante grows in his awareness of sin, and how it should be treated; compare his sympathetic weeping and swoon at the fate of Paolo and Francesca (*Inferno* V, 139–42) with Virgil's praise for his spurning of Filippo Argenti (VIII, 33–45).

11. See, for example, *Purgatorio*, XXVII, 127–9.

12. I have in mind here interpretations such as FISHER's, *John Gower*, RUSSELL A. PECK, *Kingship and Common Profit in Gower's Confessio Amantis* (Carbondale and Edwardsville: Southern Illinois University Press, 1978), and PAUL MILLER, 'John Gower, Satiric Poet' in *Gower's Confessio Amantis: Responses and Reassessments*, ed. A.J. MINNIS (Woodbridge, Suffolk: Boydell and Brewer, 1983).

13. That Gower considered this clerical audience when composing Latin poetry is apparent from his dedication of the *Vox Clamantis* to Thomas Arundell, Archbishop of Canterbury; see MACAULAY, *Works*, IV, 1–2.

14. Quoted by JACQUES DERRIDA in 'Living On: *Border Lines*' (trans. James Hulbert), in *Deconstruction and Criticism* (New York: Continuum, 1979), p. 104.

15. See *Canterbury Tales*, I, 3167–86.

16. 'Here, using an example, he denounces those princes, or anyone else, who brings about war unlawfully.'

17. See, for example, the marginal note beside Bk I, 2705: 'Salomon. Amictus eius annunciat de eo.'

18. I discuss this point more fully in 'our englisshe', pp. 46–7.

19. See 'oure englisshe', pp. 43–7.

20. See FISHER, *John Gower*, pp. 60, 93.

21. Nicholson's research into the textual variations of the manuscripts has shown convincingly that many of what Macaulay thought were authorial revisions are in fact the work of bookshop scribes rendering the usual inconsistencies found in texts produced by multiple hands ('Gower's Revisions', p. 139). Nonetheless, the four manuscripts of the *Vox Clamantis* and MSS. Stafford and Fairfax of the *Confessio* seem to Nicholson as well to 'support the belief that Gower supervised copying and production' (p. 136). On the bookshop production of *Confessio* manuscripts, see also A.I. DOYLE and M.B. PARKES, 'The Production of Copies of the *Canterbury Tales* and the *Confessio Amantis* in the Early Fifteenth Century', in *Medieval Scribes, Manuscripts and Libraries: Essays Presented to N.R. Ker, ed. M.B. Parkes and Andrew G. Watson* (London: Scolar Press, 1978), pp. 163–210.

22. An intriguing re-examination of Chaucer's sense of the book as *idea* has been offered by JESSE M. GELLRICH, *The Idea of the Book in the Middle Ages: Language Theory, Mythology, and Fiction* (Ithaca, NY: Cornell University Press, 1985).

23. Derrida's actual term for this encumbering is 'invagination'; 'Living On', pp. 97–101.

12   The Romance of History and the Alliterative *Morte Arthure**

LEE PATTERSON

In this last chapter of a larger study of historicism and medieval studies, Lee Patterson articulates the proposition that medieval historical consciousness is always at issue, always to be negotiated. Divided between the contradictory impulses to find ahistorical exemplars in the past but also to escape such repetitive patterns and the traditional ideologies they sustain, many of the romances offer self-reflexive commentaries on these issues. A historical romance such as the alliterative *Morte Arthure* not only creates the past, but meditates on that very process, and the use and abuse of historical precedent.

Sometime about 1353, as French fortunes in the war with England were sinking toward their nadir, King John of France commissioned Pierre Bersuire to provide him with a translation of Livy's *History of Rome*. In his preface Bersuire disclosed John's motives in commissioning such a work. 'It is indeed true', he said,

> that excellent princes, the wiser they are the more they will want to learn
> about the virtuous deeds and remarkable works of the princes of
> antiquity, about the martial genius, the intelligence, and the industry
> with which these men conquered lands and territories, built empires and
> kingdoms, and founded, fostered, defended, and governed their empires,
> holding them through a grand succession that endured at length; so that
> modern princes can in the same way defend and govern their lands,

* Reprinted from LEE PATTERSON, *Negotiating the Past: The Historical Understanding of Medieval Literature* (Madison, Wisconsin: The University of Wisconsin Press, 1987), pp. 197–230.

defeat and dominate foreigners, discomfit enemies, defend their subjects, and aid their friends.[1]

But despite Bersuire's rotund promises, Livy did King John little good. In 1356 he was captured by the English at the disastrous battle of Poitiers, spent the next four years a prisoner in England, and the following four ineffectively searching for a way to act out his restless gallantry. Fortunately for France, he died in 1364 and left the kingdom in the capable hands of his son Charles the Wise.

In turning to Livy in his time of need, King John strikes the modern observer as hopelessly quixotic, but according to the standards of his day he was being both high-minded and sensible. Indeed, his remarkably successful son not only owned a copy of Bersuire's Livy but commissioned a steady stream of similar translations, in part for the same practical reasons as his father, in part for larger concerns both humanistic and political.[2] Any attempt to specify medieval historical interests must be alert both to this variety of motives, at work within individual projects as well as across the spectrum of historical writings, and to a common denominator of instinctive deference, even submissiveness, before the past. As has often been noted (but rarely explored), this is a deference that renders elusive what we would take to be a genuinely historical consciousness. Indeed, the most common of medieval historical writings, those that moralise the historical record into illustrative instances of success and failure, vice and virtue, are manifestly ahistorical: the past is rendered not as a process that has its own temporality but as a storehouse of disconnected and timeless *exempla* that assume authority precisely because they are no longer timebound. Nevertheless, we should remember that medieval writers also used the past historiographically – sometimes to delineate an instructive chronology of secular empire, more commonly to apprehend the plan of providential dispensation – and it would be a mistake to assent too quickly to the common proposition that the Middle Ages lacked a historical sense. Rather, we would do better to see the medieval historical consciousness as always at issue, at times emerging toward an authentic apprehension of temporality and periodization, at other times retreating under the pressure of various ideologies toward reification and idolization.[3]

The most powerful of these ideologies, as I have suggested, was the fundamental definition of present legitimacy in terms of descent from an omnipotent past. *Verum quia vetus* is a medieval proverb that expresses a ubiquitous theology of origins in force across the whole range of medieval culture, and nowhere more visibly than in the political world. The disruptions of medieval political history were typically healed with the soothing continuities of a founding legend, and insecure rulers bolstered their regimes by invoking honorific if legendary precedents. The degree to which these political imperatives determined the kind of literature that was produced in the Middle Ages is not sufficiently appreciated; nor is the even more important fact that this literature continued throughout its medieval life to concern itself with essentially historiographical issues, issues such as the relation of individual action to historical process, or the use and abuse of historical precedent itself. My concern in this chapter is with just this self-reflexiveness, and specifically with the extent to which narratives that are now designated as romances (and hence as fictions largely unconcerned with historical reality) in fact meditate both upon the paradox of their own production – as historical fabrications designed to legitimise political power – and upon the problematic enterprise of reconstituting, from within history, a prehistorical origin. My particular focus here is upon the fifteenth-century Middle English poem, the Alliterative *Morte Arthure*, but I want to preface my discussion of that poem with more general and wide-ranging comments upon the historiographical issues that typically inhabit medieval romance.

1

[As we have already seen in the previous chapter], the discontinuities of English political history foreclosed the attempt to trace a genuinely historical line of descent from a common origin. Anglo-Saxon hegemony was achieved by displacing Britain's original Celtic inhabitants and was itself sustained only by accommodating Scandinavian interlopers, and even this heavily qualified sovereignty was abrogated by the events of 1066. Furthermore, the subsequent Anglo-Norman supremacy was both challenged from below and, more seriously, subject to the fragmentations occasioned by its own inner dynamic. Moreover, when Henry II ascended the disputed throne in 1154, he was as both duke of Normandy and king of England faced with a tangle of conflicting loyalties that required a firm assertion of royal sovereignty. Part of his effort at self-legitimisation was literary. It is doubtless easy to overestimate Henry's role as a patron of letters, and Plantagenet patronage was by no means confined to the king.[4] But much of the court literature of the period shows patterns of interest that are consistent with Henry's political needs, most explicitly in the Latin and Anglo-Norman chronicles that recorded his *gestae* and those of his ancestors, works written in Latin by Aelred of Rievaulx and in the vernacular by Jordan Fantosme, Wace, and Benoît de Sainte-Maure.[5] But of more lasting importance were the legendary histories – or, as we now call them, romances – that, for all their undoubted reliance upon oral narratives, found both their literary inspiration and political purpose in Geoffrey of Monmouth's *Historia regum Britanniae*.[6]

The historiographical purpose of Geoffrey's project, to put a complex matter simply, was to replace the Augustinian dismissal of secular history that had inspired Bede's authoritative *Historia ecclesiastica* with a Virgilian narrative that located historical legitimacy not merely in terms of the development of the church but within the larger world of history itself.[7] Yet the claim of Geoffrey's *translatio imperii* was not only that legitimacy could be transferred through the long reaches of historical time without dilution, but that the legitimising force at the origin was itself unproblematic. And as we have seen in the previous chapter, the Trojan story that Virgil passed on to the West, and that Geoffrey rewrote, called into question both the nature of that originating energy and the very linearity by which it was transmitted. This was a questioning that Geoffrey not only did not evade but that, in his often wildly parodic and ideologically unconstrained speculations, he eagerly exploited.[8] For Geoffrey's *Historia* tells of a refoundation that is accomplished only by the destruction of the very past it seeks to reenact: the founding father Brutus is himself a paricide, the preeminent Arthur is of dubious paternity and is supported by a prophet born of an incubus, the country's monarchical history riven with generational violence, and its story as a whole consists of alternating periods of internecine self-destruction and imperial warfare directed against the Rome from which it took its origin. The *Historia regum Britanniae*, in sum, is a *Gründungsage* that undermines the very ground upon which it rests: when, in one of its most emblematic incidents, the foundations of Vortigern's tower give way, an excavation reveals a pool inhabited by two fighting dragons, symbols of the perpetual strife upon which history is founded and which it continually reenacts. In short, Geoffrey's seminal text is what Judith Shklar has called a 'subversive genealogy', a 'myth that expresses the outrage of those who know all the evils of the world and recognize their necessity'.[9] It is a myth of origins that deconstructs the origin.

At about the time of Henry's uneasy accession to the throne Wace not only translated the *Historia* into Anglo-Norman but, according to Layamon, who later translated Wace's version into English, presented a copy to Queen Eleanor.[10] Moreover, the two great themes of Geoffrey's work – the Trojan foundation of Britain and the preeminence of Arthur – were not only immediately exploited for purposes of political legitimisation but served throughout the later Middle Ages, as we shall see, as central sources for English monarchs eager to bolster their often unsteady hold upon the throne. And yet these rewritings of Geoffrey remained, despite their immediate ideological purpose, powerfully conditioned by the subversive impulses that had motivated Geoffrey in the first place. Appropriately enough, Geoffrey thus became a source who transmitted to his inheritors the very instability that he saw as haunting all merely historical origins.

The continued disruptions of English dynastic history – including the fourteenth-century depositions of Edward II and Richard II, and the chaos of the middle years of the fifteenth century – meant that the English monarchs who succeeded Henry, unlike the Capetian and Valois kings of France, looked back not upon an unruffled descent from a founding father (Charlemagne) but

instead upon a political genealogy broken by violence and impeached by its
own discontinuities. Hence it was in England that the historiography of
legendary origins flourished with special vigor. To be sure, not just Britain
but virtually every European nation claimed descent from a common origin at
Troy: in his *Troy Book*, begun in 1412, Lydgate lists not just Britain as a
Trojan foundation but also France (Francus), Venice (Antenor), Sicily (Sycanus),
Naples (Aeneas), and Calabria (Diomedes), and throughout the Middle Ages
other writers contributed many other instances — including Dudo of Saint-
Quentin's early-eleventh-century assertion that Normandy had been founded
by Antenor. But while on the Continent the claim to Trojan origin was
asserted perfunctorily in the course of pursuing other interests, in England it
remained a powerful instrument of royal propaganda. This is illustrated by
Lydgate's own poem, for instance, which was commissioned by the future
Henry V only a dozen or so years after his father had seized the crown — the
same Henry who had earlier had made for himself a deluxe manuscript of the
finest Trojan poem written in the Middle Ages, Chaucer's *Troilus and
Criseyde*.[11] Even more telling is the fact that the authoritative version of the
Troy story, and the ultimate source for Lydgate's poem, had also been
commissioned by an English monarch: the *Roman de Troie* was written early
in Henry II's reign by Benoît de Sainte-Maure, who was later to provide the
king with a genealogical history in the *Chronique des Ducs de Normandie*.[12]

This correlation between political instability and Trojan historiography,
while not prescriptive, does serve to indicate that the Trojan narrative served
English monarchs as a legitimising device. Yet it also never lost its capacity
to call into question the very purpose for which it was designed. There are
various ways in which this subversiveness becomes manifest in medieval
Troy narratives. For one thing, virtually every version of the story opens
with an attack upon the authenticity of the others, a self-justifying gesture
that necessarily undermines the authority of the entire enterprise — especially
given the fact that texts claiming to be Trojan histories ranged from the
eyewitness reports of Dares and Dictys to the elaborate Silver Age *imitatio* of
Joseph of Exeter's *Bellum Troianum* the sober prose of Guido delle Colonne's
Historia destructionis Troiae, not to mention the widely divergent vernacular
versions. And for another, a continual theme of Trojan historiography is the
inexplicable nature of the events themselves: as Guido says, 'Even if these
many woes were pleasing to the gods, still, the original cause of these things,
as trifling as unimportant, rightly troubles human hearts.'[13] But for our
purposes, the most telling evidence of the instability of the Trojan story is
the generic instability of its various instantiations. The literary history of
Troy begins with the 'diaries' or *ephemeroi* of Dares and Dictys, texts that
unequivocally proclaim their historicity. But Benoît's 26,000-line rewriting
elaborately amplifies these originating documents with the addition of
extended amorous subplots, creating a generic instability that is then enacted
throughout the subsequent history of the form. On the one hand, Guido delle

Colonne not only translates the narrative into Latin prose but subordinates the romantic subplots to the martial exploits and political machinations that constitute the *narratio rei gestae* of medieval historiography. And yet on the other hand, Benoît's lovers were often detached from their historical context and used as instances of the erotic life, and nowhere more completely than in Boccaccio's *Filostrato*, where their significance derives not from their historical value but from the service they can render to the author's own courtly life. It is only, then, with Chaucer's *Troilus and Criseyde* that these conflicting registers are reunited in a complex balance, allowing the story to speak once more to historical concerns. And yet the uncertain status of the very narrative that medieval secular historiography invoked as its founding moment is implied by Chaucer in his designation of his source as 'Lollius', by which he seems to have meant a mumbler (from the ME *lollen, lullen*) with classical pretensions (hence the Latinate suffix *-ius*).

Although necessarily brief, these comments on the medieval historiography of Troy mean to suggest that the various tensions and contradictions that inhabited medieval thinking about history per se were registered at the level of textuality as a generic vacillation between history and romance, an instability that itself put into question not merely the authenticity of a particular narrative, or even of historiography as a whole, but the legitimacy of the historical life itself. Very much the same problematic may be seen at work in the development and deployment of the Arthurian legend, and is articulated in all its complexity in the Alliterative *Morte Arthure*. Again, it is Henry II who first appropriated the Arthurian aura for political purposes, as Wace's translation of Geoffrey's *Historia* suggests. In fact, Henry's court was something of a center of Arthurian literature, much to the irritation of its more Latinate members.[14] The works of Thomas of Britain and Marie de France were probably read in court circles, although probably not written there, and Chrétien de Troyes' first two romances, *Erec et Enide* and *Cligès*, have affiliations with Angevin interests that argue for an English provenance.[15] There is as well the fantastic *Draco Normannicus* (c. 1168) by Stephen of Rouen, a bizarre poetic composition that conflates Merlin's prophecies, Breton nationalism, romanticised French history, and Arthurian eschatology in order, apparently, both to exalt Henry and deflate Breton hopes for Arthur's return.[16]

Arthur's grip upon the medieval political imagination extended well past the twelfth century. In 1278 Edward I also had the tomb of his *quondam* predecessor opened and the remains transported to the high altar at Glastonbury, an event that was only the most dramatic of his many Arthurian observances.[17] So potent, apparently, was the Arthurian legitimisation that it could be invoked in even the most illegitimate of contexts. When in 1321 Thomas of Lancaster was conspiring with the Scots to overthrow Edward II he went under the pseudonym 'King Arthur',[18] and when Roger Mortimer succeeded six years later in dethroning Edward he staged a 'Round Table' tournament that invoked Arthurian pretensions that his family had had for three generations.[19] Given these strategies of division, it is clear why Edward III tried to reappropriate the Arthurian legend to the monarchy by founding the Order of the Garter with its own Round Table.[20] But this repossession was necessarily temporary: at the end of the Middle Ages Henry Tudor encompassed himself with Arthuriana, including naming his eldest son 'Arthur'. When history is negotiable the future always has the last word.

Both in their first form and in their later versions, the Arthurian legends, like the Trojan, are persistently marked by the paradox of their origin. Fabrications used to affirm a historical past, their historical authenticity is from the beginning at issue: history, it seems, comes into existence and into question simultaneously. In his *Gesta regum Anglorum*, written in the early 1120s, William of Malmesbury had issued a call for a historian who would rescue 'warlike Arthur' from the lying fables of the Britons and provide him with the truthful history he deserved.[21] Geoffrey's mockingly brilliant response aped the forms of historical accuracy that William and his fellow historian Henry of Huntingdon had established but placed them in the service of an elaborate and excessive counterfeit. Far from rescuing Arthur from factitiousness, Geoffrey's book served to ignite a controversy. William of Newburgh's commentary was the most explicit – and best informed – attack upon Geoffrey, but it was hardly the only one. Gerald of Wales, for instance, despite his heavy reliance on Geoffrey throughout his *Itinerarium Galliae*, (re)told a malicious story about the demonic properties of the *Historia*, and as late as the mid-fourteenth century Ranulph Higden cast doubt on the authenticity of Geoffrey's account.[22] But the most severe challenge to the historicity of the Arthurian story came not from historians – most of whom simply included an abbreviation of Geoffrey in their own accounts – but from the continued existence of the British fables that Geoffrey's work was supposed to repress. The Arthurian romances inevitably surrounded their chronicle cognates with an aura of fictiveness, casting upon historiography a shadow of incredibility. In the late-twelfth-century *Chanson des Saisnes* Jean Bodel had already chauvinistically devalued the matter of Britain as 'vains et plaisants' (line 7) in comparison to the historically true matter of France, and Arthurian writing was never able to divest itself of this dubiousness.

The formal effect of this fact is that Arthurian romance, often used for purposes of political authentication, defines for itself a complicated relationship to the question of its own authenticity. Two brief examples Chrétien's *Le chevalier au lion* and the Middle English *Sir Gawain and the Green Knight*, can prepare us for the more extended analysis of the Alliterative *Morte Arthure*. In the *Roman de Rou*, written before 1174, the Anglo-Norman historian Wace had recounted his journey to the forest of Brocéliande in quest of the marvels that were, he had been told, to be found there. But Wace found nothing but a forest, and he concluded bitterly,

Merveilles quis, mes nes trovai,
Fol m'en revinc, fol i alai,
Fol i alai, fol m'en revinc.
Folie quis, por fol me tinc.

I sought marvels, but I didn't find any. A fool I returned from there, a fool
I went there, a fool I went there, a fool I returned from there. I sought
folly, I consider myself a fool.[23]

Now at the beginning of *Le chevalier au lion*, Chrétien has the Arthurian
knight Calogrenant recount to his chivalric companions *his* visit to
Brocéliande. Calogrenant did in fact discover a marvel, a fountain with
dramatically magical properties and a huge knight who defended it from
interlopers. Calogrenant enacted the fountain's magic – by pouring water on
a stone he summoned up a violent storm – but was then humiliatingly
outjousted by the fountain's defender. He concludes his account with a
summarising statement that alludes to Wace, although now the words have a
very different meaning:

Ensi alai, ensi reving,
Au revenir por fol me ting.
Si vos ai conté com fos
Ce c'onques mes conter ne vos.

Thus I went, thus I returned, and in returning I consider myself a fool. So I
have told you, like a fool, that which I never before wished to tell.[24]

Both journeys were quests for validation and both ended in folly, but their
terms are sharply at odds – a disparity that measures the difference between
Wace's history and Chrétien's romance. Wace rebukes himself for having
tried to validate a fable with the experience of the eyewitness, but
Calogrenant's self-rebuke is ethical: first he failed as a knight, and now he has
brought shame upon himself by his admission of failure. Not that Calogrenant
ignores the demands of historiographical authentication: on the contrary, he
enjoins his audience by reminding them that he is himself the eyewitness to
the events he recounts:

Et qui or me voldra entandre,
cuer et oroilles me doit randre,
car ne vuel pas parler de songe,
ne de fable, ne de mançonge.
[Don maint autre vos ont servi,
Ainz vos dirai ce que je vi.]

And now whoever wishes to understand, he ought to yield me his heart
and his ears, for I do not wish to speak of a dream, nor of a fable, nor of a

lie. [Many others have offered you those, but I will tell you that which I saw.]²⁵

Moreover, throughout the romance Chrétien verifies Calogrenant's story by almost flippantly returning his heroes over and over again to the fountain that Wace could not find: it functions as the story's central locale, appearing no less than five times. By thus ostentatiously confecting the evidence that Wace labored so hard to discover, Chrétien is calling into question the historiographical mode of verification per se. But his purpose is not to dismiss it by implicitly charging it with a similar factitiousness – as if by fabricating evidence in his text he were suggesting that all forms of textual assertion were equally fabricated – but rather to set it aside as irrelevant to the deeper meanings at which his romance is aiming. For the verification to which both Calogrenant's tale and Chrétien's romance aspire, a passive witnessing is not satisfactory – just as Calogrenant's folly is more profound than Wace's. In fact, Calogrenant's words are made true or redeemed not by the mere existence of the fountain but by the heroism of Yvain, who avenges his comrade's defeat with his own victory over the fountain's defender. Yvain had vowed to return to the court with 'true evidence' (line 899: 'anseignes veraies') and a 'witness' (lines 1348–49: 'tesmoing') of his victory, and in marrying his enemy's widow and taking on the defense of the fountain he becomes himself the proof of his own success, living evidence that his words are true. It is, then, ethical verification that Chrétien's romance seeks to define: words, whether they be narratives or oaths, fables or personal accounts, are true not because they correspond to the historical world but because they impose an imperative upon the man who speaks. Language is *made* true, in short, by the ethos of chivalry.

This principle is exemplified throughout Yvain's adventures, in which the greatest folly is to speak empty words, whether they be the vaunting boasts of Kay, the unconsidered advice of Gawain, or the unkept promises of Yvain himself. In sum, Chrétien plays his romance off against the simplistic concept of authentication that motivates Wace's foolish journey. Far from evading the norms of historiographical verification – what Bede had called the *vera lex historiae* – Chrétien confronts and transcends them by asserting the priority of his own conception of narrative truth.²⁶ For just as Calogrenant's tale provides the model for subsequent actions in the world of romance, so the romance as a whole is directed to a historical world that has fallen away from old ideals and must be inspired by fictively generated norms of rectitude. 'Or est Amors tornee a fable' (line 24), says Chrétien in the prologue, and the task of his narrative is to provide a model of virtuous behavior that will make true that which is now only 'fable et mançonge' (line 27). This is the folly of the wise, the *stultitia praedicationis* (1 Cor. 1:21) that is exemplified in the fabling of the biblical parables that Calogrenant had himself allusively invoked in his introductory injunction to his audience to open their ears and hearts (see lines 169–74, cited above, and Matt. 13:14–15, Mark 8:18).

Another text that exploits the distinction between history and romance – the factual and the fictive – for strategic purposes is *Sir Gawain and the Green Knight*, which frames its Arthurian narrative with references to the fall of Troy and Brutus' conquest of England. The poet's purpose is not to persuade us that he is writing history – no poem about a green giant who replaces his severed head at will could ever have such pretensions – but rather to tell us that his story's range of relevance includes the pattern of British history as Geoffrey described it. If we do then locate the poem in this context, certain otherwise-muted themes become visible. When Brutus first conquered the island he suppressed the giants who were its native inhabitants, but the poem suggests that these original creatures are in some sense still at large, and with them the spirit of divisiveness that tragically undermined the Arthurian project and that reappears in this poem as Morgan le Fay's malevolent jealousy. Gawain's culpable if unknowing compact with these forces, then, has more than an individual significance, and his *untrawþe* to his own ideal self is as well a betrayal of the ideal court of which he is the representative. Obviously the poem is no political allegory, but in locating its subtle meditations on personal and cultural failure within a historical context it both speaks to a fourteenth-century England torn by dissension and comments on the meaning of the historical process per se.[27] Like Benoît's *Roman* and Geoffrey's *Historia*, *Sir Gawain and the Green Knight* is a fabrication – a romance – that tries to tell a truth about history. Moreover, in defining as its central value *trawþe*, and then committing itself to a magical narrative, the poem forces us to recognise that the crucial events by which history is shaped often present themselves in unprepossessing and even deceptive forms.

Finally, if the formal status of these texts can be seen as itself relevant to the problematic of historical action that they confront, we should also be aware that their thematic interests are similarly paradoxical. For they bespeak a historical imagination located between a past that is thought to be all-powerful (*verum quia vetus*) but is in fact pliable, and a present that feels itself to be always in need of support but is in fact intransigent in its demands. The result, in general terms, is an overwhelming concern in these texts with just these subterranean shuntings of influence and authority that bind together 'then' and 'now', 'it was' with 'it might have been'. These texts not only create the past but meditate upon that process, committing themselves to the endless negotiation that constitutes historicism. Specifically, the issues raised by this discussion can provide us with an interpretive purchase upon Arthurian literature, and in particular upon one of its finest Middle English representatives, the Alliterative *Morte Arthure*. The history of the genre and the history of the times are mutually inscribed in this poem, providing occasions of form and theme that allow for a meditation on the meaning of history per se – for, that is, a historical consciousness.

2

The Alliterative *Morte Arthure* is a work that despite its major importance has not yet achieved a secure place in the canon of English literature. Perhaps, then, a summary will not be out of place. The poem retells the story of Arthur's nearly successful campaign against the Roman emperor Lucius, a campaign that functions as the major episode in Geoffrey of Monmouth's account of the Arthurian tragedy. Challenged by Lucius to pay tribute to Rome, an act of homage dating back to Julius Caesar and recently reconfirmed on the British side by Uther Pendragon, Arthur not only rejects submission but asserts instead his own claim to the imperial throne. The outraged Lucius assembles his allies and marches into France, where Arthur – having paused to exterminate the monstrous giant of Mont St Michel joins him in battle. Arthur destroys Lucius and his host, reduces the city of Metz, then enters Italy and marches on Rome. The few senators left alive are eager to crown him emperor, but the night before his coronation Arthur is visited by a terrible dream, in which he is at once enrolled as one of the Nine Worthies and then subjected, like them, to the tyranny of Fortune's wheel, on which he rises only to be thrown down. The next morning he learns from an English pilgrim named Sir Cradoke that his regent in Britain, Mordred, has formed a liaison with Guenevere and seized the throne. Returning home, Arthur immediately suffers the loss of his chief retainer Gawain, who heroically if foolishly attacks Mordred's massive force with a handful of men, and then tracks Mordred down in the West where the final battle is fought. In this version of the story, both men are definitively killed: there is a *rex quondam* but no *rex futurus*.[28]

The poem survives in a single manuscript of about 1440, but was probably composed in the form in which we now have it about forty years earlier.[29] Recent scholarship has shown that some of the details almost certainly refer to the deposition of Richard II in 1399,[30] although these are by no means the only historical allusions, nor does the poem speak only to a single event in the life of the times. It has usually been thought that Arthur's invasion of Europe bears an unmistakable relevance to the adventures of Edward III in France, and indeed the fact that both campaigns have the same *casus belli* – the English king's refusal to pay homage to a foreign monarch and his subsequent claims to the foreign throne – makes a comparison inevitable.[31] This range of historical relevance suggests that the poem may well have been composed over a considerable period of time, through a process of accretion and revision familiar to medieval literature, and that it embodies a kind of historical layering, with level laid on level. In fact, as we shall see, this geological structure is a part of the poem's subject as well as of its form.[32]

Moreover, while the poem resists any restricted or exclusive application to the issues of any one time, it insists upon rendering its world with the kind of circumstantial detail we associate with fact, not fiction. Whether he has relied upon his own experience of the Hundred Years' War or upon literary accounts such as the *Life of the Black Prince* by the Chandos Herald, the poet has immersed his narrative in the gritty particulars of late-medieval military life.[33] Not only are the grim details of the battlefield undisguised by the cultic language of chivalry, but the effects of war on society as a whole are rendered with a dispassionate attention that is all the more moving for its self-restraint.[34] More generally, the poem aspires throughout to representational fidelity, carefully including specifics of dress, diplomacy, language, geography, and chronology – Arthur's campaign can be followed on both map and calendar[35] – that are so precisely rendered that critics have considered the poem an anti-romance, an epic, and a pseudochronicle.[36] Interestingly enough, the poem itself shows an unusual awareness of its place in the tradition of Arthurian literature. It recognises that there are two streams of Arthurian writing, 'romaunce' (lines 3200, 3440) and 'croncycle' (lines 3218, 3445), but locates itself at the source of both by designating them as later developments and calling itself a history: 'herkenes now hedyrwarde and herys this *storye*' (line 25).[37] The point is not to make a claim for veracity although based largely on Wace's translation of Geoffrey, the poem includes, as we shall see, large chunks of ostentatiously fictive material – but to insist that its focus is upon the historical world and its meaning.[38]

For it is not realism for its own sake that informs the attention to specificity. In its quest for historical meaning, the poem insists that what must be raised to significance is not a schematic outline of events but the historical world in all its random particularity. The itinerary of Arthur's triumphant sweep through France and Lorraine, across the Alps and into Lombardy and Tuscany, is studded with place names that serve to locate this campaign in a world that is reassuring in its historicity and yet troubling in its diversity, at once recognisable and alien. We are throughout reminded that Arthur's enemies, for all their conformity to the codes of medieval warfare, are foreigners who literally speak a different language. This fact is significantly insisted upon just as Arthur reaches the frustrated conclusion of his campaign. While walking in the Italian countryside the king engages a pilgrim in conversation in the 'Latin corroumppede all' (line 3478) that, we are told, is the local language, and it is only after the pilgrim has similarly replied that Arthur realises by his accent that he is conversing not with an Italian but with a fellow Englishman – with, indeed, a knight of his own chamber, Sir Cradoke.[39]

Arthur inhabits a world that is not merely various but fragmented, and whose disunities witness to the attritions of time. The war between Arthur and the Christian emperor Lucius reveals Christendom to be shattered within itself, just as the language of Christendom, Dante's 'latino . . . perpetuo e non corruttibile', has become 'Latin corroumppede all'.[40] This is apparently a world grown old, a *mundus senescens* declining into its last age.[41] But decadence inevitably implies restoration, and there is much in the poem that would encourage us to see in Arthur the agent of historical renewal.[42] For one thing, his campaign against Lucius is presented as part of the inevitable process of *translatio imperii*, the westering of empire from Troy to Rome, where it will eventually serve as, in Father Chenu's words, 'a providential preparation for the age of Christ'.[43] As the *pax Augusta* was the cradle in which Christ was first born, so a renovated Empire will provide the context for his rebirth.[44] The idea of *translatio* was already, as we have seen, an important theme in Geoffrey's *Historia*. Brutus is not merely a Trojan refugee but a Roman exile, expelled for having inadvertently slain his father. He at once embodies the Roman line — he is Aeneas' great-grandson — and stands as a deadly challenge, and he founds in Britain the nation that will become Rome's greatest rival.[45] Geoffrey structures his narrative on just this Rome-Britain opposition, but while Rome is thrice subdued it is never finally conquered: the British are on each occasion undone by treachery at home. Arthur's campaign against Lucius, then, is in the *Morte Arthure* as in Geoffrey's *Historia* both the summation of these efforts and an analysis of their failure.

The *Morte Arthure*, however, goes well beyond Geoffrey and the other versions dependent on him in stressing both the legitimacy of Arthur's claim on Rome and the eschatological meanings that his imperial ambitions imply. When Lucius' ambassadors demand tribute of Arthur, Geoffrey has him first reply by asserting that the right of conquest supersedes any historical precedents: 'Let him who comes out on top carry off what he has made up his mind to take!'[46] Only after thus dismissing the claims of history does Geoffrey's Arthur then invoke them, with breathtaking inconsistency, on his own behalf. But the poet of the *Morte Arthure* suppresses the argument from might entirely, and has his Arthur speak only to historical rights: 'Myne ancestres ware emperours' (line 276), he says, and later adds, 'Myn enmy . . . ocupyes myn heritage, þe Empyre of Rome' (lines 642–3). The past provides not only a precedent, as with Geoffrey, but a coherent lineage that has been broken and must now be restored. The Emperor Lucius is defined throughout as a usurper, and nowhere more explicitly than in the speech flung in his face by Arthur's tactless ambassador Gawain:

> And þe fals heretyke þat emperoure hym calleʒ,
> That occupyes in errour the empyre of Rome,
> Sir Arthure herytage, þat honourable kynge,
> That all his auncestres aught bot Vtere hym one,
> That ilke cursynge þat Cayme kaghte for his brothyre
> Cleffe on þe, cukewalde, with crounne ther thow lengeʒ,
> For the vnlordlyeste lede þat I on lukede euer!
>
> (Lines 1307–13)

The reference to Cain is only a small part of the defamation to which the poem subjects the Emperor. His allies are designated not just as from the

East, as in Geoffrey, but specifically as heathens, 'Sowdanes and Sarazenes owt of sere landes' (line 607).[47] Before undertaking the campaign Arthur's knights swear solemn vows on the 'vernicle', the veil with which Veronica wiped the face of Christ and that was preserved at Rome.[48] Arthur's knights are embarking upon a quest that is in part to recover the holy relics of Christendom, and as the campaign proceeds Arthur is embraced with an aura of election. As he walks the fortifications before Metz, he is warned to take cover but replies with equanimity that 'a corownde kynge with krysom enoynttede' (line 2447) need fear no casual attack. In short, we are made aware that Arthur is engaged not merely in a war of territorial ambition but in a crusade; and as he approaches his coronation at Rome, he is already planning to extend his conquests toward the hoped-for destination of all medieval monarchs, the Holy Land, where he will, he says, 'reuenge the Renke that on the Rode dyede' (line 3217). Given this coalescence of political and religious motifs, both the reader and Arthur might be forgiven the thought that he is to become not merely a Roman emperor but that last emperor for whom the Middle Ages had waited so long, the 'prince of the west', as 'Mandeville' put it, who 'shal conquer the Holy Land with helpe of othere Cristene' and for whom the withered tree of Paradise shall again bear fruit.[49]

That Arthur is not the agent of a providential history is the meaning of both the dream of Fortune and Cradoke's message about Mordred's rebellion. Having tried to restore a divided political world to its original (and final) unity, Arthur is recalled home by a division that continues to fester within his own nation and his own family.[50] That he bears some responsibility for his failure is clear, as he himself almost too eagerly acknowledges; but while the kind and degree of this responsibility are at the center of most critical discussion, they are not, I think, finally at the heart of the poem.[51] Rather, it is the very pattern of expansion and collapse that is the poem's deepest concern, the rhythm of striving and disappointment, of aspiration toward transcendence followed by a tragic submission to the iron law of historical recurrence. This is the pattern that is enacted in the poem's geography and chronology, and that in the image of the Wheel of Fortune is given a philosophical embodiment. But it is not, we should be careful to note, a philosophy that the poem single-mindedly espouses. Rather, the theme of recurrence functions as one element in a complex and difficult meditation on the meaning of historical action in a world in which history is given and not made.

3

We can make the terms of this meditation clearer by examining in detail the two major additions that the poet makes to his source: Gawain's foraging expedition — undertaken while Arthur is beseiging Metz — and the dream of Fortune itself. Apparently a romance intrusion in a poem that aspires to representational fidelity, the foraging expedition has suffered almost total critical neglect, although I believe it provides a paradigm of the poem's method and meaning.[52] The episode begins when Arthur sends Gawain and some French allies in search of forage, but instead of finding supplies they become engaged in two separate actions against the enemy. The first is a single combat between Gawain and a pagan warrior called Priamus, in which the Arthurian knight is victorious. The second is against a huge enemy force en route to raise the siege. The French, intimidated by the disparity in numbers, try to retire, but in a series of heroic speeches Gawain goads them on and together French and English achieve a magnificent victory, returning to Arthur in triumph.

Now in constructing this episode our poet relied upon two sources. One is the *Fuerres de Gadres* (or *Foray of Gaza*), a self-contained narrative attached to the twelfth-century *Roman d'Alexandre*.[53] In the *Fuerres* the foraging expedition is sent out by Alexander while he is besieging Tyre. The Greeks discover some cattle but are immediately attacked, first by a small group of knights, then by a huge army of Gadarenes en route to relieve Tyre. Here the disparity in numbers also elicits heroic speeches and deeds, although now the argument is over who will forgo the opportunity for heroic achievement in order to return for help, and only after a gallant (and interminable) dispute is Alexander finally summoned to rescue the few Greeks who now remain. Despite this minor difference, however, it is clear that the *Fuerres* provided the basic structure for Gawain's expedition, and the reliance is in fact also enforced by several similarities in detail.[54]

But in the *Morte Arthure* our poet chose to substitute for the first battle against the Gadarene knights the single combat between Priamus and Gawain. Here too there is a source, creating the total effect of an interpolation inset within an interpolation. The source in this case is a late-twelfth- or early-thirteenth-century chanson de geste called *Fierabras*, a crusade poem that deals with the Charlemagne, Roland, and Oliver legend.[55] In the *Fierabras*, the severely wounded Oliver engages the pagan giant Fierabras in single combat, a responsibility that has fallen to him because Roland, offended by a slight from Charlemagne, has refused; and Oliver not only defeats Fierabras but converts him to Christianity. But from this high-minded beginning, the chanson de geste declines into frivolity. The peers get themselves trapped in a luxuriously provisioned Saracen castle, and it is not long before the crusade has subsided into an Eastern wish fulfillment of maidens to be seduced, magic trinkets to be fiddled with, and (best of all) Saracens to be killed.

What could have been the motives of the poet of the *Morte Arthure* in alluding to this improbable material? To begin to answer that question, we need to understand what each of the two sources could themselves have been thought to mean. In the *Fierabras* Oliver's initial championing of the

Carolingian court against its pagan enemy stands as an ideal of Christian heroism that passes judgement on the rest of the poem. The purpose of the crusade is to recover the relics of the Passion, and it is Fierabras, conqueror of Jerusalem and Rome, who possesses them. In defeating and converting Fierabras, then, Oliver has in effect accomplished the crusade single-handedly. But the starkly simple crusading ideology – 'Paien unt tort e crestiens unt dreit'[56] – is here somewhat troubled. For if the poet carefully contrasts Oliver's humility and loyal self-sacrifice to Fierabras' arrogant contempt, he also contrasts it to Roland's pride, to Charlemagne's indolence, and to Ganelon's treachery; and the narrative as a whole shows how thoroughly compromised the crusading ideology has become. By the end of the poem, in fact, it is to be found embodied not in Charlemagne's peers at all, but rather – ironically – in the converted pagan Fierabras.

The *Fierabras* is, then, a poem about the corruption of the crusading spirit: in their foray into Saracen territory the Christians have become mired in the faithlessness they have come to punish. The Alexandrian *Fuerres de Gadres*, the episode's other source, provides a similar interpretive context. Set in the Holy Land – the battle takes place in the highly significant Vale of Josephas or Jehosephat, as the *Morte Arthure* itself notes[57] – and deploying the traditional motif of a conflict between heroic self-fulfillment and submission to a larger cause, the *Fuerres* also gestures toward the crusading ideal. But the legions of Alexander are on no pilgrimage to a holy place but rather a futile journey to the ends of the earth; and when they arrive there, at the gates of the Earthly Paradise, they will be denied entrance and told to retrace their steps. For them the capture of Jerusalem is not the climax of their efforts but just one step on a meaningless circuit.[58] The poet of the *Morte Arthure* has therefore interpolated, as seemingly victorious episodes in Arthur's campaign, fragments of two failed heroic expeditions, making the point clearer by repetition while at the same time allowing each fragment to reveal the meaning of the other.

But while our poet's interpretation includes the meanings proffered by his two sources, separately and together, it goes beyond them, even to the extent of providing both a historiographical statement and a comment upon his own strategies of allusion and revision. He not only passes judgement upon the Arthurian project but in the details of the episode analyzes its failure by focusing on the ideology of allusion itself, whether its context be political or literary. The single combat between Gawain and Priamus might be supposed to be a sign of Arthur's eschatological destiny, especially since the Oliver-Fierabras contest stands itself as a norm of crusading rectitude. But in fact the more dubious context established by the whole of the *Fierabras* controls its presentation here and redirects its force, as several crucial revisions show. For what is unsettling here is that the *Morte Arthure* omits the very topos of conversion that gives the episode its raison d'être in the *Fierabras*. Priamus is a pagan, but at no point does he ask for baptism or lament its

absence, as does Fierabras.[59] The point is underlined by the presence in both
texts of magic fluids. Fierabras, among other relics of the Passion, improperly
possesses flasks filled with the fluid with which Christ was embalmed, and
whenever wounded by Oliver he simply douses and heals himself. This detail
is more than a mere romance exoticism, for it functions to underline the
contrast between Fierabras' constantly restored body and his unregenerate
soul, which requires and receives another, symbolic laving. Priamus' magic
fluid is of a different order, however, as is his paganism. He is in fact not a
Saracen but a classical warrior, heir to the heroic virtues of the antique world
and descended, he tells us, not only from Hector of Troy and Alexander but
also from Judas Maccabeus and Joshua (lines 2602–5). He embodies, in short,
the virtue of the non-Christian world as it is later to be manifested in the
figure of the Nine Worthies. Appropriately, then, his flask 'es full of þe flour
of þe four well / þat flowes owte of Paradice' (lines 2705–6), clearly a
reference to the aqua vitae discovered by Alexander in his journey to the
Earthly Paradise.[60] With this balm Priamus heals a wound that would
otherwise prove fatal to Gawain, but he neither asks for nor does he receive
in return a baptismal anointing.[61] It appears that in this poem there is no
superior fluid by which the essence of pagan heroism can be redeemed.

As a brief allegory of the transactions of past and present this episode
represents the appropriation of the old, Alexandrian values by the new order.
Priamus initially identified himself as 'apparaunt . . . ayere' (line 2606) to the
classical world, but after his defeat he realises that his virtue will pass in the
Christian era to Arthur: '*He* will be Alexander ayre, that all þe erthe lowttede,
/ Abillere þan euer was sir Ector of Troye' (lines 2634–5). Gawain's defeat of
Priamus is a metaphor for historical transition, a *translatio virtutis* from past to
present. But if the dominion of the present over the past is asserted, so too is
the continuity between them. For the axial fact of discontinuity, the entrance
into history of Jesus Christ, is here barely acknowledged.[62] Inevitably, then,
value is conveyed in only one direction, from past to present: Priamus can
heal Gawain's wounds but cannot himself be spiritually healed. Nor is the
inheritance that he hands over subject to any redemptive transformation: the
past is superseded but the act of supersession is itself without spiritual or
even historical value. Classical heroism is transferred but not transformed, and
no answer is given to the question of how Arthur, invested with Alexander's
force, can avoid Alexander's fate. Moreover, if the past authenticates the
present it cannot be itself redeemed, cannot, that is, be seen as valid because
it humbly prepares for a present that is inarguably different and better. There
is here no typology, no old dispensation prefiguring a new. We are offered
instead a wholly secular patrimony, a natural process of succession; hence
Priamus' name, in allusion to the Trojan patriarch. It is only a brief step from
here to the Nine Worthies on the Wheel of Fortune, a vision of history that
undermines the very possibility of meaningful historical action.

But let me not move ahead to Arthur's dream without first stressing the fatal economy of this kind of historical consciousness. The poem sees the past as harboring a legitimising authority of such value that it must be retained even if it costs the present its own historical identity. Arthur must be another Alexander even if it means that his career will enact the same curve of aspiration and disappointment. Not that this risk is lightly undertaken. The fear of recursion haunts the poem, and if it sees the past as uniquely valuable it ascribes to the present a desire for ascendancy, an ardor for selection and control that would grant to the past only so much survival as the present would wish. The stance toward the past remains as aggressive as Gawain's attack upon Priamus. When, in the subsequent battle against the men of Lorraine, Gawain urges on his troops, he compares them favorably in point of honor to their 'elders' (line 2867), Absolon and Unwine, types, in scriptural and Germanic legend respectively, of rebellion against the father[63]; and when Arthur's knights first promote the campaign against Lucius they urge it in terms of redeeming and so surpassing the ancestral past. 'Now schall we wreke full wele the wrethe of oure elders' (line 321), says the Welsh king, and King Lot adds, more ominously, 'It es owre weredes to wreke the wrethe of oure elders' (line 385).[64] Moreover, since Uther Pendragon paid tribute to Rome the war is for Arthur personally a way to cancel a filial shame. And yet, with bitter irony, his efforts are undone by his own rebellious son Mordred: there is, it seems, no end to filial antagonism.

It is to be expected, then, that generational hostility should run in both directions: sons not only challenge their fathers but are themselves at risk from paternal violence. When the foraging party is sent out by Arthur he makes it clear that the Frenchman Florent is in immediate charge but that Gawain, denominated here and nowhere else in the poem as 'Wardayne' (lines 2494, 2678, 2740), is to maintain an ultimate authority. Moreover, the relationship between Gawain and the Frenchman has a familial value: Florent addresses him as 'Fadyr' (line 2735), describes himself as 'bot a fawntkyn vnfraystede in armes' (line 2736), and Gawain urges them to attack the enemy because they have 'faughte noghte þeire fill this fyftene wynter' (line 2822) but refuses to help them until they are challenged by more than the 'gadlyngez' (line 2854) and 'boyes' (line 2856) of the enemy's first wave. But Gawain's paternal condescension has telling consequences. Among the English contingent is 'Chastelayne, a childe of þe kynges chambyre / [And] warde to sir Wawayn' (lines 2952–3), and the only significant casualty in the encounter is precisely this youth, overmatched by a Swedish knight. The point is not just Gawain's failure as warden, which matches the later and more deliberate failure of Mordred, appointed by his father as 'Wardayne' (lines 650, 3523) of England. Rather, we see expressed in Gawain's failure to protect Chastelayne a dark and terrible motif that weaves itself throughout the narrative: the sacrifice of children.

This theme comes to us first in a lurid, almost comically grotesque form. The giant of Mont St Michel, in a detail unique to this version, feeds on 'crysmede childyre' (line 1051) roasted on spits, a scene whose horror is perhaps disarmed by its fairy-tale context. But we are forced to recall it in less protected circumstances when at the end of the poem the dying Arthur, in another unique detail, commands that Mordred's children 'bee sleyghely slayne and slongen in watyrs' (line 4321).[65] The thematic import seems clear: just as the present feels itself tyrannised by the past so does it dominate the future, conveying a burdensome legacy of not only heroic achievement but also intolerable violence. It is this motif, moreover, that gives special point in the description of the Nine Worthies to the designation of Charlemagne and Godfrey of Bouillon as 'childire' (line 3328) and the insistence – present only in their cases – that they achieved their positions only by inheritance: Charlemagne is 'the kyng son of Fraunce' (line 3423), Godfrey 'sall of Lorrayne be lorde be leefe of his fadire' (line 3432). Historically belated, they are above all children who will bear the burden of the example and fate of their ideological father, the first Christian worthy, Arthur, just as Arthur is himself subject to the fatal prototype defined by Alexander. But let us not forget that if the *moderni* of whatever period are tyrannised by the past, it is a past that they have themselves empowered. The reality, the poem suggests, is far different. When Alexander is finally granted a literal rather than a merely textual existence in the poem, in the portrait that appropriately stands at the head of the Nine Worthies, he is revealed to be 'a lityll man that laide was benethe: / His leskes laye all lene and latheliche to schewe' (lines 3278–9). Far from being a figure of incomparable achievement, he is in fact an almost shocking representation of the impotent father.

I have been investigating here the genealogical and psychological meaning of historical repetition. We should always remember that the great defense against repetition is the destinal linearity entailed by the linked ideas of *translatio imperii* and the crusade. I have suggested that the foraging episode, despite or perhaps because of its conspicuous irrelevance, is the point at which the effort to sustain a linear conception of historical process breaks down. It is here that the present is revealed to be not a fulfillment of the past but a reenactment, and where the value that is conveyed from past to present is finally seen to have been illusory, an authority projected onto the past by the present and then read back in impossibly exaggerated terms. The literary analogue to this process is the tyranny of the source, and it is a striking fact that for all his revisions the poet does not deviate from the essential meaning of either the *Fierabras* or the *Fuerres de Gadres*. Written as poems about the secularisation of the crusading ideology, they remain in their new habitat precisely that, never able to invest chivalric action with a meaning beyond itself. The layers of literary history reveal themselves to be identical, successive pages that are all inscribed with the same disabling message. Just as Arthur is recalled to Britain to confront the sins of his past, so the corpus of medieval literature can only recall the reader to the knowledge of his irreparably flawed origin.

The dream of Fortune both represents historical recurrence and functions in the narrative as the agency of recall. But in its detail it bespeaks a concern to place this historiography within the economy of the heroic life. The dream falls into two distinct parts. In the first Arthur is lost in a wood filled with savage beasts, including lions that 'full lothely lykkyde þeire tuskes, / All fore lapynge of blude of [his] lele knyghtez' (lines 3234–5). Terrified by these 'foule thyngez' (line 3237), Arthur escapes 'to a meadowe with montayngnes enclosyde, / The meryeste of medill-erthe that men myghte beholde' (lines 3238–9). Here are vines of silver adorned with grapes of gold, every fruit that flourishes on earth, and birds on every bough – details that recall unmistakably the Earthly Paradise.[66] It is here that the second, longer movement of the dream takes place. Lady Fortune and her bejeweled wheel descend from the clouds with eight of the Nine Worthies.[67] Six of the eight (Alexander, Hector, Julius Caesar, Judas Maccabeus, Joshua, and David) have already fallen from the wheel; they first issue a collective lament – 'That euer I rengnede on þi rog, me rewes it euer!' (line 3272) – and are then individually described and given a few lines of regret to speak. The two remaining Worthies (Charlemagne and Godfrey) are preparing to mount the wheel: ' "This chair of charbokle," they said, "we chalange hereaftyre" ' (line 3326). Lady Fortune then places Arthur on the wheel, gives him a scepter, diadem, and a 'pome' (line 3354) or orb engraved with a map of the world 'In sygne þat [he] sothely was souerayne in erthe' (line 3357), and proffers him the fruit and wine of the garden. But at midday her mood changes: she berates Arthur, whirls the wheel about, and crushes him beneath.

The 'philosophre' (line 3394) to whom Arthur turns for an interpretation tells him, with the smug obviousness of the medieval moralist that his 'fortune es passede' (line 3394) and that he should prepare for death: 'Schryfe the of thy schame and schape for thyn ende' (line 3400). But both in its structure and in its inclusion of the Nine Worthies the dream has a broader relevance. The concept of Fortune inevitably expresses a historiography of recurrence: Alexander is the prototype whose achievements are endlessly, and meaninglessly, reenacted. Arthur's dream is itself, ironically, part of this reenactment. When Alexander reached the Earthly Paradise he demanded tribute and was given a stone with the remarkable property that when placed in a scale it outweighed everything set against it but when covered with a light sprinkling of dust it was itself similarly outweighed. Alexander's own philosopher, Aristotle, interpreted this Wonderstone (as it came to be known) as representing Alexander himself: he is now the weightiest thing in the world but when in the grave and covered with dirt will become insignificant. Demanding tribute, Alexander received an object that marked the limits of the very sovereignty it was supposed to acknowledge,[68] just as the Earthly Paradise itself stood as an impassable limit to his geographical conquests.[69] So too for Arthur, whose venture into the Earthly Paradise of the dream that stands at the end of his journey reveals a similarly dark message, and one also to be expounded by a philosopher. The gestures toward chronology in the presentation of the Nine Worthies, then, are revealed to be empty signs that can only recall an alternative view of time by which to measure the insufficiency of this one. Arthur follows upon classical and Jewish heroes but remains simply a Christian version of the same thing – Christianity is a distinction without a difference, just as Charlemagne and Godfrey follow upon Arthur but derive from his example no guidance that might allow them to shape their ends differently. When in the *City of God* Augustine attacked the pagan's cyclic conception of history he cited a phrase from the Psalms: 'In circuitu impii ambulabunt' – 'The wicked will walk in a circle' (Ps. 11:9).[70] It is precisely this tragic view of history that stands, almost a millennium later, as the brooding truth at which the hero arrives.

Moreover, the structure of the dream is itself repetitive: Arthur turns first from the *oscura selva* to the garden, then from the laments of the fallen worthies to his own elevation.[71] Twice he is presented with a monitory teaching and twice he turns aside. This is a pattern of recognition and evasion that continues into the philosopher's exposition of the dream. For while the philosopher insists that the dream shows Arthur that all is *vanitas vanitatum* he nonetheless celebrates Arthur's fame as one of 'nynne of þe nobileste namede in erthe' (line 3439; and see lines 3444–5). Similarly, while Arthur is told to prepare for his end by penitential lament and ecclesiastical endowment, he is also informed that the opening scene in the wild wood foretells trouble at home. If Arthur does 'amende [his] mode', as the philosopher enjoins, 'And mekely aske mercy for mede of [his] saule' (lines 3454–5), then who will free Britain from Mordred's barbarism, whose atrocities Cradoke is soon vividly to detail (lines 3523–56)? Cradoke is himself, in fact, a pilgrim who now lives the life of penance to which Arthur has been directed, but it is a life which is, for the moment at least, closed to the king. Participation in the historical world is simultaneously proscribed and required, both revealed as without value and imposed as a duty. But for this duty to be taken up, the poem suggests, the emptiness of the historical process must be simultaneously acknowledged and repudiated. It is just this double act of recognition and evasion that the dream of Fortune both records and, in its reception, occasions. Doubled in its own structure, then, the dream gives rise to two equally conflicted imperatives, the philosopher's disjunctive interpretation and the mixed message of Cradoke, whose example urges pilgrimage to Rome but whose words send Arthur back to his final battle in England.

The final movement of the poem – the return to England, the death of Gawain, the mutual annihilation of Mordred and Arthur – records the nature of action in a world that no longer believes in history. That participation in the world is itself a mode of penance is of course a common medieval attitude. Man is tested by the world, and the whirligig of time, meaningless in itself, finds its significance in the trials it imposes on the individual soul.

Throughout its course the poem has entertained the possibility that its events are to be understood not eschatologically, as part of a providential *consummatio saeculi*, but rather penitentially, in their effect on the soul. The vow on the vernicle – a pilgrim's badge – can be read this way, and so can Arthur's battle with the giant of Mont St Michel. As he leaves to climb the mountain, he laconically tells his companions to wait behind, 'Fore I will seke this seynte by my self one' (line 937); and Bedivere later sarcastically refers to the giant's huge corpse as a 'corsaint' (line 1164) and suggests that it should be enclosed in silver like a relic. In reminding us that Mont St Michel was a popular pilgrimage shrine, this byplay raises disquieting questions. Ought the battle between Arthur and the giant to be placed in the same apocalyptic category as the Archangel Michael's battle with the dragon?[72] Or ought it not rather to be read with reference to Arthur's own human limitations, as a confrontation with an unbridled appetitive self that embodies some of Arthur's own preoccupations? Is it, in other words, an eschatological event and so relevant to the largest of historical movements, or is it rather penitential, relevant only to the spiritual progress of a single hero? Finally, when Priamus is defeated by Gawain he confesses that he was 'hawtayne of herte' (line 2612) and has been 'for cyrqwitrye schamely supprisede' (line 2616), a literal act of penance that might cause us, at least in retrospect, to revalue this episode by placing it in a pattern of significance that is less apocalyptic than confessional.

It is in the final movement of the narrative that this penitential theme, implicit throughout, threatens to dominate the meaning of the poem as a whole. *Disce mori* – learn to die – is one of the great watchwords of late-medieval spiritual life, and everywhere present in these final confrontations is the ideal of the good end. Religious values coalesce about the figures of Gawain and Arthur in their final acts of self-fulfillment. The dead Gawain is represented by his stricken king as a martyred innocent whose blood must be 'schrynede in golde, / For it es sakles of syn, sa helpe me oure Lorde' (lines 3991–2); and Arthur himself dies in the odor of sanctity: 'He saide "In manus" with mayne one molde whare he ligges, / And thus passes his speryt, and spekes he no more' (lines 4326–27).

But lest we too easily assume that the poem has finally been chastened into abandoning its eschatological ambitions, we must note in closing two contra-indications. One is the refusal to abandon the language of crusade that has for so long sustained Arthur's imperial ambitions. Even now that he is fighting an internecine civil war at home in England the poem insists, against all logic, that the religious imperatives that validated his earlier efforts are still in effect. Mordred's allies are as much pagans as those who supported Lucius, and both Gawain and Arthur exhort their men in terms that derive from crusading literature. 'We sall ende this daye alls excellent knyghtte', says Gawain, 'Ayere to endelesse joye with angells vnwemmyde' (lines 3800–1), and Arthur later promises the same reward: '3if vs be destaynede to dy to-daye one this erthe, /

We sall be hewede vnto heuen or we be halfe colde' (lines 4090–1). The
poem's unwillingness to forgo this crusading rhetoric, and the ideology that
supports it, witnesses to a deeper unwillingness to hand the narrative over to
Fortune and so to narrow the range of its relevance to a merely individual fate.

The other unsettling element of the poem's final movement is the presence
of an insistent desire for closure that refuses to be accommodated to the usual
patterns of religious fulfillment. Gawain's hopeless attack on Mordred is the
act of a man, says Mordred, 'þat wold wilfully wasten hym selfen' (line 3835),
and after he is gone Arthur proclaims that 'my were [is] endide' (line 3957)
and hastens after Mordred despite warnings that his forces are fatally
insufficient. In these acts of almost nihilistic finality we witness a pattern of
behavior that harks back to traditions more ancient even than Christianity.
We inevitably call to mind the futile concluding gestures of other heroes –
men such as Bryhtnoth and Beowulf, Siegfried and Njal, Turnus and Achilles.
These are men whom history failed, whose time never came, and for whom
only a fierce nobility made their situation endurable. The *Morte Arthure* is a
poem that supplicates the past in order to speak to the present, and in its
conclusion it achieves an almost incantatory power by which to measure
tragic failure. As Arthur returns home to the west to be slain by his own
sword at the hands of his own son, so the poem returns to the deepest
sources of heroic poetry in an act of solicitation that courts possession.
Perhaps now we can understand some of the reasons why the poet concludes
his poem with his hero's irremediably ambiguous genealogy:

> Thus endis Kyng Arthure, as auctors alegges,
> That was of Ectores blude, the kynge son of Troye,
> And of sir Pryamous the prynce, praysede in erthe;
> Fro thythen broghte the Bretons all his bolde eldyrs
> Into Bretayne the brode, as þe Bruytte tellys.

> (Lines 4342–6)

4

'For God's sake let us sit upon the ground / And tell sad stories of the death
of kings' (3.2.155–6). Richard II's invitation to rehearse the repertory of royal
tragedies, his own included, correctly assumes that the relationship between
monarchy and tragedy is reciprocal. One side of that mutuality – the tragic
prescription of a noble protagonist – is familiar enough, but we less often
remember that most kingly stories, and especially medieval ones, are
profoundly, distressingly unhappy. Nor was this a fact that medieval monarchs
avoided. Like his Shakespearean counterpart, the historical Richard II also
seems to have had an affinity for sad stories, choosing as his political patron
saints neither his immensely popular father (the Black Prince) nor his equally
popular grand-father (Edward III) but two of the least successful of English

kings, the sanctified Edward the Confessor and the 'martyred' Edward II, whom Richard assiduously promoted for canonisation.[73] And as we have seen, when even the astute Henry II and the manly Edward III chose to assume the Arthurian aura they were simultaneously darkened with the shadow of the Arthurian fate. If kings wanted national heroes to exemplify and authorise their own heroism, they seem also to have wanted them, paradoxically, to have come to tragic ends. In part this insistence on final adversity can be understood as an inevitable aspect of the ethic of the *Fürstenspiegel*: prideful in their emulation of the great heroes of the past, monarchs are subjected to the compensatory message that all heroism comes to dust. But moral explanations are as partial here as elsewhere, as is the almost atavistic superstition that by gazing upon the downfall of our ancestors we can avoid downfall ourselves. On the contrary, these narratives deliberately complicate moral response, soliciting our engagement by both episodic complexity and empathic identification. The hero's fall is cause not for righteous celebration but for tears.

Perhaps it is in these tears that we find this literature's deepest apologetics. The hero is a man condemned to historical action even when everything proclaims its futility, and royal worldliness imposes a burden on both soul and body. Arthur, as we have seen, must forego the certain consolations of the penitential way to return to the vain heroics of another battle, and he is not alone in this sacrifice, as other poets show about other kings. In canto 7 of the *Purgatorio* Dante describes in the Valley of the Princes one of his gentlest locales, the habitation of those melancholy rulers who were seduced from their true end by the magnificence of their royal means and are now imprisoned in a gilded imitation of their own gardens. Correlatively, when at the end of the *Chanson de Roland* Charlemagne is told to reassume the crusade his eyes fill with tears and he pulls helplessly at his beard. '"Deus", dist li reis, "si penuse est ma vie!"'[74] Denied Roland's opportunity for heroic *desmesure*, Charlemagne must submit to a life in history that requires him to bear up the weight of temporality itself, a life that has already lasted (the poem tells us) more than two hundred years. As a royal apologetics, these moments aim not at elevation but at sympathy: it is less the king whom we are to admire than the man who must be king whom we are to pity. This is an empathy that encourages us to forego criticism in the recognition that royal prerogatives are at best only consolations for the heavy imposts of the public life. The pathos of monarchy solicits our political consent, and tragic spectacle becomes a final, ironic justification for the recursive futility of the historical life.

Notes

1. While the whole text is unpublished, the preface is printed by JACQUES MONFRIN, 'La traduction française de Tite-Live', *Histoire littéraire de la France* (Paris: Imprimerie

Nationale, 1962), 39.359–60; see also JEAN RYCHNER, 'Observations sur la traduction de Tite-Live par Pierre Bersuire (1354–6)', *Journal des savants* (Oct.-Dec. 1963): 242–67. A presentation picture from the fifteenth-century MS B.N. fr. 259 is reproduced in MILLARD MEISS, *French Painting in the Time of Jean de Berry: The Boucicault Master* (London: Phaidon, 1967), fig. 431 and p. 56.

2. JACQUES MONFRIN, 'Les traducteurs et leur public en France au moyen âge', *Journal des savants* (Jan.-Mar. 1964): 5–20.

3. Among the many discussions of medieval historiography, those most useful to the argument presented in this chapter are R.W. SOUTHERN, 'Aspects of the European Tradition of Historical Writing', *Transactions of the Royal Historical Society*, **20** (1970): 173–96; **21** (1971): 159–79; **22** (1972): 159–80; M.-D. CHENU, 'Conscience de l'histoire et théologie au XIIIᵉ siècle', *Archives d'histoire doctrinale et littéraire du moyen âge*, **21** (1954): 107–33, appearing as chapter 5 of his *Nature, Man, and Society in the Twelfth Century*, trans. Jerome Taylor and Lester K. Little (Chicago: University of Chicago Press, 1968); ARNALDO MOMIGLIANO, *Essays in Ancient and Modern Historiography* (Middletown: Wesleyan University Press, 1977), especially chs 8 and 12; F.P. PICKERING, *Augustinus oder Boethius? Geschichtsschreibung und epische Dichtung im Mittelalter – und in der Neuzeit* (Berlin: E. Schmidt, 1967), and ch. 3 of his *Literature and Art in the Middle Ages* (Coral Gables: University of Miami Press, 1970); BERNARD GUENÉE, 'Histoires, annales, chroniques: Essai sur les genres historiques au moyen âge', *Annales*, **28** (1973): 997–1016, and his *Histoire et culture historique dans l'Occident médiéval* (Paris: Aubier, 1980); ROGER D. RAY, 'Medieval Historiography through the Twelfth Century: Problems and Progress of Research', *Viator*, **5** (1974): 33–59; ERNST BRIESACH (ed.), *Classical Rhetoric and Medieval Historiography*, Studies in Medieval Culture 19 (Kalamazoo: Medieval Institute Publications, 1985), and essays on historiography published in a special issue of *Medievalia et Humanistica*, n.s., **5** (1974) by AMOS FUNKENSTEIN, MARJORIE REEVES and ROBERT HANNING. It was HANNING's fine '*Beowulf* and Heroic History', pp. 77–102, that first provided me with a definition of my subject.

4. On Henry II as a patron, see WALTER F. SCHIRMER and ULRICH BROICH, *Studien zum literarischen Patronat im England des 12. Jahrhunderts* (Cologne: Westdeutscher Verlag, 1962), pp. 27–203; DIANA B. TYSON, 'Patronage of French Vernacular History Writers in the Twelfth and Thirteenth Centuries', *Romania*, **100** (1979): 180–222, 584; and RETO R. BEZZOLA, *Les origines et la formation de la littérature courtoise en Occident, 500–1200*, Vol. 3, pt. 1 (Paris: Champion, 1963).

5. Aelred wrote a *Genealogia regum* for Henry while he was still duke of Normandy but after he had been designated as Stephen's heir (1153–4) and a *Vita et miracula* for the translation of Edward the Confessor in 1163; JORDAN FANTOSME, *Histoire de la guerre d'Ecosse* (1174–5); WACE, *Roman de Rou* (1160–74); BENOÎT DE SAINTE-MAURE, *Chronique des Ducs de Normandie* (c. 1174). That the author of the *Chronique* and the *Roman de Troie* (see above, p. 111) are the same Benoît is demonstrated by CARIN FAHLIN, *Etude sur le manuscrit de Tours de la Chronique Ducs de Normandie par Benoît* (Uppsala: Almqvist and Wiksells, 1937), pp. 141–72. There were, of course, many other historical works composed during Henry's reign (e.g. the *Gesta consulum Andegavorum* by JEAN DE MARMOUTIER, c. 1164–73), but it is doubtful that they should be ascribed to royal patronage; see BROICH's survey, *Studien zum literarischen Patronat im England*, pp. 27–42, and ANTONIA GRANSDEN, *Historical Writing in England c. 550 to c. 1307* (Ithaca: Cornell University Press, 1974), pp. 219–68. Broich also excludes Jordan of Fantosme's *Histoire* from the direct circle of patronised writings, but see TYSON, 'Patronage of French Vernacular History Writers', pp. 193–201.

6. Despite the fact that throughout the Middle Ages the categories of what we have come to call 'history' and 'romance' blended insensibly into each other, it would be wrong to think that medieval writers had no awareness of or concern for the difference between the fictive and the factual. *Historia est narratio rei gestae*: Isidore of Seville's authoritative definition – derived from CICERO's *De inventione* 1.19.27 and endlessly repeated throughout the Middle Ages – accurately reflects the medieval view that history is an account of that which was done and is to be distinguished from fable. For a discussion of this important medieval awareness, see GUENÉE, *Histoire et culture historique dans l'Occident médiéval*, pp. 18–43, 77–128. In the present chapter I am concerned with texts that self-consciously and deliberately override this basic distinction between the factual and the fabulous, history and romance, for their own strategic purposes.

   On the meaning of the word and the genre *romance* in Middle English, see PAUL STROHM, 'The Origin and Meaning of Middle English *Romaunce*', *Genre*, **10** (1977): 1–28; KATHRYN HUME, 'The Formal Nature of Middle English Romance', *Philological Quarterly*, **53** (1974): 158–80; and JOHN FINLAYSON, 'Definitions of Middle English Romance', *Chaucer Review*, **15** (1980–1): 44–62, 168–81. It is clear from these studies that the fictive nature of romance was always recognised, but that this did not necessarily disqualify such a work from entertaining historiographical interests.

7. Perhaps the clearest understanding of Geoffrey's historiographical purpose was offered at the end of the twelfth century by WILLIAM OF NEWBURGH, who bitterly attacked Geoffrey on three grounds: (1) that he substituted *conficta, fabula*, and *ridicula figmenta* for the *historica veritas* of *noster Beda*; (2) that he exalted the Britons to the level of the great civilizations of the classical past, as if Arthur were the equal of Alexander, Julius Caesar, and Caesar Augustus; and (3) that he presented the demonic Merlin as if he were another Isaiah. In sum, William saw that Geoffrey was replacing Bede's ecclesiastical history with a relentlessly secular narrative that claimed for itself the authority of the classical past, a claim that was enforced by invoking modes of narration (e.g. the legitimising role of the prophet) derived from scriptural history. For William's comments, see the Preface to his *Historia Regum Anglicarum*, translated by Joseph Stevenson, *The Church Historians of England*, Vol. 4, pt. 2 (London: Seeleys, 1858), pp. 400–1.

8. While this is unfortunately not the place for a full discussion of Geoffrey's book, the view I am presenting of it here is consistent with that set forward by VALERIE I.J. FLINT, 'The *Historia Regum Britanniae* of Geoffrey of Monmouth: Parody and Its Purpose. A Suggestion', *Speculum*, **54** (1979): 447–68.

9. JUDITH SHKLAR, 'Subversive Genealogies', in Clifford Geertz (ed.), *Myth, Symbol, and Culture* (New York: Norton, 1974), p. 141.

10. On the date and the relation of Wace's poem to Henry, see BROICH, *Studien zum literarisch en Patronat im England*, pp. 65–77, TYSON, 'Patronage of French Vernacular History Writers', pp. 193–6, and JOHN S.P. TATLOCK, *The Legendary History of Britain: Geoffrey of Monmouth's Historia Regum Britanniae and Its Early Vernacular Versions* (Berkeley: University of California Press, 1950), pp. 467–8; on the now lost translation by Geoffrey Gaimar, see TATLOCK, pp. 452–6.

11. This is the Campsall manuscript, described by R.K. ROOT, *The Textual Tradition of Chaucer's Troilus*, Chaucer Society, 1st ser., 99 (London: Kegan Paul, Trench, Trübner, 1916), p. 5. The *Troilus* also figures in another less likely, political context: despite the fact that English books hardly ever crossed the Channel, the ambitious dukes of Burgundy bolstered their substantial Trojan collection with at least one and perhaps two copies of Chaucer's poem. See ELEANOR HAMMOND, 'A Burgundian Copy of Chaucer's *Troilus*', *Modern Language Notes*, **26** (1911): 32; and

for the literary milieu, RUTH MORSE, 'Historical Fiction in Fifteenth-Century Burgundy', *Modern Language Review*, **75** (1980): 48–64.

12. See above, n. 5.

13. GUIDO DELLA COLONNE, *Historia destructionis Troiae*, trans. Mary Elizabeth Meek (Bloomington: Indiana University Press, 1974), p. 9; see also pp. 10, 43, 114, 146–7.

14. In his *Speculum caritatis*, AELRED OF RIEVAULX has a monastic novice confess to being moved to tears by *fabulae* about 'an Arthur of whom I know nothing' (ed. A. Hoste and C. Talbot, *CCM* 1 [Turnhout: Brepols, 1971], 2.17.51, p. 90), while his disciple PETER OF BLOIS, in a *Liber de confessione* intended for a more general audience, complains about the lachrymose effects of fables about Arthur, 'Gangan' (Gawain?), and Tristan because they preempt emotions that should be directed to Christ (*PL* 207: 1088–9). Behind these complaints stands Augustine's guilty weeping for the death of Dido in *Confessions* 1.13.

15. On Marie de France, see BROICH, *Studien zum literarischen Patronat im England*, p. 37 n. 50, and E.A. FRANCIS, 'Marie de France et son temps', *Romania*, **72** (1951): 78–99; on Thomas of Britain, BARTINA WIND, 'Nos incertitudes au sujet du "Tristan" de Thomas', in *Mélanges de langue et de littérature du moyen âge et de la Renaissance offerts à Jean Frappier* (Geneva: Droz, 1970), 2.1129–38; on Chrétien, see CONSTANCE BULLOCK-DAVIES, 'Chrétien de Troyes and England', *Arthurian Literature*, **1** (1981): 1–61; ANTHIME FOURRIER, *Le courant réaliste dans le roman courtois* (Paris: A.G. Nizet, 1960), pp. 160–74, who reads *Cligès* as anti-Angevin, while ERICH KÖHLER, *Ideal und Wirklichkeit in der höfischen Epik* (Tübingen: M. Niemeyer, 1956), trans. from the 2nd edn of 1970 by Eliane Kaufholz as *L'aventure chevaleresque* (Paris: Gallimard, 1974), sees Chrétien's oeuvre as promoting Angevin interests.

16. For a full summary, see BEZZOLA, *Origines et la formation de la littérature courtoise en Occident*, pp. 126–39; for commentary, BROICH, *Studien zum literarischen Patronat im England*, pp. 88–92, and J.S.P. TATLOCK, 'Geoffrey and King Arthur in *Normannicus Draco*', *Modern Philology*, **31** (1933): 1–18, 113–25. On Arthur as an Angevin hero, see GORDON H. GEROULD, 'King Arthur and Politics', *Speculum*, **2** (1927): 33–51.

17. ROGER SHERMAN LOOMIS, 'Edward I, Arthurian Enthusiast', *Speculum*, **28** (1953): 114–27.

18. *Calendar of Close Rolls, 1318–23* (London: Longman, 1895), pp. 525–6; MAY MCKISACK, *The Fourteenth Century* (Oxford: Clarendon Press, 1959), p. 68.

19. MARY GIFFIN, 'Cadwalader, Arthur, and Brutus in the Wigmore Manuscript', *Speculum*, **16** (1941): 109–20.

20. For Edward III's Arthurian interests, as well as the assimilation of the king to the Arthurian model by his admirers, see WILLIAM MATTHEWS, *The Tragedy of Arthur: A Study of the Alliterative 'Morte Arthure'* (Berkeley: University of California Press, 1960), pp. 187–90.

21. ERICH AUERBACH, *Literary Language and Its Public in Late Latin Antiquity and in the Middle Ages*, trans. Ralph Manheim (New York: Pantheon, 1965), p. 191.

22. For Gerald of Wales, see A.C.L. BROWN in *Speculum*, **2** (1927): 449–50, and E.K. CHAMBERS, *Arthur of Britain* (London: Sidgwick and Jackson, 1927), pp. 268–76; for Ranulph Higden, see the *Polychronicon*, ed. C. Babington and J.R. Lumby, Rolls Series (London: Longman, 1865–6), 5.337–9; JOHN TREVISA, who translated the *Polychronicon* in the 1380s, attacks Higden for doubting Arthur's historicity.

23. WACE, *Roman de Rou*, ed. Hugo Andresen (Heilbron: Gebr. Henninger, 1879), 2.284, lines 6717–20.

24. CHRÉTIEN DE TROYES, *Le chevalier au lion*, ed. Mario Roques (Paris: H. Champion, 1965), p. 18, lines 577–80.

25. The first four lines are from ROQUES's edition, lines 169–72; the lines in brackets do not appear in the manuscript printed by Roques, but are correctly printed as authentic in the edition by WENDELIN FOERSTER (Halle: Niemeyer, 1887), lines 169–74.

26. In the Preface to his *Historia ecclesiastica*, BEDE defines the *vera lex historiae* as a reliance upon 'common report' (*fama vulgata*), by which he means the 'countless faithful witnesses who either know or remember the facts'; see *A History of the English Church and People*, trans. Leo Sherley-Price (Harmondsworth: Penguin Books, 1955), p. 35.

27. On the historical situating, see THEODORE SILVERSTEIN, 'Sir Gawain, Dear Brutus, and Britain's Fortunate Foundling: A Study in Comedy and Convention', *Modern Philology*, **62** (1965): 189–206. In *Old English and Middle English Poetry* (London: Routledge and Kegan Paul, 1977), DEREK PEARSALL notes that this kind of historical preface occurs in six alliterative poems and calls it 'something of a signature of alliterative poetry' (p. 158).

28. When this chapter was first written, the best edition was by VALERIE KRISHNA (New York: Burt Franklin, 1976). It has now been superseded by MARY HAMEL's excellent *Morte Arthure: A Critical Edition* (New York: Garland, 1984), which contains a hundred-page introduction, elaborate notes, bibliography, and glossary. Although I have been unable to take advantage of Hamel's supporting materials, I have checked my citations against her text. A recent survey of criticism is provided by KARL HEINZ GÖLLER in a collection of essays he has edited, *The Alliterative Morte Arthure: A Reassessment of the Poem* (Cambridge: D.S. Brewer, 1981), pp. 7–14.

29. The manuscript is Lincoln Cathedral MS 91, written by ROBERT THORNTON; there is a facsimile with an introduction by D.S. Brewer and A.E.B. Owen, 2nd edn. (London: Scolar Press, 1977). On Thornton, see the important articles by GEORGE R. KEISER, 'Lincoln Cathedral Library MS. 91: Life and Milieu of the Scribe', *Studies in Bibliography*, **32** (1979): 158–79, and 'More Light on the Life and Milieu of Robert Thornton', *Studies in Bibliography*, **36** (1983): 111–19.

30. LARRY D. BENSON, 'The Date of the Alliterative *Morte Arthure*', in Jess B. Bessinger, Jr and Robert K. Raymo (eds), *Medieval Studies in Honor of Lillian Herlands Hornstein* (New York: New York University Press, 1976), pp. 19–40.

31. See GÖLLER's summary of the critical debate, *Alliterative Morte Arthure*, pp. 11–14.

32. As evidence, let me cite just two instances – one large, one tiny – of awkwardness that bespeak a poem in process. In the dream of Fortune, the evidence of Arthur's good fortune is not the triumph he has just achieved but his earlier victory over King Frollo of France, which has not in fact been previously mentioned in the poem (lines 3345–6, 3404–5); second, the line that describes Mordred's allies as including the Montagues (a crucial piece of evidence for Benson's argument on dating) is metrically defective: 'With the Mownttagus and oþer gret lordys' (line 3773). It may be that we see here the hand of a scribe, whether Thornton or an earlier copyist.

33. In 'Edward III and the Alliterative *Morte Arthure*', *Speculum*, **48** (1973): 37–51,

GEORGE R. KEISER argues for literary sources; and see JOHN FINLAYSON, '*Morte Arthure*: The Date and a Source for the Contemporary References', *Speculum*, **42** (1967): 624–38. Personal experience is invoked, most recently, by JULIET VALE, 'Law and Diplomacy in the Alliterative *Morte Arthure*', *Nottingham Medieval Studies*, **23** (1979): 31–46.

34. See, for example, the gruesome description of the death of Gawain (lines 3840–59) and the accounts of the taking of Metz (lines 3068–71) and Como (lines 3110–27). It has often been argued, especially by WILLIAM MATTHEWS, *Tragedy of Arthur*, that this is an antiwar poem, but such a reading overvalues certain details at the expense of larger interests (as I hope to show) as well as ascribing to the poet a narrow moral purpose that ill befits his commitment to the tradition of heroic (i.e. martial) poetry. For a useful discussion, see JOHN BARNIE, *War in Medieval English Society: Social Values in the Hundred Years War, 1337–99* (Ithaca: Cornell University Press, 1974), pp. 147–50.

35. VALERIE KRISHNA prints a useful map in her edition (there have of course been scholarly disputes over the details of the journey); for temporal references, see lines 64, 78, 415, 436, 462, 554, 625, 634, 1006, 2371, 2482, 3078, 3145, 3176, 3183, 3900, 4057 (an incomplete list). The campaign begins on New Year's Day with the arrival of Lucius' ambassadors and concludes the same autumn with Arthur's death, in October or November.

36. For these labels, see, respectively, KARL HEINZ GÖLLER, *Alliterative Morte Arthure*, p. 16; JOHN FINLAYSON, in the introduction to his edition (Evanston: Northwestern University Press, 1967), pp. 6 ff., where he compares the poem to the chansons de geste; and C.S. LEWIS, 'The English Prose *Morte*', in J.A.W. Bennett (ed.), *Essays on Malory* (Oxford: Clarendon Press, 1963), p. 26, where he berates the poem for its 'vast contradictions of known history scrawled across a whole continent'. One of the best accounts of medieval attitudes toward historical legend may be found in LEWIS, *The Discarded Image* (Cambridge: Cambridge University Press, 1964): 'I am inclined to think that most of those who read "historical" works about Troy, Alexander, Arthur, or Charlemagne, believed their matter to be in the main true. But I feel much more certain that they did not believe it to be false. I feel surest of all that the question of belief or disbelief was seldom uppermost in their minds. That, if it was anyone's business, was not theirs. Their business was to learn the story' (p. 181).

37. On *storye* as 'history', see PAUL STROHM, '*Storie, Spelle, Geste, Romaunce, Tragedie*: Generic Distinctions in the Middle English Troy Narratives', *Speculum*, **46** (1971): 348–59.

38. On Wace as the source, rather than Geoffrey or Layamon, see FINLAYSON's Introduction, pp. 31–2; his opinion is supported in his 1962 Cambridge dissertation.

39. This passage, and Chaucer's 'a maner Latyn corrupt' from line 519 of the Man of Law's Tale, are discussed by JOHN BURROW in *Medium Aevum*, **30** (1961): 33–7.

40. DANTE, *Convivio* 1.5; in the *De vulgari* 1.1 this immutable language is called *grammatica* and identified with both Latin and Greek, but is regarded not as prior to the vernaculars but as *secundaria*, an artificial abstract drawn from the living if corrupted *diversa vulgaria*.

41. This theme is well discussed in relation to other late-medieval English writing by JAMES DEAN, 'Time Past and Time Present in Chaucer's Clerk's Tale and Gower's *Confessio Amantis*', *ELH*, **44** (1977): 401–18, and in 'The World Grown Old and Genesis in Middle English Historical Writing', *Speculum*, **57** (1982): 548–68.

42. See, e.g., Augustine, *Enarrationes in Ps. 38.9*: 'Looking, therefore, upon sin, upon mortality, upon time flying by, upon moaning and labor and sweat, upon ages succeeding one another without rest, senselessly from infancy into old age – looking at these things, let us see in them the old man, the old day, the old canticle, the Old Testament. But if we turn to the inward man, to the things that are to be renewed, let us find . . . a new man, a new day, a new canticle, the New Testament – and we shall love this newness so that we shall not fear there any oldness.' Quoted by Gerhart B. Ladner, *The Idea of Reform* (Cambridge: Harvard University Press, 1959), pp. 236–7. While Augustine's renewal is personal rather than historical, by the twelfth century, as Amos Funkenstein ('Periodization and Self-Understanding in the Middle Ages and Early Modern Times', *Medievalia et Humanistica*, n.s., **5** [1974]: 3–23) points out, Augustine's radical separation of 'the course of the *civitas dei peregrinus in terris* from that of the *civitas terrena*' had been overcome, most explicitly by Otto of Freising. For Otto, the great promoter of the idea of *translatio imperii*, the Augustinian scheme is used in the service of a historiographical attitude that is at heart anti-Augustinian.

43. Chenu, *Nature, Man, and Society in the Twelfth Century*, p. 185 (see note 3).

44. Werner Goez, *Translatio Imperii* (Tübingen: Mohr, 1958); Robert Folz, *The Concept of Empire in Western Europe*, trans. S.A. Ogilvie (London: Edward Arnold, 1969); Charles T. Davis, *Dante and the Idea of Rome* (Oxford: Clarendon Press, 1957).

45. In *The Vision of History in Early Britain* (New York: Columbia University Press, 1966), Robert Hanning argues that Brutus' early history was originally, in the *Historia Britonnum*, a device to cut him free from the Roman past: 'The Britons are a new order, free from the traditions of war and vengeance which in effect condemn the individual of the old society before he can help himself' (p. 105). But in its new context in Geoffrey's *Historia*, in which Britain is bedeviled precisely with war and vengeance, Brutus is now seen to have brought his past with him in the very effort to separate himself from it.

46. Geoffrey of Monmouth, *History of the Kings of Britain*, trans. Lewis Thorpe (Harmondsworth: Penguin, 1966), p. 233. For the Latin, see Edmond Faral (ed.), *La Légende Arthurienne*, Vol. 3 (Paris: H. Champion, 1929), p. 249: 'et qui fortior supervenerit ferat quod habere exoptavit.'

47. Lucius is also accompanied by heathens from the Baltic lands – 'Pruyslande' and 'Lettow' (lines 604–5).

48. The structure of this episode derives from the *Voeux de paon* by Jacques de Longuyon (1312), a narrative poem loosely attached to the Alexander romances; in the original the Alexandrian heroes vow to do great deeds upon a baked peacock, a device our author significantly revises in a religious direction. The *Voeux de paon* provides as well the first literary account of the Nine Worthies. Perhaps also relevant is the satiric *Voeux du héron*, which uses the premise of Jacques de Longuyon's poem to provide a bitterly anti-English account of the beginnings of the Hundred Years' War; see B.J. Whiting, 'The Vow of the Heron', *Speculum*, **20** (1945): 261–78.

49. *The Bodley Version of Mandeville's Travels*, ed. M.C. Seymour, EETS 253 (London: Oxford University Press, 1963), p. 49; cf. EETS 153 (London: Oxford University Press, 1919), p. 45. The opening lines of the poem cater to the hopes for Arthurian success by summarising the narrative as if it recorded only the victory over Lucius (lines 22–5).

50. C.L. Regan, 'The Paternity of Mordred in the Alliterative *Morte Arthure*', *Bulletin*

bibliographique de la Société Internationale Arthurienne, **25** (1973): 153–4, argues that the poem knows nothing of Arthur's incestuous begetting of Mordred, but there are in fact several clear references to Mordred's irregular genealogy (lines 3741–4, 3776) as well as some less explicit allusions (lines 689–92, 4062, 4174).

51. MATTHEWS, *Tragedy of Arthur*, sees Arthur as culpable from the beginning by engaging in an imperialistic war; JOHN FINLAYSON, 'The Concept of the Hero in *Morte Arthure*', in *Chaucer und seine Zeit: Symposion für Walter Schirmer* (Tübingen: M. Niemeyer, 1968), pp. 249–74, argues instead that it is only after the defeat of Lucius that Arthur's behavior becomes culpable; while LARRY BENSON, 'The Alliterative *Morte Darthur* and Medieval Tragedy', *Tennessee Studies in Literature*, **11** (1966): 75–87, suggests more thoughtfully that the poem records the conflict of two goods, 'the Christian detachment that is necessary for ultimate happiness even on this earth and the complete engagement with an earthly ideal that is necessary for heroism' (pp. 80–1). All of these readings – and others – share the common assumption that the poem's *raison d'être* is ethical judgement. To be sure, here as elsewhere in medieval literature the reader is invited to pass judgment and to extract a moral from his reading; but it would be a mistake to regard this self-justifying process as the single purpose toward which all of the elements of the work are directed.

52. Only FINLAYSON, Introduction, pp. 18–19, has provided any critical commentary; he suggests that in its explicit romanticism and individualism the episode marks the point at which Arthur's campaign loses its moral justification. The reading that follows, although different, is consistent with this interpretation.

53. The *Fuerres* is printed in *The Medieval French Roman d'Alexandre, 2: Version of Alexandre de Paris*, ed. E.C. Armstrong *et al.*, Elliott Monographs 37 (Princeton: Princeton University Press, 1937), pp. 60–127.

54. See MATTHEWS, *Tragedy of Arthur*, pp. 44–6.

55. *Fierabras*, eds A. Kroeber and G. Servois (Paris: F. Viewig, 1860). This source was first proposed by R.H. GRIFFITH, 'Malory, *Morte Arthure*, and *Fierabras*', *Anglia*, **32** (1909): 389–98. JOHN FINLAYSON, 'The Alliterative *Morte Arthure* and Sir Firumbras', *Anglia*, **92** (1974): 380–6, suggested that the direct source was one of the two Middle English translations. The points I wish to make about this source are the same in either case.

56. *La chanson de Roland*, ed. Joseph Bédier (Paris: H. Piazza, 1964), line 1015, p. 86.

57. 'Was neuer siche a justynge at journé in erthe / In the vale of Josephate, as gestes vs telles, / When Julyus and Joatall ware juggede to dy' (lines 2875–7). Jehosephat is the locale not only for this confrontation but for Titus' battle against the Jews when he revenged Christ's death – recounted in the ME *Siege of Jerusalem*, from which the poet probably got the detail – and, of course, for the Last Judgment. The *Fuerres de Gadres* gestures toward these two progressively more exalted contests but is unable to elevate its own battle to either level. Julius and Joatall do not appear, to my knowledge, in the *Fuerres*, and the allusion has not been explained; Hamel calls these names 'meaningless and certainly scribal' (p. 348, note to lines 2876–7).

58. Interestingly, the full version of the *Fuerres de Gadres* was heavily influenced by the crusading narrative of William of Tyre; see *The Medieval French Roman d'Alexandre, 4: Le Roman de Fuerre de Gadres D'Eustache*, ed. E.C. Armstrong and Alfred Foulet, Elliott Monographs 39 (Princeton: Princeton University Press, 1942), p. 23.

59. *Fierabras*, lines 1510–12 (p. 46); *Sir Ferumbras*, ed. Sidney J. Herrtage, EETS, ES 34 (London: Trübner, 1879), line 760.

60. MATTHEWS, *Tragedy of Arthur*, p. 62. For this theme, and others relevant to the poem, see MARY LASCELLES, 'Alexander and the Earthly Paradise in Medieval English Writings', *Medium Aevum*, 5 (1936): 31–47, 79–104, 173–88. Matthews stresses throughout the analogy between Arthur and Alexander, a comparison that was present at the legend's learned origin when Geoffrey of Monmouth drew upon the Alexander stories for his account of Arthur; see J.S.P. TATLOCK, *The Legendary History of Britain* (Berkeley: University of California Press, 1950), pp. 312–20. It is relevant to note that according to the most recent paleographical report, the Thornton MS originally began with the *Morte Arthure* and that a prose *Alexander* was added later, apparently as an appropriate introduction: see KEISER, 'Lincoln Cathedral Library MS. 91', pp. 177–8.

61. Unfortunately, the useful edition by LARRY D. BENSON, *The Death of Arthur* (Indianapolis: Bobbs-Merrill, 1974), includes an emendation at this point – derived from Malory – that makes Priamus ask for baptism (p. 189). Hamel, on the other hand, argues that since Priamus asks to be allowed 'to schewe schortly my schrifte and schape for myn ende' (line 2588) he must already be a Christian; see p. 340, note to lines 2587–8, and HAMEL's 'The "Christening" of Sir Priamus in the Alliterative *Morte Arthure*', *Viator*, 13 (1982): 295–307. But Priamus asks Gawain for this opportunity 'for sake of *thy* Cryste' (line 2587), and there is no reason to think that the poet did not assume that virtuous pagans conducted their final moments on earth in much the same way as did Christians.

62. Priamus first asks Gawain, 'Will thow, for knyghthede, kene me thy name?' (line 2619), and Gawain replies by falsely identifying himself as a chamber knave; Priamus then asks Gawain his identity 'fore the krisome þat þou kaght þat day þou was crystenede' (line 2636) and Gawain replies with the truth. While the purpose of this conversation is uncertain, Priamus' invocation of the baptismal anointing at once acknowledges its historical existence and reminds us of its absence in this narrative.

63. On Absalom's revolt against his father, David, see 2 Kings 13–18. Of Unwine we know only that his name means 'son born beyond hope' or 'the unexpected one' and that he did not succeed his father Eastgota: see R.W. CHAMBERS, *Widsith* (Cambridge: Cambridge University Press, 1912), pp. 219, 254; R.M. WILSON, *The Lost Literature of Medieval England* (London: Methuen, 1970), pp. 7–8.

64. These details, and the insistent foregrounding of the theme of generational conflict, are unique to the *Morte Arthure* among the chronicle versions.

65. Arthur's motives are of course dynastic, but the *Morte Arthure* adds a detail to the traditional narrative that suggests that this effort by the past to control the future will in the event be undone: Mordred has, we are told, gotten Guenevere with child (lines 3552, 3576), and of her fate and the child's the poem tells us nothing.

66. See JOHN FINLAYSON, 'Rhetorical "Descriptio" of Place in the Alliterative *Morte Arthure*', *Modern Philology*, 61 (1963): 1–11. There are three descriptions of pleasant landscapes, the first two (in the episodes of the giant and of Priamus and Gawain) prefiguring in their naturalism the supernaturalism of the third description in the dream of Fortune. The placing of these episodes links these three crucial thematic moments together, three episodes that are in narrative terms expendable. They also foreground the motif of wilderness and paradise,

which is part of the poem's larger eschatological theme; on this motif, see GEORGE H. WILLIAMS, *Wilderness and Paradise in Christian Thought* (New York: Harper, 1962).

67. The most complete discussion of the Worthies in the *Morte Arthure*, and in general, is by HORST SCHROEDER, *Der Topos der Nine Worthies in Literatur und bildender Kunst* (Göttingen: Vandenhoeck & Ruprecht, 1971), pp. 309–18.

68. In the *Morte Arthure* this pattern is ironically enacted by Lucius, who demands a tribute from Arthur that is then paid with silver caskets enclosing the bodies of Lucius himself and his senators.

69. In at least one Alexander romance, the orb is referred to as a 'pome'; Lascelles, 'Alexander and the Earthly Paradise in Medieval English Writings', p. 42. On the conjunction of sovereignty, the garden, and the *Reichsapfel*, see TERRY COMITO, *The Idea of the Garden in the Renaissance* (New Brunswick: Rutgers University Press, 1978), pp. 8–9.

70. AUGUSTINE, *De Civ. Dei* 12.14. Augustine did not of course mean that in pre-Christian times history actually was cyclic but was attacking rather what he took to be the ruling idea of classical historiography. For a criticism of this now common (mis)conception, see MOMIGLIANO, *Essays in Ancient and Modern Historiography*, pp. 179–204, esp. pp. 184–5 (see note 3).

71. A possibly Dantean background to the dream is discussed by MARY HAMEL, 'The Dream of a King: The Alliterative *Morte Arthure* and Dante', *Chaucer Review*, **14** (1979–80): 298–312.

72. For a wholly positive, although not explicit apocalyptic, reading of the battle with the giant, see JOHN FINLAYSON, 'Arthur and the Giant of St Michael's Mount', *Medium Aevum*, **33** (1964): 112–20. Also relevant to this kind of reading is the notion of giants as representatives of an evil at once primitive and terminal, as in the monstrous figures Gog and Magog, who came to embody the barbaric tribes whose depredations would mark the coming of the last days.

73. See McKISACK, *Fourteenth Century*, p. 498 (see note 18).

74. This is the last line of the *Chanson de Roland*.

13 *The Flower and the Leaf* and *The Assembly of Ladies*: Is There a (Sexual) Difference?*

ALEXANDRA A.T. BARRATT

Barratt exercises some of the reading strategies developed by feminist gynocritics – the study of women's writing – to question the traditional arguments for attributing anonymous, early literature to men. Barratt proceeds by carefully uncovering the presuppositions and logic of old-style philological approaches, then experiments with the opposite assumption. The female narrators of *The Flower and the Leaf* and *The Assembly of Ladies* cannot be taken as irrefutable proof of female authorship, yet this proposition foregrounds different features of special interest to women in both texts, features hitherto masked by the assumption of male authorship.

Modern feminist literary criticism takes it for granted that sexual difference exists in writing; that is, that 'gender informs and complicates both the writing and the reading of texts'.[1] Although there is dispute about what precisely it is that constitutes women writers as a distinct literary group, and where the 'difference' resides, there does not seem to be much doubt among feminist literary critics that it exists, and can be perceived. There is even a distinct branch of literary criticism – gynocritics – which deals with the interpretation of works written by women.[2] It is significant, however, that most feminist criticism has been concerned with nineteenth- and twentieth-century texts, whose female authorship is an accepted fact of literary history. What of texts from earlier periods, especially the Middle Ages, which are so often anonymous? How do critics and scholars decide the gender of anonymous authors, if there is no infallible stylistic indicator of a writer's gender? Arguments for a woman's having possibly written an anonymous literary work may tell us as much about prevailing orthodoxies as the

* Reprinted from *Philological Quarterly*, **66** (1987): 1–24.

problem of gender which they claim to elucidate.

It is an unwritten law of literary scholarship, so deeply embedded that it does not have to be made explicit, that anonymous texts are assumed to be written by males. If asked to justify this assumption, its proponents would argue that most known writers in the Middle Ages were men, so it is probable that most anonymous writers of the same period were also male. There are obviously flaws in this argument – women might well be more anxious to conceal the fact of their authorship than men (the phenomenon of women writers' male pseudonyms in the nineteenth century is possibly analogous to the medieval situation) – but its worst feature is its cumulative negative effect. It becomes circular and self-fulfilling. If most named authors are men, then so too are most anonymous writers; any one anonymous work is almost certain to be assigned to a male writer; and that attribution itself becomes part of the argument for assigning the next anonymous writing to a male. The burden of proof is always left with those who wish to argue for a female writer. If for a while this assumption were reversed, so that in every case female authorship were assumed unless the contrary could be proved, the results might be instructive!

In the meantime, it is less demanding to examine, as paradigmatic, the case of two poems of the fifteenth century which some have claimed for women authors, and some of the arguments which have been put forward on both sides. *The Flower and the Leaf* first appeared in print in Speght's 1598 edition of Chaucer's poems,[3] so initially it was attributed, along with a large number of other apocryphal poems, to a prestigious male author. But there were doubts about this attribution, and in 1897 Skeat declared that the poem was not Chaucer's but probably written by a woman because, as a narrative poem of the dream-vision type (though not actually a dream – the narrator does not fall asleep but goes through dream-like experiences which are clearly to be interpreted allegorically) it has, as all such poems have, a narrative persona who, as we learn towards the end, is female.[4] As a female narrator is an uncommon phenomenon, Skeat suggested that the 'authoress' who composed *The Flower and the Leaf* also wrote *The Assembly of Ladies*,[5] a somewhat inferior poem which also has a female narrative persona, as the end of the first stanza reveals. Right from the start, therefore, the question of female authorship became entangled with the apparently independent question of whether or not the two poems were by the same poet. But this complication was not gratuitous. Skeat was willing to countenance one woman fifteenth-century poet but not two, for he argued that women writers were so rare that the same one must be responsible for both these poems with female narrators. Skeat's view has not gained wide acceptance; G.L. Marsh, writing in 1906, pointed to the flaws in Skeat's argument:

It depends fundamentally upon the assumption that because the author purports to have been a woman, woman she must have been. Insistence upon this point implies . . . that no man would have used so simple a device as concealment of sex. . . .[6]

And he goes on to argue that cross-sexual writing was not unknown in the Middle Ages, a point we will return to later. Moreover, Skeat had argued that, apart from the ballad of the Nutbrown Maid, there are no pre-1500 poems which claim to be written by a woman; 'Therefore, the argument seems to run, these two poems which do purport to be by women, must be both by the same woman; because no two women in England in the fifteenth century could have written poetry.'[7] (Skeat nowhere makes this step in his reasoning explicit, but Marsh's interpretation is correct.) So far, the analysis is strictly logical; but the conclusion he goes on to draw is startling. Instead of querying Skeat's assertion about the absence of women writers before 1500 – and a quick search through any moderately comprehensive collection of Middle English lyrics would throw up at least a dozen with female personae, if not by female writers – he concludes:

> It would seem more reasonable to say that because Professor Skeat finds no record of early English women poets, therefore these poems were not by women at all.[8]

His own position on the question of authorship is:

> The author of [*The Flower and the Leaf*] may have been a woman; but was probably not the same person as the author of [*The Assembly of Ladies*]. And it should not be assumed on the present evidence that the author was a woman at all.[9]

The arguments about authorship took a strange turn in the early 1960s, when Ethel Seaton claimed both poems for the Lancastrian knight Sir Richard Roos. She attacked Skeat's attribution of *The Assembly of Ladies* to a woman on much the same lines as Marsh but also brought forward a new argument against female authorship of both poems:

> If a woman wrote these two skilful poems, why is not her name known for her very rarity, as are those of Marie de France, Christine de Pisan, Anne de Graville, or Margaret of Navarre?[10]

This argument is interesting for its assumptions that women poets were rare and that any rare fact was likely to be recorded; but the women writers on whom she relies are not a homogeneous group. We know that Marie de France wrote her poems only because she chose to say so in the text and we know very little, if anything, about her from other sources; there is both internal and external evidence of Christine's writing activities but she was a professional; Marguerite of Navarre and the obscurer Anne de Graville were of high social rank and also lived at a time when anonymity was generally less common. One might also ask why, if skill is the criterion for the preservation of a writer's name, the name of the Gawain-poet is unknown?

Miss Seaton also had a new argument specific to *The Flower and the Leaf* – that a reference to Livy at ll. 530–2 of that poem 'would come more naturally from a man than from a woman of the period'.[11] Now here is a quite unexamined assumption about women's tastes in reading. If the argument were that a fifteenth-century woman would be unlikely to be able to read Livy in the original, it would deserve serious consideration; but in fact it is part of Seaton's argument that the author of *The Flower and the Leaf* probably used a French translation as Sir Richard Roos would be no more likely than a lady to be a reader of classical Latin prose; it would seem that Duke Humphrey, who was closely associated with Sir Richard, had a French translation of Livy in his library:

> There is every probability that Sir Richard handled it and read in it, the more easily for its being French.[12]

But there is no reason why a woman writer should not have read Livy in this French translation, unless one is convinced that women never read Roman history.

The poems' most recent editor, Professor Pearsall, is ambivalent towards the question of their female authorship. He argues that it was not unknown for a male writer to use a female persona, and cites, following Marsh, some poems by Deschamps and Lydgate's 'balade sayde by a gentilwoman which loued a man of gret estate'.[13] This poem, which only one manuscript attributes to Lydgate, is indeed a *ballade*, in other words a lyric, not narrative, poem; it is only seven stanzas long and hardly can be said to present a fully-developed narrative persona. (No one has yet produced a long narrative allegorical poem of the type of *The Flower and the Leaf* by an indisputably male writer using an unequivocally female persona and this paper will later argue that such a phenomenon would be unlikely in the Middle Ages.)

However, having taken away with one sceptical hand Pearsall gives back double measure with the other:

> if we do accept that both poems are by women, there is certainly no need to assume, with Skeat, that poetesses were so rare in the fifteenth century that they must be by the same woman.[14]

He goes on to cite the authors of some of the Findern poems, Christine de Pisan and other mid-fifteenth-century French courtly ladies. But Pearsall is really much more interested in disputing the supposed common authorship of the two poems, hence his willingness to countenance two English women poets. Here and elsewhere,[15] he argues that the same poet wrote *The Assembly of Ladies* and the romance *Generydes* and that *Generydes* is unlikely to have been written by a woman. He gives no explicit reason for this but implies that *Generydes* is the work of a *professional* writer and that no women were professional writers in the fifteenth-century (except Christine de Pisan?); therefore *The Assembly of Ladies* is not by a woman either but 'with its smooth versifying and effortless padding, must be the work of a practising [sc. = professional?] poet. . . . *The Flower and the Leaf* looks more like the work of a non-professional poet, perhaps a woman.'[16] The number of unspoken assumptions continues to grow: there is now a distinction between professional and non-professional, — or maybe practising and non-practising — poets, and nothing 'professional' can be deemed the work of a woman writer!

None of the arguments put forward either for or against the female authorship of *The Flower and the Leaf* and *The Assembly of Ladies* is totally convincing. But one argument, though not conclusive, deserves more respect than it has been hitherto accorded, and this is the oldest argument of all — the female narrative persona. The generation which grew up with the distinction between 'Chaucer the poet' and 'Chaucer the pilgrim' as an article of faith naturally is ready to dismiss Skeat's faith in the phenomena as naive and simplistic. But did it not contain a substratum of good common sense? The distinction in medieval narrative poetry, especially when the action is a dream or has dream-like characteristics, between the poet and the narrative persona is by no means as clear cut as that which exists between, say, Robert Browning and Porphyria's lover or T.S. Eliot and Prufrock. There seems to have been a strong assumption in the Middle Ages that the two overlapped considerably, even if they were not quite identical. As Donaldson has said, 'the several Chaucers must have inhabited one body, and in that sense the fictional first person is no fiction at all. In an oral tradition of literature the first person probably always shared the personality of his creator. . . .'[17]

The most useful discussion of the question has come about in a quite different context, that of the controversy over the authorship of *Piers Plowman*. There, the possible identification between Will the Dreamer who has been long in land and the putative poet William Langland is of vital importance. Kane argues that

thirteenth- and fourteenth-century French and English authors, writing various kinds of narrative poems in which a first-person narrator recounts a succession of fantastic incidents represented as experienced either awake or in a dream, would conventionally identify the narrators with themselves. Such identification was obviously not intended to be complete. At the same time it was necessarily deliberate.[18]

and later writes

if no fourteenth-century dream-vision poem exists in which the dreamer who recounts the vision is a total fiction . . . then to maintain that the Will of *Piers Plowman* is such a fiction is to posit a very remarkable exception. . . . The greater likelihood is that the concept of the wholly fictitious first-person narrator in a fourteenth-century poem is anachronistic.[19]

The Flower and the Leaf and *The Assembly of Ladies* are modelled on such thirteenth-and fourteenth-century poems, as their early attribution to Chaucer bears mute but eloquent witness, and Kane's arguments, that the 'wholly fictitious first-person narrator' is anachronistic and that there is a deliberate, though incomplete, identification between the dreamer and the poet, are directly relevant to them.

If one were setting out to construct a completely fictitious narrative persona who enjoyed no continuity at all with the subject creating him, the most obvious of ploys would be to give him a sex other than that of the poet. There is nothing more basic to one's sense of self than one's sexual identity. If, then, *The Flower and the Leaf* and *The Assembly of Ladies* were indeed by male poets, we would have two indisputable cases of the 'wholly fictitious first-person narrator' about whose existence Kane is sceptical. In effect, then, we may choose between two improbable possibilities: two women poets; or two wholly fictitious women personae. The former alternative seems the less unlikely.

It is hard to think of any evidence within a poem that could indisputably prove to everyone's satisfaction that the writer was a woman. Even when, as in the case of Marie de France's *lais*, the writer declares 'Marie ai nun, si sui de France', there is no proof that 'Marie de France' is not the narrative persona of a male (or female) writer. And sexual difference is not to be perceived 'cold', as it were. If we know that a poem is by a woman, then we are likely to find — or think we find — further internal evidence; but will it ever be possible to identify and isolate textual characteristics so exclusive to women writers as to make confident attribution of an anonymous poem to a woman possible?

It remains to consider whether, and if so how, our perception of a poem changes if we accept it as written by a woman. A presupposition about the gender of a writer does indeed affect our choice of those elements in a literary work which we foreground, but this choice is likely to be linked with whatever stereotypes currently prevail about sex-roles and the characteristics of gender. What new features of *The Flower and the Leaf*, then, might receive an emphasis in the late twentieth century, if we are willing wholeheartedly to accept the theory of female authorship? First, the fact of female authorship — itself unusual in medieval poetry — foregrounds any unusual, non-conventional features of the poem. This is particularly fruitful in the case of a poem which was described by Marsh as 'a tissue of conventionalities'[20] and by its most recent editor as 'entirely conventional in themes, imagery, and machinery' though he does go on to point out that in it 'convention is accepted and integrated in a rich, coherent, and meaningful pattern'.[21] It is always hazardous to suggest that elements in a medieval poem are not conventional, but the conventionality of *The Flower and the Leaf* has been exaggerated. It deviates somewhat from the tradition within which it was written, so that it might even be seen as undermining it. The poem clearly belongs to the genre of 'medieval allegorical dream-vision' and is closely related to the debate-poem genre. But, paradoxically, it is a dream-poem without a dream (the narrator stays awake throughout); without personification allegory (the companies of the Leaf and the Flower are 'real' men and women, neither dream-figures nor personifications of abstract qualities, though they do have a representative function); and a debate-poem in which no debate takes place. David Harrington, in the only recent article on the poem, points out that the poem 'is not a traditional literary debate. It lacks the balance and characteristically indecisive conclusions of such debate poems as the *Owl and the Nightingale* and the *Parliament of Three Ages*, or perhaps the debate portion of Chaucer's *Parliament of Fowls*'.[22] Unlike, again, the *Owl and the Nightingale*, there is no acrimonious wrangling between two widely-different approaches to life; indeed, another notable feature of *The Flower and the Leaf* is the prevalence of modes of complementarity and co-operation, rather than of competition. As Harrington notes, 'There is no hint of rivalry between the groups of people.'[23] In other ways, too, the poem asserts its individuality, its quality of otherness; it does not always say what we expect.

The Narrator does not reveal that she is a woman until four-fifths of the way through the poem; but that moment changes the reader's perception of all that has gone before (an experience which would not have been available, or necessary, to an audience listening to the poem, who would presumably have been aware from the start that the speaking voice of the author and/or narrator was female). But in spite of this late, and surprising, revelation of gender, the Narrator remains a self-effacing figure; if she is indeed 'wholly fictitious' and does not enjoy even continuity of sex with her creator she is remarkably thinly characterised, until the very end of the poem. She offers few narrative comments, and these are unremarkable.

The action opens with the Narrator (conventionally) unable to sleep –

> As I lay in my bed, sleepe ful unmete
> Was unto me
>
> (17–18)

– but, contrary to convention, there is no good reason for her sleeplessness. She is not suffering from unrequited love or a lover's cruelty; in fact she seems to be that most unusual phenomenon, a happy and contented narrator. Even she finds her condition somewhat surprising:

> but why that I ne might
> Rest, I ne wist, for there nas earthly wight,
> As I suppose, had more hearts ease
> Then I, for I nad sicknesse nor disease.
>
> Wherefore I mervaile greatly of my selfe,
> That I so long withouten sleepe lay.
>
> (18–23)

The explanation for this composure and self-sufficiency, which would be almost unnatural in a male narrator, is to be found at the end of the poem: the narrator is a follower of the Leaf – of chastity and fidelity, of strenuous and virtuous activity. Pearsall notes that conventionally at this point the narrator falls asleep, utters a complaint, or goes out to console himself for his mistress's cruelty[24]; our narrator, logically enough as she is unable to sleep, goes out for a walk at a most industriously female early hour, intending to listen to the song of the nightingale, and as she walks

> a path of litle breade
> I found, that greatly had not used be,
> For it forgrowen was with grasse and weede,
> That well unneth a wight might it se.
>
> (43–6)

which leads to 'a plesaunt herber' enclosed by a hedge so thick

> That who that list without to stond or go,
> Though he would all day prien to and fro,
> He should not see if there were any wight
> Within or no. . . .
>
> (67–70)

Again, this is a commonplace, but is also the kind of imagery of secrecy, enclosure and impenetrability which, it has been suggested, more recent women poets use.

Here we find our first example of complementarity: the narrator does hear her (traditionally female) nightingale, but not until she sings in response to the song of the (male) goldfinch, the bird later associated with the lazy and frivolous Company of the Flower:

> And when his song was ended in this wise,
>
> The nightingale with so merry a note
> Answered him that all the wood rong. . . .
>
> (98–100)

It is this combined song, as line 127 shows, which ravishes the narrator into a trance-like state of perfect contentment; she has her heart's desire, which is not happy love but Paradise:

> Whereof I had so inly great pleasure
> That as me thought I surely ravished was
> Into Paradise, where my desire
> Was for to be. . . .

(113–16)

The Company of the Leaf, whom she then observes, are described at great length, much greater length than the rival Company of the Flower. The first feature that we might stress is their sexual segregation: a company of ladies enters first, whose leader is also a woman, and only later the male groups. The ladies are associated with images of circularity:

> all they yede in maner of compace.
> But one there yede in mid the company
> Soole by her selfe. . . .

(163–5)

they sing a roundell (176) – a poem with a circular structure – and their singing is a matter of reciprocity between the lady of the company and the rest:

> And she began a roundell lustely . . .
> And than the company answered all
> With voice sweet entuned. . . .

(176–80)

At this stage, then, we witness a perfectly harmonious, self-fulfilling and self-sufficient female community bound together by communal, complementary, artistic activity; collective without an internal hierarchy except for the presence of a leader marked out from the others by her solitariness, her initiation of the song, and her surpassing beauty:

> of beauty she past hem everichon.

(168)

For no obvious reason the narrator constitutes herself as observer and judge of their individual performances. At this moment, she hints to the vigilant reader at her own gender by implicitly claiming to be able to assess 'womanliness' –

> I might avise hem, one by one,

Who fairest was, who coud best dance or sing,
Or who most womanly was in all thing.

(187–9)

– though the company themselves are not engaging in any such competition.
But before she can come to any conclusions about their relative merits, a
crowd of soldiers – 'Of men of armes . . . such a rout' (196) – bursts in on
this idyllic female community. In contrast to the ladies, they do not engage in
a circular dance, in co-operative or reciprocal song but compete in the linear
and destructive jousts. Whereas the ladies (apart from 'the lady of the
company') all seem to be equal, there are far more hierarchical distinctions
among the men. There is a clear-cut division between the 'men-at-armes' who
are trumpeters or heralds, and the nine kings-of-arms. They are followed by
another company of 'herauds and pursevaunts eke' (232), followed in turn by
a group of nine knights, each accompanied by 'three hensh-men' (252), and
by another 'rout' of armed knights. The male group is presented as more
fragmented and differentiated than the female. They are also more competitive:
nothing comes of the Narrator's attempt to judge the ladies' beauty,
musicianship or womanliness, but 'tho that crowned were in laurer grene'
(289) definitely win the jousting by main force.

While the male and female groups sit together under the tree –

>   every lady tooke ful womanly
> By the hond a knight, and forth they yede
> Unto a faire laurer

(302–4)

– the Narrator observes the arrival of the Company of the Flower. Unlike the
Company of the Leaf, sexually differentiated from the start but with the two
groups later adopting complementary roles, they are sexually integrated, and

>   came roming out of the field wide,
> Hond in hond, a knight and a lady.

(325–6)

But they are not socially homogeneous, for they are preceded, not by
heralds, but by 'ministrels many one' (336). Their dance and song in honour
of the daisy never reaches a decorous conclusion, as did the song of the
ladies of the leaf –

>   as soone as they goodly might
> They brake of both the song and dance.

(299–300)

– for it is rudely interrupted by overpowering heat followed by a disastrously
destructive hail storm.

In spite of their obvious contrasts, the two companies are not hostile towards each other nor do they engage in any overt competition or debate as to their rival merits. On the contrary, the Company of the Leaf goes to the aid of their rivals out of a sense of compassion:

> And whan the storm was cleane passed away,
> Tho in white, that stood under the tre –
> They felt nothing of the great affray
> That they in greene without had in ybe –
> To them they yede for routh and pite,
> Them to comfort after their great disease,
> So faine they were the helplesse for to ease.
>
> (372–8)

The initiative in this is taken by the Lady of the company, who takes the 'queen that was in grene' by the hand; she is followed in this act of condescension by the ladies and only then do the knights follow suit. With their counterparts they all make themselves useful cutting firewood, gathering herbs for sunburn, and preparing salads. The Lady of the Leaf then invites the Lady of the Flower to dine, and both groups go off amicably together. Our last glimpse of them is one of harmony, as they pass on their way, singing together, for the Lady of the Leaf works by the incorporation of others to gain their adherence and co-operation, not by harsh moral criticism.

It is thus surprising to find, when the Narrator seeks an explanation of what she has seen, that the Company of the Flower are so reprehensible and incur such critical judgment from a follower of the Leaf. The difference between the two groups is not so simple as merely the opposition of sensuality and continence.[25] The Company of the Leaf is an inclusive group: it includes some women who have rejected sexual expression (the virgins who bear branches of *agnus castus*); some who demonstrate total fidelity in love; and, significantly, some women wearing laurel chaplets, who have chosen a life of strenuous, virtuous activity –

> such as hardy were and wan by deed
> Victorious name which never may be dede;
> And all they were so worthy of ther hond,
> In hir time, that none might hem withstond.
>
> (480–3)

It is the women as much as the men who wear laurel as is clear from lines 158 and 495. And yet they are praised unequivocally for their physical bravery; they must be the precursors of Spenser's Belphoebe and Britomart. In contrast, the Company of the Flower are lazy and frivolous rather than sexually dissolute –

    such that loved idlenes
And not delite of no busines
But for to hunt and hauke, and pley in medes,
And many other such idle dedes.

(536–9)

It is not so much chastity as activity which enables one to rise above the
transitoriness of the temporal world and which is presented as the ideal for
women. The narrator obtains this interpretation and guidance from an
authoritative female figure whom she addresses as Madam and who addresses
her as 'My doughter'. While it would be absurd to argue that the female
exegete is necessarily the product of a female writer, it is perhaps slightly less
so to point out that all the authority figures in this poem are female – the
explicator and the two queens, who it turns out were the goddesses Diana
and Flora. What is more, the Narrator not only seeks guidance from an
authoritative female figure, she also accepts her authority when questioned
about her own allegiances –

    to whome doe ye owe
Your service? and which woll ye honour? –

(572–3)

and the validation and approval that her choice gains (577–81).
    Perhaps, though, the most fertile passage to reassess in the light of an
assumption that a woman wrote it, is the envoi. The author sends her poem
out into the world with maternal solicitude as if it were a young girl –
uneducated and uncultivated, shy, prone to blush, liable to be criticised for
brazenness and bare-faced presumption, finding crowds an ordeal, inadequate
and with no control over who is likely to witness her shortcomings:

O little booke, thou art so unconning,
How darst thou put thy self in prees for drede?
It is wonder that thou wexest not rede,
Sith that thou wost ful lite who shall behold
Thy rude langage, full boistously unfold.

(591–5)

One might then read this poem as idealising female autonomy and
structures in which men take a subordinate place; as showing a distinct
preference for co-operation and complementarity rather than the divisiveness
of dialectic; as refusing the conventions of the dream and the debate but
nonetheless presenting its own ideas, directly and discreetly. Such a reading is
as much a compendium of late-twentieth-century stereotypes of female
psychology as Skeat's arguments are of late-nineteenth-century ideas; but the

poem has not been forced to yield these insights. They can be quite legitimately drawn from the text. On the other hand, while they are not features which would have come into focus except through the lens of a willingness to accept that the poem was written by a woman, they certainly cannot be regarded as arguments for female authorship.

One's first impression of *The Assembly of Ladies* is of how different it is from *The Flower and the Leaf*, and astonishment that anyone ever seriously believed that the same author wrote the two poems. The mere presence of a female narrative persona in both seems to have taken precedence in the minds of scholars over the obvious dissimilarities. In this poem we know the narrator is female right from the start, she does fall asleep, and she does meet figures of personification allegory who all identify themselves as such. The narrator is in the forefront of her dream and emerges convincingly as a fictional construct whose gender is directly related to the theme of the poem. There is therefore more room to see the narrative persona as separate from the poet and, possibly, of a different gender.

It is generally agreed that *The Assembly of Ladies* is not a good poem. Often inept, it is hard to interpret coherently but presents a number of interesting features if we are prepared seriously to entertain the possibility that a woman wrote it. The poem presents us with what must be one of the most hesitant and unself-confident narrators ever to appear in a medieval dream-poem, and one has the distinct impression that this is not a deliberate irony perpetrated by the poet. The Narrator is dependent on men; although all the characters who appear within the dream are female, the poem itself is framed by a conversation in which the Narrator draws validation from a male audience. The Narrator is wandering around with four other ladies, as the 'fift, symplest of all'(7).

> And yit in trowth we were nat alone:
> Theyr were knyghtis and squyers many one.

> (13–14)

It is only as a result of the repeated questioning prompted by her apparent aimlessness and her pallor, and the encouragement, not to say coercion, of one of these men that she tells her tale. Paradoxically, she contradicts this account of the poem's genesis as elicited by male insistence when at the end of the poem she tells how she awoke and

> went and made this booke,
> Thus symply rehersyng the substaunce
> Because it shuld nat out of remembraunce.

> (740–2)

Immediately her male audience voices its approval:

Now verily your dreame is passyng goode
And worthy to be had in remembraunce

(743–4)

but his curiosity is still not satisfied: what does she intend to call it? (We shall later see that within the dream the narrator exhibits considerable anxiety about the signifying process.) The Narrator not only produces the name she has hit on for her creation but seeks the knight's approval, which is duly given:

As for this booke, to sey yow verray right
And of the name to tel the certeynte,
'La semble de Dames', thus it hight;
How thynk ye that the name is? 'Goode, parde!'

(750–3)

The poem, then, presents a paradigm of women's writing (for regardless of whether the poet is or is not a woman, within the poem the Narrator is presented as a woman who turns her dream-experience into a book) as generated by the demands of a male audience and depending for validation both of its intrinsic value and the way in which it presents to the outside world on that same source of approval.

Whether deliberately or not, the poem presents an interesting picture of female depression, confusion and uncertainty, though Pearsall sees 'pert self-confidence'[26] and John Stephens 'self-satisfied stubborness'![27] When we first meet her, the Narrator is wandering in a garden maze 'As a womman that nothyng rought' (18) (is she carefree or just indifferent?)[28] apparently seeking something or someone, and surprisingly pale. It is the dream experience itself which has induced her state, making it unlikely that it has been 'the journey towards enlightenment and middle age' for which Stephens argues.[29] That experience, she tells the inquiring knight, started in that very same maze when the Narrator became separated from her female companions. It is interesting throughout the poem to note the narrator's ambivalent attitude towards her women companions; she competes with them and yet is, literally and metaphorically, lost without them. Her affiliation needs are strong and unsatisfied. The wandering in the maze is initially a co-operative activity –

My felawship and I, bi one assent,
Whan al oure other busynesse was done,
To passe oure tyme in to this mase we went –

(30–2)

but quickly breaks up into individual effort, with some of the fellowship even offending against the conventions of the maze by stepping 'over the rayle'

(42). The narrator feels she has gained an advantage – 'I gate my self a litel avauntage' (44) – but is so tired by her efforts that she can go no further and instead comes to a 'herber' where, it seems, the rest of her companions also hope to arrive, so that she feels obliged to wait for them:

> A litel while thus was I alone,
> Beholdyng wele this delectable place;
> My felawshyp were comyng everichone
> So must me nede abide as for a space.
>
> (71–4)

The Narrator has been more successful than her companions in penetrating that maze but, perhaps because success means separation from the group, it makes her anxious. Reflecting on the past and sighing deeply, she falls asleep.

Within the dream, the Narrator becomes even more passive and uncertain, lapsing into the security provided by a succession of authoritative female personifications who provide her with detailed instructions. She no longer has to take any initiative, but only to respond. Perseverance appears first and tells the Narrator that she and her companions have been summoned by Lady Loyalty to a council in seven days' time. Attendance is obligatory –

> And more she badde that I shuld sey
> Excuse ther myght be none nor delay.
>
> (111–12)

She is told that they must all come with mottos embroidered on their sleeves and dressed in blue. Perseverance urges assertiveness –

> And be nat ye abasshed in no wise,
> As many as bien in suche an high presence;
> Make youre request as ye can best devise
> And she gladly wil yeve yow audience
>
> (120–3)

– and promises a guide, Diligence. The Narrator asks if she should bring any men (the question is indeed 'weakly motivated')[30] and is both surprised and faintly horrified to hear that she may not, for reasons that are left obscure:

> 'Yit,' quod I, 'ye must telle me this cace,
> If we shal any men unto us calle?'
> 'Nat one,' quod she, 'may come among yow alle.'
>
> 'Nat one?' quod I, 'ey, benedicite!
> What have they don? I pray yow, telle me that.'

264

'Now, be my lif, I trowe but wele,' quod she,
'But evere I can beleve ther is somwhat,
And for to sey yow trowth, more can I nat.'

(145–52)

Further detailed instructions follow before the Narrator lets Perseverance
leave, but by then the Narrator claims to have received some much-needed
self-confidence:

'Yowre comfort hath yeve me suche hardynesse
That now I shal be bold withouten faile
To do after youre avise and counsaile.'

(187–9)

She sets off with her guide. When she arrives she finds one companion, a
gentlewoman, already there (this seems to reverse her waking experience)
and equipped with the necessary clothing. She is worried that she may have
missed the others,

'But this I dowte me gretely, wote ye what,
That my felaws bien passed by and gone,'

(246–7)

is reassured that they have not yet arrived, but gently cautioned,

It is non harme though ye be there afore.

(252)

It's not an offence to be early! But the narrator continues to need reassurance
that she is acceptable: her next anxiety is her dress –

So than I dressid me in myn array
And asked hir if it were wele or noo.
'It is,' quod she, 'right wele unto my pay;
Ye dare nat care to what place so ever ye goo.'

(252–6)

She also continues to fret about the absence of her companions: when
Countenance asks where they are, she replies:

      they bien comyng echeone,
But in certeyne I knowe nat where they be.
At this wyndow whan they come ye may se;
Here wil I stande awaityng ever among,

For wele I wote they wil nat now be long.

(297–301)

While she is waiting, our attention is drawn to the fact that the Narrator, unlike the other characters in her dream, has no 'word' or motto embroidered on her clothing: only the clothing she has been instructed to wear provides her with a signifier. But when she says,

And for my word, I have none, this is trewe;
It is inough that my clothyng be blew
As here before I had comaundement.

(312–14)

is she defiant or uneasy? In any case, this deficiency perhaps forms a link with the Narrator's obsession with names; practically none of the personifications volunteers her name, the Narrator always has to ask.

Complementing the passive, unself-confident Narrator are the excessively controlling personifications: for instance, the Narrator is told that Perseverance

wil telle yow every thyng
How ye shal be rulyd of your comyng

(377–8)

and the Narrator and her friends pledge absolute obedience, though even in that they depend on external approval – they lay bets not only on who is best dressed but also on who will receive the most praise.

Perseverance approaches, claiming the privileges of an old friend, and asks the Narrator about her own and her friends' mottoes. Here her anxiety at her voicelessness and failure to conform to the group comes out clearly:

Whan they begynne to opyn theyr matiere
There shal ye knowe her wordis, by and by.
But as for me I have none verily
And so I told to Countenaunce here afore;
All myn array is bliew, what nedith more?

(409–13)

When Lady Loyalty grants them audience, the first eight ladies obediently present their bills of complaint but the Narrator – the voiceless one, who relies on her blue dress to signify rather than a motto – hangs back. Pearsall calls her behaviour rude but it can also be read as hesitant and in harmony with her lack of assertiveness and low self-esteem throughout the poem. She can hardly bring herself to voice her own sorrows, for this would force her to admit her own emotional needs:

266

'Ye have rehersed me these billis alle,
But now late se somewhat of youre entente.'
'It may so happe peraventure ye shal.'
'Now, I pray yow, while I am here present.'
'Ye shal, parde, have knowlache what I ment . . .'
'Now, goode, telle on, I hate yow, be seynt Jame.'
'Abide a while, it is nat yit my wil.'

(680–90)

When she finally speaks it is to reveal depression, a desire for death, and a profound sense of grievance.

The interpretation of the poem from line 680 onwards is highly problematic but vitally important. The Narrator's own complaint should provide a climax, yet it is hard to know what exactly she is saying. The problems start with lines 680–1 (quoted above). Who is speaking here, and who is addressed? In his edition, Pearsall notes, 'Lady Loyalty speaks, turning to the fifth lady, the authoress, who has not yet presented her complaint. She is reluctant to do so and replies rather rudely (682, 690), but is eventually prevailed upon.'[31] Skeat also says Lady Loyalty speaks at lines 680 and 689.[32] If we follow this interpretation, then in lines 694–707 the Narrator is speaking directly to Lady Loyalty, the *ye* of lines 696–8. But, then, who is the female figure to whom the Narrator refers in the third person at lines 699 and 705?

Without hir help that hath al thyng in cure
I can nat thynk that it may long endure;

(699–700)

Of hir goodenesse besechyng hir therfor
That I myght have my thank in suche wise
As my desert deservith of justice.

(705–7)

Pearsall does not offer any guidance or even indicate that a problem exists; he merely cites verbal parallels from Chaucer and Lydgate. It seems unlikely that the figure is Lady Loyalty if she has just been addressed in the second person; possibly she is some other female authority-figure such as the Virgin or Lady Fortune – the latter Skeat's suggestion if she is not Lady Loyalty[33]; but if so her introduction is surprisingly abrupt as neither has appeared before in the poem. In the parallel lines from Chaucer's *Man of Law's Tale*, the phrase 'hir that hath my life in cure' is used by the Sowdan of Constance, with whom he has fallen passionately in love; and certainly, if these two stanzas (699–707) were an independent poem we would not hesitate to see them as referring to the poet's love-object. One is driven to the conclusion that the narrator is talking about another woman whom she loves. Startling as this may seem it is perhaps even more startling that no one has previously suggested this as the obvious meaning of the text.[34]

But in fact it seems unlikely to me that it is Lady Loyalty whom the narrator addresses at lines 682 ff.; Stephens rightly describes the exchange as 'downright childish'[35] and Pearsall no doubt has this passage in mind when he refers to 'the narrator's pert self-confidence'. I suggest that the speaker of lines 680–2 is the Narrator's original interlocutor, the Inquisitive Knight. (When the Knight speaks at the end of the poem at line 743 he is not introduced by name either.) The interchange then reinforces the relationship that was evident between them at the poem's opening – his inquisitiveness, her, possibly coy, reluctance. (There are verbal echoes, too: the lines 'But now late se somwhat of youre entente', and 'Now, goode, telle on, I hate yow, be seynt Jame' echo 'Telle on, late se, and make no taryeng' [23]. The Narrator's response – 'Abide a while, it is nat yit my wil' [690] echoes her earlier 'Abide,' quod I, 'ye be an hasti one' [24].) The Narrator, then, is still addressing the Knight parenthetically in lines 697–98, and there is no reason to dispute that it is Lady Loyalty who is referred to at lines 705 and 699.

We can thus safely restore this extremely conventional poem to the literature of heterosexual love. But the discussion of this particular passage has perhaps helped to emphasise that we all make far more assumptions than we are ready to admit in reading and interpreting medieval poetry; and that challenging one assumption about a poem may well lead on to a fresh look at other aspects of the text.

Lady Loyalty's response to the bills of complaint, once they have all been articulated, is strange. Having initiated the whole idea of their presentation, all she does is promise to refer them to 'oure court of parlement'. She provokes action, and then frustrates it. The women appear satisfied –

> For as us thought we had oure travel spent
> In suche wise as we hielde us content

(732–3)

– but it is surely from tears of frustration that the Narrator awakes:

> All sodainly the water sprang anone
> In my visage. . . .[36]

(736–7)

Once awake, she is still torn between her dependence on male approval and her need for support from her companions: her last words to the Inquisitive Knight are:

> Now go, farewele, for they cal after me,
> My felawes al, and I must after sone.

(745–6)

The poem as a whole, then, presents a picture of female helplessness, dependence on others, particularly men, and frustration, in a Narrator whose only power lies in deliberate unco-operativeness, who refuses to communicate verbally, or does so only with reluctance. I do not believe that this was the conscious intention of the poet, which seems more to have been to present her as touchingly artless and ingenuous. But truth will out. If the poet, as distinct from the Narrator, is a woman, she has certainly depicted her sex in a flattering light – Stephens' remark that the Narrator 'is hardly a suitable vehicle through which to express the vindication of women'[37] is fair comment. Nor has she demonstrated much competence as a poet. There is no reason to assume that women writers always do either of these things: but she has given us a glimpse, perhaps unwitting, of the dark side of women's consciousness, if we are willing to see it.

We may conclude, then, that readings of texts for which female authorship is assumed will not invariably throw up the same features of interest. In *The Flower and the Leaf* can be discerned a woman-centred ideal of virtuous activity, presented with some literary nonconformity in an ambience of complementary and co-operation, all admirable female characteristics. But in *The Assembly of Ladies*, such a reading highlights less admirable characteristics of uncertainty, lack of self-esteem and dependence on men. This should be no surprise as women writers, though fewer in number than men in the Middle Ages, presumably demonstrated a similar range of preconceptions, obsessions and prejudices, not to mention the same variation in sheer literary competence. The 'difference' is perhaps not so much sexual as individual.

Notes

1. *Writing and Sexual Difference*, ed. E. Abel (Brighton: The Harvester Press, 1982), p. 1.

2. ELAINE SHOWALTER, 'Towards a Feminist Poetics' in *Women Writing and Writing About Women*, ed. M. Jacobus (London: Croom Helm, 1979), pp. 25–6.

3. E.P. HAMMOND, *Chaucer: A Bibliographical Manual*. (New York: Macmillan, 1908; repr. New York: Peter Smith, 1933), pp. 423–4.

4. *The Complete Works of Geoffrey Chaucer*, 6 vols (Oxford: Clarendon Press, 1894), 6:xii.

5. W.W. SKEAT, *The Chaucer Canon* (Oxford: Clarendon Press, 1900; repr. New York: Haskell House, 1965), p. 139.

6. G.L. MARSH, 'The Authorship of "The Flower and the Leaf"', *JEGP*, **6** (1906–7): 375.

7. Art. cit., ibid.

8. pp. 375–6.

9. p. 380.

10. ETHEL SEATON, *Sir Richard Roos: Lancastrian Poet* (London: Rupert Hart-Davis, 1961), p. 296.

11. Ibid., p. 319.

12. Ibid.

13. *'The Floure and the Leafe', and 'The Assembly of Ladies'* (London: Nelson, 1962), p. 14. All quotations from both poems are from this edition. In general modern non-feminist critics claim a lack of interest in authors' genders, belied by the amount of effort they devote to refuting arguments for female authorship.

14. Ibid, p. 15.

15. *'The Assembly of Ladies* and *Generydes', RES*, n.s. **12** (1961): 229–37.

16. *The Floure and The Leafe*, p. 20.

17. E.T. DONALDSON, *Speaking of Chaucer* (London: The Athlone Press, 1970), p. 10.

18. G. KANE, *Piers Plowman, The Evidence for Authorship* (London: The Athlone Press, 1965), p. 57.

19. Ibid., pp. 57–8.

20. G.L. MARSH quoted by PEARSALL, pp. 51–2.

21. PEARSALL, p. 52.

22. D.V. HARRINGTON, 'The Function of Allegory in *The Flower and the Leaf'*, *Neuphilologische Mitteilungen*, **71** (1970): 249.

23. Ibid., 250.

24. p. 131.

25. Harrington comments, 'The activities of the two contrasting parties . . . do not specifically demonstrate for us in concrete dramatic form the victory of chastity over idleness' (250).

26. PEARSALL, p. 58.

27. JOHN STEPHENS, 'The Questioning of Love in *The Assembly of Ladies'*, *RES*, **24** (1973): 137.

28. See Stephens' discussion, p. 131.

29. p. 140.

30. As Stephens points out, p. 135.

31. p. 169.

32. *Chaucerian and Other Pieces* (Oxford: Clarendon Press, 1897), p. 538.

33. Ibid.

34. John Stephens reads this part of the poem entirely differently. He quotes ll. 680–1 and notes 'the awkward shift in personae'; 'It is possible that *ye* and *youre* refer respectively to *Avisenesse* and the narrator, but the imprecision momentarily fuses the two' (p. 138). (Avisenesse is the secretary who at the request of Lady Loyalty has read aloud the eight previous bills.) But Stephens goes on to refer to 'the altercation between the narrator and *Attemperaunce*' which 'delays the presentation of the final bill' (138–9) by which presumably he means the dialogue in ll. 682–92. Attemperaunce is the chancellor first mentioned by name at 1.508 and apparently

Stephens reads the four stanzas beginning at 1.512 as describing Attemperaunce rather than Lady Loyalty. But Lady Loyalty is certainly the speaker at the end of the four-stanza description who accepts the bills, summons Attemperaunce to take them to Avisenesse and then instructs Attemperaunce to send for Avisenesse to read the bills aloud. So Stephens seems to be saying that at ll. 680–1 Lady Loyalty is speaking first to Avisenesse the secretary and then turns to the Narrator, while Attemperaunce speaks at ll. 683 and 689. The text does not, however, give any indication of these changes of speaker.

35. p. 137.

36. Another contentious point of interpretation; Pearsall notes, 'Skeat suggests that the water was thrown in her face by her companions to wake her up; this seems rather drastic. Perhaps the spray from the fountain caught her face as her head nodded in sleep.' (pp. 170–1)

37. p. 137.

14 Why was *Lady Isabel and the Elf-Knight* the Most Popular Ballad in Europe?*

STEPHEN KNIGHT

Stephen Knight argues that critical methods which focus on sources or characterisation are inappropriate to the study of traditional ballads, which are best considered in their thematic groups. Even though texts survive only rarely from the medieval period, the ballads work through discourses and latent structures which are medieval in origin. The most popular of these narratives both presents and contains a challenge to a patriarchal order which is deeply anxious about female independence and sexual autonomy, on both economic and psychological grounds.

I

This paper has two purposes. One is to provide an answer to its title question, and in doing so to suggest that such questions are proper ones: that other categories such as aesthetic value, genre, formal excellence, moral insight are less primarily relevant to analysis of cultural phenomena than is a study of the relations between those phenomena and the social formations that produce and consume them.

The second purpose is to practise a set of comparative techniques. A comparison of the many versions of a 'text'; a comparison of such versions across languages; a comparison of that multiple phenomenon with its social context and social impact. These comparisons all act against conventional and restrictive practices common in literary study: restrictions to one language

* Reprinted from SNEJA GUNEW and IAN REID (eds), *Not the Whole Story: Tellings and Tailings from the ASPACLS Conference on Narrative* (Sydney: Local Consumption Publications, 1984), pp. 5–13.

and nation, to the imaginary confines of one text, and to 'literature' itself – a self conjured into being to legitimise the academic and *litterateurish* self, wilfully and wishfully severed from its social world.

Another mode of comparison will be with the techniques of reading text and context developed in medieval studies. The inadequacies of recent ballad criticism largely stem from their being located within literary criticism of the 'new critical' kind. The texts of a ballad itself offer little for the scrutinising eye beyond a certain naive charm. The old kinds of scholarship and folkloric studies offered more material, but it had no relation with the text as a structure; the ballad was merely a surface to destroy in the process of excavation.

Medieval literary analysis, on the other hand, draws its strength from the context – social, intellectual, theological – to which the texts themselves naturally and consistently refer, and this essay will presume and implicitly argue that this is the proper method for ballad analysis as well.

Ballads themselves survive only rarely from the medieval period, and then they tend to be atypical, like the largely tuneless, somewhat bookish fifteenth-century Robin Hood texts. But the forms of language, mimesis, structure and social reference in the ballads all indicate that while some may not have been recovered even until the nineteenth century, the context of discourse they represent is medieval. The method of comprehension offered here is that which appears to be highly informative in the case of medieval genres like romance, fabliau and drama, that is a reading of the text as social document, not as an alienated, individualised and transhistorical message.

II

Lady Isabel and the Elf-Knight is the title given by F.J. Child to the group of ballads he prints as his 'Ballad no.4' (1882, I, pp. 22–62). Six versions appear there and more are scattered through the five volumes, in ten parts, of the first edition of his collection; references to the addenda are in the 'Index to Ballad Titles' in Volume 5.

Child said 'of all ballads this has perhaps obtained the widest circulation' (p. 22) and his survey of its dissemination across Europe is by far his longest preface to any ballad. The scope of *Lady Isabel* is stressed by Bronson, who calls it 'one of the most impressive of all the ballads for the geographical sweep of its popularity and vital tenacity' (1959, p. 39). He supports this by printing no less than 141 tune variants.

There are no early manuscript or printed versions of the ballad, which implies a long existence outside literacy and its socio-cultural connotation, if the ballad is not a recent art-creation. Child considers this an early ballad (hence its low number in his collection) and the antiquity of the non-English versions supports that conclusion. Child feels its most ancient form is observed in the Dutch *Halewijn*, which he judged 'Far better preserved than the English and marked with very ancient and impressive traits' (1882, I, p. 24); Nygard agrees with this assessment (1958, p. 327).

This paper is not concerned with the quest for a single antique and so notionally authoritative text, but with the structural core or 'essence' of the ballad, its basic narrative pattern and inherent function. This core can be reconstructed and summarised like the structure of a folk-tale by comparing versions and considering how differences are related. The process of core (or 'essence') and variants can be broadly associated with historical development, since the earliest texts appear 'essential' and there are many later-appearing stages of variation, especially to euphemise challenging core features of the ballad. But at the same time the 'essential' text survives alongside and sometimes within its variations. Development is not linear and historical, but multiplex and ideological, charting different types of response to the basic pattern of the ballad.

Here the text taken as typical of the 'core' of the ballad (no. 1 in Appendix 2) is Child's no. 4a, entitled by him *Lady Isabel and the Elf-Knight*, from here on referred to as *LIEK*.

III

The study of *LIEK* has been restricted to traditional paths. H.O. Nygard's work is a good example. He surveys the ballad across many languages and tries to construct a historicist stemma. This leads to several odd results, such as having to assume *LIEK* is spurious, because it is in several respects (including title) unlike British variants recorded previously (1958, pp. 297–316). Elsewhere he follows another type of authority-quest, source study (1961). As he summarises it, the story of *LIEK* has been traced to, among other things, solar myth, the Old Testament, 'Judith and Holofernes', a story which has certainly affected the names in some versions) and *Bluebeard* – which may indeed be related to *LIEK* in an indirect manner.

However, if ballads are considered in terms of social function, it soon becomes clear that they form coherent thematic groups, not single source-oriented structures. *LIEK* itself belongs to the 'Mysterious Lover' group, where a strange (in both senses) travelling man appears to a woman alone. He offers sexuality, sometimes marriage. She normally masters him, though there are some substantive variants where he is an agent of her punishment for a former infidelity (to a man), e.g. *James Harris/The Demon Lover* (Child no. 243).

This whole group stands in related opposition to a group of 'Daughter's Lover' ballads like *Clark Saunders* (Child no. 69), where the family takes vengeance, usually bloody, on the daughter's deliberate choice of a lover: he has disrupted family order – by entering the house or her bedroom, by abducting her, by making her pregnant and so on. (The reflex of this is the 'Prospective Bride' like *Gil Brenton* (Child no. 5) in which she is examined for virginity.)

Another related group, perhaps a resistant sub-group of the 'Daughter's Lover', allows the daughter to retain her chosen lover against the family's will through her own courage and cunning, as in *Brown Robin* (Child no. 97) and *The Gay Goshawk* (Child no. 96). In these cases, however, the male lover appears to be consistently shown as inferior in terms of social status and/or virility. Suggesting that the wilful daughter's reward is slight is apparently a way of minimising her success and so containing the threat that this pattern offers to a patriarchal structure.

To return to the *LIEK* group: the narrative structure shared by these ballads is:

1. Woman alone in springtime.
2. Sexual rapport between her and a knightly man who is to some degree supernatural.
3. When the two are in sexual or quasi-sexual rapport, he threatens her with the death he has dealt to other women.
4. By the use of stereotypically 'feminine' actions and responses, of a non-sexual or only mildly sexual character, she disarms him.
5. She kills him either with his own weapon or in water.

IV

To move towards interpretation, *LIEK* (like the 'Mysterious Lover' group to which it belongs and many of the other 'Family Ballad' groups) dramatises tension between the daughter's personal sexual inclinations and the family's anxiety to control and then barter her sexuality for its own ends – family is almost always represented only by the male members of the family, a number of brothers and often the father (unlike the 'Prospective Bride' group shown in *Gil Brenton*, where the mother is dominant in the action).

There were strong social and economic reasons for this familial restriction on daughters. It is clear that in the past (as far as most English-speaking cultures are concerned) whatever the social standing of the family, the marriage of a daughter was seen as an important social and economic step. Her capacity to produce children was transferred with care and with a clear eye to at least an indirect share in her future productivity. At the peasant level, co-operation in labour and equipment could be expected from the link with another labouring family; at the gentry level, less directly tangible rewards would stem from the marriage – patronage of one sort or another, such as preference to posts, favoured treatment in law-courts and other official structures. In the cash-context, at a number of social levels, the return for the daughter might simply be her marriage portion, which her father would keep, nominally in her interest.

Material on marriage practices and attitudes is quite common in historical and sociological work on the family. Brief but telling passages about peasant practices appear in MacFarlane (1978, pp. 24 and 28) and those of the gentry are discussed by Stone (1977, pp. 86–9). It should be noted that this paper's discussion of attitudes to a daughter's marriage does not depend on a position in the controversy as to whether the family in earlier England was extended or essentially nuclear (see Laslett, 1972, pp. 1–89 for a controversial statement on this). While I disagree with Laslett's position, which seems an attempt to find pre-capitalist legitimation for the bourgeois nuclear family (like MacFarlane's treatment of individualism), it is in fact rare for ballads to refer to any family member who is not nuclear.

It is not irrelevant, by the way, to speak of both peasants and gentry families in the context of a ballad that uses as its personnel 'lords and ladies'. It appears that ballads about aristocratic figures were part of the cultural and ideological experience of labouring families, since the ballad community based on manor, household, large farm or, as in Buchan's research, the 'fermtoun' (1972, Pt. 1.3) shared communal interests across what later viewpoints have recognised as social classes. Such communal cultural activity ends both with the separation of the upper class into different types of education and resultant culture, and with the intervention of bourgeois training and culture. As a result ballads, when recorded in the eighteenth and nineteenth centuries, often remain in the mouths of labouring people of both genders. This has been misinterpreted on a class-based model to see the ballad as a 'down-sinking cultural good'.

V

The broad context of 'family' ballads is the anxiety about daughters making their own choice of a sexual partner and so damaging or destroying them as an object for the marriage market. Within this range, *LIEK* and its group have features which appear to be central to its dynamic success. The major unique element is the absence of the family. They may be implied in the existence of a building in which the lady often has a bower, and she does frequently wish to see them, particularly her father, before her notional death, but the essential feature of *LIEK* is that the woman both invokes and then outwits the threatening mysterious lover on her own. The only apparent contradiction to this is the 'brothers' rescue' ending, a variant where members of the young woman's family arrive in time to kill the Elf-Knight. Child is satisfied that this is late, not an abandoned element of the 'essential' ballad, and it therefore appears to represent a containing resurgence of the masculine family into the ballad, containing its unusual female force.

The isolation of the woman in *LIEK*, her sexual arousal, her competence to defend herself, all without male dominance or even assistance, must raise the question whether this ballad and others somewhat like it represent an independent voice and role for women — a feminist ballad, in short. It is certainly true that ballads were in many cases performed and, it would seem, composed by women (Lönnroth, 1978, has some Swedish examples). The large number of women among performers who transmitted ballads to their recorders may have occurred partly because in the recording period women were more likely than men to be still in touch with pre-literate, pre-scholastic culture, both because of the differential education of boys and girls and because educated women often had long-term intimate contact with uneducated servants. The oral source of a recorded transmission is often a cook, a nanny, a housemaid. But in spite of this educational imbalance, it is evident that the ballads were both produced and performed by both genders.

However, the shadow of patriarchy seems to lie heavily on the possibility of a feminist ballad. When women act independently in ballads the action seems to be problem-causing, and there is always some explicit or implicit containment of their role, like Chaucer's treatment of the Wife of Bath or Shakespeare's presentation of active women as versions of men. The same structure has been identified in Norse saga, which contains many powerful women (Clunies-Ross, 1977) and it is also observable in Celtic literature of the past.

Nevertheless, there is a sense in which some ballad-groups, including the one under discussion, do give expression to a female self-consciousness which, though oppressed, is still capable of types of resistance. This will become clear later on. But patriarchy is a supple force. Bronson (1959) describes *LIEK* as a 'bride-stealing' ballad (p. xiv) — but whose bride is she? This masculinist notion comes from Nygard's analysis (1958, p. 320), where he both privileges the man (the opening sequence is improbably called 'The Courtship', p. 261) and insists that the basis of the ballad is theft of the father's human property (p. 265).

VI

LIEK is the most extreme realisation in all the ballads of this dynamic female power, and I believe that the central reason for its popularity is that it does realise this threat to patriarchy so strongly. But that threat is treated *as a threat*, not as a natural force. A more detailed reading of each of the main functions described above shows an implicit pattern of patriarchal ideology, taking here the form of recommending auto-repression to young women.

1. Lady Isabel is aroused by a horn and invites the knight in: he leaps through the window and remarks on her taking the initiative. They ride together to the wild wood.

2. He is the elf-knight. He has killed many women and will now kill her.
3. Either:

    A. By restful, stereotypically feminine calming, she lulls him to sleep, and kills him with his own dagger.

Or:

    B. She uses maidenly modesty as a trick to push him into water and drown him.

This pattern is not hard to understand in the context of anxiety about a daughter's sexuality. In 1, female sexuality is active and outside socialised control – she invites him in through the window, they ride out into the woods on stolen horses. In 2, by diabolising the hero to a degree, the dangers of such an instinctive sexual reaction are implied: her own 'elf-like' behaviour, judged from the family viewpoint, is displaced onto the knight and made a threat. In 3, by instrumentalising traditionally passive female practices, which range from modesty to delousing, she defeats the threat of the elf-knight; that is, she becomes auto-repressive. The daughter is culturally urged to see danger in releasing her own sexuality and is further urged that she can only save herself from this threat by traditional and stereotypical female passivity.

So much is plainly an effective piece of patriarchal ideology, the family controlling the daughter on those crucial occasions when it is absent. And the travelling lover is not merely a symbol of her own 'elvishness': he is also a pragmatic figure. Meeting a stranger and going away with him was both the ultimate threat to the family's power over the girl, and a common occurrence – like modern runaways. The intrusive male lover is always a credible threat to the family's control of a daughter – a travelling knight, a wandering scholar, a roving sailor.

VII

Though the structure discussed so far is effective, and especially powerful because of its unusual female force, this is only part of the ballad-group's ideological function. Condensed with the message about female auto-repression is another statement about female sexuality, which is seen from a male viewpoint more sharply, even more incisively.

It is noticeable that the mimetic viewpoint of the ballad varies a good deal. That is a common formal feature of many early ballads, a part of what Gummere calls their 'leaping and lingering' (1907, pp. 90–2). Stemming from a non-individualist epistemology, the result is often to broaden the ideological force of the ballad. In *LIEK* a male viewpoint is developed as well as Lady Isabel's. The elf-knight is surprised when invoked, an interchange of viewpoint follows, and the final scene is basically experienced as his 'ain' view of being stroked, lulled, killed, even taunted after death (a particularly important event in defeat within a shame-oriented culture).

Related to this emergence of a male viewpoint is the fact that the ballad implicitly realises a sexual narrative. The knight is aroused sexually: implied in *LIEK* by the horn and the leap through the window. In other versions she will pluck a flower and he will leap up from the bush, or some other version of that symbolism. They will ride together into the *wild* wood; then he is *lulled* to sleep in her lap; finally he is killed in a way which suggests castration. His own dagger is appropriated for the job in *LIEK*; elsewhere he is beheaded or plunged into water. (In *Bluebeard* his last, successful, wife returns to him his bloodstained key after penetrating the forbidden room. The potency of the bloody key as a motif of insecure sexual and financial power may have worked backwards through *Bluebeard*, changing the plot to arrive rationally at this dynamic climax.)

To summarise these details: condensed within the story about the social control of female sexuality there is a story that expresses individual masculine fear of that same force. It is the story of a single sexual encounter where the man weakens and dies through the power of a woman who is still vigorous when, he feels, she ought to be still and vigour-less.

VIII

This second and latent structure in the ballad may well explain why he should be an elf-knight, not a demon. As a lone travelling knight he is a male fantasy of sexual adventure, and it is interesting to note that elves are not normally thought in European folklore to be murderous (Nygard, 1958, p. 310). The figure is evaluatively marginal, capable of conveying a threat and also of being a projection of male sexuality. The strain placed on this overdetermined elvishness indicates where the patriarchal ideology is most strenuously at work. It is also of interest that in *James Harris* (Child no. 243), where the travelling lover is the agent of punishment for a woman's past infidelity, he is a true demon: the projection there is entirely punitive (or sadistic), not erotic.

Condensed though they are, the outer, social and familial anxiety and the inner masculine anxiety do not have the same resolution. (This inner – outer distinction is a considered one, not a mere replication of the traditional bourgeois 'society and individual' model. Loss of honour, public status and social power are not associated with the threatened castration, as they are with the loss of a daughter in the 'Daughter's Lover' ballad-group.) The wish of the familial structure was fulfilled in the story, in that the daughter repressed her sexuality, but it is noticeable that a residual anxiety remains. She very rarely returns home and then only in a perfunctory way (Nygard, 1958, p. 278), so familial containment is absent or sketchy. A similar strain derives from the suggestively erotic refrain (of which there are many versions). It recurs throughout the ballad – a feature which is, from one viewpoint, subversive of the auto-repressive structure, and, from another, a reason why that structure is so important.

Limited though the containment may be at the social and familial level, it is much greater than that provided for the inner masculine anxiety. This only foresees a curtailed and painful ending, with symbolic castration and death.

IX

So both latent structures of the ballad have residual tension, especially the latter. That is a normal feature of successful cultural phenomena, especially the great popular successes, and that brings to a dynamic conclusion the tensely balanced ideological conflicts of the ballad.

By now an answer has been collected to the question in the title of this paper. *LIEK* was the most popular ballad in Europe because its fiction condenses particularly acute aspects of patriarchal anxiety, namely the control of women and their sexuality at both the social and personal levels. Resolutions are offered at the social level in terms of feminine auto-repression, but there is an unresolved fear at the inner and personal level: that latter fear is itself generated by the disparity between ideology and reality at the social level. If women are repressed socially then they are most formidable where their physical powers are quite plainly superior to men and where social repressions do not adequately operate – namely, in the sexual encounter where women have much greater endurance.

That answers the question, but answers it from a basically male viewpoint. Not, I hope, from that of the author of this paper, but from that of the patriarchal dominance of culture. The feminine viewpoint in the ballad is brought to auto-repression; the male viewpoint emerges and becomes of dominant, even narcissistic, interest. How does this square with the strong feminine component in ballad-creators and ballad audiences? Obviously women may well be bearers of patriarchal ideology, or it would not in fact be a dominant force. Yet at the same time it is not hard to conceive of some at least of the female part of the audience finding *LIEK* compulsively interesting as a statement of the experienced pressure of a patriarchal world, and also as a coded statement of the existence of certain powers actually held by women within that world.

This is also true of the 'Daughter's Lover' group of ballads, many of which indicate how wrong and foolish the family males are to attack the daughter's lover, how they destroy daughter and family along with the intrusive male. There is more than a trace of the pressure of historical feminism, or at the very least an alternative viewpoint, in some of the ballads, and that is presumably because they are not a gender-linked form in terms of production and consumption. Few ballads, however, express that pressure in as dramatic and conflictive a way as the 'core' or 'essential' version of the 'Mysterious Lover' group, *Lady Isabel and the Elf-Knight*.

X

So far this has been a discussion of the 'essential' ballad typified by *LIEK*. But it has many variant versions, and these (like those of purely literary texts, almost always ignored) are in a real sense a guide to the responses of audiences in their re-creation of texts as they are transmitted and consumed. Obviously, for many, the dynamic power of *LIEK* was valuable – hence its 'vital tenacity' in Bronson's phrase (1959, p. 39). But the pattern of variants indicates that it was sometimes too dynamic, and containment by variant is a discernible process. There are a number of examples, but I will deal with only two here, one containment for each of the two latent structures of the ballad.

The first exists in an additional sequence often attached to *LIEK*: the 'parrot' ending (no. 2 in Appendix 2). These variants presumably all have the same origin in that some performer altered the ballad and others assented to and re-used that version. (Bronson records 66 uses of the 'parrot' ending among his 141.) It is a powerful variant indeed and apparently only exists in English (Nygard, 1958, pp. 281–2 and 296).

In the extra scene, the daughter returns home and the parrot knows where she has been. In return for material comforts, the parrot conceals its knowledge, telling the father that its noise was caused by a cat visiting the cage – but the daughter has driven the cat away.

The effect is a further and final containment of the woman. In one particularly popular version of this variant she is herself named Polly, the traditional parrot-name. The woman returns to her house as the parrot does to its cage: cats and elf-knights are driven away, material comforts are resumed (as Bluebeard gave his wife access to all his riches, forbidding only one, apparently, sexually symbolic room). This ending operates basically in terms of the social and familial structure of the ballad, but it also has general force as a reducer of the independent and sexual role of the woman – she is presented finally in a patriarchal mode, as a bird in a gilded cage.

XI

The other euphemised variant of *LIEK* that I want to raise here is actually described by Child as a quite different ballad, *The Elfin Knight* (Child no. 2, *EK* from here on: 'Scarborough Fair' is a well-known version. See No. 3 in Appendix 2). Child said that this ballad had borrowed stanzas 1–4 from *LIEK* and that its last two stanzas were incomprehensible (1882, p. 13). Nygard thought *LIEK* had borrowed its opening from *EK* (1958, p. 310). However, the construction and meaning of the ballad become quite clear once it is seen as a contained variant of *LIEK*.

EK, which itself has many versions, especially in Bronson (1959), employs the well-known folk-lore motif of the 'impossible tasks' structure as the conflict function to replace the sexual conflict function of *LIEK*. This is a drastic euphemisation of the sexual threat of the woman, an encounter of wits rather than genitals. To cover all the sexual material latent in *LIEK*, however, the 'impossible task' section had to be developed to such an extent that it filled all but the first four and last two stanzas – hence Child's interesting but wrong-headed notion that the intervening stanzas were the core of the ballad and that the opening and closing were inauthentic and mysterious (1882, p. 13).

Being a variant of *LIEK*, *EK* asserts the auto-repression that young girls should feel when faced with travelling men, but this structure is euphemised because the conflict is one of wit rather than physicality. The social and familial pattern of *LIEK* is represented in a diluted form. In this respect the containing function of *EK* is like that of the 'parrot' version of *LIEK*. But *EK* does more than this. It is the inner masculine-anxiety structure of *LIEK* that is most strikingly euphemised by the variation found in *EK*. This is clear from the ending, in which the knight returns to his wife and children rather than suffering an impotent death. Not all of *EK* is as blandly un-anxious as that ending: it euphemises *LIEK*'s threat, rather than dissipating it. The refrain about the wind blowing a plaid away is implicitly sexual, indeed more direct than most of the spring-time implications of *LIEK* refrains like 'Ay as the gowans grow gay'. There is also material in the verses that, by relatively distant symbolisations, realises to some degree the personal male fear of sexual women which was more overt in *LIEK*.

The curious exchange of refrain in the last stanzas (which was part of Child's problem with them) indicates the knight's defeat and his acceptance of a non-oppressive sexual position originally feminine – this is a displaced version of the castration images of *LIEK*. Other material in the ballad seems to turn from male aggression to female triumph, albeit in a discussion of sexual relations, not in their enactment.

Marriage is the offer by the elf-knight, but this seems itself a euphemisation. When he demands that to win 'marriage' from him the girl sew him a shirt, he employs a motif very common to mysterious lovers and other would-be seducers. The word 'sark' means shirt or chemise, and many of its early usages have a sexual context (not unlike 'petticoat'). I suspect but cannot yet prove a colloquial sense of 'vagina' for 'sark' and the seamlessness presumably means virginity. (I wonder what sailors thought was meant by the famous ship's name, 'Cutty Sark': cutty means 'tight-fitting'. On its figurehead the 'sark' is a diaphonous chemise . . . the latent meaning may be directly erotic.)

Whatever the exact significance of the knight's remarks, the girl appears to understand them clearly, and responds in similarly obscure but apparently sex-linked form. She has an acre of good 'ley-land' (no doubt pronounced 'lay-land'), which he is to plough with his horn. This seems frank enough, in a moderately disguised way. But as she goes on, the scale of his effort is made minuscule, his equipment makes such acre-ploughing an impossible task indeed. This seems a displaced castration image, and the real reason why the knight so huffily returns to wife and children. The girl has been too powerful for him in sexual wit, if not, like Lady Isabel's innuendoes, in sexual practice.

Even in its distinctly contained and euphemised variants, *Lady Isabel and the Elf-Knight* remains a dynamic ballad, realising the serious threat to patriarchal order posed by the vigour of sexually awakened woman. The same force is dealt with in other ballad-groups, especially those I have called 'Daughter's Lover' and 'Prospective Bride'.

Seen in a comparative way, across versions, across languages, against their medieval origins, and particularly across the all too frequently created gap between literature and society, many of the ballads that have survived appear both to present and contain a challenge to patriarchal simplicities as part of their challenge to a whole phalanx of undesirably authoritarian postures and practices. It is apparently because *Lady Isabel and the Elf-Knight* does all these things with such dynamic and complex condensation that it was the most popular ballad in Europe.

Appendix 1 Methodology

For the purposes of this paper 'ballad' is merely taken to mean texts of the sort published by Child and Bronson. It is generally recognised that Child's canon was restrictive, particularly in the light of the many songs discovered in the USA and also in the context of folk-tale studies. But even keeping only to Child and Bronson, there is a huge amount of material, and elementary patterns and tests of methodology may be worked out there with some confidence – that is the process I am currently engaged in, of which this paper is part.

Very many ballads were sung, and many tunes have survived. The discussion in this paper takes no account of performance and music. This goes against the trend of ballad studies to some degree, and for several reasons. One is that my knowledge in this area is not sufficiently sophisticated to deal confidently with a musical sociology of the ballads – not yet at least. But I do not see that as a disabling disadvantage, because another reason for this paper's non-musicality is that the emphasis on music in the ballads has had the effect of a new type of aestheticism, a way of restricting discussion to mere admiration. An approach not as inauthentic as old style 'literary appreciation', but in its way quite as far from comprehending socio-cultural function.

Finally, a speculation. In discussing the inherent meaning of ballads in this paper, I have on several occasions used terms from Freud's *The Interpretation of Dreams* (1976). This is not a casual borrowing. I would be prepared to argue that the patterns outlined here bear a remarkable resemblance to the basic structuration of dreams described in his Chapter VI – and not because I started with that terminological model. It was when I was halfway through the analysis that I realised what was happening and recognised the usefulness of Freud's terms and categories.

Briefly, the inherent compression of the ballad-story responds to Freud's elementary form of 'condensation'; the significant motifs throughout the variants are examples of 'representation' and these may well include a type of 'displacement' as in the transfer of 'elvishness' from Isabel to the knight. More important structural relations are visible between ballad and dream. The double latent structure of *LIEK*, both female auto-repression and male castration anxiety, is a version of Freud's structural 'condensation', and a number of features of the ballad are therefore 'over-determined'. The 'parrot' ending is, in terms of the whole *LIEK* ballad-group, a 'secondary revision' and the substitution of the 'impossible tasks' function in *EK* for the implicit sexual encounter is a structural 'displacement'.

I am not suggesting that Freudian content-analysis has any special role in comprehending these ballads and their function: I am sceptical about that for several reasons (among them the non-individualist ontology and the earlier familiar model inherent to the ballad, apart from any feminism-oriented doubts), but I think it is possible that Freud's mechanics of dream-structuration and his ways of reading a text can be separated from his own use of them. I suggest they may be the most useful part of his work for an analysis which is seeking the latent meaning of the manifest cultural product.

Appendix 2 Texts

1. *Lady Isabel and the Elf-Knight*

> 1. Fair Lady Isabel sits in her bower sewing,
>   Aye as the gowans* grow gay.
>   There she heard an elf-knight blawing his horn.
>   The first morning in May.
>
> 2. 'If I had yon horn that I hear blawing,
>   And yon elf-knight to sleep in my bosom.'
>
> 3. This maiden had scarcely these words spoken
>   Till in at her window the elf-knight has luppen.*

---

* gowans – daisies; luppen – leapt

4. 'It's a very strange matter, fair maiden,' said he,
   'I canna blaw my horn but ye call on me.

5. 'But will ye go to yon greenwood side?
   If ye canna gang I will cause you to ride.'

6. He leapt on a horse, and she on another,
   And they rode on to the greenwood together.

7. 'Light down, light down, lady Isabel,' said he,
   'We are come to the place where ye are to die.'

8. 'Hae mercy, hae mercy, kind sir on me,
   Till ance my dear father and mother I see.'

9. 'Seven king's daughters here hae I slain,
   And ye shall be the eight o them.'

10. 'O sit down a while, lay your head on my knee,
    That we may hae some rest before that I die.'

11. She stroakd him sae fast*, the nearer he did creep,
    Wi a sma charm she lulld him fast asleep.

12. Wi his ain sword-belt sae fast as she ban* him,
    Wi his ain dag-durk sae fair as she dang* him.

13. 'If seven king's daughters here ye hae slain,
    Lye ye here, a husband to them a'.'

(Refrain repeats in every stanza.)

2. *LIEK* 'parrot' ending

> She leapt on her milk-white steed,
>   She led the dapple grey;
> She rid till she came to her father's house,
>   Three hours before it was day.
>
> 'Who knocked so loudly at the ring?'
>   The parrot he did say;
> 'O where have you been, my pretty Polly,
>   All this long summer's day?'
>
> 'O hold your tongue, parrot,
>   Tell you no tales of me;
> Your cage shall be made of beaten gold.
>   Which is now made of a tree.'

---

* fast – firmly; ban – bound; dang – struck.

O then bespake her father dear
  As he on his bed did lay:
'O what is the matter, my parrot,
  That you speak before it is day?'

'The cat's at my cage, master,
  And sorely frighted me,
And I calld down my Polly
  To take the cat away.'

3. *The Elfin Knight*

My plaid awa, my plaid awa,
And ore the hill and far awa,
And far awa to Norrowa,
My plaid shall not be blown awa.

1. The elphin knight sits on yon hill,
    Ba, ba, ba, lilli ba
  He blaws his horn both lowd and shril.
    The wind hath blown my plaid awa.

2. He blowes it east, he blowes it west,
  He blowes it where he lyketh best.

3. 'I wish that horn were in my kist*,
  Yea, and the knight in my armes two.'

4. She had no sooner these words said,
  When that the knight came to her bed.

5. 'Thou art over young a maid,' quote he,
  'Married with me thou il wouldst be.'

6. 'I have a sister younger than I,
  And she was married yesterday.'

7. 'Married with me if thou wouldst be,
  A courtesie thou must do to me.

8. 'For thou must shape a sark* to me,
  Without any cut or heme,' quote he.

9. 'Thou must shape it knife-and-sheerlesse,
  And also sue it needle-threelesse.'

---

* kist – chest; sark – shirt;

10. 'If that piece of courtesie I do to thee,
    Another thou must do to me.

11. 'I have an aiker of good ley-land,
    Which lyeth low by yon sea-strand.

12. 'For thou must eare* it with thy horn,
    So thou must sow it with thy corn.

13. 'And bigg* a cart of stone and lyme,
    Robin Redbreast he must trail it hame.

14. 'Thou must barn it in a mouse-holl,
    And thrash it into thy shoes soll.'

15. 'And thou must winnow it in thy looff*,
    And also seck it in thy glove.

16. 'For thou must bring it overe the sea,
    And thou must bring it dry home to me.

17. 'When thou has gotten thy turns well done,
    Then come to me and get thy sark then.'

18. 'I'll not quite my plaid for my life;
    It haps* my seven bairns and my wife.'
        The wind shall not blow my plaid awa.

19. 'My maidenhead I'll then keep still,
    Let the elphin knight do what he will.'
        The wind's not blown my plaid awa.

(Refrain repeats in every stanza, with variants as indicated in the last two stanzas.)

---

* eare – plough; bigg – build; looff – palm; haps – covers.

References

BRONSON, B. *The Traditional Tunes of the Child Ballads* (Princeton University Press, 1959).

BUCHAN, D. *The Ballad and the Folk* (London: Routledge, 1972).

CHILD, F.J. *The English and Scottish Popular Ballads*, 5 vols (Cambridge: Harvard University Press, 1882–98; repr. New York: Dover, 1965).

CLUNIES-ROSS, M. 'Women in Early Scandinavian Myth and Literature', *Refractory Girl*, **13–14** (1977): 29–37.

FREUD, S. *The Interpretation of Dreams* (London: Penguin, 1976).

GUMMERE, F.B. *The Popular Ballad* (Boston 1907, repr. edn. New York: Dover, 1959).

LASLETT, P. (ed.), *Household and Family in Past Time* (Cambridge University Press, 1972).

LLOYD, A.L. *Folk Song in England* (London: Lawrence and Wishart, 1967).

LÖNNROTH, L. 'Sir Olof and the Elves' (manuscript trans by M. Karlsson-Lillas as 'Herr Olof och Alvorna'), in *Den dubbla scenen* (Stockholm: Prima, 1978), pp. 81–111.

MACFARLANE, C.B. *The Origins of English Individualism* (Cambridge University Press, 1978).

NYGARD, H.O. *The Ballad of Heer Halewijn* (University of Tennessee Press, Knoxville, 1958). See also his essay 'Child Ballad no. 4: Ballad Source-Study', reprinted in *The Critics and the Ballad*, ed. M. Leach and T. Coffin. (Carbondale: Southern Illinois University Press, 1961), pp. 189–203.

STONE, L. *The Family, Sex and Marriage, 1500–1800*. (London: Weidenfeld and Nicolson, 1977).

Notes on Authors

DAVID AERS holds a Personal Chair in the School of English and American Studies at the University of East Anglia, Norwich. His most recent books are *Community, Gender and Individual Identity: English Writing, 1360–1430* (Routledge, 1988), and an edited collection, *Essays on English Communities, Identities and Writing* (Harvester Wheatsheaf, 1992).

ALEXANDRA A.T. BARRATT is Associate Professor of English at the University of Waikato. She is editor of *Women's Writing in Middle English* (Longman Annotated Texts, 1992) and is working on an edition of the medieval English translator, Dame Eleanor Hull.

SHEILA DELANY is Professor of English at Simon Fraser University. Her most recent books are a translation, with commentary, of Osbern Bokenham's *A Legend of Holy Women* (University of Notre Dame Press, 1992), and *The Naked Text: Chaucer's* Legend of Good Women (University of California Press, 1993).

LAURIE A. FINKE is Director and Associate Professor of Women's and Gender Studies at Kenyon College. She is the author of *Feminist Theory, Women's Writing* (Cornell, 1992) and co-editor with Martin Shichtman of *Medieval Texts and Contemporary Readers* (Cornell, 1987) and with Robert Con Davis of *Literary Criticism and Theory: Greeks to the Present* (Longman, 1989).

SHEILA FISHER is Associate Professor of English at Trinity College, Hartford. She is editor, with Janet Halley, of *Seeking the Woman in Late Medieval and Renaissance Writings* (Tennessee, 1989) and author of *Chaucer's Poetic Alchemy: A Study of Value and its Transformation in the* Canterbury Tales (Garland, 1988). She is currently working on a study of women and systems of exchange in *The Canterbury Tales*.

STEVEN JUSTICE teaches in the Department of English at the University of California at Berkeley. He is author of a number of articles on medieval literature, especially *Piers Plowman*.

STEPHEN KNIGHT is founding Professor of English and Cultural Studies at De Montfort University, Leicester. His most recent works on medieval literature are *Arthurian Literature and Society* (Macmillan, 1983) and *Chaucer* (Basil Blackwell, 1986). He is currently working on a study of the Robin Hood tradition.

JILL MANN is Professor of Medieval and Renaissance English at the University of Cambridge. Her most recent book, *Geoffrey Chaucer*, was published in Harvester's

Feminist Readings series in 1991. She is currently editing *The Canterbury Tales* for Penguin Books.

ANNE MIDDLETON is Professor of English at the Department of English at the University of California at Berkeley. She is preparing a study of Langland, to be called *Piers Plowman as Life Work: Vernacular Identity and Literary History*.

R. BARTON PALMER is Professor of English and Communication at Georgia State University. He has just published *Guillaume de Machaut: Three Love Visions* (Garland, 1992), the fourth volume in a continuing series of editions and translations of the narrative works of Chaucer's French contemporary.

LEE PATTERSON is Professor of English at Duke University. His most recent book is *Chaucer and the Subject of History* (Routledge, 1991).

STEPHANIE TRIGG is Senior Lecturer in English at the University of Melbourne. Her edition of *Winner and Waster* was published by EETS in 1990, and she is currently writing *The Making of Geoffrey Chaucer: The Exemplary History of Medieval Studies*, a study of the discourses of Chaucer criticism.

R.F. YEAGER is Professor of Literature and Language at the University of North Carolina at Asheville. He is the author and/or editor of four books and numerous articles on *Beowulf*, Chaucer, and Gower, including most recently *John Gower's Poetic: The Search for a New Arion* (D.S. Brewer, 1990). He is presently completing concordances to the French and Latin poetry of Gower.

Further Reading

Medieval poetics: theories of language and representation

AERS, DAVID, *Piers Plowman and Christian Allegory* (London: Edward Arnold, 1975).

ALLEN, JUDSON BOYCE, *The Friar as Critic: Literary Attitudes in the Later Middle Ages* (Nashville: Vanderbilt University Press, 1971).

——*The Ethical Poetic of the Later Middle Ages: A Decorum of Convenient Distinction* (Toronto: University of Toronto Press, 1981).

ARTHUR, ROSS G., *Medieval Sign Theory and Sir Gawain and the Green Knight* (Toronto: University of Toronto Press, 1987).

BOITANI, PIERO, *English Medieval Narrative in the Thirteenth and Fourteenth Centuries*, trans. Joan Krakover Hall (Cambridge: Cambridge University Press, 1982).

BOITANI, PIERO and ANNA TORTI (eds), *Poetics: Theory and Practice in Medieval English Literature*, The J.A.W. Bennett Memorial Lectures, 7th Series, Perugia, 1990 (Cambridge: D.S. Brewer, 1991).

BURROW, J.A., *Ricardian Poetry: Chaucer, Gower, Langland and the Gawain Poet* (London: Routledge, 1971).

CLANCHY, M.T., *From Memory to Written Record: England 1066–1307* (London: Edward Arnold, 1979).

COLISH, MARCIA L., *The Mirror of Language: A Study in the Medieval Theory of Knowledge* (rev. edn Lincoln: University of Nebraska Press, 1983).

DINSHAW, CAROLYN, *Chaucer's Sexual Poetics* (Madison: The University of Wisconsin Press, 1989).

ECO, UMBERTO and COSTANTINO MARMO (eds), *On the Medieval Theory of Signs* (Amsterdam: John Benjamins, 1989).

FEWSTER, CAROL, *Traditionality and Genre in Middle English Romance* (Cambridge: D.S. Brewer, 1987).

GALLACHER, PATRICK J. and HELEN DAMICO (eds), *Hermeneutics and Medieval Culture* (Albany: State University of New York Press, 1989).

GANIM, JOHN M., *Style and Consciousness in Middle English Narrative* (Princeton: Princeton University Press, 1983).

GELLRICH, JESSE M., *The Idea of the Book in the Middle Ages: Language Theory, Mythology, and Fiction* (Ithaca and London: Cornell University Press, 1985).

KELLY, DOUGLAS, *Medieval Imagination: Rhetoric and the Poetry of Courtly Love* (Madison: University of Wisconsin Press, 1978).

KOLVE, V.A., *Chaucer and the Imagery of Narrative: The First Five Canterbury Tales* (London: Edward Arnold, 1984).

MIDDLETON, ANNE, 'William Langland's "Kynde Name": Authorial Signature and Social Identity in Late Fourteenth Century England', in Lee Patterson (ed.), *Literary Practice and Social Change in Britain, 1380–1530*, The New Historicism 8 (Berkeley: University of California Press, 1990), pp. 15–82.

MILLER, JACQUELINE, *Poetic License: Authority and Authorship in Medieval and Renaissance Contexts* (New York and Oxford: Oxford University Press, 1986).

MINNIS, A.J., *Medieval Theory of Authorship: Scholastic Literary Attitudes in the Later Middle Ages* (2nd edn Aldershot: Scolar, 1988).

MINNIS, A.J. and A.B. SCOTT, *Medieval Literary Theory and Criticism c1100–c1375: The Commentary Tradition* (Oxford: Clarendon Press, 1988).

NICHOLS, STEPHEN G., *Romanesque Signs: Early Medieval Narrative and Iconography* (New Haven: Yale University Press, 1983).

PEARSALL, DEREK, *Old and Middle English Poetry*, Routledge History of English Poetry 1 (London, Henly and Boston: Routledge and Kegan Paul, 1977).

——(ed.), *Manuscripts and Readers in Fifteenth-Century England: The Literary Implications of Manuscript Study*, Essays from the 1981 Conference at the University of York (Cambridge: D.S. Brewer, 1983).

——(ed.), *Manuscripts and Texts: Editorial Problems in Later Middle English Literature*, Essays from the 1985 Conference at the University of York (Cambridge: D.S. Brewer, 1987).

——(ed.) *Studies in the Vernon MS* (Cambridge: D.S. Brewer, 1990).

ROBERTSON, D.W., *A Preface to Chaucer: Studies in Medieval Perspectives* (Princeton: Princeton University Press, 1962).

——*Essays in Medieval Culture* (Princeton: Princeton University Press, 1980).

ROBERTSON, D.W. and BERNARD HUPPÉ, F., *Piers Plowman and Scriptural Tradition* (Princeton: Princeton University Press, 1963).

RUSSELL, J. STEPHEN (ed.), *Allegoresis: The Craft of Allegory in Medieval Literature* (New York and London: Garland, 1988).

TURVILLE-PETRE, THORLAC, *The Alliterative Revival* (Cambridge: D.S. Brewer, 1977).

YEAGER, R.F., *John Gower's Poetic: The Search for a New Arion* (Cambridge: D.S. Brewer, 1990).

The contexts of medieval poetry

AERS, DAVID, *Community, Gender and Individual Identity: English Writing, 1360–1430* (London: Routledge, 1988).

——(ed.), *Medieval Literature: Criticism, Ideology and History* (Brighton, Sussex: Harvester, 1986).

——(ed.), *Essays on English Communities, Identities and Writing* (London: Harvester Wheatsheaf, 1992).

ALFORD, JOHN A. (ed.), *A Companion to Piers Plowman* (Berkeley and Los Angeles: University of California Press, 1988).

BARRATT, ALEXANDRA A.T. (ed.), *Women's Writing in Middle English* (London: Longman, 1992).

BURROW, J.A., *Medieval Writers and their Work: Middle English Literature and its Background 1100–1500* (Oxford: Oxford University Press, 1982).

COLEMAN, JANET, *English Literature in History 1350–1400: Medieval Readers and Writers* (London: Hutchinson, 1981).

DELANY, SHEILA, *Writing Woman: Women Writers and Women in Literature, Medieval to Modern* (New York: Schocken, 1983).

——*Medieval Literary Politics: Shapes of Ideology* (Manchester: Manchester University Press, 1990).

GREEN, RICHARD FIRTH, *Poets and Princepleasers: Literature and the English Court in the Late Middle Ages* (Toronto: University of Toronto Press, 1980).

HEFFERNAN, THOMAS J. (ed.), *The Popular Literature of Medieval England*, Tennessee Studies in Literature 28 (Knoxville: University of Tennessee Press, 1985).

LAWTON, DAVID A. (ed.), *Middle English Alliterative Poetry and its Literary Background* (Cambridge: D.S. Brewer, 1982).

LE GOFF, JACQUES, *Time, Work and Culture in the Middle Ages*, trans. Arthur Goldhammer (Chicago: University of Chicago Press, 1980).

MEDCALF, STEPHEN (ed.), *The Later Middle Ages*, The Context of English Literature Series (London: Methuen, 1981).

OLSON, GLENDING, *Literature as Recreation in the Later Middle Ages* (Ithaca and London: Cornell University Press, 1982).

PATTERSON, LEE (ed.), *Literary Practice and Social Change in Britain, 1380–1530*, The New Historicism 8 (Berkeley and Los Angeles: University of California Press, 1990).

———*Chaucer and the Subject of History* (London: Routledge, 1991).

SIMPSON, JAMES, *Piers Plowman: An Introduction to the B-Text* (London and New York: Longman, 1990).

STOCK, BRIAN, *The Implications of Literacy: Written Language and Models of Interpretation in the Eleventh and Twelfth Centuries* (Princeton: Princeton University Press, 1983).

Modern critical theory and medieval poetry

BLOCH, R. HOWARD, *Etymologies and Genealogies: A Literary Anthropology of the French Middle Ages* (Chicago and London: University of Chicago Press, 1983).

CARMICHAEL, VIRGINIA, '"Green is for Growth": Sir Gawain's Disjunctive Neurosis'. *Assays* 4 (1987): 25–38.

COLETTI, THERESA, *Naming the Rose: Eco, Medieval Signs, and Modern Theory* (Ithaca and London: Cornell University Press, 1988).

DRAGONETTI, ROGER, *La Vie de la lettre au Moyen age: le conte du Graal* (Paris: Éditions du Seuil, 1980).

FISHER, SHEILA and JANET E. HALLEY (eds), *Seeking the Woman in Late Medieval and Renaissance Writings: Essays in Feminist Contextual Criticism* (Knoxville: The University of Tennessee Press, 1989).

'Gay and Lesbian Studies', *Medieval Feminist Newsletter*, 13 (Spring 1992).

LAWTON, DAVID, 'The Subject of *Piers Plowman*', *Yearbook of Langland Studies*, 1 (1988): 1–30.

SAPORA, ROBERT WILLIAM, JR., *A Theory of Middle English Alliterative Meter with Critical Applications*, Speculum Anniversary Monographs 1 (Cambridge, Mass.: Mediaeval Academy of America, 1977).

SHOAF, R.A., *Dante, Chaucer, and the Currency of the Word: Money, Images, and Reference in Late Medieval Poetry* (Norman, Oklahoma: Pilgrim, 1983).

———*The Poem as Green Girdle: Commercium in Sir Gawain and the Green Knight*, University of Florida Monographs, Humanities Series, No. 55 (Gainesville: University Presses of Florida, 1984).

SPEARING, A.C., *Medieval to Renaissance in English Poetry* (Cambridge: Cambridge University Press, 1985).

———*Readings in Medieval Poetry* (Cambridge: Cambridge University Press, 1987).

VANCE, EUGENE, *Mervelous Signals: Poetics and Sign Theory in the Middle Ages* (Lincoln and London: University of Nebraska Press, 1986).

VANCE, EUGENE and LUCIE BRIND D'AMOUR, (eds), *Archéologie du Signe* (Toronto: Pontifical Institute of Medieval Studies, 1983).

Vitz, Evelyn Birge, *Medieval Narrative and Modern Narratology: Subjects and Objects of Desire* (New York: New York University Press, 1989).

Wittig, Susan, *Stylistic and Narrative Structures in the Middle English Romances* (Austin: University of Texas, 1978).

Zumthor, Paul, *Essai de poétique médiévale: Toward a Medieval Poetics*, trans. Philip Bennet (Minneapolis and Oxford: University of Minnesota Press, 1992).

Debates in contemporary medieval criticism

Aers, David, 'The Good Shepherds of Medieval Criticism', *Southern Review*, **20** (July 1987): 168–85.

Allen, Peter L. and Jeff Rider (eds), 'Reflections in the Frame: New Perspectives on the Study of Medieval Literature', *Exemplaria*, **3** (1991).

Bloomfield, Morton W., 'Contemporary Literary Theory and Chaucer', in Donald M. Rose, (ed.) *New Perspectives in Chaucer Criticism* (Norman, Oklahoma: Pilgrim Books, 1981), pp. 23–35.

Brownlee, Marina S., Kevin Brownlee and Stephen G. Nichols (eds), *The New Medievalism* (Baltimore: The Johns Hopkins University Press, 1991).

Finke, Laurie A. and Martin B. Shichtman (eds) *Medieval Texts and Contemporary Readers* (Ithaca and London: Cornell University Press, 1987).

Fradenburg, Louise O., '"Voice Memorial": Loss and Reparation in Chaucer's Poetry', *Exemplaria*, **2.1** (1990): 169–202.

——'Criticism, Anti-Semitism, and the *Prioress's Tale*', *Exemplaria*, **1** (1989): 69–115.

Frantzen, Allen J., *Desire for Origins: New Language, Old English, and Teaching the Tradition* (New Brunswick and London: Rutgers University Press, 1990).

——(ed.), *Speaking Two Languages: Traditional Disciplines and Contemporary Theory in Medieval Studies* (Albany: State University of New York Press, 1991).

Frantzen, Allen J. and Charles L. Venegoni, 'The Desire for Origins: An Archaeological Analysis of Anglo-Saxon Studies' *Style*, **20** (1986): 142–56.

Jauss, Hans Robert, 'The Alterity and Modernity of Modern Literature', *New Literary History*, **10** (1979): 181–227.

Leupin, Alexandre, 'The Middle Ages, the Other', *Diacritics*, **13** (Fall 1983): 22–30.

Middleton, Anne, 'Medieval Studies', in Stephen Greenblatt and Giles Gunn (eds), *Redrawing the Boundaries: The Transformation of English and American Literary Studies* (New York: MLA, 1992), pp. 12–40.

Nichols, Stephen G. (ed.), 'The New Philology', *Speculum*, **65** (1990).

Patterson, Lee, *Negotiating the Past: The Historical Understanding of Medieval Literature* (Madison: University of Wisconsin Press, 1987).

Stock, Brian, *Listening for the Text: On the Uses of the Past* (Baltimore and London: The Johns Hopkins University Press, 1990).

Wasserman, Julian and Lois Roney (eds), *Sign, Sentence, Discourse: Language in Medieval Thought and Literature* (Syracuse: Syracuse University Press, 1989).

Index